TELEVISION REWIRED

The Rise of the Auteur Series

MARTHA P. NOCHIMSON

UNIVERSITY OF TEXAS PRESS
AUSTIN

Requests for permission to reproduce material from this work should be sent to:
   Permissions
   University of Texas Press
   P.O. Box 7819
   Austin, TX 78713-7819
   utpress.utexas.edu/rp-form

∞ The paper used in this book meets the minimum requirements of ANSI/NISO
Z39.48–1992 (R1997) (Permanence of Paper).

LIBRARY OF CONGRESS CATALOGING-IN-PUBLICATION DATA

Names: Nochimson, Martha, author.
Title: Television rewired : the rise of the auteur series / Martha P. Nochimson.
Description: First edition. | Austin : University of Texas Press, 2019. | Includes
   bibliographical references and index.
Identifiers: LCCN 2018038437
   ISBN 978-0-292-75944-2 (cloth : alk. paper)
   ISBN 978-1-4773-1895-9 (pbk : alk. paper)
   ISBN 978-1-4773-1847-8 (library e-book)
   ISBN 978-1-4773-1848-5 (non-library e-book)
Subjects: LCSH: Television series—United States—History and criticism. |
   Television writers—United States—History and criticism. | Television producers
   and directors—United States—History and criticism. | Television authorship—
   United States.
Classification: LCC PN1992.8.S4 N634 2019 | DDC 791.45/75—dc23
LC record available at https://lccn.loc.gov/2018038437

doi:10.7560/759442

Let everything happen to you: beauty and terror.
Just keep going. No feeling is final.

Rainer Maria Rilke, *Book of Hours: Love Poems to God*, I, 59

CONTENTS

INTRODUCTION

The David Effect

I f you want to survey positive recent changes in the United States, you could do worse than to join me in considering television, the American television series to be precise, taking 1990 as our starting place. That was the year when *Twin Peaks*, a series created by David Lynch, an artist new to the medium working in collaboration with established TV writer Mark Frost, birthed the possibility of television art. *Twin Peaks* beckons as our portal to auteur television and a new aesthetics of mass-media storytelling, and I invite you to take a journey of discovery with me through that door.

Of course, as a medium dealing with images, sound, framing, and music, television had always been possible to ponder in terms of its aesthetic. Indeed, we are long since past the start of a burgeoning conversation on that subject that includes the work of Jason Mittell, Steven Peacock, Jason Jacobs, Douglas Howard, Martin Shuster, Sarah Cardwell, Jane Feuer, George Toles, Kim Akass, and Janet McCabe, and other pioneering critics and scholars in television studies. My own first book, *No End To Her: Soap Opera and the Female Subject* (1992), made claims for a televisual aesthetic in daytime drama in its heyday, during the 1980s.[1] All of these studies have broken some ground in creating a critical context within which to conduct increasingly improved conversations about entertainment TV. At the same time, *Twin Peaks* has brought the foundational studies to a crossroads. We have reached a point at which it has become necessary to establish some crucial distinctions, not yet made. I hope my book will be a useful starting point.

As the American television series develops, it is not only useful but urgent that we stand back from everything that has already been said about its aesthetic. In 1990 *Twin Peaks* put an end to the total domination of all series by enforced formulaic "narrative" practices. These originally limited, indeed erased, the possibility of the art of storytelling in the medium of television but were so familiar and naturalized that even the most discerning critics had lost touch with how disabling they were, certainly for the artist. We had become inured to what early television passed off as narrative: although it was much criticized, we had become oblivious to the fact that it was not only generally trivial but also only barely a form of storytelling. Storytelling is an art; and series television began as a story product offered to the public by a fast-growing business. Our understanding of television aesthetics needs to be reevaluated in the light of how limited the pre-*Peaks* medium was in comparison with the artistry that Lynch modeled.[2]

The pre-*Peaks* television series were a commodity. Ironically, they appeared at a time when movies were accorded a place as a form of expression. The 1952 Supreme Court Miracle decision gave movies the protections of the First Amendment of the Bill of Rights, already granted to print literature. This decision would cover series television too, but only technically. What passed for storytelling on American television when the decision was handed down was not expression. There is some hyperbole in this assessment, but the excessive damage that early television did to the narrative experience for the mass-entertainment industry cannot be overstated.

Before *Twin Peaks*, the TV series was hopelessly divorced from both the classical, long recognized, humanizing elements of telling stories *and* the modern transformation of narrative that was well underway. The pre-*Peaks* series embraced the classical convention of conclusive, sharply etched fictions but was not classical. It arrived at a time when the inconclusive, indeterminate modernist art of storytelling was cresting; but, although it utilized images of contemporary life and emanated from modern technology, it was not modern. It was neither classical nor modern because it lacked those connections to culture that have always been understood as the core of storytelling. In its beginning, in the 1950s, the American TV series existed in a commercial bubble. It was closer to being a thing than an expression about the world around us, like the products that it existed only to sell, at least from the perspective of the people in control of television.

Before *Twin Peaks*, television story product could be considered in the financial context of the business of storytelling but not in the context of narrative art. To speak of art television is to begin a conversation with unlimited ways of focusing on the auteur television that Lynch inaugurated. It is also to foment curiosity about the changes in story product that suddenly took place after Lynch's first *Twin Peaks* series went on the air.

Because of what I have discovered from speaking with David Lynch and the new auteurs who followed him (of which much more below), I choose to enter the conversation through a tradition of speaking about art that runs through Horace (65 BC–8 BC), Sir Phillip Sidney (1554–1586), and Percy Bysshe Shelley (1792–1822) to T. S. Eliot (1888–1965). It is a tradition that understands the artist to be the crucible in which individual talent and expression are fused with the intellectual, moral, ethical, and philosophical life of the culture. Story product severed the traditional link between narrative pleasure and knowledge of the ferment of ideas around it: "Oh, this? It's just entertainment." But art had traditionally been viewed as entertainment, as enunciated by Sidney when he spoke of it as a vehicle of instruction and delight, and as the loam of meaning, as described by Shelley when he unblinkingly called poets the "legislators of the world" in his essay "A Defence of Poetry."

These "legislators" clashed on many points. However, all who take part in this tradition share a deep belief in the connection between art and the great ideas being generated by culture. I stand on their shoulders as I emphasize the emergence of individual expressiveness and cultural connection in post-*Peaks* auteur TV storytelling. At the same time, I use the light that they shed on the history of narrative to explore the very different effect that *Twin Peaks* had on post-*Peaks* industrial story products. As the post-*Peaks* auteurs began to use the medium of television, they became part of a new branch on the evolutionary tree of television. There is a profound difference, which I seek to uncover, between the birth of the post-*Peaks* television series steeped in the art of storytelling worthy of inclusion in the traditions of art commented on by Horace, Sidney, Shelley, and Eliot and the evolution of televisual story products toward increasingly sophisticated visual and aural technology, performance and direction, and even an interesting theme here and there.

At present, appreciation of the growing sophistication of post-*Peaks* American TV series and of early pre-*Peaks* signs of that potential is lively and increasing. However, distinctions between aesthetic improvement in enduringly disconnected entertainment commodities and the aesthetics of an expressive, fully connected art of storytelling have not yet been fully acknowledged in television studies. David Lynch made television a potential platform for modernist art and thereby an enduring vehicle of delight and instruction in the ways of the modernist upheaval and a potential legislator of a new knowledge of reality. The freedom he modeled contrasts with the constricted practices of manufactured story product that is disposable, mechanical, and divorced from modern ideas of the real, despite its sophisticated technological use of the medium of television. But distinguishing between the Lynchian modeled art of television storytelling and story product is not as simple as it might seem. On the journey ahead we shall need to create a clear definition of modernism as it relates to our discussion and as precise a definition as possible of the nature of the formulaic story product.

Although the newly arisen art of storytelling contrasts with the traditions that spawned "TV things," I do not intend to say that the writers who made them were handed a list of rules or any explicitly codified instructions. Rather, as toilers within the prevailing pre-*Peaks* televisual culture they were expected to participate in certain unwritten, extremely repressive, and culturally disconnected practices. In searching for a name for those practices, which I encountered myself when I wrote for television, I have hit on "formula" as a convenient term. It is a word used vaguely in the industry and by entertainment journalists to indicate repetitive, clichéd, stale, depersonalized approaches to entertainment. By contrast, we shall become more specific here. In order to illuminate more clearly what changed with *Twin Peaks*, although we cannot produce a set of rules for formula television, we can give names to the parts of the story-product template and outline what that template made possible and what it made impossible. At the same time, in these introductory pages, I shall show how I am using the complex and often debated concept of modernism as a way of distinguishing story product from the auteur series.

STORY PRODUCTS: OUT OF DATE AT THE STARTING GATE

Giving story product its due, we need to acknowledge that it circulated an abundance of genres and styles of entertainment contrivances over the decades, beginning with the domestic comedy *I Love Lucy* and the police drama *Dragnet* in 1951 and moving forward to generate a rich inventory of variations on the basic merchandise. Here is a quick, highly selective overview of the diversification: in the 1950s *Father Knows Best*, *Lassie*, and *The Honeymooners*; in the 1960s *The Twilight Zone*, *The Fugitive*, *The Man from U.N.C.L.E.*, *Star Trek*, and *Columbo*; in the 1970s *All in the Family*, *The Mary Tyler Moore Show*, *M*A*S*H*, *The Rockford Files*, *Happy Days*, and *WKRP in Cincinnati*; and in the 1980s *Hill Street Blues*, *Star Trek: The Next Generation*, *Remington Steele*, *St. Elsewhere*, *Murder, She Wrote*,

Moonlighting, and *MacGyver*. Domestic comedy evolved; workplaces as new versions of family-like life appeared. Series television also began to offer witty, more inventive variations on the crime/action drama and introduced fantasy and science fiction. The shows differed in cleverness and ingenuity, but they had this in common. Their writers worked as industrial technicians, not artists. This is not to say that these writers never infused formulaic television with some personal insight or new ideas; as we shall see, they did so to a limited extent. But pre-*Peaks* writers knew that they were being paid for industrial products and expressed that awareness in their metaphors for their trade, factory images like "laying pipe" and "making sausage."

To this day, professionals who write formula television use industrial images to describe their work. Alongside the vibrant tradition of formula writers who experience formula as a straitjacket is another tradition of writers who speak of it with pride. One of the most enthusiastic and positive self-portraits of the formulaic craft comes from Shonda Rhimes, a successful producer and writer of more recently devised formula television (the producer of *How to Get Away with Murder*, which we shall discuss in due course). Rhimes is an interesting figure in formulaic television for many reasons. She broke the color bar with *Grey's Anatomy* in 2005, becoming the first black woman to write and produce a series; nevertheless, she speaks about her craft as if it were still 1951. In her recent autobiography, *Year of Yes: How to Dance It out, Stand in the Sun and Be Your Own Person*, Rhimes says of her days as a fledgling writer: "So I learned to lay track quickly. Artfully. Creatively. But as fast as freaking lightning. Lay some fiction on it. Smooth some story into that gap. Nail some imagination around those edges."[3] Rhimes vividly conveys the kind of industrial understanding that storytelling should be fun and full of speed as it envelops passive viewers and drives them toward an inevitable denouement. At that point there are no loose ends, or as few as possible, but also no possibilities, only certainty, a world narrowed to one circumscribed destination: THE END. The train trip ends here, at this station; think no further on this.

Rhimes is talking about what I am going to call the "perfect narrative." I have extracted this term from a conversation I had with David Simon, the creator of *The Wire* and *Treme*, among other television series.[4] Simon was, of course, using the term ironically, to invoke the static, airless, dissociated quality of formulaic television. Rhimes, in her enthusiasm for becoming part of the business of storytelling, appears oblivious to the way formulaic television *reduces* the scope of storytelling in order to make the series run on tracks, no matter what the subject, tone, or genre; nor does she appear to consider the implications of that diminishing force. We shall not share her exhilaration about her craft; rather we shall share Simon's ironic perspective. We shall observe how formula TV requires a "perfect hero" and reduced sensory palette of visuals and sounds to ensure that there are few distractions from the progress of the perfect hero along the tracks of the perfect narrative, distractions that would disturb the passive viewing experience fabricated by formulaic television story products.

The perfect narrative and its perfect hero, the quintessential ingredients of the template for formulaic story products, with their emphasis on how one person towers over a series of plot complications and achieves definitive closure, represent a simplification of the traditional narratives that have situated human beings at the center of a coherent universe since the Renaissance. But classical narratives were not perfect in the deadly sense of the word. They pulsated with complex understandings of thinking contemporary to them. Conversely, story products are the death rattle of a worldview that began a long, slow death more than 100 years ago with the rise of modernist literary art. That break with the past is generally understood to have begun roughly in 1890 in Europe and then kicked into high gear with the groundbreaking literature of James Joyce, Virginia Woolf, and Franz Kafka. Histories of modernism tend to narrate the entrance of American fiction on the scene shortly afterward, with the work of the likes of William Faulkner. Or it may be that American storytellers got there first and that Faulkner was part of a historical line of modernists who supplanted traditional storytelling as far back as the extraordinary American literature of the early to mid-nineteenth century. Perhaps literary modernism began with Nathaniel Hawthorne, Edgar Allan Poe, and Herman Melville, preceding Joyce, Woolf, and Kafka by seventy years or more. (As we shall see in chapter 2, the modernism of Poe is, according to David Chase, part of what inspired him in his creation of *The Sopranos*.)

Whenever it began, to speak of modernity is to speak of a cultural shift in Western societies that swept all areas of knowledge and means a plethora of different things to different people. My use of the term in this study may best be illustrated by the following parable. When I first met David Lynch in person in 1994, to get a sense of where he stood philosophically, I asked him what he thought of Plato's image of the relationship of reason, passion, and instinct as the driver of a chariot (reason) and the two horses (passion and instinct). He replied, "But what if no one is driving the chariot?" That, I would say, is modernism in its essence. In more conventional terms, my use of "modernism" will invoke the spirit Lynch implies, that of a radical shift away from traditional beliefs in the inherent meaning of our daily reality represented by closed structures, absolute values, continuity, definitive solutions, certainties, and unified identities. Increasingly, through the offices of modern physics, philosophy, art, and psychology, the modern world sees itself in terms of a discontinuous, random, uncertain universe of boundless energy inside and outside of us, ceaselessly moving particles, and relative cultural and linguistic systems.

I shall elaborate further on this in due course. However, as we explore the television auteurs as the newest branch of Shelley's fellowship of literary legislators, we shall be speaking of how American art television tells its stories within a modern era. Modern narrative portrays human life as a voyage into fear and wonder, sometimes branching out into the part of surrealism that overlaps psychology and physics, sometimes branching into the mysteries of philosophical and sociological relativism.

By contrast, when series television instituted the perfect hero and the perfect narrative—hyperbolic exaggerations of the kind of human control that was part of narrative form and characterization in traditional storytelling—it did so in the teeth of a modernity in which they were no longer thought possible, welcome as they might be to an audience cheered by their simplistic images of solved problems and happy endings. This mechanistic approach to narrative closed its eyes to images of what was emerging in science, philosophy, and psychology: a huge, complex universe of indeterminate psychic flow and time and space in liminal flux. When, in succession after David Lynch, David Chase created *The Sopranos* and David Simon created *The Wire*, this "David effect" was nothing less than a new mass-media connection to a high-culture literary modernism that knew itself to be a revision of the classical view of reality and often commented reflexively on its relationship to the masterworks of its predecessors.

The kind of cultural connection that the David effect made possible for television narrative is analogous to the modernist connections forged with traditional literature by the great storytellers of print fiction, as when Faulkner created a modern narrative by contrasting it with a classical antecedent.[5] Faulkner grounds his disturbing modernist novel *The Sound and the Fury* in opposition to Macbeth's sublimely nihilistic speech in William Shakespeare's play: "Out, out brief candle! / Life's but a walking shadow, a poor player, / That struts and frets his hour upon the stage, / And then is heard no more. It is a tale / Told by an idiot, full of sound and fury, / signifying nothing" (act V, scene 5). Macbeth speaks of the idiotic meaninglessness of his life in beautifully crafted iambic pentameter. In his novel about the Compsons, a disintegrating upper-class southern family, Faulkner reflects a transition in the twentieth century from classical meditations on meaninglessness to the experience of chaos. Faulkner's first chapter plunges us into the mind of Benjy Compson, a brain-damaged man of thirty-three who is unable to form language into coherent thought, so that we literally experience life as a "tale told by an idiot" with no cultural protections from its random formlessness.

The first words of Faulkner's novel immerse us in a world of random particles: "Through the fence, between the curling flower spaces, I could see them hitting. They were coming toward where the flag was and I went along the fence. Luster was hunting in the grass by the flower tree. They took the flag out, and they were hitting. Then they put the flag back and they went to the table, and hit and the other hit." Shakespeare has his protagonist conceptualize dissociation; Faulkner gives us the experience of dissociation. Shakespeare's gorgeous language saves us from that experience and shelters us from Macbeth's horror of the nothingness he feels. For Shakespeare's audience, there remains an objective structured reality denied to Macbeth because of his moral decay. Faulkner's language is, of course, an aesthetic reproduction of Benjy's dissociated outbursts, but no linguistic or intellectual structure guarantees an objective, meaningful universe for Faulkner's reader. Constructing a literary contrast with an old masterpiece, Faulkner emphasized his revised vision of the real as subjective, discontinuous, and relative.

The new American auteur television series also knows itself to be a revision, in this case of its TV predecessors. The David effect reenvisions familiar characters—the detective, the gangster, the police officer, and more—from a modernist perspective that binds us not to the vacuum of the factory-tooled narrative machine but to cutting-edge science, art, philosophy, and psychology. As television auteurs connected television to vital and dynamic storytelling, they made many changes in the form and tone of series narrative. With their "off-track" storytelling, they neither needed nor wanted a perfect hero or a diminished sensory palette. And they did not cater to the childish desire for unequivocal clarity at any price.

CAN YOU SHOW ME A HERO?

A nonformulaic television series has no use for the perfect hero, who guarantees that the reader will travel smoothly and directly on the tracks described by Rhimes. The perfect hero is immune to context; conversely, the modernist worldview to which contemporary storytelling is linked invokes the enormity of larger circumstance. In modernist thinking, physical, political, and psychological contexts dwarf or sharply condition human initiative and power and puzzle the understanding. When series television began again as an art, it revolted against the formulaic practice of cutting to measure circumstance and context in story products that never measure up to the powers and comprehension of the perfect hero. The essence of the formulaic version of perfection is that the context of the action is reduced to a foil for the perfect hero's progress toward closure, so that he or sometimes she moves smoothly along the frictionless track that the writers have put down, whether we are talking about a detective, a police officer, a cowboy, or a comically dissatisfied wife.

Unvaryingly, the perfect narrative is a story that presumes a severely limited number of possibilities, rather than either the rich dimensionality of the problems imagined by classical society or the endless potential for randomness, discontinuity, and contradiction reflected by the modern view of the universe. In the very small fictional universes of formula TV cut down to the size of the powers of the perfect hero, he (usually in pre-*Peaks* TV) is the character who can cleverly isolate the pertinent elements among the very limited number that surround him and manipulate and master them until all possibilities are excluded from the terrain except those that generate closure. The perfect hero of formulaic series television unfailingly makes the series universe small and cozy in each episode as he masterfully brings control and clarity and above all a clear ending.

In opposition to this, the works of Lynch, Chase, and Simon have no hero, only protagonists who repeatedly discover the immensity of their contexts as the story unfolds. Lynch, Chase, and Simon do not believe in heroes; nor do the other series creators who followed in their footsteps—Eric Overmyer, Matt Weiner, and Lena Dunham. In a completely different spirit from for-mulaic storytelling, the contexts of *Twin Peaks* and post-*Peaks* nonformulaic television get bigger and more open as the series and episodes unfurl, not only running the story off the tracks but disturbing the very idea of tracks. Moreover, in storming the castle of "story product," nonformulaic television places the very notion of standard closure, the destination of those storytell-ing tracks, under siege. In nonformulaic TV, the riptides of a vast universe render closure a dubious prospect.

What I am calling a nonformulaic protagonist is the central figure of auteur series; the protagonist may believe in his or her power to master circumstances, but that is not the perspective of the new auteur series. It has become fashionable to label this character an antihero, but I shall dispense with that term in discussing art television, with apologies to all who have come to rely on it. It is a concept inimical to modernist storytell-ing. The antihero depends as much as does the perfect hero on a fictional world of rigorously diminished possibilities. Dale Cooper in *Twin Peaks*, Tony Soprano in *The Sopranos*, and Jimmy McNulty in *The Wire* are all foundational examples of what the protagonist has become in nonformulaic TV storytelling. They are vividly characterized against the prevailing idea of formula TV's perfect hero but not as its opposite precisely because they do not operate within the same conception of context. The opposite of formula TV's perfect hero inhabits this reductive context as the perfect villain, whose perfection is constituted as reduction of evil, or wrongdoing, to exactly the size that the perfect hero can eradicate. When we observe the consequences of the arrival of the TV auteurs for the formulaic television series (chapter 7), we shall find a use for the term "antihero." Once the perfect villain became the central figure of a formulaic series, he or she became an antihero and all that implies for a perfectly criminal or even evil antihero in a perfect narrative. But that is getting ahead of our story. Nonformulaic TV, the major subject of our voyage, has no perfect heroes or villains and no antiheroes.

Rather, the protagonists conceived of by television auteurs are beset by an enormous, limitless world where the signposts are unclear and are always subject to contexts bigger than themselves. Tony Soprano (James Gandolfini) is a ruthless criminal, but he controls very little. He is neither a perfect hero nor a perfect villain. He lives within a psychological context blurred by internal slippages and discontinuities shooting out of the subconscious, as David Chase imagines it, within complex external circumstances where anything is possible, even the bending of the time/space continuum. FBI agent Dale Cooper (Kyle MacLachlan) lives within quite a different context, but he has in common with Tony a universe whose immensity is beyond manipulation and control. As we shall see, if Cooper is to have any hope of understanding Laura Palmer's death, the central event of Lynch's series, he must let go of the desire to control and open himself to the universe beyond ordinarily conceived limits. Police detective Jimmy McNulty (Dominic West), in *The Wire*, is a protagonist inhabiting a still different context, within which the many layers of social systems and the conflicting energies that collide and flow within them leave no opening for the heroics of the formula TV policeman; there is barely room for closing cases. Unlike the perfect hero of formulaic TV, who is a supreme puzzle solver, bringing unity and harmony to the pieces of a problem that originally seemed perplexing; in modernist nonformulaic television, for example, the protagonists imagined by Lynch, Chase, and Simon are confronted with pieces that do not fit, not just initially, but inherently. It is a modernist thing.

As they united television with the modernist view of the essential randomness and chaos of reality, Lynch, Chase, and Simon mocked the absurdity of the harmonized pieces of formulaic television's perfect narrative and the concept of the hero who might bring that harmony, much as Faulkner's *The Sound and the Fury* derided delusional concepts of a harmonized universe throughout his novel and especially at its extraordinarily powerful closure. At the very end of the novel, pathetic, damaged Benjy Compson has one of his frequent tantrums and can only be comforted by a reassuring carriage ride around the Civil War monument at the center of town, but only if he is driven around in the circle in the only way that he recognizes as familiar. When one of the Compson family servants, inexperienced in Benjy's requirements, directs the carriage horse toward what it turns out is the "wrong way," Benjy begins bellowing at the top of his lungs and does not stop until the carriage is rerouted the other way around the statue, the "right way."

The searing irony of this concluding moment is that the driver who sets things right is achieving the "perfection" of satisfying a highly damaged human being, unable to tolerate a break from routine, or formula as we might say for our purposes. This is Faulkner's distillation of what old storytelling structures are, the answer to a deeply felt, irrational demand for a bogus harmony, which turns out to be nothing more than a familiar pattern that has been elevated idiotically into an illusion of absolute reality. After talking with many of the new television auteurs, I would say that this resembles, if in harsh terms, their metaphors for formula TV storytelling and the way they view the relationship between the formulaic hero and the conditioned television audience.

A nuanced account of this television history must acknowledge that Lynch did not emerge out of nowhere. An impatience with the manufactured, hollow, demented idea of perfection embedded in formula TV writing did exist in early American television, even if for quite a while it went no further than the kind of subversion we see in the unintended feminism of *I Love Lucy* or the rare glimpse of social problems in the short-lived *East Side/West Side*. That series served up flashes of overwhelming cultural issues, but only to resolve its plots according to the schedule of the perfect narrative.

More obstreperous were Rod Serling's embattled and highly original episodic journeys into *The Twilight Zone*, which intentionally shocked the audience into thinking about the rough edges of what was considered normality in the United States. However, try as Serling might, he could only intermittently escape the neat formulaic closure mandated by television's on-track narrative architecture. Consider "Where Is Everybody?"—Serling's early *Twilight Zone* episode about a man wandering around a completely empty town, not knowing who or where he is. The man becomes more and more desperate as a telephone rings. When he answers the call, he hears only an automated voice on the other end. His solitude is increasingly painful. We too become enmeshed in and a bit disoriented by his ordeal of uncertainty. But at closure both the protagonist and the viewer are "rescued" from the threat of a context larger than the normality that the protagonist yearns for. When we learn that our hero is in solitary confinement as part of an experiment run by the United States Army, normality is restored. Serling, a crucial pioneer in early television in his attempts to disturb the perfect narrative and unbalance the perfect hero, was a major influence on David Chase, who carried the torch further than Serling could.

As the various civil rights struggles took hold in American culture from the 1970s onward, some TV series intentionally tried to connect with cultural contexts but could not break away from the constraints of formula represented by either the perfect hero or the perfect narrative. Stories about working women and feminism appeared, for example, in *The Mary Tyler Moore Show* and *Moonlighting* but were always smoothly brought to perfect closure, always disconnected from the ambiguities, discontinuities, and indeterminacies of how gender plays out in the American workplace. Norman Lear brought forth a slew of comedies that acknowledged, with some originality, the presence of racism, bigotry, and sexism, including *All in the Family*, *The Jeffersons*, and *Maude*. And we need to acknowledge how important Lear's success was when he gave audiences some images of the political upheaval around them in their daily lives. But only rarely did any of these innovative shows trouble the entrenched story-product formulaic experience. The main character Archie Bunker (Carroll O'Connor) was perfect in his unfailingly erroneous conclusions about life. The show rarely opened up the modern traumas of irresolution, indeterminacy, or ambiguity that a real Bunker experiences.

However, the few instances in which Lear managed to disturb the formulaic narrative product were impressive. For example, in "Gloria, the Victim" (3.23), Gloria (Sally Struthers), Bunker's daughter, is raped. For sexist reasons, he succeeds in stopping her from bringing charges against the rapist, never taking into account that the man is now free to rape other women or even Gloria again. The complexity of Bunker's "success" is sharply etched. In the final words of the episode Archie, euphoric at having kept Gloria under his control, triumphantly proclaims, "We protected our own," suggesting formulaic closure. At the same time, the camera pans to Gloria, who does not look like a damsel who has been rescued from her distress. On the contrary, her entire body silently screams with terror and disorientation, clearly still wracked with tension. This leaves space for the spectator to ponder Archie's "heroism," since his bringing of order and closure has a scent of the delusional about it. It was a flash of something beyond the machinations of the characters, pointing toward some interesting ambiguities in some larger context beyond Bunker's closed front door.

Traces of social problems became more and more common within the formulaic TV simulacrum after 1970. But the conventional pre-*Peaks* story product did little more than name cultural disturbances, since by closure any truths about them that might have complicated the final vacuous harmonies of the perfect narrative had been eradicated. *Columbo* is a pre-*Peaks* detective series that often brought up social issues within a cleverly conceived dance between the perfect Los Angeles Police Department detective and the perfect villain of the week, but the show never referenced the complexities either of the issue or of the LAPD. Where had the Los Angeles context gone? Columbo's police department is completely configured to facilitate the formulaic progress of the *Columbo* plot. As we shall soon see, there is a world of difference between this and the way David Simon's *The Wire* connects us with the overwhelming problems of crime and punishment within the social reality of the Baltimore Police Department and the other social systems with which it interacts. Where *Columbo* grew from the tradition of formulaic writing, Simon's storytelling grew from his vision of the Baltimore context; context was not, as in *Columbo*, a pro-forma representation of a landscape through which those formulaic tracks run. *Columbo* made room for the presence of some trendy new cultural issues on TV but always only as they might exist in the story-product vacuum.

Consider the *Columbo* episode "By Dawn's Early Light" (4.3), in which British actor Patrick McGoohan starred as the villain, Col. Lyle C. Rumford, the head of a military academy for boys. Rumford is a martinet who runs the academy with a merciless, mysogynist discipline that borders on the sociopathic. As Columbo uncovers the crime that the colonel has committed, old sexist verities are questioned, but formula is not. A macho individualist run amok, Rumford is an aberration that must be caught and contained so that ordinary life can proceed "properly." Intriguingly, McGoohan was the star and unacknowledged creator of *The Prisoner*, a British television series of roughly the same period, in which he pioneered the kind of modern TV storytelling of which *Columbo* did not even dream.

The Prisoner, which preceded Columbo by three years, also questions traditional male stereotypes, but it does so in a profoundly nonformulaic way. Its episodes connect viewers with modern unanswered questions about reality, which appears to be a complex set of boxes within boxes of illusions. The nameless protagonist of *The Prisoner* played by McGoohan is a former action hero (a very perfect hero) who is kidnapped and finds himself in a hermetically sealed, contextless village from which he tries unsuccessfully to escape in each episode. Even when he does seem to escape in the series finale, it is not at all clear whether his liberation is an illusion or not. As creator of *The Prisoner*, McGoohan ruminates on the plight of being trapped in formula television; as a character in "Dawn's Early Light," he is simply trapped. While *The Prisoner* must surely have had some effect on the horizon of possibility understood by American television's creative community, the desire to tell the story of a protagonist who engaged with the random nature of an ambiguous reality had little effect on network production decisions until *Twin Peaks*. American formula television was still making sure that Benjy got driven around the town square in the correct order.

ENTERTAINING NEW DESIRES

Admittedly, comparing the effect of formula TV with the spectacle of pathetic, brain-damaged Benjy bellowing for what is reassuring and familiar at the end of *The Sound and the Fury* is cruel. But the comparison does make the point that from the modernist point of view the perfect TV hero and the perfect narrative are a futile fiction verging on the absurd, pandering to a desire for passivity and reassurance. The auteurs who make nonformulaic television seek to inspire another kind of desire. Nonformulaic television encourages a desire for active, mature engagement. Unlike formula TV, it does not lay out a clear map of the action to manipulate the viewer into accepting the rules of the story unfolding and experiencing a standardized feeling of relief and satisfaction at closure. Lynch, Chase, and Simon (each in his own way) raise questions about whether it is really entertaining to succumb to a story as opposed to engaging it. Nonformulaic TV prefers less manipulation.

In describing to me what he does as a television writer, Matt Weiner, one of David Chase's protégés and the creator of *Mad Men*, argued that all drama involves manipulation but that in art there is a tension between the familiar elements of control and the sincere vision of the artist.[6] As I restate this for our purposes, the familiar elements of control to which he refers are what I have been talking about as formulaic limits on storytelling. The tension between sincerity and manipulation that he invokes is, as I understand it, a tension between the fountainhead of art, the uncontrollable subconscious, and the rationally controlled forms that culture mandates as the vehicles for public utterances.

In formulaic storytelling, any conflict between the unsupervised subconscious and the standardized narrative is negated or kept to a bare minimum, while Lynch and Chase as television auteurs are deeply immersed in their subconscious creative energies, as they said to me in their own ways. So is Eric Overmyer, David Simon's co-creator of *Treme*, one of a very modernist (and very underappreciated) new nonformulaic television series. Simon himself did not mention the subconscious but rather spoke of bearing witness to what is going on in our culture in a way that invokes another strain of sincerity that pits the asymmetries of social observation against the symmetries of formulaic narrative. As we shall see, Lena Dunham's creation of an unprecedented women-centered series, *Girls*, takes still another road away from passivity and consolation. In her storytelling, she invokes the body in the narrative process in a way that summons up cutting-edge thinking that reverses the mind/body hierarchy and creates tension between the expected limits of narrative order and corporeal immediacies, discontinuities, and mysteries.

The power and enigmas of the wild regions of human experience in non-formulaic television are what lure audience desire beyond its comfort zone toward dynamic imaginative adventure and the artist's truth. It is precisely this desire that formulaic TV forbids. We can see this clearly when we look at the contrasting ways in which formulaic and nonformulaic television addresses audience desire, particularly in a series pilot. The pilot of a formulaic series sets up a desire for answers. The pilot of a nonformulaic series sets up a desire for questions. The formulaic series stirs audience curiosity about how the perfect hero will solve the dilemmas of the series. The nonformulaic series incites audience curiosity about what the ground rules of this fictional universe might be and generates the possibility that there are no clear rules. It also incites curiosity about how to function on such a terrain. The traditional formulaic pilot depends on a simplistic desire for certainty and conclusiveness. The pilot of the nonformulaic series connects with our braver desire for wonder as it exposes human and cultural mysteries before our eyes.

We are all familiar with the way formula TV invites us to expect a new solution to an episode of crime and punishment that will be given to us each week (*Law and Order*, for example). We need do nothing more than passively wait. We wait longer for the continuous formulaic series to give us solutions (for example, *Breaking Bad*), but the passivity is the same. (Many readers will be surprised to see *Breaking Bad* classified as a formulaic series; in chapter 7, on post-*Peaks* formulaic TV, we shall explore in detail why this classification is appropriate.) Wholly different is the nonformulaic invitation to active imagination, for example, in *Mad Men*. The main title begins with a room dissolving around a man carrying a brief case, sending the man into free fall, which suggests that everything we believe to be solid and real is imaginary and that ordinary life consists of falling into the unknown of reality—and yet, oxymoronically, the illusion of the substantiality of concrete daily life persists. We shall discuss the tantalizing contradictions in this introduction to the series in detail in chapter 5. Here let us say that the main title is an incentive to wonder, not to wait. Our journey will explore how nonformulaic television irritates us and stimulates us to thoughts that connect us with the problems and frustrations, as well as the joys, that we experience in our lives.

ENTERTAINING NEW DEVICES

Part of the way old television series made audiences believe in the diminished world of the perfect hero and his perfect narrative and put us into a passive relationship with the story was to standardize the sensory range of what the audience sees and hears to promote an undisturbed clarity markedly different from the way we see and hear in real life. The more intoxicating the standard images, the greater the passivity. In nonformulaic TV, the reverse is true. An expansive desire is authorized by a sensory range that shocks and teases the audience into activity.

Generally what we see and hear in formula TV is reduced to the tunnel vision of the perfect hero who is following clues, so that we are not distracted from the tracks on which he or she is gliding toward the perfect ending. We see and hear only what will make us expect, believe, and delight in the success of the hero at closure. Sometimes formula television raises its investment in rendering the audience passive to the level of grand spectacle. Post-*Peaks* formula series like *Game of Thrones* proudly tell their stories using expensive, massive sets. And older formulaic shows like *Columbo* indulged in expensive, technologically intricate location shooting. But their spectacles are soporifics, while the astonishment of nonformulaic television comes from a visual and aural poetry that augments looking/seeing and hearing/listening, disturbs stock reactions, and makes us think and feel.

So much that we see in *Twin Peaks, The Sopranos*, and *The Wire* jolts us out of unimpeded surrender to the plot action and the protagonist's perception so that we are free to contemplate the context in which the series is set. The disturbing visuals and sound are an organic part of the nonformulaic narrative, not, as in formulaic TV, merely an interesting decoration. For the sake of economy, *Twin Peaks* will serve as an example of what has happened to the sensory palette of art television. If we consider only two of the many stunning, provocative, comic, mysterious visuals in *Twin Peaks*, we can see that art television revolutionizes narrative visualization. I am speaking of the strangely compelling sensory details in moments like those in the pilot, when agent Dale Cooper is in the Twin Peaks hospital morgue examining Laura Palmer's corpse. While Cooper is in the process of discovering an important clue, a bit of paper on which is printed the letter "R" under the fingernail of the dead girl at the center of the series, the florescent lights in the morgue ceiling blink on and off. A slight buzz is audible.

The intermittent disruption caused by the blinking, humming ceiling light is not part of a reduced sensory presence that narrows the attention of the audience to Cooper's plot action. Quite the reverse: it lures the viewer, through sensory pleasure, away from that kind of diminution of storytelling. It makes us think of the disruption of the flow of electric energy in the room as a mysterious presence in itself. There are many such displays of energy in *Twin Peaks*, as it is both released and repressed. This is not just a clever device, as we might find in formulaic story products as a momentary gleam of wonder in a train of events and details that will inevitably be reabsorbed into the certainties and resolutions of formula. The vibrant, dramatic, odd presence of energy distracts us from Cooper's control of his examination of a clue, a distraction that points us toward the larger physical context of Laura's death. It is a distraction that conditions our understanding of Cooper's role as a detective, the universe in which the life and death of Laura Palmer are set, and human action in general. The vision here creates an entirely new kind of context for narrative in entertainment that characterizes an entirely new category of television series.

As I initially struggled to think about how I would talk about the varieties of wonder produced by the new auteurs, I was troubled by a strong sense that I had vocabulary for speaking of formula in television but not enough vocabulary for speaking of television that breaks free of it. I felt that lack tied me down just as it did the pioneers of discussion of television aesthetics. They were adept at talking about the aesthetics (such as they are) of formulaic entertainment but not of its distinction from auteur television, which I believed and believe needs to be understood as something apart from business as usual in the mass media. Through a long process of trial and error, confusion and exhilaration, I found my vocabulary for expression of my perspective when I spoke with the new television auteurs. I offer my experiences with them in this book for whatever use they may be to my colleagues and all those interested in the new delights of American entertainment.

GOING TO THE SOURCE

In many ways, the point for me of talking with auteurs was to find a way to report on what is oblique and indirect about their creative processes so that I could validate my perceptions of how television had changed and also so that I could think about the tensions auteur processes create within the production circumstances of television. Auteurs speak and work very differently from formulaic writers. They restrict themselves to thinking about their work as it fits the parameters of industry practices. When I began my research, I could easily document the processes of formulaic writers because of my own practical experiences with the formulaic craft of network soap opera. I had worked on five shows. I knew how constricting the environment is.

Perceiving the differences between interviewing auteurs and interviewing formula writers came naturally to me because I had a great deal of experience as a formula writer in network soap opera. After I finished working in the industry I could verbalize aesthetic qualities in soap opera of which almost all of my former colleagues were unaware. But while I was writing I could not have told anyone anything about them. For this reason, I am not surprised that even the most intelligent, well read, and perceptive of my soap opera colleagues were hard pressed to link what they believed with what they wrote (nor could I when speaking of my own work)—so formulaic were the requirements of the genre.

The best members of the community making formulaic television did want to talk about how they did what they did, but they were likely to interpret a question about their work as being about tone, rhythm, emotionality, and texture, not about vision. They expressed to me a sense that what they were as people automatically and unconsciously determined those aspects of their writing. Indeed, from my experience of writing soap opera and what I understood from colleagues who wrote for the most successful formula television, it did not matter very much what any of them thought except for a remark here or there in the scripts. When I interviewed writers working on nighttime formulaic shows, I got the same impression. For example, when I interviewed Terry Winter while he was creating *Boardwalk Empire*, he gleefully told me that what he was trying to do was give the audience the opposite of what it expected. Whatever you think will happen, he told me, the opposite will happen. In hindsight, I realized with surprise that Winter was talking about the same pleasure expressed by Shonda Rhimes in speeding her story along the tracks; he just built his tracks with more guile.

The interviews that I conducted with the auteurs discussed in this book were immensely different. There was usually an initial period of discomfort because no one in the industry is used to speaking about their worldview in conjunction with their work. To do so may seem like a forbidden pleasure to the auteur, simply because of the industrial context. But, given a fortuitous rapport with an interviewer, auteurs will plunge in and splash around. David Lynch and David Chase were originally reserved with me but soon became freely articulate. Eric Overmyer, whose career began in the theater, was more comfortable with far-ranging discussions of meaning and philosophical positions. Matt Weiner, an extremely articulate man, at first expressed his sense that many of his colleagues would call the kind of conversation that I wished to have with him "precious." But he ultimately seemed to enjoy it. For

David Simon, by contrast, a conversation about meaning, context, and philosophy was immediately familiar and comfortable. He is used to initiating such discussions, so, if he did not expect to have that kind of conversation with an interviewer, he took no time at all to acclimate himself.

It was also of interest and importance to me to learn of how the auteur is, from time to time, somewhat stymied by the collaborative process. In the heat of production, working with talented colleagues on whom auteurs depend, but who are overly influenced by the omnipresent tendency toward formulaic writing in the industry, they may receive intense pressure to take the formulaic route. An example of a situation like this is the disagreement that took place in *The Sopranos* writer's room with respect to the disappearance of a Russian gangster in "Pine Barrens" (*The Sopranos*, 3.11). In this episode, Christopher Moltisanti (Michael Imperioli) and Paulie Gualtieri (Tony Sirico) drive to the Pine Barrens to bury Valery (Vitali Baganov), a tough Russian gangster they think they have killed. But he not only leaps out at them when they open their car trunk but escapes into the deep snow of the Jersey winter. They fire at him as he flees but can never ascertain whether or not they killed him. It was Chase's very firm decision to leave the question unanswered, but the writers argued about whether or not that was the best way to handle the phantom Russian. Terry Winter, a key staff writer and the future creator of *Boardwalk Empire*, tried very hard to convince Chase to pay off the unanswered question in a future episode. Winter was speaking formula discourse. Chase was responding with the new nonformulaic approach. Winter continued to be a very important member of the team, but Chase kept a steady hand on the wheel.

The obliqueness of the auteur requires the luxury of time in order to reach an understanding with him/her. The standard industry twenty-minute interview with an auteur is all but pointless. The more time, the better. It is a disorienting but rich experience.

My many years of speaking to David Lynch have been like floating through the layers of a palimpsest. When I first interviewed Lynch in 1990, I wanted to confirm my own intimations of the seriousness of his art in opposition to the climate of discussion at that time, which was based on assumptions that he was a trickster, a kind of camp terrorist exploiting the media for notoriety. When I visited Lynch in Los Angeles, he greeted me from the cabin of his pickup truck with a twinkle in his eye, sounding much like Gordon Cole in *Twin Peaks* (1990–1991 and 2017). I was not sure what was ahead for us. But his seriousness as an artist was soon evident. Just as quickly his modernist engagement with the subconscious was undeniable. Although no school of psychology was specified, Lynch liked what I said about Carl Jung. We looked at paintings together, talking about not categories of meaning but what art does to the observer inside. Lynch spoke of inner life often. It was a natural progression for me to digest our discussion and then write *The Passion of David Lynch*, about the connection between his work and the inner lives of characters and audience. I wrote that book at a time when everyone else was trying to fit Lynch into genre categories or commenting on his hair, his voice, or some "groovy" line in one of his films. My first years of talking to him connected me and my readers to his art heritage, but not as fully as after I spoke with Lynch in March 2010, when he revealed his connections to the extremely old worldview of the Indian Holy Vedas and to the new worldview of quantum mechanics.

Lynch had accepted my references to Jung as a serviceable way of talking about his worldview, but he had not previously revealed to me his own point of reference, which related consciousness to composition of matter, as Jung did not. When I told him I had studied physics as part of my research about his films from *Lost Highway* (1997) to *Inland Empire* (2006), he opened up to me about his interest in both modern and ancient physics. In this portion of our 2010 interview, Lynch spoke of the unified field of consciousness, which is at the center of a structured universe and accounts for the existence of matter. He talked about the unified field, which is a central consciousness, the source of everything, including matter:

> DAVID LYNCH: It's eternal. Unbounded. Has no boundaries. It's infinite. It alone is. . . . Now this unified field is a field of infinite intelligence, infinite, infinite creativity, infinite bliss [Lynch makes an explosion sound], infinite bliss, infinite love, infinite energy—
>
> MARTHA NOCHIMSON: —and power?
>
> DAVID LYNCH: Infinite power. Infinite. Infinite peace, by the way. Infinite peace. Very important for this time. Now, the Vedas are the laws of nature. I don't know how many. The words are called mantras. And they are made up of syllables. So what they say is that after every single syllable there's a gap. Maharishi says this gap is critical. And there's another syllable and a gap. And another syllable. And they make up the words. . . . That which is heard. Heard as a sound, as a vibration. That's the Vedas.

In that interview Lynch permitted me to connect him and his art with extremely specific inspirations that make his storytelling a conduit for television audiences to both the most ancient belief systems and the most modern scientific thought. "At this very moment, Martha Nochimson," he said to me on March 28, 2010,

> there are almost an infinite number of universes as big or bigger than our universe. Almost an infinite number. It's so huge and what are they really? What are they really? This unified field is this transcendent, this medium—life—is beneath everything, and permeates everything, and is above everything. It is everywhere. Here, there, and everywhere. And one of these days, the quantum physicists—there's another whole thing—they may really believe, well, not this guy [Niels] Bohr, but they may really believe in the unified field. But they don't have the experience of that unified field. Now you take a kid in school who gets a grant from the David Lynch Foundation to learn transcendental meditation. They get this technique to dive within, to transcend. They're experiencing that exact same unified field that those people have discovered in their equations and in their thinking. And that's the thing. That's the subjective science. Gives them the experience of that. So Maharishi says it's knowledge *and experience*. What's missing is the experience. You can experience it. And when you experience it you say, "Wait a minute. This is what life's all about."

David Chase spoke repeatedly of his admiration for Lynch and how *Twin Peaks* had inspired him to follow his own vision. As an artist, Chase had not needed to interview Lynch to pick up the torch from him. As a critic, however, I had to know what was going on with someone I perceived as the most influential man in the mass-entertainment industry, a breaker of tracks. He was and still is. Chase had been inspired to do work on the basis of his own intuition of how film and television are dreamlike even when the action is ostensibly taking place within ordinary reality.[7] In our conversations, I became privy to the way Chase's mind works imaginatively, which gave me insight into his benchmark series. In an e-mail of October 28, 2013, Chase displays his fascination with the way ideas and impressions grow and connect over the years through chance and the beautiful indirection of the imagination as it internally weaves experiences:

"What is your interpretation of the following unspooling of events?" his e-mail begins:

> In 1997 I wished to end the first season of *Sopranos* with a song. Because of New Jersey and because I loved the song I decided on "State Trooper" from Bruce Springsteen's "Nebraska." I went to Steven Van Zandt about it

who had told me, "If you want to use Bruce's music, make sure it's the one you want because you're only going to get one chance." At that time, Bruce was licensing his music less, I think, than he does now. I stuck with "State Trooper." It ended the first season. I still thrill to it now. (Though I haven't seen it in 15 years.)

2. In getting ready to air the same first season of the series—all the episodes including the last were now shot and edited—a main title sequence was needed to begin every episode. What came to me was the drive from the Lincoln tunnel, thru NJ, to home in North Caldwell. We went out, shot thousands of feet of car shots through industrial Turnpike Jersey highway and edited it down (gifted editor Sidney Wolinsky). You, the audience, saw it every week.

3. Years later I made movie about a rock and roll band from New Jersey in the mid to late 60s. Van Zandt did the music. Springsteen was alluded to.

4. The other day I received an email from Jon Landau, Springsteen's producer, with a link to Springsteen's website inviting me (and I'm sure many others) to see a video they'd made. The video used the song, "Dream Baby, Dream." You know me and dreams. The song was GREAT. I thought right away of using it for the end of my next film (about whose subject matter you seemed to express a lot of surprise. "What gave you THAT idea?") If I make the film I will use DB,D.

5. I researched "Dream Baby, Dream" and learned Bruce did not write it. Unusual for him. That it was a 1970 song by a duo called Suicide. A techno pre-punk band from New York. Springsteen was described as a fan. Techno pre-punk? Bruce Springsteen?

6. I You-Tubed an original performance by the band from way back in the early 1970s (almost just the period where Not Fade Away ends). It's great. And though the song was not "Dream Baby, Dream" there was no mistaking its influence on "State Trooper," both the "lonely" aural space and the singer's ghostly whoops. Beautiful.

7. I played another YouTube Suicide video and this was comprised only of early 1970's shots from a car (in black and white) moving through an industrial landscape of smokestacks, factories and a head-on POV shot of the highway ahead through the windshield.

Thoughts?

Many. Chase's generous sharing of his process with me helped me to reflect back on *The Sopranos* in ways that conditioned chapter 2, as you will see.

David Simon similarly broke up stock responses about *The Wire* when he spoke to me about the problem of writing a socially conscious story:

> I'm always getting in trouble with ideologues, because nothing is clean. The reporter in me just has to say that police shooting is awful, and that police shooting is not as bad as that, but it's still pretty bad, but this one [some quintessential police brutality situation] isn't what you think it is. And I can look at the overall and say yes, law enforcement has by dint of its misuse as a form of social control and racial control brutalized the black community unnecessarily and with clear systemic bias for generations. I can say that. But then if you give me the guts of the shooting I don't immediately have to strain it through the systemic [a political formula]. Okay, well what happened? At a certain point I'm dealing with a man who got shot or a woman who got shot and a police officer who shot them. . . . There are individuals who come to that moment not just as functions of race and class but as individuals with free agency that has to be considered as well.

This was part of his response to some questions I asked him about *Between the World and Me*, Ta-Nehisi Coates's book about racism in America. I had introduced Coates into the conversation early in the interview to give us a common point of reference. I guessed that Simon would know the book, and I was correct and then some. Simon not only knows Coates's work but has participated in panels with him and was, at the time, working with him on plans for a new television series that unfortunately never came to fruition. But Simon took pains to say that he values Coates not because he agrees with him about everything, but because Coates is a rigorous thinker who interrogates his conclusions and his own prejudices. He gave as an example the first time he met Coates on a *New Yorker* panel about race. Simon questioned the furor about the situation in Ferguson, Missouri, when Michael Brown, a young black man, was shot by police while he was holding his hands in the air. Simon stunned the crowd when he told them he could not call it murder because the evidence just was not there.

A heated discussion followed, then Coates, the son of a former Black Panther as well as a historian committed to telling the story of prejudice in America, spoke up. As Simon told it,

> He [Coates] said, "The reason you don't want to do that [call it murder if it is not] is that it weakens your argument." He's looking at it from the perspective of someone who has not covered police work for what it was

and what it should have been. He doesn't have that background. But he said that if you make claims that can't be sustained then the legitimacy of your argument regardless of its validity overall become vulnerable. And I said exactly. He summed it up in one sentence. And it came to me over my shoulder when I most needed to have what I was saying affirmed. I love his ability to see with clarity.

My interview with Simon confirmed that he was firmly committed to creating 360-degree characters and situations that could not be characterized in terms of the one-sided ideological ideas about *The Wire* held by many people, including many who admire the series. Before I spoke with Simon, I was inclined to look at the show anachronistically myself. I understood that it was multidimensional, not narrowly ideological, but I approached it for the most part in the spirit of the Book of Ecclesiastes in the Judeo-Christian Bible, hardly a connection to modernist thinking, although it is built on a relativistic perspective. Simon made me look more carefully at his complex, cutting-edge mode of storytelling:

> Listen, a lot of people say that drama is real life with the boring parts left out. That's an old saw. And to an extent if that weren't true then every drama would look like a Frederick Wiseman movie. I love Frederick Wiseman and I find great value in what he does; it's not drama. So it's [*The Wire*] not documentary. It is trying to tell the story that you believe is the most legitimate and powerful that you can tell, given the reality you're trying to vet. And saying that this is an admission that if you want the piece not to be a fundamental lie at its core, you have to let in the notion that not everything is a perfect narrative, and it isn't. It isn't. At a certain point your villains behave in noble ways and your heroes disappoint you in certain circumstances. And certain people do not get revenge when they deserve it.

I thought he had handed me my Ecclesiastes interpretation on a silver platter, with its poetry about there being a season for everything, and its observation that, out under the sun, "the race is not to the swift, nor the battle to the strong, neither yet bread to the wise, . . . but time and chance happeneth to them all" (9:11). But when I introduced the idea at that point, he debunked it, saying the Ecclesiastes and the Book of Job were both distasteful to him because they counseled resignation, an interpretation that I am not alone in disagreeing with. However, the point was not to argue the issue with Simon but to find out what he thought. And find out I did. Simon broke me free of my own predispositions, and any residual stock responses. Ecclesiastes as he saw the book is the last thing he intended in his portrait of the immense variety of life in *The Wire*. On the contrary, he told me he was always amazed

> when people watched *The Wire* and were like, "Well, there's nothing to be done." That it was urging that everything is fucked. No, this is an argument for society, for the city. This is an argument for us. This is what needs to be attended to. To me, I have the same tonalities [in *The Wire*] that I had when I was a journalist. Let's go look at what's actually happening on the ground and write about it and make people give a shit.

He added that he was writing to help the audience to see that it is complicit in cultural problems by failing to attend to what is actually going on and that allowing ourselves to be distracted is at the bottom of how things became as bad in America as they have become.

Uta Briesewitz, the first and most important cinematographer on *The Wire*, also helped me to shape my vision of the series, though more as a matter of confirmation than revision. I came to my book believing that *The Wire* had been completely misconstrued as cinema verité. She confirmed my opinion by expressing her frustration with this misconception. In Briesewitz's words from the transcript of our interview:

> **UTA BRIESEWITZ:** I wouldn't call it a documentary look. For me a documentary look I would describe as something that seems more spontaneous, more hand held.
>
> **MARTHA NOCHIMSON:** And less composed.
>
> **UTA BRIESEWITZ:** And less composed. I think he [David Simon] wanted it real. He didn't want it stylized in terms of beautifying the environment. He wanted Baltimore to look as real as possible. But that still means I lit those African American faces very carefully. I think there's a lot of beauty in those portraits. And I lit them very carefully so therefore sometimes it was a little bit frustrating that people were not getting it. If my cinematography was mentioned it was described as gritty. Just because the environment is gritty I wouldn't call the cinematography gritty.

As will become apparent in the following chapters, I had similar experiences of discovery and/or confirmation during all my interviews and when I carefully scrutinized what Lena Dunham had said as opposed to what had routinely been said about her by entertainment journalists and scholars alike. Without talking with the auteurs, as you will see, I could not have become as fully aware of how their art is filled with their acknowledgement of the limits of language. I have often thought that it was exposure to their physical presence more than their words that impacted my understanding of their work, even in the case of my interviews with Weiner, which were almost always on the telephone. Something was added to their words by the sensory tone and immediacy of speaking together and speaking to each other that broke me free for a lively, uncaged understanding of new television. Presence, that intangible element in interviews, became a potent part of my escape from an obstructive discourse about television. I found in that powerful and communicative sense of presence a way to understand how it is possible for there to be such a thing as auteur television when the medium is so collaborative.

Their commonalities have to do with their rejection of laying train tracks or pipe or making sausage and the standard hero. They have to do with the breadth of vision that they each brought to creating a series: individual vision, auteur vision, a counterforce to the business of storytelling. They each understood the protagonist as a figure in a large landscape, a large universe that he or she could neither control nor understand. And they saw their narratives as what I am calling part of modernist culture, the understanding of reality as beyond human certainty, beyond human limits, or beyond cultural traditions and systems. They all in their own ways verbalized the importance to them of silence and the limits of language in constructing characters, scenes, and the overarching sense of the series as a whole. They could not speak their truths within the limits of verbal language and prevailing concepts, that is to say, within the limits of formula television. While they were all concerned with context, it was the silence of the context, the need to portray it through nonverbal gesture, images, music, and tone. Of course, as artists, not disciples of some standardized practice or philosophy, they do not conceive of context in the same way. O, the delicious abundance and revelations of those differences that I now share!

THE SECOND TIME AROUND

The theme of this introduction has been connection, a new tradition of expressive, nonformulaic television that is bonded to culture and to life. In speaking of the nonformulaic series I shall analyze the remaking of series television as an organic link between the history of modern literature and the mass media. In this introduction, I have mapped a number of contrasts between the disconnects of early formulaic television and the lively cultural connections with culture that emerged with *Twin Peaks*. I have indicated that a series of conversations with new television auteurs has helped me to make important distinctions in the history of television entertainment. However, what follows will not be a neat polarization of formulaic and nonformulaic television. The modernity of the cultural and contextual connectivity in nonformulaic television varies a great deal from artist to artist; and the development of new kinds of formulaic television in response to the new television auteurs has sometimes blurred the line between themselves and nonformulaic artistry. Since *Twin Peaks*, formulaic TV has become a different kind of product. What kind? We shall see. The first six chapters to follow will articulate the massive differences among the varieties of storytelling practiced by television auteurs. The seventh chapter will excavate the changes in formulaic storytelling that have occurred because of the mere existence of nonformulaic TV, a second-wave formula television that will henceforward be referred to as Formula 2.0.

The Formula 2.0 television series is now a massive category of entertainment that is also part of the legacy of auteur television. The primary goal of our discussion of this development in the culture industry will be to sharpen distinctions between a series that is built on bona fide modernism and a series that refers to new developments in cultural thinking but in which the perfect narrative and perfect hero are alive and well, if slightly different in appearance. The disconnect from culture is almost fully retained in 2.0, while it provides the illusion that it is a new and improved form of fun and diversion. But there will also be another, more intriguing goal: to isolate those 2.0 series that veer tantalizingly toward modernist art narrative, never really making the leap from story product but briefly opening new doors for the mass audience. If they are not art, they nevertheless represent opportunities, albeit diminished by the limits imposed by story-product manufacture, for speculating about aesthetics in formula TV.

Finally, I shall provide a "Coda" about David Lynch's 2017 series, *Twin Peaks*. For we are floating in a moving river. The TV story has already been altered since I began researching and writing about it. David Lynch is dreaming again, and those of us who are interested in television as a medium of art as well as entertainment will do well to dream with him about some new questions and feel the rush of new possibilities already in progress.

THE FOUNDING TITANS

·

Men without Formula

CHAPTER 1

DAVID LYNCH, *TWIN PEAKS*

DAVID LYNCH: I think at the bottom of everything is the super string. Unmanifest, self-referral consciousness. The Unified Field. That, they say, is perfect symmetry. When spontaneous sequential symmetry breaking starts, the little strings appear. Forces come from this symmetry breaking and act upon the particles. The whole thing starts to grow and change. But really it's all consciousness.
MARTHA NOCHIMSON: The source of time and space is consciousness?
DAVID LYNCH: Yes, the source of everything.

> —David Lynch, in-person interview with author, March 18, 2010

Toward the end of 1989 American film schools were ablaze with the news that David Lynch, already well known as an independent filmmaker, was about to make his television debut. I was teaching at the Tisch School of the Arts at New York University at the time. Because of a provocative lecture I had given on *Blue Velvet*, students pulled me aside regularly to tell me about the imminent arrival of *Twin Peaks*. They felt that something new was on the horizon. And they were right.

Lynch's art background was the diving board from which he had leaped into film and would also inform his plunge into television. The resulting series could not be typical. Did any television writers at that moment have roots in art school or such a powerful creative connection with the untrammeled energy of the subconscious? Could any one of them say to me, as Lynch did, "90 percent of the time, I don't know what I'm doing"? Did any of them have a horror of being asked to explain their work? (Lynch asks, "How dare they?" It is a question that results from the kind of awe the artist feels for the immense forces that he serves but neither comprehends nor masters.) Lynch's art television was thus born to be the domain of powerful, profound energies, not trivial, perfect plotting. To call the original *Twin Peaks* a work of modern art is only appropriate.

Twin Peaks had little or no relationship to the formulaic television that had gone before it; it was the first taste of art television for the TV audience. It was immeasurably significant, but it was not a complete release from formulaic dissociations. The original *Twin Peaks* has a rocky history. In *The Passion of David Lynch: Wild at Heart in Hollywood*, I have already documented important differences between Lynch and his co-creator Mark Frost, and there were even greater differences between Lynch and the American Broadcasting Company (ABC), the network that produced and distributed the series. Neither Frost nor ABC understood that Lynch was not working within the strictures of story product. Did they even know how circumscribed the familiar TV practices were? My experiences with ABC as a writer suggest they did not; nor would they know how to be introspective about their demands on Lynch. The paucity of thought about how television is written forces most network executives to work from a gut feeling of what feels familiar and what feels alien and to howl like Benjy when the carriage drives the wrong way around the monument.

Frost, committed to making a television show that was lively, fresh, and filled with striking visual images, nevertheless did not grasp the originality of Lynch's concept of mystery or detectives. He made clear to me that he thought of series protagonist Special Agent Dale Cooper (Kyle MacLachlan) of the Federal Bureau of Investigation (FBI) as part of the Sherlock Holmes tradition. However, Holmes is a character made for perfect television narratives, a detective who narrows the world severely as he reduces the millions of details of reality to a perfect trail of clues and a tight, clear, indisputable closure.[1] Frost was oblivious to the contrasts between Cooper and this tradition: Cooper discovered a bigger and more mysterious world with every step he took into his investigation of the death of Laura Palmer (Sheryl Lee). When Lynch removed himself more and more to do postproduction on his film *Wild at Heart* (1990) in the second season of the series (from episode 8 until the double episode that concluded the series), there was an escalating collapse into formulaic entertainment contrivance. Happily, with the series finale, Lynch miraculously stopped the runaway train and took his show off the tracks completely, as we shall see.

In its inception, Lynch's creation of his TV series was totally informed by his personal vision, his sensitivity to what the medium of television offers the storyteller, and his faith in the power of the imagination. His rejection of the perfect hero and the perfect narrative has become the model for art television, not because Cooper is a prototype, but because he is a paragon of freedom from formulaic constraints. (For a detailed discussion of the perfect hero and the perfect narrative, see "The David Effect" in the introduction.) Most of the members of the creative television community with whom I have spoken who were involved in making nonformulaic series have told me how seeing the first seven episodes of *Twin Peaks* shattered the once impermeable boundaries of formula television for them. What happened after the first "magic seven" in the production history of *Twin Peaks*, then, is crucially pertinent to our study, since circumstances might have meant the end of the new beginning for the auteur television series.

Lynch chose to make a series about a detective because mystery is what interests him and what he believes is most interesting to the majority of people, mystery at the highest level of curiosity involving the most far-reaching drive to understand the enigmas of the universe and the human condition. His story about a beautiful dead girl, Laura Palmer, was not calibrated to the low level of formula mystery stories that close down our perception of the world to include the number of clues necessary to reach narrative conclusion. Instead, Lynch sought to show the cosmic ramifications of Laura Palmer's death and would have followed through with a narrative of how they reverberated limitlessly, if production circumstances had not gone wrong. This chapter is about how he built that boundlessness into the first seven episodes of the series and reinserted it into the closure of the series, opening up the possibility of *Twin Peaks* (2017), with which this study will conclude.

Lynch was not an avid television watcher or enthusiast when he made *Twin Peaks*. Rather, television presented itself to him intuitively as an extension of what he was already doing with cinema. He immediately understood that television offered all the space for visual storytelling of film but more room for considering the element of time in narrative. Lynch grasped as no one else yet has the temporal opportunities inherent in the medium of television. ABC gave Lynch only a limited opportunity to play with televisual time and space in 1990–1991.

Lynch used that opportunity successfully to offer the audience the incandescent Dale Cooper, who distinguishes himself from all TV detectives who came before him by seeking answers in dreams, visions, and symbolic rituals and finding only questions. It is now common knowledge that Laura was killed by her father, Leland Palmer (Ray Wise), who was possessed by a malign spirit who calls himself BOB (Frank Silva). But how fully is it understood that the enigmatic fusion of Leland and BOB destroys the seeming closure of the case? Is there a full realization of the enormity of the changes Lynch made to the script that was handed to him as the blueprint for the series finale? The last episode transforms the solution of the crime into a new set of questions and a shattering revision of formula conventions that multiplied the complications surrounding Laura's death just when clichéd TV would have narrowed them into air-tight closure.

Because ABC had considered the case closed in 2.9, the show had dwindled into a formulaic set of episodes in which a new antagonist, this time a perfect villain named Windom Earle (Kenneth Welsh), dragged Cooper into the role of perfect hero and threatened to send the series careening toward oblivion until Lynch made a last-minute save. Thus, we need to understand the first shift of American television beyond formula in terms of three distinct processes: industry events; the storytelling that unfurled on the television screen; and the contrast between the first seven episodes and the central episodes between episode 2.1 and 2.20 that descended into what become more and more trivial formulaic storytelling. This is crucial if we are to comprehend both the brilliance of the way the series began and its miraculous recovery.

A DETECTIVE AND HIS CONTEXT

In its approach to storytelling, the universe of *Twin Peaks* unravels the universe of Sherlock Holmes. Sir Arthur Conan Doyle's detective was appropriate for his time and represented the contemporary prevailing positivist zeitgeist of 1897–1927. Sigmund Freud and Carl Jung had only begun to disseminate their ideas; quantum physics and the theory of relativity, which exploded contemporary ideas about matter and time, were formulated well after the Holmes series began. All of these were to change the social landscape, but they were only glints in a few eyes when Holmes reigned supreme as the prototypical detective. Pre-*Peaks* TV detectives, however, who to a man or woman imitate Holmes, are rooted in a long-dead zeitgeist instead of the contemporary thinking of fin de siècle America with which Lynch connects his audience through Cooper. Lynch comments on the diminished capacities of the Sherlockian detective in *Twin Peaks* through the person of Albert Rosenfield (Miguel Ferrer), the FBI's most brilliant forensic investigator in the series, an amusing and interesting but not ultimately successful factotum. Rosenfield's uncanny Sherlockian ability to see into the role of material clues is dazzling, but he is too narrowly focused. Cooper is amused by Albert and gives him his due. Albert is able to tell Cooper the composition of the rope with which Laura Palmer was bound the night she died, but the information, though impressive, creates no progress toward a solution of the crime or a deeper understanding of the crime and its context, Cooper's true goal.

Albert is restricted to a laboratory, cut off from the larger world. By contrast, *Twin Peaks* is filled with uncircumscribed and unbounded terrain of the ceaselessly moving particles capable of infinite possibilities of quantum mechanics and Vedic creation mythologies that so fascinate Lynch.[2] Lynch uses Cooper's dreams and waking visions and the sensory palette of images to disturb our expectations by suggesting the energy in things unrecognized by both the controlling intellect of a Sherlockian detective and marketplace masters of buying and selling. The trivialization of matter is particularly represented in those masters of the *Twin Peaks* marketplace, Ben Horne (Richard Beymer) and Jerry Horne (David Patrick Kelly), who see in the mysteries and majesty of Ghostwood Forest only the basis of a real estate deal. Their greed, rapaciousness, and intent to pollute the world around them for profit represent the pessimism about human culture that has been typically linked to modernist art. But if Lynch is painfully aware of the destructive power of commodification, another influence on him accounts for the ever-present sense of something positive beyond the world of business transactions.[3]

Lynch has been inspired by his sense of the power of the subconscious, but not because he has read Freud and Jung. Rather, he has experienced that power in himself, in works of modern art by Francis Bacon, Jackson Pollock, and Edward Hopper and in the modern art of cinema, such as the films of Orson Welles, Federico Fellini, Billy Wilder, and Alfred Hitchcock.[4] He has been inspired by quantum mechanics, not by reading the works of Niels Bohr or Werner Heisenberg but through a friendship with physicist John Hagelin. He has been inspired by the physics of the Eastern Vedic worldview, which adds another plane of reality to the terrain in this series, and gained insight through his meditation practice, which began in the 1970s. All of these shape the context of *Twin Peaks*, which combines the mysteries of human consciousness with a sense of the particle realities identified by physics, surging under the appearance of solid matter. These yield a keen awareness of the misinterpretation of the terrain of the marketplace by most of the characters.[5] They also are crucial to the *Twin Peaks* audience.

Knowing Lynch's influences and that they are his own poetic transformations of current ideas, not straight quotations of rigorous academic or scientific ideas of physics, psychology, and Vedic religion, is important to our understanding of the role of context in the storytelling Lynch intended. The messengers of darkness from beyond who, like BOB, are behind Laura's death and the interpenetration of the positive and negative energy of the Red Room, which affect Cooper as he searches for answers, derive from that aspect of Lynch's private worldview and give us a story that puts an auteur spin on his modernism. Lynch's interest in Vedic vision combines with his admittedly basic introduction to ideas about matter in quantum mechanics to create the larger context of mystery of which Laura's death is only a small

FIGURE 1.1. *BOB, a figure of darkness from beyond who combines Vedic and quantum mysteries.*

part. The expansive, ambiguous world of *Twin Peaks* marbles darkness and light, optimism and pessimism, a far cry from the polarized, diminished world of the formulaic Sherlockian television detective.

SPECIAL AGENT DALE COOPER: "WHAT'S THE MATTER?"

When Lynch was preparing *Twin Peaks* for release as a DVD boxed set, he added to each episode a new prologue spoken by the Log Lady (Catherine Coulson), the mystic truth-teller of the town of Twin Peaks. Sitting in her cabin in all her sybilline, besweatered glory holding her log, she became Lynch's way to highlight his blend of the ordinary and the visionary and to bend to his own vision the formulaic tactic of the prologue, which usually enhances the sense of certainty about the meaning of what is to follow. Instead, Lynch challenges the certainty that had crept into his series after the original seven episodes, against his desire. The prologue to the first episode, after the pilot, is a good place to begin delving into the nature of what *Twin Peaks* introduced into American entertainment that set it apart so dramatically from formula television: "I carry a log. Yes. Is it funny to you? It is not to me. Behind all things are reasons. Reasons can even explain the absurd. Do we have the time to learn the reasons behind the human being's varied behavior? I think not. Some take the time. Are they called detectives? Watch—and see what life teaches."

Lynch was breaking with pre-1990 television by inviting the audience to work to understand his story instead of riding along tracks that had been put down in the second season by formulaic writing. The richness of this simple prologue is startling. The Log Lady suggests at the same time the possibility of understanding if we try, the likelihood that we are not used to trying, and the existence of models for us to learn from: detectives. A transmutation of our idea of detectives will come later, both in the episodes themselves and in future prologues. Here Lynch builds on the prologue to the pilot in which Lynch nudges us to think of Laura in terms of her relationship to a very large cosmic context: "It [Twin Peaks] encompasses the All. It is beyond the fire, though few would know that meaning. It is a story of many but begins with one, and I knew her. The one leading to the many is Laura Palmer."

The prologues are vehicles for deepening our first impressions of his series, that the interesting questions bear on our sensibilities and our relationship to the largest reality that exists, not on the comparatively much less important question of "Who killed Laura Palmer?"—the trivializing focus of marketers.

Lynch took the opportunity of the *Twin Peaks* DVD boxed set to undercut the marketers and make us look anew at the invitation in the episodes of the first season in a larger context. At first the invitation is disguised as pleasant humor. In our first glimpse of Cooper, as he is driving to Twin Peaks to investigate Laura's death, he is dictating a message for Diane. We are never told who or what Diane is; this is among the initial nudges for viewers to have fun doing some imaginative work. We are left to deduce from the clues embedded in Cooper's behavior as he dictates into a tape recorder, giving her details about the weather and his expenses that place him firmly, for the moment, within familiar marketplace coordinates of ordinarily conceived time, space, and money. Diane, his disembodied assistant back at the home offices of the FBI, whom we never see or hear in the original series, becomes a running joke, but a joke with serious undertones. When Cooper records messages for Diane, he seems completely within our comfort zone: the detective as we know and understand him. With his crisp grasp of order and facts, Cooper will surely put an end to the disarray of a shocking crime in Twin Peaks—just like the *ur*-detective of the mass media, Sherlock Holmes. But Diane's persistent invisibility playfully insinuates a phantom into Cooper's solid world.

Similarly, even before we meet Cooper, the images of the main title montage of objects and bodies seem to be solid representations of a terrain that is beautiful and familiar, except for the lap dissolves among them that create just a tinge of mystery about the relationships among different forms of matter and the fast and slow motion of the natural energy of water. Once the body of Laura Palmer is discovered, little by little Lynch intensifies the presence of an uncanny activity in ordinary things that becomes increasingly important in understanding the mystery of this one dead girl as the series proceeds.

Lynch asks us, for example, to focus on the ceiling fan upstairs in the Palmer home at the moment that Sarah Palmer (Grace Zabriskie), Laura's mother, discovers that Laura is not in her bedroom, an atypical choice at such an emotionally charged time, when we know that Laura is dead. Such fans are literally "part of the furniture" in mystery stories, often atmospheric markers of an exotic or seedy setting for the drama of human emotions, but always stable, the part of the detective story that will not suddenly change in front of our eyes, as characters often do. Here the fan achieves a presence that is as indeterminate as the human situation it looms above, because the sound design encourages us to listen to the air churning loudly through the fan's revolving blades in a new way. The air is a counterforce, a power already there before the fan begins to move, made more visible and audible by the humanmade machine. As Sarah Palmer runs up the stairs, something else is set in motion aside from her anxiety; there is an energy aside from hers in her home.

A similar effect occurs when Lynch comes in for a close-up of the curled telephone cord left dangling when Leland drops the phone after being told of his daughter's death by Sheriff Harry S. Truman (Michael Ontkean) while he is talking on the phone to his distraught wife. As the cord hangs there, the vibration of Sarah's despairing voice continues to course through its looped wire. The long take of this phone cord is another atypical directorial choice. But as the first season of Twin Peaks progresses, such choices become the norm and redefine the audience's ideas about the relationship between energy and instruments of culture. Cinematographer Uta Briesewitz, who created the look of David Simon's The Wire, has commented on the mesmerizing art of Lynch's visualization of the story. She was stunned by Lynch's decision to stay on the telephone cord and also not to cut between Sarah and Leland, as would be standard procedure in a formulaic series. Lynch's decision to hold viewer attention on one person much longer than in the conventional way of approaching the scene, as Briesewitz says, lets things sink in for an active viewer response, instead of telling the audience what and how to think through formulaic editing.[6]

It is not a coincidence that we see the fan and phone cord as we have never seen objects before at the very moment when we watch Laura's parents discover her death. Lynch's construction of Cooper's investigation encourages us to see animate materiality as so crucial to the case that it is being given parity with the human drama. This is one instance in which Laura's death becomes a path into perception of the All, which the Log Lady has asked us to think of as the final destination of the inquiry about Laura. As Sarah makes her heartbreaking discovery, we look at a ceiling fan as well as at her face; when Leland drops the phone at the news of Laura's death, Lynch opts for a long pan down the telephone cord, which is given almost as much emphasis as the reaction shots of Laura's father and mother. Interpretations of these choices as merely interesting stylistic devices not only miss the point of the rhetoric of the series but also miss the point of how this expanded sensory palette changed the horizon of expectations for television.

This is an important early moment in which Lynch's influences from Vedic vision and quantum science combine to make us see and hear differently. He does this not because he is a theorist, or because he is proselytizing for a religion, but because he is an artist sensitive on a subconscious level not only to the percolating ideas of our time about matter but also to the way ancient cultures are connected with modern ideas. They are part of the 90 percent of his work that he himself does not consciously supervise. Watching the first season and the series finale of *Twin Peaks*, we hear and see differently than we do in formula TV because we are engaged with a work of art, and transformation is at the soul of the relationship between the spectator and the artwork. Sight and sound here do not render us passive before the mechanics of the plot. Rather, they disturb the plot to jolt us from submitting to images and noises that will support the perfect hero and his perfect plot. Instead, we are encouraged to actively surrender our stock responses and engage our own imaginations in a way that will bring us into communion with the zeitgeist of our time and our own lives.

Sensory connection with the great ideas of our time creates a path for our imaginations toward the All. In Vedic terms, vibrating sound is shaking up the illusion of solidity in both the image of the ceiling fan and the phone cord. In quantum terms, Sarah's voice moves in particle form through a phone cord, while her body is in a room miles away, so she is effectively in superposition, metaphorically in two places at the same time. An enigmatic connection between objects and sound vibrations is made here and also in the image of the ceiling fan. In Lynchian terms, a small town in Washington is visible as an environment more charged than the ordinary flat, lifeless terrain of conventional detective stories, which are routinely filled with coursing energies, but only those of human desires.

In all ways, the town of Twin Peaks is enveloped in energy. Images that call our attention to the air coursing through the majestic Douglas firs do not forward a perfect plot or aid a perfect hero. They pull us toward the larger context of everything that is going on, as do the images of trees misted over with clouds and water cascading forcefully over the falls below the Great Northern Hotel and flowing gently as it becomes a stream below the falls. There is a drama and a modulation in the energy of the landscape, as in the emotions of the people in it. Similarly, electricity, which is merely part of an inert backdrop in formula television storytelling, is perceptible here as energy coursing through the wiring and tubing in which it is encased, as in the flickering of light and buzzing sound of electricity in the hospital morgue and later in the sign at the brothel One Eyed Jacks. And the night scenes in the forest are filled with the typical Lynchian image of partial, only dimly illuminating flashlights, suggesting how small our resources are in the face of huge, unknown energies out there in the world we barely see and barely know. Lynch fuses our subconscious apprehension of what is around us with a sense of the animate world the way the marketplace never constructs it. We become nonformulaic detectives too.

It is not just nature and mechanisms that are touched with a different kind of vigor in this series. The materiality of the human body is also unconventionally depicted with a mysterious energy of its own. In Cooper's dream of the Red Room, the energy of speech reshapes the familiar cadences of the spoken language. An uncanny energy of dance moves the body of the Little Man (Michael J. Anderson), Cooper's host. When the Little Man rubs his hands together, the gesture releases the electric energy. The body of Audrey Horne (Sherilyn Fenn), the daughter of town entrepreneur Ben Horne (Richard Beymer), is also sometimes depicted as a flow of spontaneously animated particles. In the pilot, when she mischievously alarms the Scandinavians that her father hopes will invest in his Ghostwood project and sends them packing by telling them about Laura's death, Audrey is consciously using her young, sexy body in a conventional way to undermine Ben's plans out of high-spirited teenaged rebellion. But in the next episode, alone in her father's office, an alternate visualization of her body appears: she undulates sensuously as though her body was simply flowing in the air and she has gotten out of its way to allow it to happen.

In episode 2, Audrey breaks into dance in the Double R Diner to a tune on the jukebox, the same tune that the Little Man dances to in Cooper's dream. Like his, her body seems to make visible the flow of particles that takes place without anyone making it happen. It is this aspect and her odd concentration on physical objects that make the mutual fascination between her and Cooper part of the mystery that surrounds Laura. Leland Palmer's body also breaks into dance in the same mysterious way, not with Audrey's

FIGURE 1.2. *Audrey Horne's body has a dancing particle life of its own.*

mysterious beauty, but as a form of the pain and distress inflicted by his entanglement with BOB. These fissures in ordinary perception are not as startling as the transformation of Fred Madison (Bill Pullman) into Pete Dayton (Balthazar Getty) in *Lost Highway*, but they do prefigure Lynch's more daring later visualizations of matter as being as open and filled with possibilities as are human sensibilities and emotions.

Much closer to what Lynch has shown as the uncanny flow of energy in materiality in more recent work is the meshing of Leland Palmer and BOB, which Lynch builds up to very gradually. Initially, BOB seems to be a figment of Sarah Palmer's imagination. But slowly, as other people see him, he takes on a more equivocal existence. BOB's full implications as part of the Laura Palmer murder mystery only become available in episodes 13 to 17. With BOB's murder of Maddy Ferguson (Sheryl Lee), his entanglement with Leland as the vehicle for the deadly assault makes BOB and Leland more than one and less than two as Laura's murderers. We are forced by the limitations of the language to use the plural "murderers." But there is no true plural here, but rather something that quantum mechanics has shown to be possible and yet inexpressible in the language and concepts that we have at our disposal: superposition. In this phenomenon discovered experimentally by quantum physics, one particle appears simultaneously as two. This is not an aspect of physics that Lynch knows about theoretically in an experimental or an intellectual way, but it has been suggested in less technical terms to him by John Hagelin.[7]

In Lynch's imagination, the energy of matter has been translated into a source of communication with the human subconscious, as we see in the extraordinary scene in which Cooper mobilizes the Twin Peaks police department for an experiment with rocks, bottles, and a blackboard to further his inquiry about the murder. In this scene, Lynch fuses the contextual evocation of energy and matter with detection, tantalizing us with the way connection with the cosmic universe around us and the subconscious intersects with detection if we are open to the larger picture. Cooper brings the police to a woodland glade and has Sheriff Truman and his team establish a glass bottle on a stump precisely sixty feet and six inches from a blackboard and a table set up with doughnuts and coffee for refreshment. The scene is filled with large choreographed, dramatic gestures; it is a ritual of connection among people, between people and things, and between law and the subconscious. Cooper tells them it is anchored in a dream he once had that both made him concerned for the plight of the people of Tibet and led him toward the kind of mind-body method of investigation he is now conducting. When Cooper asks Sheriff Truman to read the names (all of which begin with "J") that he has written on the blackboard in sequence, when Cooper stands by the blackboard and throws a rock at the bottle to coordinate the sound of the name with what happens to the rock and the bottle, Lynch is reconfiguring the universe of action, context, and human interiority in televisual storytelling. What do we gain from all this? A sense that every action, every life and every death, is a part of the All, not an atomized event to which Sherlock can put a period. We expand!

Of course, Cooper's dream about Laura at the end of episode 1.2 is Lynch's bombshell introduction of human interiority into the American television series and his fusion of the energy of the subconscious with the modernist understanding of materiality. Cooper has a dream in which he sees BOB, MIKE (Al Strobel), Laura, and a small man dressed in a red suit. At first, BOB and MIKE present themselves to the dreamer, as though they were talking to him. Then Cooper sees himself as an old man in a mysterious Red Room with an interesting floor design of zigzag lines, seated across from Laura and the Little Man. They speak oddly. A slouchy jazz melody plays. The Little Man dances and shakes. Laura kisses Cooper and whispers something in his ear. When Cooper awakens, his hair is standing at a 90-degree angle to his head in an antic vertical cowlick. He calls Sheriff Truman and tells him that he knows who killed Laura Palmer.

FIGURE 1.3. *The Red Room is an introduction to the mysteries of reality blocked by the illusions of the marketplace.*

It is somewhat unusual for television detectives to have dreams about their cases, but not unprecedented. The truly groundbreaking aspect of Cooper's dream is the interconnection it suggests between an odd materiality buried in Cooper's subconscious and the obliqueness of words, images, and sounds in the process of communication and understanding. The Log Lady's prologue to Cooper's dream in episode 1.2 sets us up to expect something along these lines when she tells us, "Sometimes ideas, like men, jump up and say, 'Hello.' They introduce themselves, these ideas, with words. Are they words? These ideas speak so strangely. All that we see in this world is based on someone's ideas. Some ideas are constructive. Some are destructive. Some ideas can arrive in the form of a dream." The interrogative cast of the prologue in general is noteworthy. Specifically, it questions the traditional importance of words in communication.

In Cooper's dream, the words that Laura and the Little Man speak are neither transparent nor direct. The Little Man talks about gum and suggests that the girl with him, his cousin, only looks like Laura, while Cooper insists that she is. Laura talks about her arms bending back; and when she speaks into Cooper's ear, we cannot hear her. As we discover, he cannot consciously retrieve the words either, though he feels that they are inside him somewhere. We discover the significance of the gum and arms that bend back in later episodes. At the same time, the oddness of the material in the dream also speaks to us, neither more clearly than the words nor less meaningfully. We now know that when Lynch recorded the dialogue of Laura and the Little Man he asked them to speak the words backward. He then replayed the recording in reverse to achieve a sense of the spoken work that calls at least as much attention to tone and rhythm as it does to verbal meaning. The dancing body of a man who is not the standard size of adult men also calls attention to physicality rather than attributing plot significance to what we are watching. In other words, Lynch is powerfully asking the audience to actively develop questions about everything, even though the dream is bracketed by the plot question about who killed Laura. The effect on audiences was galvanizing. No one came away untouched by the electricity created by Cooper's dream. It loomed as large in audience experience as the standard question about whodunit.

Crucially, we do and we do not leave ordinary reality to experience these things. This is a dream, but it is a dream mysteriously and compellingly connected with reality. This is an expanded view of ordinary reality unprecedented in television, part and parcel of Cooper's investigation and the cosmos within which it takes place, to which the Log Lady prologues become a poetic bridge. Her poetry leads toward how we approach knowledge, toward questions, toward the seething energy of matter and the equally seething energy of human emotion and impulse. She provides few ordinary clues; rather, she is a forceful presence as an enigmatic reader of and listener to the world of matter. It is a mystery that points toward the enigma of matter rather than toward the smaller mystery of Laura's death, though the two are interconnected ultimately.

Lynch also uses sound and music to create an audience distance from the marketplace of illusions and a proximity to the auteur point of view of the series. Kate McQuiston's *We'll Meet Again: Musical Design in the Films of Stanley Kubrick* serves as an excellent jumping-off point for discussion of Lynch's nonformulaic use of music in *Twin Peaks*. The conventional use of sounds in serial television is almost completely to establish the "reality" of the setting. The conventional use of music in the television series is to pump up the audience's empathy with the feelings of the characters and to rachet up the audience's experience of drama or suspense and sometimes of comedy. For the most part there was not a great deal of concern about whether the music in pre-1990 television was diegetic, emanating from a source, like a radio inside the scene, or nondiegetic: an application of music on the soundtrack for purely manipulative reasons. As McQuiston points out, one of Kubrick's main uses for music is to render ambiguous whether the music is diegetic or nondiegetic.[8] Consideration of the relationship of sound, music, and the diegesis, apart from formulaic emotional manipulation, is an interesting way of understanding one of Lynch's most nonformulaic approaches to television.

I am most comfortable discussing the use of music and sound in episodes that Lynch specifically directed. Other directors were able to work with Lynch's images in some cases but rarely with nonformulaic sound design, of which he is a master. Most of the music in the first seven episodes, regardless of director, is what I shall call "context music" rather than character themes or music that directly addresses character emotions. Instead of telling us how to feel about the action on the screen, it poses questions, invites us to fill in the scene with our imaginations.[9]

The disruption of the scenes with images and sound that expand our sensory experience of the series is complemented by a different kind of juxtaposition, just as disruptive, but with a completely different edge. Alongside of the images and sounds that convey the surges of energy behind what seems to be solid and static are images that conjure for us how the marketplace relentlessly manufactures objects that mime the appearance of nature but are depleted of its energy. From this contrast grows an unorthodox view of marketplace objects as comic appearances, stiffly nailed, stuffed and shellacked, and absolutely silent, that add up to less than they should. This apparition of stuffed and shellacked objects is epitomized by the rooms in the Great Northern Hotel.

From one point of view, Ben Horne's establishment is alive with the many universes that spring up in each of the rooms. From another, it is a monument to the rigor mortis of an American commercial culture of pseudo-nature. To alert us to the lumpish deadness of marketplace images of the world of objects and bodies, Lynch's camera takes time out from recording human events to crawl over the bedposts in Cooper's room that look like tree trunks and a gun rack over Cooper's bed that holds the gun in place with objects that look like goat horns. The rooms at the Great Northern that we see from time to time are all decorated in that manner and often feature stuffed birds, mounted fish, and heavily varnished nature paintings, sometimes embellished by the stuffed corpses of birds in bas-relief against a shellacked sky. These images have a certain antic inertia. Walls are completely wood paneled; and unlike the Log Lady's living log, they stand as a bulwark against living energy. Industrial fossilization of the natural is everywhere in *Twin Peaks*: heads of dead stuffed animals pop up in all sorts of rooms; and the objectified portrait of Laura as prom queen threads through the series and substitutes for her. Laura's cousin, Maddy Ferguson, is murdered by Leland/ BOB in front of a cheesy varnished idyllic nature painting in the Palmer house, against which she is brutally thrust. Ben Horne and others walk into his wood-paneled office as if they are walking onto a stage. All these are evidence of cultural petrifications of the world.

From this perspective, the activities of the marketplace, even the drug trade in Twin Peaks' criminal underworld, become visible as imitations of life, blockages of authentic experience. In this series, drugs are not mind expanding but rather usurp human sensibility to make expansion impossible, much as BOB does when he takes over a character. Laura is the flash point of both these constraints, as both drugs and BOB fight to possess her. This use of images to conjure a vision of the enormity of life and the perverse cultural initiatives that diminish it in our eyes is the stamp that lifts the series above the level of melodrama and ordinary detective fiction.

As long as Lynch was actively involved in the early episodes, and played with his storytelling with artistic freedom, the series was marked by what we can call with some justice the quantum poetry of open forms, a vision of matter roiling under and behind the artificial stasis of culturally created surfaces. Until the near-fatal turn that the series took while Lynch was less connected to it, Cooper seemed destined to surmount the nailed, stuffed, and shellacked world of the marketplace through the power of a greater vision of energies coursing beyond it. In being able to see beyond ordinary cultural constructs, Cooper seemed to be becoming adept at forming partnerships of sorts with messengers of good from beyond cultural limits and developing a way of seeing messengers of evil for what they are. He was becoming a detective in a cosmic sense: not a master of illusory control in the tradition of formulaic TV detectives, but a master of receptivity to reality. He did not reach that mastery, and it is impossible to say precisely what the investigation of the death of Laura Palmer would have looked like if Lynch had been able to avoid the problems that beset his series. But we can say more about the modernist vision of good and evil that Lynch began to evolve with the first seven episodes.

TIDINGS FROM THE UNIFIED FIELD

Serious evil and human hope and goodness butt heads within the quantum reality of infinite possibility that Lynch dramatizes in the first season of *Twin Peaks* in a way that says much about the originality of Lynch's vision. As suggested earlier, most quantum physicists believe that the whole enterprise of ethics and morality has been shaken, perhaps fatally, by the randomness of the swerves and flows that they have discovered in the behavior of particles. The founding father of quantum science, Niels Bohr, declared that anyone who is not terrified by quantum mechanics does not understand the situation. However, the Vedas, Lynch's other source of poetic inspiration, are founded on an ancient optimism about the unified structure of the universe beyond the illusions of solid materiality in everyday life. That part of his poetry explains why Lynch is not terrified.

In the first season, Lynch rooted his depiction of the wonder of possibility in an oxymoronic simultaneity of limitlessness and stability: the infinite nature of particle combination and the unified field at the heart of the cosmos. In *Twin Peaks*, in the "beyondness" of the All, something stable inheres that guarantees the possibility of a clear division between good and evil in the larger context, though not in the marketplace in which we humans live. Some, with cause, will identify this aspect of Lynch's cinematic poetry as religious, since the Vedas are the holy books of an ancient religion. Similarly, some will maintain that a belief in absolute good and evil is not by its very nature modernist. I suggest that the simultaneous existence of the ambiguous marketplace and the unified field of the beyond in *Twin Peaks*, a work of art and poetry, is the essence of discontinuity and enigma in modern art. It suggests the modernist oxymorons perhaps more fully than a total commitment to randomness, which after all can be understood as a perfect narrative of sorts. In any case, there is that doubleness in *Twin Peaks*, the dissociations of the marketplace and the unified field of the Vedas, visualized by messengers from the larger cosmos that are both good and evil. As long as Cooper is able to see and hear the messengers, both the good and the evil, he remains distinct from the perfect hero of formula television as a protagonist who is aware of and connected to a sense of a context bigger than he is.

BOB is a perfect metaphor for the fear of many of the powerful quantum theorists (of which Niels Bohr is the major example) that the distinctions between good and evil must disappear in a quantumverse. But, although BOB may run amok in the marketplace in Lynch's 1990 series, in the larger scheme of things he is balanced out by other forces. It is only human confusion (leading to fear) about the illusory material plane that gives BOB his power within the marketplace. While Cooper is receptive in the first season, his fear is kept in check by his openness to vision and the messengers from beyond the marketplace. Openness is the only way that human beings can find liberation from the marketplace, since the messengers cannot directly give guidance or salvation. They can only convey limited and/or comforting revelations.

One of these messengers, the Giant (Carel Struycken), appears to Cooper while he is lying on the floor in episode 2.1, having been shot in the first season finale. He makes a point of letting Cooper know that supportive forces exist that he can call on but also makes it clear that he cannot say more than that. The conflicted energies of the invasive, destructive, murderous BOB, and MIKE, a former collaborator, who is now dedicated to opposing BOB, having become aware of the unified order at the center of the universe, are silent on how destructive energies fit into the larger picture. The Log Lady tells us in her prologues to the episodes that she cannot reveal the source of her knowledge. As poetic figures intertwined with the images of a physical world in flow, they are not figments of anyone's imagination but rather signs of a universe in which we human beings are not completely enclosed either within our own psyches or within a closed system of matter but rather can be innately connected to motivating energies from outside of ourselves.

Lynch has taken his inspiration for BOB from evil presences in the Vedas called Rakshasas.[10] (Of course, this poetic embodiment of evil has no parallel at all in experimental quantum physics.) Vedic Rakshasas are malign shape-shifting beings that enter the space of ordinary human lives to cause trouble, as does the owl, a bird that figures in the Vedas as an evil spirit, not figuratively or mythologically, but in reality. This is where knowing that Lynch is inspired by the Vedas not Jung's collective unconscious assumes special importance for the study of *Twin Peaks*. The archetypes that Jung discusses as structures deep within the collective unconscious as the animators of human actions and impulses are understood by him to be purely in the mind. But in the Lynch-influenced episodes of *Twin Peaks* they are part of the external reality, as they are in the Vedas.

Lynch told me directly more than once that he considers these beings real, but he is speaking of a poetic reality that gives a body and name to the impact on humanity of energies from beyond the parentheses that we have drawn around what we have decided culturally to consider the limits of the real. Lynch does not literally believe that there are Rakshasas and messengers among us, for as a human being he makes a very clear distinction between reality and making movies and television. However, as an artist, in the fiction of *Twin Peaks*, Lynch has poetically created BOB, his version of a Rakshasa, to visualize the dire problems associated with being stuck in the illusions of the closed marketplace.

I am not aware of benign messengers in the Vedas that serve as the source of the positive messengers in *Twin Peaks*; I surmise that Lynch invented the Giant under pressure from ABC to solve the case in the second season. The Giant may suggest the beyond of the marketplace, but he is also very much implicated in directly giving Cooper some fairly pointed clues, as we shall see below, in riddles that require a minimum of imagination to fathom. This is quite different from the more Lynchian Red Room, in which indirection, ambiguity, and mystery defy simple rational translation. The Red Room points toward an infinite range of possibilities for us, by destroying any and all discrete boundaries between life and death, the terrain of society and cosmic space, and materiality and immateriality; the Giant points toward a form of closure. While MIKE and BOB convey the modernist fear of a chaotic, immoral universe, in the 1990–1991 version of *Twin Peaks* the Red Room conveys something different, solace and reassurance.

When Lynch's personal vision in *Twin Peaks* connects us to the most searching and enigmatic ideas of science as well as to ancient ideas, between the two we are confronted by metaphors both for reassurance and for stark realities: how extremely difficult it is within the marketplace to deal with evil and to defend goodness. In *Twin Peaks*, our usual defenses—law, physical force, rationalization—do not work, and our best defenses turn out to be questions. But there are more than questions involved in Lynch's consolations, which are uncharacteristic of modernist art.

I have already said that nonformulaic TV does not offer the comforting optimism that has historically been mandatory in formulaic television. This would seem to conflict with a reading of the reassurances offered by the father of nonformulaic American television, David Lynch. But let us consider. While Lynch offers consolation of a sort in *Twin Peaks*, it is not the typical consolation that all is well, now buy something. Lynch testifies to the suffering of the world—he told me more than once "there's a lot of it out there"—and he also testifies, and this is the consolation, that the suffering generated by the marketplace is not all there is. That is quite a different matter from producing the kind of perfect narrative and perfect hero that compress the world of the narrative so that suffering, confusion, and death can be totally erased.

Lynch offers a powerful yet highly enigmatic reassurance that acknowledges the tenacity of the illusions that constitute the constraints of the marketplace and generate suffering and disorientation. And it is that complex approach to the enormity of his context that inspired both David Chase and David Simon. They do not propose a context remotely like Lynch's but instead propose some form of positive possibility beyond the problems caused by human and cultural limitations, while they are quite clear on the human comedy and tragedy. Cooper's ultimate dark predicament at the end of *Twin Peaks*, brought about by the interference of contextual industrial forces beyond Lynch's control, only added to the way his legacy pointed away from formulaic perfect narratives and perfect heroes for nonformulaic television auteurs who came after him.

HONEY, I SHRUNK THE UNIVERSE

After the first season finale, episode 1.7, formulaic elements began to appear in *Twin Peaks*, as Lynch temporarily distanced himself from the show. With the details of production history we now have, while this distancing did take place, it is impossible to say why it happened.[11] There are competing testimonies: Lynch has claimed that he never did distance himself; Mark Frost told me that Lynch left him "all alone." But the absence of Lynch as a writer and director in season 2 is indisputable. He only wrote one episode, 2.1, and directed only 2.2 and 2.7 before he returned to direct the series finale, 2.21.

Lynch was at the time working on the postproduction of *Wild at Heart*, which many (including me in a previous commentary) had assumed to be the reason his attention had turned elsewhere. However, I now think that *Wild at Heart* need not necessarily have distracted him. It is possible that Lynch allowed it to because he was discouraged about *Twin Peaks* and alienated from it by ABC's successful demand for a definitive solution to the mystery of Laura Palmer's murder, a reasonable demand from the network perspective within the context of formulaic television but utterly contrary to the art television that Lynch was writing. The supposition that Lynch was smarting from the interference in his art and withdrew instinctively makes sense to me, because when Lynch returned and exerted full artistic control over the final episode of the series, his verve returned. The series had been canceled, so ABC probably had no reason to police him at that point.

In hindsight it is clear that Lynch was working under (likely painful) constraints from the beginning of season 2. Although the end of the first season pointed beyond conventional plotting, the new season was laying the groundwork for the kind of perfect narrative that went against Lynch's grain. The show was now preparing viewers for the moment of revelation in 2.9 that Leland Palmer killed his daughter. Episode 2.1, the only one in season 2 that Lynch directed and wrote, was seeded with increasingly pointed clues that Leland was possessed by BOB, paving the way for Cooper to make a definitive identification of the murderer. At the same time, it was preparing the audience for the narrative that would begin when the mystery of Laura's murder ended by introducing a new character named Windom Earle. If the story about Laura was reining in Cooper's connection to an unfathomable universe beyond cultural illusions of limits in order to reach a formulaic closure, Windom Earle was the perfect villain who would reduce Cooper to the status of standardized perfect hero with no connections to anything but a perfect narrative.

Earle is first mentioned in episode 2.1, which briefly alludes to his escape from an institution for the criminally insane. He is introduced to the audience as Cooper's former partner at the FBI and former nemesis, an unfortunate part of Cooper's past. As their past began to play increasingly large roles in the narrative, the scripts lost the Lynchian stamp. The plot became a set of tracks that was supposed to lead to an obligatory formulaic "big battle" between Earle, representing all that is good, and Cooper, representing all that is bad. Cooper was scripted by Mark Frost, Robert Engels, and Harley Peyton to lose the battle with Earle in the series finale, a total defeat that might be construed as a form of rebellion against the perfect narrative. However, that would be a misconstruction: as television writers know, a perfect defeat is just as formulaic as a perfect victory. Neither allows for the modern vision of indeterminacy, ambiguity, complexity, or discontinuity. When Lynch returned to direct and reconfigure the script of the series finale, however, he revoked Earle's standing as the perfect villain and recaptured for American television its first incredibly exciting nonformulaic closure. A close—but economical—look at 2.1, 2.9, 2.10, and 2.21 will tell the tale of how we almost lost David Lynch's legacy.

In 2.1, we see a transition beginning that will move the series from non-formulaic storytelling to formula. In this episode Lynch was stubbornly preserving some of his vision but capitulating as well. The tension between the Log Lady prologue and 2.1 is greater than the tension between the prologues and the episodes in season 1. Episode 2.1 starts the season off by moving Cooper toward control, while the Log Lady prologue has only questions about life. "X-rays see through solid or so-called solid objects. There are things in life that exist, and yet our eyes cannot see them. Have you ever seen something startling that others cannot see? Why are some things kept from our vision? Is life a puzzle? I am filled with questions." In this episode, Cooper is also filled with questions, but those that he cannot answer remind us of the glory of *Twin Peaks* that is about to pass. He begins the episode very much out of control, lying on the floor of his hotel room, a continuation from the season 1 finale, at the end of which he was shot. In his weakened condition, Cooper is visited by some interesting people who are unable to help him before he is rescued by Sheriff Truman: an old waiter at the Great Northern and a Giant. In fact, he is visited by the Giant twice, once at the beginning of the episode and once at the end. In these encounters what he cannot do about the case is much more compelling than what he can do, as I shall discuss in due course.

The rest of the series is highly formulaic. Windom Earle, as perfect villain, turns the world of *Twin Peaks* into a chessboard, an image that quintessentially evokes the limits of formulaic television. Once Earle becomes Cooper's antagonist, clues narrow down the story through association with chess moves and black and white pieces. But even before that, Cooper's conduct of the case about Laura's death starts to narrow toward a conclusion when he discovers that it is Leland Palmer who killed his daughter. Episode 2.1 starts the formulaic ball rolling by setting up red herrings to tease the audience about the answer to the question of "Who Killed Laura Palmer?" Red herrings are the mark of formula. In nonformulaic storytelling, lateral elements add depth and broadness to the universe. In formula narratives, they are only there to be eliminated. The red herrings are supported in 2.1 by the elaboration by Cooper and Rosenfield about the narrative sequence of the events of the night Laura died, which Rosenfield has discovered through his Sherlockian forensics.

But 2.1 is not completely cut off from the large universe invoked in the first season. It also continues the collateral stories begun in season 1, which are being set up for future season episodes, about the lives of people not directly implicated in Laura's death. The most interesting of these are the love triangle of Big Ed Hurley (Everett McGill), Norma Jennings (Peggy Lipton), and Nadine Hurley (Wendy Robie); the troubled relationship between Major Garland Briggs (Don S. Davis) and his son Bobby (Dana Ashbrook); and Audrey Horne's indirect declaration of her love for Cooper through her self-initiated undercover adventure at a brothel in Canada just across the border from Washington called One Eyed Jacks. These perform an enlargement of the story that is neither a clue nor a red herring, but a way of enriching formula storytelling. They are not about the universe, but they broaden the range of formulaic television and are the best aspects of the formulaic episodes in season 2. They will be recalled in the coda, when I discuss what Lynch did with his Twin Peaks story when he was given full artistic control by Showtime cable network in *Twin Peaks* (2017).

The traces of nonformulaic storytelling to which we are bidding farewell at the very beginning of the episode are most important at the moment for our purposes. They constitute the loose ends that Lynch picks up again when he returns to direct and essentially rewrite the last series episode. The first minutes of 2.1 are the last of such narrative until the end of the series. These disorienting, poignant moments are devoted to the question of fear. Dale Cooper is lying on the floor bleeding, completely helpless, with no assistance in sight. A superannuated waiter arrives with warm milk but is unable to comprehend that Cooper needs a doctor despite several requests from the

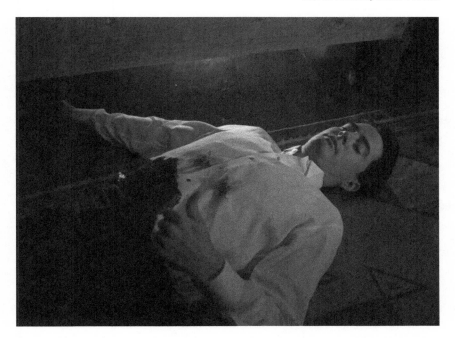

FIGURE 1.4. *Dale Cooper's receptivity to the experience of being shot is one of the last captivating Lynchian touches as the series slid toward formulaic narrative.*

prostrate man. The tone is strangely gentle and comic. Clearly Cooper needs care. Yet the old waiter's dogged pursuit of his own concerns—which include hanging up the phone instead of calling for help and twice walking out of the room and back for one more word irrelevant to Cooper's predicament— draws neither ire nor impatience from Cooper. When the obtuse old fellow bends down to have Cooper sign the room service tab, Cooper asks if the price includes a gratuity. This scene both teases our formulaic expectations and actively generates a different, nonformulaic delight by refusing to gratify them. This is compounded when a Giant appears to Cooper and gives him clues but no medical help. Cooper remains placid, fascinated by three riddles that the Giant tells him (each of which bears on the Laura Palmer case), and gives the Giant his ring, as in a fairy tale. The scene distills the new devices and desires of auteur television.

The doorway shimmers in our sight just past Cooper's prone body, empty, and we are torn between longing for and expecting the obligatory rescue and being captivated by Cooper's musings about his situation, which he records for Diane by starting the voice activation button merely through speaking. He describes the sensation of being shot and thinks about the things that he regrets and might miss. But the most important thing he says is about fear. Being shot is not as bad as he thought it might be "as long as you can keep fear from the mind." Indeed, he muses, you can say that about almost anything in life. We drift far from the plot into a realm in which questions are raised about the connection between the mind and the body and about how we cope in general with a world we cannot control. Just about the time when we almost long for Cooper to lie on the floor for a much longer interval, Harry Truman and his deputies Hawk (Michael Horse) and Andy (Harry Goaz) show up to bring us back to the newly laid narrative tracks.

The tracks lead to episode 2.9, in which the mystery of who killed Laura is declared solved when Cooper identifies the killer as Leland Palmer, Laura's father. When Lynch added the Log Lady prologue to this episode, he positioned the solution as a kind of illusion in a nuanced, poetic way, but that message can only be received by those who have already understood his initial vision and what has happened to it. We are now in a position to understand her words: "So now the sadness comes, the revelation. There is a depression after an answer is given. It was almost fun not knowing. Yes, now we know. At least we know what we sought in the beginning. But there is still the question, why? And this question will go on and on until the final answer comes. Then the knowing is so full there is no room for questions." What she says points away from the finality indicated in the script of 2.9, written by Mark Frost, Harley Peyton, and Robert Engels, which was fully intended to conclude the story of Laura's murder and in which Lynch's vision was reduced to the parameters of formula television.

It is important to note, however, that the form of closure in Laura's story in 2.9 is as impressive as a formulaic closure gets. It must be recognized as formulaic not because it is uninteresting and fails to move the audience, but because it packs its punch by keeping the story firmly within the limits of clarity and resolution and manipulating the audience with its illusory reassurances about human control. Formulaic storytelling at its highest level of achievement can push some pretty powerful emotional buttons with its consolations and clarity, and 2.9 is formula at its most effective. The discovery scene vividly and intensely stimulates audience desire for the most lyrical, noble form of perfect hero, which Cooper becomes as he traps Leland Palmer and then shepherds him to death with a priestly kind of absolution. It is riveting, but here Cooper is towering above circumstances with such a vengeance that he is even in control of the path to eternity. This is not the story that Lynch had been telling. Cooper is moved subtly onto those formulaic tracks put down by Frost, Peyton, and Engels. It is a spectacle that moves us to tap into our most deeply felt illusions about life and death.

The discovery scene is efficiently prepared for with a great deal of dialogue recapping what has already happened. In the traditional style of detective fiction, Cooper then assembles all the potential helpers and suspects. The dialogue during this meeting reaches a pitch of formulaic clarity when Cooper enumerates a list of all the "techniques" he has used, reducing the strangeness of the subconsciousness and the flow of the physical world to a series of boxes that he checks off: "Bureau guidelines, deductive technique, Tibetan method, instinct, and luck. But now I find myself in need of something new, which, for lack of a better word, we shall call magic." This trivializes the mystery of the All that we have experienced and substitutes the clarity that formulaic detection fiction demands. Moreover, the scene trivializes the original sensory palette of the series, reduced from its initial mystery to a mere adjunct of the perfect narrative. As Cooper says the word "magic," lightning flashes, whitening the screen and raising his authority to a formulaic level of absolute power. The same happens when he hears Laura tell him that her father killed her. The subconscious loses its initial complexity and becomes the servant of human control.

Similarly, when Leland is cornered and BOB forces him to kill himself, Cooper assumes the kind of control over life and death that is the fundamental delight of formulaic TV, holding Leland as he dies in a Pietà-like image, talking Leland "into the light" without fear and with the certainty that Laura has forgiven him. How can the audience resist the thought that the path to death, even for the worst of us, can be so gracefully charted by a very good man? It is meticulously acted, well directed, and represents Frost's finest hour as a formula writer—a mixed distinction in this case—but it was not Lynch's (or anyone's) auteur vision. Frost, in collaboration with Peyton and Engels, tapped the power of what Lynch had established only in order to shut it down. The thrill of questioning has been reduced to the bliss of a fantasy of human control over the terror of death. And the original thrill stayed shut down for the next twelve episodes.

The collapse became total and devastating in 2.10, in which BOB disappears along with all of the messengers, the modernist enigmas about materiality, and the power of the subconscious. The most extraordinary and obvious violation of Lynch's vision is the sudden declaration that BOB is gone. At the end of 2.9, Sheriff Truman, a simple man who believes in the evidence of his eyes and common sense, is so deeply affected by the mysteries of the Leland/BOB entanglement that even he knows that no final end has been reached. "Where is BOB now?" he asks. Harry's question is answered by a tracking shot into the nighttime woods to a burst of uncanny light, out of which flies a predatory owl, claws bared. BOB, who has previously been associated with owls, is still there. This image should not be confused with nonformulaic uneasiness; it is borrowed from formulaic horror movies, which reinforce their premises that horror is an uncanny invasion of perfect human culture. There is nothing modernist about the protection of audience illusions that their society is perfectly transparent and positive if undisturbed by alien elements. The horror movie owl image has nothing to do with the true ambivalence about the marketplace that we find in early *Twin Peaks*.

But even formulaic ambivalence is erased almost immediately in 2.10. Sarah Palmer, isolated and alone in the first season of the series, is suddenly surrounded by the complete placidity of a community static in its unity as people assemble with picture-postcard food brought to help Sarah mourn Leland's death. This is not a modernist discontinuity but rather the result of bad writing and the abandonment of Lynch's poetry. In contradiction of the final image of 2.9, Cooper is scripted to reassure Sarah Palmer that BOB is gone forever in 2.10. And he is, for the time being. *Twin Peaks* has shriveled to a place menaced by perfectly nasty eccentrics and homicidal psychopaths—the principal lunatic being perfect villain Windom Earle, the fodder of formulaic television.

When *Twin Peaks* collapsed, Cooper was reduced to being a man in trouble with the FBI, the victim of a plot against him by some newly arisen subversive forces at the bureau and part of a melodrama that pitted him against Earle, whose wife, Caroline (Brenda E. Mathers), had betrayed him with Cooper a few years before. The new fuel for the old duel was provided by Cooper's season 2 love interest, Annie Blackburn (Heather Graham), a former nun who looks remarkably like the now dead Caroline. Words, bodies, and things no longer have their own drama in this melodrama; they are only the setting and furniture for clichéd situations.

COOPER GIVES AWAY HIS SOUL AND SAVES THE SERIES

When Lynch returned to direct 2.21, he had to contend with a perfect hero, a perfect plot, and standardized image and sound. As a result, he had to think of a way of honestly making the finale continuous with his vision and also with the character that Cooper had become. To do these things, Lynch took the drastic step of literally disposing of the script by Frost, Peyton, and Engels that he was handed and improvising the last episode right on the set.[12]

If we contrast the texts of the never-televised paper script that I was given by Lynch's office with what Lynch improvised for the screen, it becomes clear that the changes he made play out the problem of Cooper's fear, but not on the terms of his collaborators. In the script Cooper is afraid of the powerful Earle, who is dramatized defeating him, a definitive victory for evil.

What we saw onscreen was Cooper defeated by his own fear of Earle, who is nothing but BOB's puppet. That fear makes Cooper susceptible to BOB and reconfigures the series to return to the large vision of the first seven episodes and the power that people have if they can—as Lynch's characters say so often—protect themselves from fear. This is a crowning achievement for Lynch and a beautiful example of his fusion of modernist chaos with a reminder of higher possibilities of connection to an ordered universe beyond the marketplace.

Had Lynch directed script #29 (episode 2.21), as written, it would have driven *Twin Peaks* unalterably back into the box created for detective fiction by Arthur Conan Doyle through the prominence in Cooper's last hours of a Windom Earle, dramatized by Frost, Peyton, and Engels as an updated version of Professor James Moriarty. This is what we would have seen. Cooper's futile attempt to rescue Annie would have led him, not to the Red Room, but to both a surreal dentist's office and a huge, similarly surreal room-sized black-and-white chessboard floor measured out with painful precision, which would serve as the battlefield on which he is bested by Earle and his sidekick, BOB. We would have seen a mentally ill, monomaniacal Earle browbeat Cooper into giving him his soul.[13]

But we did not. In Lynch's revision of the confrontation, Cooper's futile attempt to rescue Annie leads into the Red Room, with all the cosmic indeterminacy that location suggests. There we find that Cooper *only thinks that Earle is his main adversary*. Events in the Red Room reveal that Earle has been possessed by BOB, who is the source of Earle's terrible behavior and Cooper's fear of BOB that is his undoing. In Lynch's version, Cooper is defeated by his own reductionist thinking. In some ways the finale can be seen as a metatext that dramatizes from Lynch's perspective what happened to Cooper as a result of the formulaic writing on the show. When Lynch decided to make the Red Room not the surreal dentist's office the site of Cooper's final confrontation with BOB, he sent both Cooper and Earle into the Red Room not in a dream but as a space in the real world that can be accessed magically. Fear conquers them both.

When Cooper crosses over into the Red Room space now, unlike in his dream in 1.3, he is frightened and confused by its vision of its strangeness rather than receptive and curious as he once was. Laura, who was once an enigmatic source of revelation, both dark and light, is now polarized in Cooper's collapsed perspective into *either* good *or* evil. Cooper is stumped when the Little Man says to Cooper, "When you see me again, it won't be me." Granted, the simultaneous existence of one as more than one but not quite two, as Laura and the Little Man exist in his dream, might be a daunting

FIGURE 1.5. *Terror marks Cooper's second visit to the Red Room in the 1990–1991 Twin Peaks.*

prospect, but would the Cooper we first met have been resistant to the Little Man's meaning?

The paradoxes in Cooper's dream in episode 1.3 tantalized him; in the final televised episode those paradoxes drive this dwindled version of Cooper toward hysteria. He holds a cup filled with liquid coffee that morphs into a solid form of coffee and then into an oily substance. The Giant declares that he and the Little Man are "one and the same." The spaces of the Red Room permit no accurate sense of direction. Cooper wanders from one red-draped enclosure to another, but he cannot determine where he is or where he has been. The enclosures look the same, but they are not the same. A boundless fire erupts. The old waiter speaks in a palindrome, "WOW BOB WOW," which forecloses the ordinary one-way direction of language, since it can be spelled the same way forward and backward. Visibility is short-circuited as a blinding strobe light blinks suddenly in darkness.

The trauma that Cooper suffers on this terrain of liminality is conveyed through the image of a puzzling physical lesion that suddenly erupts: he bleeds from his stomach, although we have seen no external attack on him. If we have been following the tutorial that Cooper receives from the Little Man, we can recognize this bleeding as part of the quantum physics of the Red Room. Bodies may be seen to occupy the same space at the same time—as they are not seen to do under "normal" perceptual conditions. Cooper in present time is entangled with his body as it once was years before, when he was stabbed by Earle. Similarly, Annie and Caroline merge before his eyes as if their bodies were entangled as more than one but less than two. Cooper's hysterical capitulation to fear of this entanglement leads him to agree to forfeit his soul to Earle to save Annie. Then a laughing BOB tells Cooper that Earle has no power. However, Cooper's soul has been compromised, by a faux bargain. BOB has him in his power. Cooper's fear—not Earle—leads to his domination by a fiendish doppelgänger that is and is not him.

When we next see Cooper, Doc Hayward and Sheriff Truman are hovering about him. Cooper goes into the bathroom, ostensibly to brush his teeth. But he does not. Instead, he reveals to us that he is the doppelgänger of Cooper, not the original visionary. He repeats multiple times in savagely mocking tones the words of concern that he had moments before, with seeming sincerity, spoken to Sheriff Truman and Doc Hayward: "How's Annie?" When Cooper's mirror reflects BOB and Cooper smashes his head against the glass,

FIGURE 1.6. *Cooper's possession by BOB created a nonformulaic, open finale for the 1990–1991 Twin Peaks.*

Lynch gives us an image of the mind in untenable relationship to matter. Cooper's fall into fear enables BOB, the demonic Rakshasa, to sap Cooper not only of his initial freshness and creativity but also of his concern for others and for justice.

CONCLUSION: THESE FOOLISH THINGS

In *Twin Peaks*, Lynch is in the process of developing the televisual vocabulary that appears in *Twin Peaks* (2017) in greatly expanded form as a brilliant visual vocabulary that articulates his sense of an opposition between what he sees as serious misunderstandings that lock us into a hallucinatory marketplace and the courageous openness of those who can see past it.

As written, the *Twin Peaks* finale would have deflated and trivialized the early promise of the show. Earle, the creation of the marketplace of network television, was scripted as invincible in the final episode, a denial of the possibility that Cooper originally represented. His lack of relevance to Lynch is demonstrated by his total erasure in the 2017 series. In the original series, Lynch worked with Earle because the character could not disappear; rather Lynch destroyed the fantasy of Earle's power. The series finale that Lynch filmed was not a conclusion as defined by formulaic practice in the writing of TV series. It gave us a taste of the further mysteries within which Cooper had become entangled by looking into one mystery, the death of Laura Palmer. Seeking beyond, we were shown, taps into the uncontrollable, the unexpected, the indeterminate. Beyond the possession of Leland Palmer by BOB is the possession of Cooper by BOB. It was, of course, the ramifications of that possession that took center stage in Twin Peaks (2017) and yielded to unending mystery, as we shall see.

The Sopranos and *The Wire*, which followed *Twin Peaks* (and the nonformulaic series that followed them), opened up further room for art versus the business of storytelling and demonstrate what this new art of the TV series means. They are not, as is the case with influence by formulaic television on what comes next, new versions of detection in a small town. They are not variations on the theme of possession. They do not feature another version of Cooper, Laura, or any of the *Twin Peaks* characters, or images and sound design that imitate Lynch. Rather, what we are looking for as we ponder the appearance of nonformulaic American serial television is not the substance of plots or characters or the look or sound of storytelling. What characterizes nonformulaic television is its resemblance to Lynch in that it is connected to the genuine context of modern thinking through the artistic expression of a creator. We are not looking for specific modern influences either. It does not make a television series nonformulaic to be connected with Freud,

Jung, Bohr, or Einstein. We are simply looking for connection with some important, influential modern thought, as opposed to the dissociation of the pre-Peaks formulaic TV series and its existence as story product. No dissociation, but rather cultural connection, means an active audience, the need to discover what connections are being made. This is part of the new art of the TV series too.

The shows to which we are about to give very close attention are not only nuanced and complex, as you may be anticipating, but culturally connected, as you may not be anticipating. Because they disturb the familiar dissociations of formulaic series that postulate a phantom certainty in which the modern world no longer believes, they are disturbing and thought provoking, as is modernity.

CHAPTER 2

DAVID CHASE, *THE SOPRANOS*

They [network producers] had this uncanny ability to find just the thing that made the script great. They'd go right for it. Like truffle pigs. And find it and say that's no good. And it would destroy your whole reason for wanting to write in the first place.

—David Chase, in-person interview with author, May 30, 2014

There is an expression that sometimes moves across David Chase's face: it begins with a quiet softening of the jaw and rolls up into his eyes, where a gleam of surprise breaks. I saw it for the first time at the Silvercup Studios in Astoria, Queens, during our initial interview when we were talking about how amazingly the pieces had come together for *The Sopranos*. When I reflected that it was a miracle, I saw the look. It said, "Bingo!"

Everyone who has worked in television—whether as a high-power writer/ producer/director like Chase or as a temporary academic visitor laboring on a soap opera, as I had—knows that no one can make the casting, writing, directing, acting, cinematography, sets, and myriad other details align through force of will or even talent.[1] They do or they do not. With *The Sopranos*, they did. The American media miracle strikes again, which it does with more regularity than one might suspect. Only its energy is routinely squandered, eroded over time because the weight of formula on American mass entertainment is so great. It takes a confluence of circumstances to permit a genuine spark to ignite.

Simply put, the miracle struck and endured because of Chase and because of HBO (Home Box Office). Chase's brilliance and his modernist vision were the substance. Unwavering support from HBO was the vehicle. Chase was initially pessimistic about the commercial chances of *The Sopranos*, having worked in formulaic television for almost thirty years when, in 1999, he showed up with four videotapes at the office of Richard Plepler, who was executive vice-president of HBO at the time (now the chairman and chief executive officer). After screening the first four episodes of *The Sopranos* on the tapes, Chase asked, "Do you think anyone's going to watch this?" Plepler, an elegant, cultivated man, was so amazed by what Chase had shown him that he blurted, "Holy shit."[2] According to Plepler, he and the other HBO executives knew that Chase had presented them with "something magical." The network's genuine desire at the time to give great television a platform permitted Chase to move series television along the road opened up by David Lynch.

Plepler compares Chase to Arthur Miller as a dramatist, industry acknowledgment that auteur television deserves consideration as art but also proof that it has little idea of the incendiary nature of what it is playing with. Miller is a solid, old-fashioned, left-wing realist who confirms traditional progressive ideas for audiences. *The Sopranos* is much more akin to poetry and to the perplexing surrealism of one of Chase's favorite films, Luis Buñuel's *The Exterminating Angel* (1962), a surrealist comedy in which the guests at a dinner party find themselves unable to leave the house of their host, even though nothing visible bars their way. This is not merely an interesting comparison. Chase screened the film for some of his key creative collaborators as a model for some of the most compelling scenes in *The Sopranos*. Similarly, as we shall see, *The Sopranos* takes inspiration from one of Chase's favorite American poets, Edgar Allan Poe, with his even more extraordinary surrealism before there were surrealists. It would be hyperbolic to call *The Sopranos* a surrealist work, but it would not be going too far to say that it connects American television with overlapping influences from Buñuel, Poe, surrealism, and modernist liminality.

As a television auteur, David Chase made a new storytelling covenant with the audience, releasing one of its favorite genres, the gangster story, from the box into which it had been locked. With his surrealist-flavored, modernist gangster, Chase boldly transformed the tradition of mass-media fiction about crime and made the first actual gangster story for television, all with an 86-episode stroke. Many mobsters had previously been featured on television. Not very long before *The Sopranos*, the popular television series *Wiseguy*, created by Chase's mentor Stephen J. Cannell, featured as its hero

Vinnie Terranova (Ken Wahl), a police mole in a gangster crew helmed by Sonny Steelgrave (Ray Sharkey), Vinnie's mob adversary.[3]

Wiseguy was a standard formulaic narrative setup, with one variation. Sonny Steelgrave was charismatic and quasi-sympathetic, not merely a thuggish villain. Nevertheless, the series was told from the policeman's point of view. Vinnie was a perfect hero, running the story along tracks toward Sonny's necessary arrest or death—the two formulaic alternative closures for American gangsters in the mass media. Steelgrave chose death, committing suicide rather than allowing Vinnie to place him in the cold hands of the justice system. Until *The Sopranos*, television had never had any kind of narrative told from the gangster's point of view.

There is a crucial difference between a narrative with an adversarial gangster in it and a gangster story.[4] When the gangster is merely an adversary, the story fits snugly into the perfect narrative dominated by a perfect hero who solves the problem of crime. The old Warner Bros. gangster movies in the 1930s in which the gangster was the protagonist opened up some dangerous territory through audience identification with gangsters and suggestions about the liminality of gangster identity in America.[5] These old movies have a daring modernist edge, which creates indeterminacies about the complex ramifications of American promises of upward mobility and individualism, from the first gangster film, *The Musketeers of Pig Alley* (1912), through the films made by Warner Bros. and beyond. That kind of questioning had previously been driven into the subtext, however, not only by the censors but by the formulaic requirements of mass-media narrative. When Chase created Tony Soprano and used the old Warner Bros. gangster movies he had loved so much as a boy as a jumping-off point, he took the modern liminality of the gangster figure out of the shadows.

GANGSTER IN TREATMENT

Chase put his mob boss in therapy and at the mercy of his own inner forces, thereby opening a door through which a host of familiar clichés exited and unfamiliar internal uncertainties, discontinuities, and fragmentations of the subconscious and American identity entered. The infusion of energy from the subconscious shifted the gangster plot structure. It broke up time-worn, trivialized portraits of mobsters and their satellites and caused new kinds of characters to enter the gangster environment. Chase was not employing a reliable, comforting formulaic strategy. He was canceling formula through his personal complex vision of the powerful presence of a fearful and wondrous energy that blows up perfect narratives and destroys definitively powerful perfect heroism.

Chase's artistry made Tony Soprano's fragmented inner and outer lives and his indeterminate relationship to the paradoxes of American life the center of his series. The result was a double lightning strike. Psychiatrists, as portrayed in story products, had been at least as severely trivialized as the gangster. If the mob boss had been cut to the measure of a plot with a definitive closure, so had the fear and wonder of the subconscious in stories about clean-cut cures by magisterial analysts. But Chase's narrative propelled Tony's encounters with his therapist, Dr. Jennifer Melfi (Lorraine Bracco), and his unconscious off the formulaic tracks to which both media gangsters and media therapists had been restricted.

Therapy in *The Sopranos* is no more powerful than gangster violence. As we shall see, Melfi too often had tunnel vision about what she unleashed in Tony's life through their sessions together and a far too reductive way of looking at the dreams he told her about and her own dreams about him. *The Sopranos* is marked by modernist intimations of the pervasive human powerlessness before the universe that Chase found so riveting in Poe's poem "Dream within a Dream" as an echo of his own sense of the fluctuations of reality. Poe wrote, "O God! can I not grasp / Them [the sands of time] with a tighter clasp / O God! can I not save / One from the pitiless wave? / Is all that we see or seem / But a dream within a dream?" Turning his back on the mass-media tradition of ignoring modernist anxieties, Chase's art reflected an unabated Poe-like existential panic, from Tony's first confused glance at the statue of a woman in Dr. Melfi's office, as he waits for his first therapy session, all the way to the last moment of the series, when Tony's life swirls around him and around us, only to disappear suddenly into blackness. The same panic is in Melfi too, as she takes to downing vodka before her sessions with him and tries to block her (justified) fears that many aspects of this therapeutic situation are beyond her and beyond the psychiatric framework.

Chase's narrative is not a simplistic gangster story running along tracks toward proof that crime never pays—or proof that human analysis can solve all problems—but a complex story that sets the material aspirations of a gangster and the reductionist theories of therapy against the much larger forces of the subconscious and, as the show continued, the quantum indeterminacies of time and space. The pilot episode, "The Sopranos" (1.1), immediately scrambles our expectations about both the perfect gangster narrative of crime and punishment and the perfect psychiatric story of redemption and cure. It begins to upset old conventions immediately by placing its first scene not only in a location alien to the gangster genre (the waiting room of a therapist's office) but in the very arena set aside for us to explore our vulnerability to internal forces that we can never entirely know or control. At that important moment in storytelling when we form impressions that will shape our experience of the narrative to come, mob boss Tony Soprano does not appear as the conventionally dominating figure but rather sits quietly, almost meekly, waiting to be called into Dr. Melfi's inner sanctum. At the beck and call of a female authority, he is also framed tightly between the legs of a statue of a nude female.

The image of a physically bracketed Tony raises a plethora of questions, with its silent intimations of the birth canal, female power, and his own powerlessness. As Tony's eyes move toward the upper body of the nude, the sense of his vulnerability is heightened, and the questions multiply. He is not the bearer of the famous power of the male gaze but rather experiences ocular confusion. The female image before him standing with her legs securely planted, her arms confidently crossed behind her head, her body aggressively open, and her facial expression strong and inquisitive clearly bewilders him. He is off his turf, just as we are off ours with respect to our expectations about the gangster genre.

But this image of powerful femininity slips away from formulaic expectations too. Melfi is neither the powerful figure of the clichéd therapist nor the amazon represented in the sculpture. Neither gangster nor therapist holds the reins during this first meeting, which is predictive of every indeterminate interchange, every liminal relationship in this series (recalling Lynch's question, "But what if no one is driving the chariot?"). The reduction of all the characters to puppets animated by inner forces that endlessly produce blind spots, lies, denials, self-deceptions, misunderstandings, and prejudices begins when Tony enters Melfi's office. The two briefly negotiate (silently) about who will sit in what chair. He abdicates to her the chair of control, only to wrest control from her by doubting his need for therapy and by giving her only partial truths in response to her questions.

Melfi guides a reluctant Tony toward talking about what happened on the day of his panic attack, the immediate cause of his decision to try therapy. But the session turns out to be a slippery slope that conflates truth and deception. In reporting on the catalytic day, Tony tells Melfi that it was his son's birthday, a day that began with the pleasure he took in a family of ducks that had nested in his pool, which is true. But he lies wildly, and comically, when he tells Melfi about a "meeting" with a "business" associate. The encounter was in fact a criminal attack on a character named Alex Mahaffey (Michael Gaston) who has not paid up on a loan from Tony. "We had coffee," Tony says pleasantly. In juxtaposition we see what Tony has not said to Melfi: Mahaffey dropping a tray of coffees in terror as he sees Tony's car bearing down on him. Tony gets a rush of pleasure from violence. We see subsequently, though

FIGURE 2.1. *We are privy to the joy that Tony experiences from violence, which he hides from Dr. Melfi.*

Melfi does not, that after meeting with Mahaffey he plans to solve a conflict with another garbage company by killing someone. He also has to deal with the plan of his uncle, Junior Soprano (Dominic Chianese), to "whack" a rival gangster in a restaurant owned by Tony's good friend.

There is plenty of crime in the air, but nothing that prefigures a perfect narrative. It consists of a lot of discontinuous fragments. And if Melfi seems to be substituted for the usual detective or police officer who is prefigured as a force that will stop the mob boss, the prognosis does not look good. She has no idea what she is dealing with. Maybe she does not want to know. By warning him that she "technically" would have to report anything that she hears about a crime being planned, she encourages his edited remarks about himself, whether intentionally or inadvertently.[6] The series abrogates the old contract that confirmed our hopes for justice and our hopes for human control over our inner demons. It makes a new contract to lead us to wonder about a larger context: the context of the subconscious as it escapes doctors and overwhelms everything that we do, remaining mysterious and potent.

Even in Dr. Melfi's second meeting with a more forthcoming Tony, the mobster-in-analysis story leaves a lot of loose narrative ends when he tells her about a dream in which he unscrews his penis, as if it were part of a machine. While he is looking for the man who used to fix his Lincoln to screw it back on, the dream figure of the water bird then grabs it from his hand and flies away. In the formulaic therapy session, Melfi would find a therapeutic key to Tony's panic attacks in this dream. But the fascination of what Chase has portrayed is how baffling the dream remains even after the therapist has spoken.

Melfi connects the dream bird to the ducks in Tony's pool and the image of castration to their flight from his pool once their ducklings learned to fly and the ducks disappeared. She concludes that the dream of the ducks was about Tony's fear of losing his family and that this fear lies at the core of his panic attacks. Tony is mightily impressed with her analytical powers, but should we be? The dream never becomes the key to anything. The episode leaves the meaning of the dream open to question, as in all of the episodes in which we see Tony's provocative dreams. The mechanized body, the castration image, fused with self-mutilation (Tony takes out the important screw himself), the pun on screw, and the loss of his penis feel much bigger than any conclusions drawn by Melfi in the session. Perhaps the interpretation of the dream that Tony and Melfi arrive at has some validity, but perhaps not. Melfi creates a perfect analytical narrative, but the episode portrays a very complex and liminal, inconclusive set of images. The potential meanings of the dream remain elusive and comically tenuous, especially when Tony wonders if seeing Alfred Hitchcock's *The Birds* recently had something to do with the dream.[7]

In fact, Tony and Melfi resemble both the people in *The Birds* who propose with certainty dubious explanations for the attack of the birds and the guests

FIGURE 2.2. *Dr. Melfi's office is a defined therapeutic space; the therapy, by contrast, is a vortex of discontinuity, fragmentation, and liminality.*

in *The Exterminating Angel*, who try to guess what is happening to them but cannot. In both of those films (one mentioned in the scene and the other a major inspiration for Chase), the context lifts us beyond simplistic thinking and not to a particularly comforting vision of the human condition. We can create a perfect narrative about the subconscious only if we cherry-pick the fragments that it grants us. But here Chase encourages us to go beyond the characters to realize that the dimensions of our dreams are much larger than our narratives, just as he encourages us not to shoehorn Tony into a formulaic figure of control by cherry-picking the details in the episodes. Here control of life is as much an illusion as control of the meaning of the subconscious.

Tony only seems to be the formulaic macho and potent mob boss as he blazes a trail through season 1. As the episodes unfold, he, among other things, cagily prevents his incompetent uncle Junior from gaining control of his mob crew, seeks to manage his mother's life by ensuring her a place in an upscale retirement home, takes on a seemingly profitable contract with an Orthodox Jewish rabbi who wants his son-in-law to grant his daughter a divorce under Jewish law, and kills an ex-gangster who informed on the mob, whom he comes across by accident while he is taking his daughter on a trip to inspect colleges. For every conclusive act he performs there are many more out-of-control moments of panic attacks, troubling dreams, illness, the impossible task of trying to be a loving son to his serpentine, vicious mother, and even (in season 6) a sudden experience of a parallel reality, after he is shot by Junior.

The episodes tend to structure Tony's power so that his criminal violence never really achieves the kind of definitive results that we have been taught to desire by formulaic television. *The Sopranos* distances us from those tired, automatic yearnings in ways that become most searing when Tony's motivation for violence seems to overlap with our own hatred of certain kinds of abuses. In those instances, Chase most imaginatively forces us to question our desires for immediate justice when a wrong is committed. There are numerous episodes of that type, but for the sake of brevity we shall look closely at the way it works in two representative episodes "Boca" (1.9) and "Whoever Did This" (4.9).

Everyone hates a child molester. Tony discovers in "Boca" that Don Hauser (Kevin O'Rourke), the coach of his daughter Meadow's (Jamie-Lynn Sigler) soccer team, has sexually molested one of Meadow's teammates. He arranges for one of his crew, Silvio Dante (Steven Van Zandt), to kill Hauser. The episode plays with the oxymoron of Tony's "criminally" righteous determination to kill Hauser and the restraining influences exerted on him by Melfi and by his one friend who is a legitimate businessman, Artie Bucco

(John Ventimiglia), the father of another of the girls on the soccer team. The emotional dynamics of this story defy all standard audience expectations. Most viewers will be torn between identifying with Tony's urge for a spontaneous dispatch of Hauser and identifying with the civilized solution of letting the proper legal authorities take over. Most Americans dream of vigilante justice under certain provocations, even if they would never take the law into their own hands. So the fantasy of Tony's power here is arresting. But the questions raised by Melfi and Bucco as they try to dissuade Tony are compelling too. Melfi wants to know why Tony is so driven to be the one to take charge. Bucco reminds Tony that his solution primarily makes him and the other outraged fathers feel better without any concern for the abused girl, who will have to deal with the coach's murder. In a rare moment of impulse control, Tony calls off the hit, and the police are notified about Hauser. Then Chase reveals the real surprise.

As Tony watches the newscast of a humiliated Hauser being led away in handcuffs, he is in the process of drinking himself into a stupor beyond any previous (or subsequent) inebriation. Nothing is explicitly explained to us, but Tony is clearly unable to deal with the consequences of his restraint. He careens around his house, noisily knocking into things and alarming both Meadow and his wife, Carmela (Edie Falco), by his strange orgy of self-pity. "I didn't hurt anyone," he murmurs to Carmela before passing out. If, as seems likely, Tony's need to be in charge and to make himself feel good through violence is connected to his drunken wallow, the question looms as to why this is so deeply disturbing to him. We are mesmerized, as is Meadow as she watches her father from the balcony overlooking the living room.

Machismo is not defined here in purely social/cultural terms but rather in terms of the unfathomable depths of the subconscious. Chase opens up the vulnerable underbelly of machismo and also of formulaic perfect heroism for scrutiny without giving us instructions about what to think of it. We are to do the work. This is also true of the subordinate storyline in this episode, in which Junior brutalizes his long-standing mistress and cuts off relations with her because she has carelessly let it be known that he performs cunnilingus on her, a sign of unforgivable weakness among the men of Tony's crime family. Junior suffers from his inability to stand up for his own pleasure at the same time that he expresses his weakness in rage against his girlfriend. The episode solves nothing through gangster control but fills us with important questions about men, crime, justice, and sexual entitlement in America.

Everyone in favor of animal abuse, raise your hand. This is the crime for which Tony murders one of his most unlikable, malicious captains, Ralph

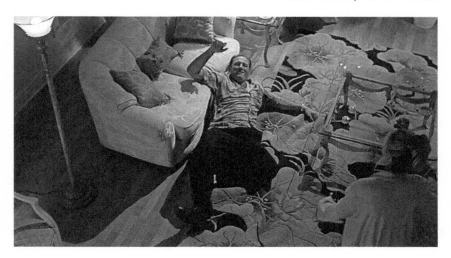

FIGURE 2.3. *We glimpse the mysteries of Tony's delight in violence when he drowns his anxieties about not hurting anyone in liquor.*

Cifaretto (Joe Pantoliano), in "Whoever Did This," an episode as intricate and enigmatic as "Boca." Again the plot hinges on Tony's illegal solution to a crime that elicits predictable rage from the viewer. At the same time, the episode hinges on creating an active questioning of our own rages. A horse named Pie-O-My jointly owned by Tony and Ralph dies in a fire that Tony cannot help thinking was caused by arson committed by Ralph for the insurance money. Audience members are likely to let Tony's guess pass for truth, since Ralph is a thoroughly despicably, greedy, sadistic thug. Tony kills Ralph in retaliation in a long, drawn-out, savage fight to the finish in Cifaretto's kitchen. Tony pummels Ralph mercilessly, and Ralph gives as good as he gets until Tony dispatches him. Ralph dies horribly. An immediate rush of satisfaction among viewers at this outcome is likely to ensue. But the possibility that Ralph did not commit the arson and thereby kill the horse for the insurance hangs over the scene. Intriguingly conflicting feelings trouble any easy response to Tony's murder of Ralph.

Ralph begins the episode with his usual ugly swaggering. Only a few minutes into the story, however, his son Justin (Dane Curley) is accidentally wounded by an arrow while he and his friend are playing, depriving his brain of oxygen. Agonized by the prognosis that Justin will either live out what time he has left in a coma or be severely handicapped, Ralph experiences, perhaps for the first time in his life, the agony of concern for another person. His sudden humanity elicits an unaccustomed feeling of sympathy for Ralph from Tony—and from viewers.[8] Then Tony and the audience learn of a stable fire in which Pie-O-My was burned alive and had to be put out of her misery. Broken hearted, animal-loving Tony visits Ralph, who is part owner of Pie.

At first Tony goes there only to inform Ralph of what has happened. But he becomes filled with certainty that Ralph set the fire to collect the insurance. Ralph responds with a fit of belligerent defensiveness, snarling that he did not do it, but enigmatically adding "So what? . . . It was a fuckin' animal!" Both Tony and Ralph have histories of lying, denial, and striking out with blind violence as Tony wished to do in "Boca." There we knew that Hauser was guilty. In this case, although Ralph is fully capable of burning a horse alive for money, he may or may not be telling the truth. The episode is ripe with possibilities in play. But unlike formula TV Chase gives us no way to end the uncertainty.

With Tony, we are caught up in a maelstrom of anger at Ralph, complicated by the memory, still fresh and painful, of Ralph murdering his pregnant goomar (mistress), who was the age of Tony's daughter. All this provokes a troubling and precipitous identification with Tony when he viciously attacks and murders Ralph. But in the aftermath, as we watch Tony summon Christopher Moltisanti to help him dispose of Ralph's corpse, Chase gives us a long time and many strange silences to weigh and balance our doubts and our desires for retribution and certainty, only to leave us with nothing but perplexity. The episode restructures the unequivocal joy of the formulaic moment when the hero finally strikes out against a nemesis. After all, the avenger is a murdering gangster himself, and the eerie silence of the aftermath of Ralph's death is filled with anything but formulaic satisfaction.

Waiting for dark so they can dispose of the body, Tony and Christopher distractedly watch the Elizabeth Taylor/Van Johnson melodrama *The Last Time I Saw Paris* (1954) on television. The striking red of Taylor's coat in the Paris snow distills its lush Technicolor wallow in overheated romantic entanglements, while Tony spoons peanut butter from a jar. Why does Chase remind us at this moment of Hollywood's version of jealousy, betrayal, irresponsibility, death, and final redemption? This scene is like a dream in which images seem to speak to us obliquely in ways that we cannot understand, especially at the end of the episode when Tony wakes up alone in the Bada Bing (the strip club where he keeps an office) after sleeping off the murder, finds a photo of Ralph's dead mistress, and literally disappears into the light of day as he exits from the dark club.

The dreamlike aspects of "Whoever Did This" are a result of the shifts of Tony's inner life from moment to moment. He moves fluidly and inscrutably through a variety of emotions toward Ralph just as he moves into and out of his subconscious, into and out of confusion and certainty, into and out of his lies in all the episodes of the series. Each episode requires us to work at moving imaginatively to intuit what lies beneath the surface of this character, a much more captivating spectacle than the crimes he commits. What is most important about this dynamic is that it constantly reminds us that what seem like his exertions of power are the enigmatic result of a flow of impulses that are driving him. This is a total unraveling of formula television, rendering Tony neither perfect hero nor antihero.

Something of the same can be said about the characterization of the women in *The Sopranos*. Chase set out intentionally to create these characters in opposition to the way women are conventionally defined and characterized by the gangster genre—or any genre. And he does.

UNFIT WOMEN

"What was Mama Corleone's first name? Mama?" Chase asked with a grin, when he spoke to me about his desire to write good parts for individuated women in *The Sopranos*.[9] Most gangster stories in the mass media and crime stories in general marginalize women characters. Even when they do not, just like some other formulaic TV genres that are rife with central female figures (domestic comedies and melodramas, for example), they lock the wife, the mother, the daughter, the mistress, the career woman, the sister, and so forth into familiar patterns. It is interesting that in reducing human identity to templates formula TV treats men and women alike. With Tony, Chase joined Lynch in giving the television audience a central character more in keeping with the modernist understanding of the fragmentation and indeterminacy of identity; and he gave women parity with respect to identity.

With Carmela Soprano and Jennifer Melfi, particularly, Chase gave American television female characterizations as mysteriously modernist as that of his male protagonist. This is not to say that he gave them narrative equality with Tony. The story of *The Sopranos* is Tony's story, not theirs. Nonformulaic television does not necessarily grant gender equality. The essence of nonformulaic characterization concerns its rejection of unequivocal identities suitable to the perfect narrative, whether male or female. Chase did write good parts for Carmela and Jennifer Melfi, as he intended, but did not give them narrative parity.[10] Chapter 6 (on Lena Dunham's *Girls*) discusses narrative parity of men and women and indeed woman-centric narrative in nonformulaic TV. Here I shall discuss the way the women in *The Sopranos* fascinate us as departures from formula clichés about female identity as they act as secondary figures in Tony's story.

Like the men in *The Sopranos*, Tony being the most exciting and fully articulated example, the identities of the women in the series are composed of pieces that do not fit together. It is almost impossible to characterize the women of *The Sopranos* with neat sound-bite generalizations. They are depicted for the most part through discontinuities, ambiguities, and indeterminacies. For the purposes of brevity essential to this study, Carmela Soprano and Jennifer Melfi will stand as examples of Chase's achievement.

In the majority of formulaic perfect narratives, in an infinite number of ways, women facilitate the perfect hero's clear, definitive, and orderly resolution of a plot problem. In *The Sopranos*, the complexity of the women becomes part of the rhetoric of indeterminacy of Tony's story, along with the dreams that bubble up from his subconscious; natural disturbances like disease and death; and the ambiguities of time, space, coincidence, and serendipity. Carmela, for example, is defined in this series by her role as Tony's wife, but she is anything but the consistent, clearly motivated wife of formula television. We see her agonize about her double life as a Christian and a mob wife, and we also see her as a woman who turns off her conscience when it suits her. We see her imitate Tony's tactics, and we see her terrified by the insecurity of a criminal life. We see her enraged by Tony's infidelity, and we see her flirting with her own desires to kick over the traces. Because of decades of media training it will be tempting to many to achieve clarity by reducing Carmela to nothing more complicated than a hypocrite, a parasite, or a status-conscious bitch. But that would require us to willfully sacrifice the richer rewards of savoring a character that thwarts our stock responses.

Carmela Soprano is a spectacular reconfiguration of the simplistic mass-media images of the generic wife, the mob wife, and the materialist American woman rolled into one shifting vortex of incommensurable desires, fears, and angers. Like Tony, she too is a strangely elliptical creation: much takes place in the silent spaces between her inner life and the words and deeds of her outer life. Consider what we see of Carmela in "Commendatori" (2.4), when her friend Angie Bonpensiero (Toni Kalem), a mob wife who is fed up with the way her role reduces her to a mere factotum, announces that she is going to divorce her uncaring, unfaithful husband. At a ladies' lunch with Angie and Rosalie Aprile (Sharon Angela), a mob widow, Carmela quite sincerely and with warm concern reminds Angie that marriage is a holy sacrament, even after hearing Angie break down hysterically because she can no longer bear her life with Tony's captain Sal "Big Pussy" Bonpensiero (Vincent Pastore). She tells them that Sal has finally returned from a mysterious disappearance. But when she heard his voice as he entered their house after all her prayers that he would come home safe, she wanted to vomit, she wanted to kill herself.

FIGURE 2.4. *Carmela channels Angie Bonpensiero when Tony returns from Naples.*

Carmela successfully deters Angie from seeking a divorce. But at the end of the episode, after Carmela hears Tony returning from a business trip to Naples, she finds herself experiencing feelings similar to Angie's. Carmela's face becomes steely at the sound of Tony's voice, in the split second before she turns to go to him. Does she feel like vomiting? Does she want to leave? To die? The moment is filled with contradictory imaginative cues for the audience, particularly as the soundtrack is ironically flooded with the nondiegetic sound of the romantic kitsch of Andrea Bocelli singing "Con Te Partirò," a lush cliché about the sadness of the departure. Carmela stands not just in opposition to formulaic devotion but in affirmation of herself as a person, like Tony, shifting among unsought impulses.

We see Carmela often moved by chaotic urges elaborately articulated. In "Full Leather Jacket" (2.8), while Meadow is waiting to hear whether she has been accepted by any of the colleges she applied to, Carmela becomes increasingly determined to keep her daughter from attending the hyperliberal and more importantly very distant University of California at Berkeley, by any means possible. First, she covertly throws a letter from Berkeley to Meadow in the garbage but repents, brushes off the coffee grounds, and gives it to her daughter. Is it laughably transgressive, mildly detestable, or purely corrupt that, though unable to permit herself to dispose of the letter, later in the episode Carmela surrenders completely to a much more unethical urge? Carmela waylays her next-door neighbor Jeannie Cusamano (Saundra Santiago) to persuade her to convince her twin sister, a lawyer with connections to

FIGURE 2.5. *Notwithstanding her protests that she stands apart from Tony's criminality, Carmela smilingly channels Tony as she commits intimidation by pie.*

Georgetown University, counting on her husband's reputation to intimidate Jeannie into helping Meadow get a recommendation for her application file.

When this does not work, she redoubles her efforts and pays an unscheduled call on Cusamano's sister at her office. The once perhaps inadvertent intimidation has now ripened into a full-blown gangster operation with a maternal twist. Carmela smiles and presents the woman with a ricotta pie (with pineapple), a domestic gesture contaminated with the unstated threat that her life is on the line if she rejects Carmela's overtures. As Carmela puts it, her eyes flashing in anger, she "wants this letter."

Who is this Carmela brandishing her pie and her husband's criminality like a weapon? What is her relationship to the Carmela who cooks to make herself the domestic center of family and friends? Or the Carmela who takes communion in her living room from Father Phil Intintola (Paul Schulze) with no one else home, in an erotically charged forbidden moment? Or the Carmela who beams when Tony exhibits affection for their son and patiently deals with Tony's impossible mother? Or the Carmela who threatens Robert Wegler (David Strathairn), the teacher of her son A. J (Robert Iler), with casually sinister irony? When she has a brief affair with Wegler while separated from Tony and he breaks it off, she implies that his life is in danger. What is her relationship to the Carmela in the astonishing episode "Second Opinion" (3.7), in which she visits psychiatrist Dr. Krakower (Sully Boyar) who tells her in no uncertain terms that she is an enabler of Tony's crimes and that her only chance to save herself and her children is to leave him? "You can never say . . . that you haven't been told," Krakower says bluntly, refusing to let her pay him with Tony's blood money. Carmela sobs, feeling the truth of his harsh judgment. But only for that moment. Carmela's character shifts, as it will, and by the end of that very day it is almost as if she has not been told.

When Carmela next sees Tony, she not only fails to leave him but digs herself deeper into living off his blood money. There is a seriocomic gap between the Carmela who sobbed in Krakower's office and the Carmela who uses her misery as a lever for dislodging Tony from his previous adamant refusal to give a donation of $50,000 to Columbia University. It is a new moment and a new Carmela who believes that she is stacking the deck in favor of her daughter, who has not gone to Berkeley after all but is a student at Columbia, a place less politically radical and closer to home. Carmela's identity seems solid but moves like the random particles of quantum mechanics and the unpredictable energies of the subconscious.

Structurally, Dr. Melfi's identity as a therapist is similarly liminal. Her role as Tony's therapist opens tantalizingly to reveal the inner shifts, contradictions, and complexity of her professional idealism, which smacks of naïve grandiosity as well as a lack of self-knowledge. As a woman and a professional person, Dr. Melfi aspires to do no less than probe and transmute the vast depths of the tangled urges of evil, a project endemic to formula drama about therapy but breathtakingly naïve within the structure of Chase's much more limitless universe. The nobility of her motives and its fit with the extremes of the optimistic American can-do mythology blinded many viewers to how unrelentingly the series resists that perfect therapeutic story.

Ironically presented, Melfi is not in a position to eradicate evil. Who is? Only perfect heroes. But Melfi, as prone as Tony is to assaults from the subconscious, repeatedly loses her grip on the enormity of the obstacles to Tony's therapy, even when she is forcefully presented with evidence. In "Guy Walks into a Psychiatrist's Office" (2.1), we see the aftermath of the end of season 1, when Melfi needs to go into hiding because Tony learns that his mother and his uncle are responsible for a recent attempt on his life and she is in danger because of knowledge that Tony's cohort may believe she possesses. Melfi realistically reevaluates her decision to treat Tony. When, after a car accident caused by a panic attack, he pleads with her to resume their therapeutic sessions, she categorically refuses. But she ultimately relents under the pressure of ambiguous, illegible, subconscious impulses.

In "Toodle-Fucking-Oo" (2.3), Melfi has a dream in which she is driving on a crowded highway and sees Tony dead or dying after a traffic accident, lying on the hood of his crashed automobile. She feels certain that she is

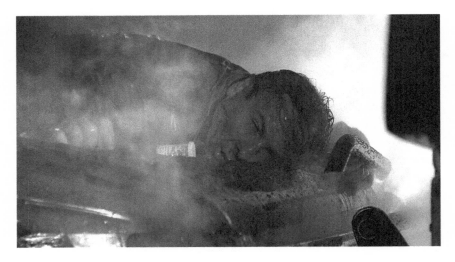

FIGURE 2.6. *Doctor, heal thyself! Melfi willfully misinterprets her patently comic dream about Tony.*

telling herself that Tony needs her and that she has to resume his treatment. At the same time, we know—and she does, too—that there is nothing unequivocal about the dream. Her dream glimpse of Tony pathetically splayed on his car hood is accompanied by a contradictory element, the song "Optimistic Voices" from *The Wizard of Oz*, sung in the altered tones of the Munchkins: "You're out of the woods / You're out of the dark / You're out of the night / Step into the sun / Step into the light." Might not these voices suggest her inner joy at being well out of her professional relationship with him no matter how pathetic his plight? The dream image and dream sound are contradictory and antic. The blend of comedy and pathos strikes a darkly parodic note. Consequently, Melfi's choice is destabilized for the audience, as is the professional judgment. Why is she not more attentive to the discrepancies in the dream? Why has she willed herself back into a dangerous situation that she already regrets?

These kinds of compelling moments in which Melfi is caught in a chaos about her intentions toward Tony occur throughout the series. One of the most important of these landmark encounters occurs in "Employee of the Month" (3.4), where it sheds some light on why she did not cut Tony loose in the second season. And even when she does finally terminate his treatment, in "Blue Comet" (6.20), her action is anything but simple, clear, and rational.

The savage rape that she suffers in episode 3.4 gives rise to another seminal dream. This time it is she who craves Tony's protection. In her dream, he appears to her in the form of a dog who tears the rapist Jesus Rossi (Mario Polit) to pieces. When the dog attacks in the dream, Melfi experiences relief: Rossi will never be brought to justice in her waking life because the police have broken the chain of custody with the evidence against him in the rape kit. She does not, as a result, ask Tony to avenge her, but she does, as a result, keep him from leaving her for a behavioral therapist as she had previously counseled him to do. How are we to define this woman who is, at the same moment, holding Tony at a professional distance and keeping him close? Audiences chose to think of this as a moment filled with underlying sexual connection between the two. Although each of them certainly has moments when unconsummated sexual impulses are in play, all of them, including this one, are only part of a much larger picture of indeterminate nonformulaic characterization. Melfi's relationship with Tony may involve some erotic charge, but it primarily involves complex questions about power, her power to cure, and the kind of violent power he commands that may seem to be at her disposal because she is his therapist. Her elusive feelings about his power and her grandiosity about her power remain undefined and troubling throughout the series, an exciting modernist form of characterization.

Melfi's character and her relationship to Tony, made up of pieces that do not fit together, reach a high of originality and ambiguity in "The Blue Comet" in the wake of a dinner party attended by Melfi and a number of her colleagues, including her own therapist. The repartee at the table is a vortex of peer pressure, the guilty pleasures of attraction to gangsters, and personal rivalry/hostility. When the conversation drifts toward the general public fascination with criminals and the rescue fantasies of women who engage in love affairs with prisoners, Melfi begins to suspect ulterior motives on the part of her therapist, Elliot Kupferberg (Peter Bogdanovich). She believes he is steering the conversation in order to needle her about what he sees as her perverse desire to continue treating Tony. When Kupferberg's wife brings up a major study showing that criminals only become more efficient at their work through therapy, Melfi becomes certain that Kupferberg has set her up. That certainty hardens when he breaks with therapeutic ethics and reveals that she is treating the famous Tony Soprano.

The scene is a tour de force that makes it impossible to draw a clear line between where a high level of intellectual discussion ends and mean-spirited personal attacks begin or to clearly see how Melfi becomes impelled to reread the seminal study of the pointlessness of "talking cures" for criminals by Samuel Yochelson and Stanton E. Samenow.[11] She is decisive in manner when she terminates Tony's treatment, but it is very difficult to take her belated dismissal of Tony as deriving from strength of character or control

FIGURE 2.7. *The termination of Tony's therapy with Melfi closes a door for both of them.*

of the situation. As always in *The Sopranos*, major decisions and actions come off as the result of buffeting by many forces. The dinner party and rereading of Yochelson and Samenow stand out as the causes for Melfi's dismissal of Tony. But questions remain about why the article, which she knows well, is having such a dire effect on her now and why she suddenly becomes exasperated by Tony after all the years of hearing him say much the same thing he says to her before she cuts him loose.

In their final session, Melfi becomes more and more agitated with every word Tony says. But by what? When she opens her office door as a signal to him to leave, Tony accuses her of immoral abandonment of him right now when his son has just tried to commit suicide. His accusation is funny and ridiculous, but at the same time her decision is unprofessionally abrupt and beyond her control. We miss the richness of the scene if we refuse to recognize Chase's deliberate ambiguity about the character, which is of a piece with the rest of the series. Melfi, like Carmela, and unlike the women in formulaic TV storytelling who exist to confirm the power of the perfect hero, serves as one more ironic, darkly humorous way of defining the mob boss's lack of control.

THIRTY YEARS

A gangster, a wife, and a therapist whose identities contravene the clichés by which such characters are usually defined: these are not what we would expect from a man with thirty years of experience writing for formula TV.

But the architect of *The Sopranos* did not expect a television career when he began working in the mass media; he thought that his television career would be a stepping stone to auteur filmmaking, not an end in itself. Inspired by the postwar Italian neorealists and Fellini, Chase imagined a journey into narrative about the impossibility of anything but contradiction and indeterminacy in the context of our nature, our culture, and the universe of random particles. But he had to step on the stones of reductive formulaic TV narrative much longer than he had anticipated. He reached his limit in 1999 and was extremely depressed by what lay ahead of him if he continued on his career path, although his work was somewhat innovative for pre-1990 TV. It just did not go far enough.

Chase's early work on one of television's early sci-fi series, *Kolchak: The Night Stalker*, gave him a chance to play with some of the humor and mystery he had seen and enjoyed on *The Twilight Zone*. *The Rockford Files* brought him under the wing of an encouraging, knowledgeable mentor, Stephen J. Cannell, a double-edged sword for Chase, who became more proficient at a craft in which he could not take pride. After *Rockford*, Chase briefly helmed his own series, *Almost Grown* (a domestic comedy), which lasted for only thirteen episodes and did not add to his career satisfaction. Immediately preceding *The Sopranos* he wrote and produced for *I'll Fly Away* and *Northern Exposure*, considered innovative and groundbreaking by many entertainment journalists and viewers. They left Chase wondering, "Is that all there is?"

Chase's extraordinary capacities had barely been tested by the pre-*Sopranos* work. Nor did it allow him to tap into the richness of a background filled with mechanical ingenuity and immense mental leaps into the unknown. When he was a child, he had busied himself by constructing complicated models. After he saw the classic movie *Frankenstein* (1931), he built a small simulacrum of the mad scientist's laboratory, complete with a tilting balsa-wood gurney. Add to this his love of music, which began when he was a very young man excited about rock and roll and the mind-expanding literature that he was exposed to in college, and you have a fascinating amalgam of craft and soaring curiosity. Like so many college students of the time, he read Carlos Castaneda's early books about Don Juan, a sorcerer who teaches the controlled use of drugs as a portal to alternate worlds. He experimented with LSD, which he took nine or ten times, but never became unhinged by it. He liked the initial rush but could see that repeated drug episodes did not lead toward liberation but toward paranoia and a lack of creativity. Furthermore, reading Carlos Castaneda convinced Chase that using drugs "without a whole belief system around it was really fourth rate."[12]

The big picture, including those glimpses beyond, became increasingly essential to the way he saw things. His large view was intimately connected with the double helix of his culture: the detail-obsessed American pragmatism of works like *The Autobiography of Benjamin Franklin*, filled with his many lists of things to do and things done; and the dream-haunted stories and poetry of the American Romantics. When he embedded his gangster story with both the American doer and the American dreamer, he leavened the commercial television industry with some of the yeast of American high culture. As Allen Coulter, one of the key directors on *The Sopranos*, says of Chase, "He's a man of many dimensions." Indeed.[13]

Chase's curiosity and daring are closest to those of his contemporary media relative, David Lynch, but many important distinctions must be made between their visions and their work. *The Sopranos* does not brush shoulders with any Lynchian religious sense of absolute good and evil moored beyond the marketplace at the center of a cosmic unified field. But Chase does share with Lynch a sense of the portals to infinity in daily life and their importance. That sense resonates with the lyrics of one of Chase's favorite songs by Pink Floyd, "Comfortably Numb": "When I was a child I caught a fleeting glimpse / Out of the corner of my eye / I turned to look but it was gone / I cannot put my finger on it now / The child is grown / The dream is gone / I have become comfortably numb." Loss of vision is a terrible loss.

By his own words, Chase is "not a religious person at all." But he has also told me that he is "very convinced that this is not it. That there's something else. What it is, I don't know. Other universes. Other alternate realities." Yet there are traces of religion of a very personal sort in his art of the glimpse behind ordinary appearances. The act of making art, as he has also said to me, is his form of prayer: not, obviously, as a form of importuning a divinity for favors and security but rather as an act of recognition, awe, and appreciation of the majesty of the cosmos, just as his questions about the way we live suffuse his series. Chase's personal sense of the contradictory combined presences of infinity and bounded everyday life is everywhere in *The Sopranos*.[14]

GLIMPSE

The temporal and spatial context within which Chase's shifting characters operate shifts as much as they do, albeit not early in the series. However, by the end of the first season, Chase has already begun to prompt viewers to engage actively in threshold experiences of glimpses of a beyond. Almost all the core characters in the series have such moments, but of course Tony's experience of alternate visions of his life is central. Tony's visions are germane not only to his character but also to the context within which the action takes place and to the action itself. His glimpses flesh out the context of the gangster action and diminish the image of gangster power and significance. Among the major glimpses is Tony's drug-induced fantasy in "Isabella" (1.12), the penultimate episode of the first season, caused by Dr. Melfi's unwise increase of his dosage of Prozac when Tony reports being under increased pressure.

Under the influence of the drug, Tony hallucinates a gorgeous, sensual, but maternal Italian exchange student, Isabella, who in his fantasy is housesitting for his neighbors, the Cusamanos, while they are away on vacation. Prozac can be understood here as a chemical facilitator of a conversation that Tony wants and needs to have with the larger, less-contained aspects of himself. He knows in some indeterminate way that his cold, self-involved, toxic mother has consented to his uncle's plans to kill him as part of a power play for leadership of the New Jersey mob. Tantalizingly, Chase does not resort to a formulaic dream message that clearly points in that direction but rather endows Tony with a fantasy of a warm, loving, comforting Italian mother that depicts the messages of the subconscious as discontinuous from the direct communication of verbal language. There is wonder here, raising many questions about how Tony's inner life works.

To add to the enigma of the situation, Chase framed the vision as another reality by asking director Allen Coulter to direct the episode à la Luis Buñuel's *The Exterminating Angel*. Buñuel's realistic photography creates an interesting sense of factuality for a situation that formulaic directors would have treated through the visual conventions of fantasy, blurred images, celestial music, and so forth. Chase did not want that. He wanted a Buñuel-like treatment for the episode so that the audience would have to work to deal with the transitions between ordinary life and the hallucination, when it turns out that there was never any Isabella next door. In this way, the Isabella drug hallucination is coded as an alternate reality, not just a blip in ordinary reality.

Tony's dreams in "Funhouse" (2.13), stimulated by fever and digestive upset, similarly endorse the inner life as another reality that overlaps ordinary daily life as we try to negotiate complicated questions. In daily New Jersey life, Tony believes but is not certain that his best friend, Big Pussy Bonpensiero, is collaborating with the FBI, giving information in exchange for the usual immunity from criminal prosecution that comes with such deals. In "Funhouse," in a dream less Buñuelesque than the hallucination in "Isabella," Tony gets his answer from the depths of his subconscious. Using special effects and arresting camera angles that signal something more than daily life, Chase treats us to a nonformulaic vision of how the subconscious operates that defies the plot-driven linearity of the usual treatment of dreams in formulaic TV.

Tony's dreams are tied to plot progress, but the images in the dreams always slip beyond the needs of plot; loose fragments provoke wonder rather than the sense that we have nailed down the function of Tony's subconscious. At the end of the six-part dream in "Funhouse," Tony's subconscious provides the necessary desperate image of Pussy himself, in the guise of a dead fish on a fishmonger's cart, who directly tells Tony what he suspects to be true: Pussy is talking to the FBI. This facilitates Tony's decision to murder Pussy. But the route to this revelation is labyrinthine and inexplicable, a convoluted progress of nonlinear images of death and doubt about mysterious people who do not appear and discontinuous dream encounters with Dr. Melfi and a female mob boss he met in Naples in "Commendatori." One of the enigmatic dream fragments takes place in a tiny red car, in which references to toilet paper send the potential ramifications of the dream flying off in all directions. Chase's dream language is evocative of much greater associations than if he took a formulaic approach to using dreams as moments when plot has to be negotiated.

The dream that outdoes all of Tony's other dreams by complicating the relationship between plot necessities and the wild energies of the subconscious is the portrait of his inner life in "The Test Dream" (5.11), which is connected with a plot line about Tony's separation from Carmela. At the end of season 4, after one too many revelations of Tony's adultery, Carmela tells Tony that she wants a divorce. He leaves the house. In the next season, Chase decided to reunite the pair by using a dream as the staging ground for Tony's decision to return home. But "The Test Dream" is rife with so much byzantine careening around heteromorphic dream vistas that it does much more than serve a plot function. It gives the linear plot a chance to go where it needs to but at the same time richly suggests the immensity of forces working on Tony as he makes what might seem a simple decision. Tony is alone at the Plaza Hotel in New York City, where he has moved temporarily because he is no longer living at his home with Carmela. If Chase was happy about using dream language to move his plot forward, he was disappointed at having the dream so tightly tied to plot. He preferred, he said, to do something more like Lynch does, tunneling into the oracular and incomprehensible associations made in the subconscious.

The dream indeed includes a number of pretty clear direct references to Tony's breakup with Carmela and his desire to return to her, but Chase does not give himself the credit he deserves for adumbrating the discontinuities of the subconscious. It bristles with a myriad of digressive images: the many television screens on which movies are shown and into which the characters disappear, if not unfathomable in their implications, at least require a lot of active work on the part of the audience. Other images concern the engagement of his daughter to a young man that Tony considers beneath her and his misfit cousin Tony Blundetto (Steve Buscemi), who has made himself a target of the fury of the New York mob and a very big political problem for Tony. These concerns often interpenetrate each other in the images. Tony is at the mercy of his inner life in his turmoil, and we are confronted with a thrilling challenge to our spectatorship.

Tony's troubled marriage is invoked by the comically surreal segments of the dream in which Carmela and Tony are getting ready to meet the parents of Meadow's fiancé, Finn DeTrolio (Will Janowitz). But these moments also elude easy analysis when the parents turn out to be Annette Bening and Vin Makazian (John Heard), a now dead policeman who was on Tony's payroll and has no connection to Finn outside the dream. Similarly slippery is Tony's continual loss of teeth during "The Test Dream." And other important transformational segments of the dream complicate even the moments that directly refer to Carmela. In one scene in which Tony and Carmela are talking, Tony moves through television screens the way Alice moves through the mirror to Wonderland. He is preoccupied at moments with *Chinatown* (1974), *A Christmas Carol* (1951), and *High Noon* (1952), which appear on random television screens for reasons that have no easily discernible connection with Tony's marital issues. Tony's "test dream" is also filled with segments in which he speaks with dead people and moments when he watches his cousin Blundetto kill New York boss Phil Leotardo (Frank Vincent), using his fingers as a symbolic gun. Tony is chased by the kind of mob typically featured in Frankenstein films and is saved by Artie Bucco, who arranges for him to have sex with his wife, Charmaine (Kathrine Narducci).

Most extraordinarily, and most elusively, the dream ends as Tony stalks his old high school coach, Coach Molinaro (Charley Scalies) but is unable to kill him because, as Molinaro points out, he is not prepared. Tony's gun shatters into pieces as he tries to fire, with the bullets dissolving into greasy fecal matter. Molinaro tells Tony that he is not the man he could have been and will never be able to silence Molinaro's criticism of him. The pervasive question in this dream, asked by many of the dream figures, is whether he is ready to do something that is never stipulated: the dream shifts between the Carmela and Blundetto situations and also larger issues about Tony's manhood and maturity. We are far beyond plot issues but at the same time right in the thick of them. The whirlpool eddies and waves of images, sounds, and associations articulate Tony's inner life with a force and a vitality that had so far not been available in formulaic American television. They entangle the active viewer in Tony's experiences of popular culture; his feelings about Carmela, his daughter, his cousin; and his fears of insufficiency. His dream places the narrative squarely within a huge context of inner and outer realities in which Tony can do no more than try to cope with the enormity of life.

This is even more true in the parallel lives of Tony Sopranos that emerge in "Join the Club" (6.2) and "Mayham" (6.3), in which Chase envisions a reality fully separate from the one in which Tony operates as a mob boss. Chase wrote me in an e-mail, "Nature is part of Our Universe and Our Universe is part of Nature and there could well be more universes or mirror universes." As an artist, Chase explores these thoughts in these episodes, telling the story of what happens to Tony after he has been shot by his uncle, Junior Soprano, whose onset of dementia has driven him to hysterically confuse Tony with an old enemy, Little Pussy Malanga. In what has largely been assumed to be a dream state while he is in an induced coma in the hospital, Tony's loss of control takes him further than ever before beyond ordinary life. He experiences an alternate life as a successful optical supplies salesman with a wife and children in a New Jersey suburb. Suburban husband Tony has risen to commercial success from a dead-end job as patio furniture salesman, the very job that gangster Tony jokingly talks about as his alternative to his life as a rich and powerful mobster. Again, Chase challenges his viewers to have some fun working with a more profound understanding of Tony and the world he lives in as he propels us to an alternate universe.

These episodes explode the fantasy that somewhere "over the rainbow" there is a better place. All realities are seemingly filled with their own pitfalls and darkness. Alternate Tony, at a convention in Costa Mesa, California, loses proof of his identity when he discovers that the briefcase and wallet that he has belong to someone called Kevin Finnerty, who somehow has taken his. Mistake? Intentional switch? Confusion. He wonders if he could be Finnerty after all. To make things darker, Finnerty may have swindled a group of Buddhist monks who insist that alternate Tony make the necessary reparations. When alternate Tony falls down a flight of stairs accidentally, he is taken to a hospital where the emergency room doctors discover evidence on an X-ray that he probably has incipient Alzheimer's disease.

This triple identity dislocation within a mirror universe—Tony, alternate Tony, Finnerty—packs a hard punch. Death, this experience shows us, is the only alternative to the strangeness of life. This we see when alternate Tony follows a clue to where he might find Kevin Finnerty and get back documents that will certify his identity. He finds an invitation to a family party in Finnerty's attaché case. When he gets to the address on the card he finds himself

FIGURE 2.8. *Tony lives a parallel reality filled with mysterious light.*

outside of a brilliantly lit, beautiful house, from which emanate the sounds of carefree merriment. A stranger outside the house, who is the double of his cousin Tony Blundetto, tries to take his briefcase—which alternate Tony refers to as his life and the stranger treats as his burden—as he encourages him to go to the party. Alternate Tony clings to his burden/life, pulling back from this glimpse of a happier place, and the transition back to New Jersey begins. He hears Meadow saying, "Don't leave us" and is transported from the Finnerty family soirée to mobster Tony Soprano's North Jersey hospital.

Questions emerge from this mirror-universe interlude like firecrackers popping and exploding into flashes of light. The two main questions that Tony takes away from his hiatus in another universe are "Who am I?" and "Where am I going?" The alternate world moments in 6.2 and 6.3 bring Tony toward the perspective of the series on the fragility of identity and toward a glimpse of something beyond the circumstances that have so far defined him. As it asks about the way our identities are entangled with our circumstances, it is also filled with a comparative sense of the way different lives that we might lead are likely to be a series of contrasting kinds of suffering. This is the richest contextualizing moment in *The Sopranos*. Chase's art provides a nonformulaic moment of eternity or infinity, as Kevin Finnerty's name implies.

The questions that emerge from the parallel reality episodes are explicitly embedded in dialogue in "The Fleshy Part of the Thigh" (6.4), when Tony grows stronger and finds himself in the company of a fellow patient, John Schwinn (Hal Holbrook), a quantum physicist from Bell Laboratories.

Context explodes still further as the two of them join another patient, Da Lux (Lord Jamar), a rapper, in his room to watch a boxing match on television with Paulie Gualtieri, one of Tony's gangster visitors. If parallel realities complicate our existence, there is still more fascinating intricacy for us to cope with, according to Schwinn. Unlike the gangsters, he is unmoved by the sports spectacle of winners and losers in the boxing ring or Paulie's bitter mutterings about everyone being alone in the world, because his discipline of physics tells him that our sense of reality is merely an illusion. Voicing the previously unvoiced vision of the entire series, Schwinn explains that he is unmoved because reality is only a soup of moving particles that are always crashing into each other. Nothing is separate; everything is connected. Separate shapes are what we choose to see. Da Lux gets it. "Everything is everything," he says, in softly surprised tones. He might well have said that everything is nothing, which would mean the same thing. Schwinn and Da Lux have put a name to what Chase has been showing us throughout the series. They have put a name to the contrast between *The Sopranos* and formulaic television as well.

TONY'S TWILIGHT ZONE—AND OURS

What can greedy, violent gangsterism mean in a reality that is a soup of particles and electrical subconscious impulses? And how is it possible to reach closure as formula understands it in such a universe? Just like definitive victory and static identity, formulaic termination through clarity and completion is not feasible within the art of Chase's storytelling. In *The Sopranos*, he seeks the experience of the contradictions of both the finality and the insecurity in an ending, a combination that more accurately reflects what happens to all of us when our lives come to a close. Chase's art seeks the return to the pain and rapture of wonder about endings that he sees in Poe's poem. The end of *The Sopranos* makes us feel the shock of Poe's metaphor of slippery, overwhelming life. Its very silence turns the termination of our time in the ordinary world of Tony and his families into an extraordinary moment, just as Poe turned a simple event on a beach into the edge of infinity. Like Poe, like Buñuel, Chase's art assumes a silent level of knowing more profound than words that we already know if we open up to that deeper part of us. Unlike the simplistic, judgmental, or illusory closures of formulaic crime stories, *The Sopranos* conclusion raises poignant questions about crime in a world of random particles and subconscious mazes of images, sounds, and allusions.

The series begins its descent toward its wide-open closure with the violence, verging on insane self-destruction, initiated by a family game of Monopoly in "Soprano Home Movies" (6.13), the first episode of the second part of the final season, and concludes with the murder of New York mob boss Phil Leotardo in "Made in America" (6.21). The violence has an air of *The Twilight Zone* about it. Indeed, at the safe house where Tony and his crew hide out during the concluding mob war with Leotardo, a very bitter episode of *The Twilight Zone* that satirizes the television industry is seen on the television. A producer is scolding a man who, as he puts it, has the temerity to aspire to the august position of television writer. *The Twilight Zone* musical theme plays, underlining the insanity of the scene: the writer, at least before Chase brought *The Sopranos* to the home screen, was the lowest man on the TV totem pole. Chase knows it, and so did Rod Serling. Instead of building to a big climax, Chase's auteuristic final episode is a study in diminishing formula.

The death of Phil Leotardo, which would ordinarily have been the major concern at the end of any conventional boilerplate mass-media gangster story (usually involving a big shoot-out), becomes anticlimactic after the mob negotiations that left Tony free to kill him. Leotardo is shot with no buildup, while he is in a gas station talking through a car window to his wife, with his twin grandchildren in the back seat. In a ghastly/funny moment, Phil's wife bolts out of the car in panic as Phil falls onto the ground. She has forgotten to put the car in park, and it rolls forward over Phil's head. This grotesque note only serves to underline the marginality of this action, which differentiates itself from the majesty accorded the boilerplate mob denouement. The most important thing about this death is that things go back to normal for the Sopranos. But what is normal? Reality is a soup of particles, as we see in the famous closing moments of the series, particles with no beginning and no end, particles in random motion, particles impossible to identify as either good or bad, welcome or reprehensible.

This gangster story ends with the Soprano family having dinner at Holsten's, a local diner, eating onion rings. Around them flow all kinds of people, strangers, some of whom are reminiscent of people they know. They look at Tony, Tony looks at them. Are they neutral? Do they mean harm? When a man who might look sinister walks into the men's room, it summons up cultural memories of *The Godfather*, when Michael Corleone went into the bathroom restaurant toilet to get a gun for an assassination. Meadow, across the street from the restaurant, is having trouble parking—things just do not fit into the places we want them to. After finally maneuvering the car into the parking space, she runs across a street with cars whizzing by. Everything is in motion. Who are all these people? Where are they going? Who are the Sopranos? Where are they going? The cut to black is the big climactic question, not a definitive answer. That is Chase's modern artistry. Almost all the public and most of the critics looked for a statement. That is the confusion about the nonformulaic series that Chase created.

Chase's conclusion to his series partakes of the modernist vision of the boundless possibilities of experience and reality; some of the tenets of surrealism, with its silences and distrust of language, and also of the relativism of the modernist approach to language. As Chase said to me (January 20, 2015) "translating a vision into the English language and then into the language of film, the dream gets worn down." Chase's post-*Sopranos* reading tells some of what his "word weariness" is about. He opened up Castaneda's early books again about three years after his final *Sopranos* season; several years after that he read for the first time Castaneda's last book, *The Power of Silence*. The book speaks of a knowledge much deeper than the rationality that constructs verbal language. Castaneda speaks of this kind of language as the "betrayer" of the deeper knowledge. Chase tends to agree with him that the problem of words is the problem of evil itself, which Castaneda defines as stupidity. "In his [Castaneda's] world, stupidity means something else. It means only listening to your stupid fucking interior dialogue. It's all about the stupid fucking interior dialogue. We fool ourselves constantly."[15] What good is the formulaic structure with its clear purposiveness and well-defined conclusions for invoking the lives of a species that fools itself constantly? Chase's use of the gangster genre in a completely original manner produces a portrait of daily lies and self-deceptions that speaks to America as a twilight zone in which reality is a strange dream of extreme emphasis on loss and gain and the ownership of things, things, things, pointing toward a larger context of reality within which formula fiction, if comforting, is absurd.

CHAPTER 3

DAVID SIMON, *THE WIRE*

Everything is messy. Everything's a tangle. I can't help but be a reporter.
—David Simon, in-person interview with author, January 21, 2016

W hen David Lynch and David Chase narrate context, they look, in their separate and distinctive ways, toward the universe/cosmos and therefore beyond ordinary perceptions of time and space. They also search the depths of the subconscious. By contrast, time, space, and the subconscious play little or no contextual role in *The Wire*. Rather, as David Simon imagines it, context is cultural and social. His portrayal of it is, for American television, an entirely fresh depiction of the dynamic interchanges of energy in social systems. The environment in American TV series is ordinarily passive, swept for travelogue images, but not depicted in terms of the interplay of racial, political, and sociological forces. On the rare occasions when such issues are raised, one carefully limited social element is isolated and one "right" perspective is established. Not so in *The Wire*. Simon's first nonformulaic foray as a television storyteller is an auteur series filled with collisions among the multiple issues tangled around the drug problem in Baltimore.

In television's first nonformulaic police show, Simon seeks complexity through immediacy, connecting his audience to Baltimore through his experiences on its streets as a police reporter and through his collaborators:

writers, directors, and actors. Like him, they have had vivid, intense personal connections with what Simon passionately calls "my city." Immediacy is as much a part of modernist art as is the rich interface with modern physics, literature, and psychology that we see in *Twin Peaks* and *The Sopranos*. Think of Walt Whitman's wild "yawps" over the rooftops and William Carlos Williams's desire to connect his readers with the blood and bone of experience of *his* city, Paterson, New Jersey:

> —Say it, no ideas but in things—
> nothing but the blank faces of the houses
> and cylindrical trees
> bent, forked by preconception and accident—
> split, furrowed, creased, mottled, stained—
> secret—into the body of the light!
> —"Paterson," Book I

Think of Wallace Stevens trying to burst free to the world and escape from mental images:

> The palm at the end of the mind,
> Beyond the last thought, rises
> In the bronze distance.
> —"Of Mere Being"

But Simon does not merely want us to touch the raw stones of Baltimore. He wants us to open our pores and take in its macro- and micro-levels of life, its seemingly infinite contradictions and discontinuities, and the ambiguities of its local history and its complex mass of social systems—and wonder and think.

And David Simon is happy to talk about all this.[1] He pivoted to series television when he began to feel that his commitments to social justice were no longer served by journalism, hoping that storytelling for a mass audience might enable him to provide better service to the public. If this sounds to you more like propaganda than entertainment, Simon could not agree more. Simon says he is a propagandist, not an artist. But his belief in balance, his rejection of polarized good and evil, and his herculean determination to avoid writing the perfect narrative for a perfect hero suggest otherwise.[2] Propaganda lacks balance, cleaves to polarization, manufactures clarity, discounts ambiguity and irony, and avoids sensory distractions from its political map of action. By contrast, *The Wire* is the ambiguous, ironic, sensuous modernist political vision of an artist.

Admittedly, it does seem like Simon is indulging in propaganda when he says, as he did to me, that *The Wire* is about how the war on drugs "got fucked." He wants us to think about what needs to be done about that. But he does not want to tell us what to do. William Carlos Williams says, "No ideas but in things." David Simon tells stories as if to say, "No ideas but in the energy of the marketplace." Lynch's marketplace is an illusion; but Simon's marketplace is the loam of the real in its "messy" flesh, blood, and nerves— his antidote not only to the perfect narrative of television but to the equally reductive and disconnected perfect social narratives circulating as if they were reality. Messy is a narrative issue for Simon. The perfect narrative is constructed to filter out the disarray, the disjunctions among the many voices of a community; however, that is where Simon finds reality as a storyteller. But what kind of narrative form reflects the living mess of Baltimore without itself being either pedantic or chaotic? To begin any discussion of *The Wire*, it is first necessary to appreciate how Simon solved this narrative problem.

Simon's narrative in *The Wire* runs parallel with the kind of disjunction that his fellow Baltimore journalist Ta-Nehisi Coates explores in *Between the World and Me* (2015), a book that Simon says is consistent with the point of view of *The Wire*. Indeed, dipping into its pages helps to illuminate what Simon's narrative structure is about. Coates, who deals in social philosophy not fiction, goes on an odyssey in the book, exploring what he sees as some serious disconnects between American thought and American reality. This odyssey began when he entered Howard University, filled with excitement at the prospect of being initiated into the secrets of higher knowledge: "I went into this investigation [college] imagining history to be a unified narrative, free of debate, which once uncovered would simply verify everything I had suspected. The smokescreen would lift and the villains who manipulated the streets and the schools would be unmasked. . . . The trouble came almost immediately. I did not find a coherent tradition marching lockstep but instead factions, and factions within factions."[3] The unified narrative that Coates had sought suddenly seemed a sinister illusion with a lock on social systems. Once the object of his quest, it became the kind of enemy that Simon finds in the perfect narrative of the formulaic TV series.

Coates calls that enemy the Dream. "The Dream thrives on generalization, on limiting the number of possible questions, on privileging immediate answers," he writes. "The Dream is the enemy of all art, courageous think-ing, and honest writing."[4] The reductivism of Coates's Dream is a disabling detachment from the complexity of our reality and holds us in a hypnotic perspectival grip that drives us to think of our situations in ways that exacerbate problems. This defines the narrative problem of *The Wire* in a nutshell.

You cannot write a grand narrative—or a perfect narrative—if you want to break the grand narrative's lock on culture. Simon had to invent a form of narrative that would not deliver Baltimore into the hands of what Coates called a unified narrative and does not thrive on "generalization" or "limiting the number of possible questions." He had to invent a narrative form that would reflect the "tangle" of people and systems that he saw with his own eyes and would take us into the city at the end of the mind. He needed to stimulate the desire that would awaken the audience from the Dream into a reality that Simon had experienced. In his narrative, no one, no perfect hero, could stand either above or beyond our unavoidable interconnection with each other; causes and effects could be confusing and even become indistinguishable from each other. He had to invent a nonformulaic narrative that would make us reject false, simplistic answers that had no bearing on the immediacy of the city. He evolved collage narrative.

COLLAGE NARRATIVE

Simon had previously tried to turn his real-life experiences as a reporter into a television series in *Homicide*, but as a formulaic series it could not challenge old ways of thinking about crime stories. Only the nonformulaic art of narrative can do that. Simon's transition from the formulaic *Homicide* to the nonformulaic *Wire*, from the conscious to the subconscious, is a passage that will not be clarified here. It is the fundamental mystery of how anecdote becomes art. But what is clear and observable is that *The Wire* leaps out of the straitjacketed structure of *Homicide*, admired for its gritty tone and mood, which Simon had created in the image of the formulaic but taboo-breaking *Oz*. *Oz* had influenced Simon to want to write a television series; it was the first indication that the medium could tell a disturbing story about the dark corners of American life and influence more people than he could from his perch at the *Baltimore Sun*.[5] By contrast, *The Wire* is not only gritty but also visionary.

The Wire, the enticing and ironic title of the series, may mislead some into expecting some version of the network cliché of invincible technology that has become the sine qua non of the crime procedural. But the show questions, among other things, the comforting formulaic expectations that TV has associated with both heroes and science. When the series begins, there is no wire; when the wire finally arrives, it provides many advantages to the police in their war on drugs but is still no match for the disarray produced by the discontinuous, fragmented, operations of the police, which are built on falsification of the life on the street.

The police department that Simon portrays in *The Wire* is ceaselessly caught between the immediacy of the Baltimore streets and the grand narratives of the city hierarchies. The police are continually required to demonstrate their effectiveness even though they are not effective. As a result, an almost hysterical reliance on "clearances" has grown up within the department, certification that a case has been solved and statistics that prove the police are making progress in fighting crime. Much of the time, the clearances, fabricated from manipulated statistics, are disconnected from the worsening drug wars in the city. The same can be said of other systemic hierarchies of Baltimore, which squander most of their energies keeping up appearances instead of actually impacting the chaotic confusion of the labor-management turmoil at the port of Baltimore; the deepening problems of the city's education system; and the incrementally corrupting commercialization of the press in the city. The narratives of *The Wire* are a bubbling, steaming stew flavored by many races and ethnicities. As we survey the narrative consequences of all the clashes and miscommunications (born of the many and conflicting disconnects between life and social systems), I shall parenthetically indicate the race of each of the pertinent characters because the racial mix is so crucial to what happens.[6]

The first members of Baltimore officialdom whom we meet in the pilot of *The Wire* are part of the racially diverse but universally ill-informed police hierarchy. Always in desperation mode because the upper police hierarchy concentrates on short-term, meaningless "buy and bust" operations, rather than well-planned long-term strategies, the police never get their hands on the drug lords who control the operation. They do not even know their names when the show begins. But one (white) cop, Jimmy McNulty, for the most part considered both insubordinate and misguided, has made it his business to research the identities of those in charge of the drug trade in West Baltimore: Avon Barksdale (Wood Harris) and his enforcer, Russell "Stringer" Bell (Idris Elba), both black.

In a formulaic procedural this would mean McNulty to the rescue. Not in *The Wire*. McNulty's capability is complicated by the war between his own intelligence and his predilection for heroic grand narratives as well as by internecine wars at all levels of the police administration. In order to depict all these complexities, Simon rejects the idea of making McNulty's story central to the series. Instead *The Wire* dramatizes the always compelling McNulty as one element of a big collage composed of juxtaposed stories and points of view. McNulty's striving to be a hero is part of a live mosaic of perspectives emanating from the essentially white middle/upper-class community and from the essentially black poor/lower-class community. These multiple perspectives flow through the city, frequently at cross-purposes, often canceling each other out, sometimes making some small inroads on the problems of Baltimore. This is the nature of the city that we see. We are figuratively with Simon in the back of a Baltimore police car, eyeballing a ceaseless and seemingly meandering dance of oppositions.

Consider the first season of the series, which is about the events that lead with almost painfully slow indirection to authorization of wiretap surveillance in the fight against the drug trade. The early episodes introduce us not to a forward-moving formula plot about people determined to do something about a well-defined problem but rather to multiple problems with little definition: a city too poor to conduct police and court business properly; a drug trade well organized by Barksdale and Bell; large numbers of hopeless people in the drug scene caught up in addiction; police, underpaid, demoralized, and lacking resources; and careerists, daunted by an impossible and racist economy, fighting for a foothold on the professional ladder, whether or not their efforts run counter to the job that they have been hired to do. We have juxtaposed images of combatants with equally compelling motives who do not understand each other, creating intimations of deepening conflicts that only grow stronger as the series unfolds.

From the first moment of "The Target" (1.1), we see how the police and the criminals are in the same boat in many ways, often looking confusedly at each other. This is evident in the first image of the show, which plunges us into the hurly-burly of a murder scene, a familiar part of the exposition of the crime procedural. In a crime procedural this would be our first view of the big murder case of the episode; here it is just one of the murders that are daily events in the poor black areas of the city. A street kid named Snot Boogie is dead. His death is a fragment, not the gateway piece of some big crime puzzle to which a perfect hero will find a solution. But fragments are the life of collages, and this one says much about the larger identity of this series. McNulty and one of the anonymous local black street kids (Kamal Bostic-Smith) sit quietly, talking about the victim. A street handle like "Snot Boogie," McNulty observes, is not fair; it is more of a contemptuous comment than a name. But the kid is not interested in what is fair. It is life. He is more concerned about why someone would kill Snot, obnoxious as he is, when a good beating would suffice. The kid communicates this raw street perspective to McNulty through a story about how he and his friends handled problems with Snot, who was more than a little peculiar. In *The Wire* there is no such thing as just another crime. Every police folder is filled with the mysteries big and small of human particularity.

It seems that Snot routinely shot dice with the other guys on a Friday night. He would always lose and at some point would always grab the pot of money and run. McNulty is incredulous that the kids kept letting Snot Boogie get away with stealing their money. "Why did you let him play?" McNulty asks. "This America, man," the kid replies. They beat Snot up regularly, but they played with him anyhow. McNulty shakes his head. This conundrum, this human comedy, is the rule not the exception in *The Wire*. This is Simon's America, writ small in his Baltimore.

Even as the wire technology begins to come into play, the context remains a seething caldron of connections through difference and misapprehension. There is a beautiful comic interlude that is a synecdoche of this state of affairs. A few episodes after the pilot, in comes "Old Cases" (1.4). It is a small peripheral moment in the series that has no bearing on the forward motion of any of the actions against drug crime, but it says everything about the world in which we find ourselves as viewers. The interlude features a rainbow assortment of police of different races and temperaments belonging to the detail commissioned to focus on major crimes, newly formed under (black) university-trained lawyer Lt. Cedric Daniels (Lance Reddick). They are full of the spirit of cooperation but thwarted by competing perspectives and the difficulty of communication. The new detail is in the process of moving into shabby rundown headquarters that embody the contempt in which the police high command holds this crew. The members of the new major crimes unit believe that they are working collectively as they strive to move a desk out of a doorway during the process of settling in. But the collective in *The Wire*, as in Snot Boogie's life with his street buddies, means a lively turbulence, contradictions, and cross-purposes.

The episode opens with the desk stuck in a doorway, with one member of the detail, the bullish and crude (white) Detective Herc Hauk (Domenick Lombardozzi), struggling to move it. He is joined by Sergeant Ellis Carver (Seth Gilliam), a quieter, more nuanced (black) man. They struggle together, at which point the elegant Daniels joins them, as they curse and strain every muscle. They are watched silently, eyebrows arched, by another member of the detail, Detective Lester Freamon (Clarke Peters), a (black) man whose quiet demeanor conceals a razor-sharp mind with a spectacular capacity for detail. When they are all at the end of their rope, Herc says, "At this rate we're never going to get it in." And they all freeze with exasperation. As the detached, amused, and silent Freamon could see, they were obliviously working at cross-purposes. Not all of them were trying to drag it *into* the room. *The Wire* is peppered with small, telling moments like this that matter because they are small versions of the big action of the series,

FIGURE 3.1. *Whither the desk? Herc and Carver struggle at cross-purposes.*

the introduction of wire technology to the Baltimore police for their war against drugs.

The big action, the arrival of wire technology, comes into play through a similar vigorous collage of disparate multidirectional intentions. It begins in episode 1.1 with McNulty's exasperation when the police lose what should have been an easy win in a murder case because Barksdale and Bell, the local drug lords, are able to intimidate most of the witnesses. Within the police hierarchy, there is no sympathy for McNulty's concerns about the miscarriage of justice—quite the reverse. When the (white) trial judge, Daniel Phelan (Peter Gerety), buttonholes McNulty about why the trial went the wrong way, McNulty feels forced to answer that the police have no effective long-term anticrime strategy. He gets in trouble because Phelan, who is also disconcerted by the botched trial, communicates his own displeasure to the (black) deputy police commissioner, Ervin Burrell (Frankie Faison). Maj. William Rawls (John Doman), a surly, often cruel (white) careerist with a fierce dedication to the police hierarchy who is in charge of the homicide unit, feels the heat.

McNulty and Judge Phelan do not form an interesting, offbeat crime-fighting team that cleans up Baltimore, as they would in on-track pre-*Peaks* procederals. Instead a series of colliding interests ends up by chance paving the way for a wire for the police. It begins with Rawls looking for a way to punish McNulty. He is not upset about losing the case so much as perturbed by the disturbance of the hierarchy, caught up in what Ta-Nehisi Coates would call the Dream. Rawls cares only that McNulty has broken the chain of command by speaking with Judge Phelan and wants to break McNulty for going outside the chain of command. But he does not find institutional support for vengeance, even though Commissioner Burrell is also more interested in the chain of command than in dealing with the immediacy of street life. Burrell comes down on the side of better management, but not because he has any connection to the actual drug problem. He senses that currying favor with Judge Phelan could be helpful to his career. When Burrell approves the new crime-fighting detail that McNulty wanted, and places it under Daniels's command, some progress is obliquely made toward a better war on drugs. Maybe. But no one was in control of the way the decision was made.

This narrative path is anything but clear and linear and is certainly not the result of the power of one character, as in formula TV, but rather the result of a potpourri of unaligned intentions, accidental outcomes, individual temperamental quirks, and bureaucratic mechanisms. No perfect hero here; events converge. First, McNulty visits his friend Terrance "Fitz" Fitzhugh (Doug Olear), a special agent at the FBI, for reasons that are not connected with his determination to make the police more effective, and by chance sees just how extensive the new surveillance technology is. He becomes enthusiastic about the possibility of electronic surveillance. Second, William Gant (Larry Hull), the one citizen who did testify for the police, is murdered by the drug lords in reprisal to send a message to the community, ratcheting up the problem of police failure to protect dutiful citizens. Third, Burrell is in an ornery mood because he was forced by circumstances into authorizing Daniels's detail.

Burrell not only does not care about the crime-fighting potential of the Daniels detail but has a personal reason to sabotage it. He does not like being pressured. The surly Rawls does his duty by assigning to the detail McNulty and Detective Kima Greggs (Sonja Sohn), a highly competent, scrupulously honest (black) woman, as well as two reasonably useful street police. Daniels requests a few more police, which gives Burrell a way to vent his dissatisfaction. He selects men whom he believes to be the worst deadbeats in the department. Happily for Daniels and Baltimore and unhappily for Burrell, he is partially misinformed. Two of the four detectives are indeed hopeless. The other two are Lester Freamon, who has been marooned in a deadend job for years, and Detective Roland "Prez" Pryzbylewski (Jim

True-Frost), a (white) cop with demonstrably bad impulse control. Freamon and Prez have bad reputations, but only because their talents have been either undiscovered or thwarted as a result of the crushing systems of lies and ill-conceived procedures in the police department. They are wizards with the new technology. Surprise: the death of Gant, the detachment of the hierarchy, and McNulty's chance meeting with Fitz yield a major crimes unit and a wire.

Once the collaboration of McNulty, Freamon, and Prez starts, the wire accumulates intelligence and information about Barksdale and Bell that will enable the police to fight them much more efficiently. As a result, it becomes tempting to see the three police as some kind of conventional heroes, but the series will not permit it. The collage structure keeps pelting them with the forces in play in a troubled city and a troubled department.

Simon fights hard against the formulaic traditions of crime TV series, not only through his complex restructuring of the threads of the police stories but also through his careful management of the threads of the stories involving the criminals, notably Omar Little (Michael Kenneth Williams), a dashing, sexually gay, Robin Hood–like (black) vigilante drug pusher, well known in West Baltimore, who robs the big drug lords to enrich himself but also to give back to the poor blacks in the ghetto who are being victimized by everyone. Omar has all the panache of the antihero who dominates circumstances through his illegal bravado, but ultimately he too is at the mercy of context. In the first season he is unable to protect his (probably racially mixed) lover, Brandon Wright (Michael Kevin Darnall), from the vengeance of Barksdale and Bell and thus becomes vulnerable to the proposition from McNulty and Greggs that he testify against Barksdale and Bell. He does get his own vengeance against them that way, by lying to McNulty and Greggs when he tells them that he was an eyewitness to Gant's murder and then lying again under oath. This victory is again a collage of local influences—professionalism, greed, vengeance, innocence, murder, and Omar. But ultimately his appealing gaming of everyone's system will, sorrowfully, not catapult him beyond context, as devoted *Wire* fans know.

At the end of season 1, technology does not reign triumphant as it does in the police procedurals; instead we are left with a standoff between the potential of the wire and the entrenched but useless police short-term policy of useless buy-and-bust tactics. Thanks to the wire, Baltimore's finest have seized a large cache of cocaine. But instead of keeping it under wraps so as not to ruin the long-term possibilities of the wire by tipping their hand to Barksdale and Bell, the department caves in to pressures to put the drugs on display for the publicity, for the short-run benefit of appearances. This time there is no help from Judge Phelan, because he is in an election year, a time when he cannot make waves, according to the grand narrative. In the world of formulaic TV, intelligent, well-intentioned Phelan would always be on tap to take the long view, and indeed he does understand that the police can continue to get information and make a more far-reaching case if they maintain the wire. But storytelling of that type denies context, at least as Simon sees it. In the grasp of the political grand narrative, Phelan has to keep his distance from what he knows to be bad policy. Once the drugs are on a table in front of the reporters, the wire goes dead. Simon's collage structure is the key to unmasking the simultaneously flawed, fragile, obstructive, repressive police/political/educational/journalistic grand narratives for what they are. Baltimore is depicted in *The Wire* as the land of bad Dreams, and one bad Dream begets another.

BAD DREAMS

From seasons 2 to 5, bad Dreams haunt Baltimore, as increasing desperation about fiscal problems mocks long-term planning and investment and inspires short-term madness. As we shall see, the worst thing about a bad Dream is that it looks so good if you do not figure in the disheveled context, as formula TV and Baltimore's bureaucracies do not. When *The Wire* places the Dreams of well-meaning characters in context, they foment chaos. In the third season, Maj. Howard "Bunny" Colvin (Robert Wisdom), a warm, intelligent (black) veteran police officer, has such a Dream that arises from his dejection about the stalled war on drugs. Exasperated beyond endurance by the futile war on drugs, without consulting the chain of command, Colvin unilaterally creates free zones for drug sales in West Baltimore where the drug trade goes on under the watchful eyes of the street police, which de facto legalizes drugs. In the fourth season, we see an attempt to destroy the conveyor belt from impoverished childhood to drug-addicted adult in West Baltimore through a pilot program in the city schools to save at-risk students. The success of this approach, which is a product of long-term thinking and investment in the future, makes no difference to a culture of short-term policies. In the final season, McNulty's Dream of better policing turns into a nightmare. In each case, Simon's collage narrative structure brings these Dreams into collision with the seething context, like rejected transplanted organs.

Major Colvin finds this out to his dismay when he creates his free zones for drugs. As he had hoped, all the surrounding streets experience a rise in the quality of life, but the zones run afoul of the law, become pits of unsanitary, destructive behavior, and change nothing in the long run. Colvin is a better man than most, and his Dream is inspired by compassion, but we are never

FIGURE 3.2. *Major Colvin glows with pleasure at Hamsterdam, but it is a time bomb for Baltimore and for him.*

allowed to forget the contextual forces arrayed against him that doom his plan from the start. Moreover, the other stories keep reminding us of the difficulty of real change in the lives of the people in these neighborhoods. Colvin is in violation of police culture from the bottom of the hierarchy to the top and finds himself continually having to lie to the men in the police command, who are kept ignorant of his illegal plans, and to the men under his command, telling them that the zones are part of a plan to get all the drug criminals together and then make a massive arrest. He also lies to the members of the drug community when he presents himself as having the authority to create the zones and insists that they can trust him.

How does Colvin's plan look once it is contextualized? The drug community wants nothing to do with his idea. The notion of a peaceful area in which they can break the law without fighting the police and inflicting all kind of violence on each other conflicts too much with what they know as reality. And the police feel the same way, once Colvin convinces them that this is now an official police project. They fear losing face and the respect of the drug sellers if they no longer harass and beat them. Both sides intuit that the free zones go against the laws of the jungle that they understand as reality. The drug dealers expect buy-and-bust violence and hostility from the police. It is part of the narrative. Unlike the perfect heroes of formulaic television, Colvin is in a precarious and worsening position as he dreams big, driven to unethical and illegal behavior to make life better for the people who live in the poor, black district, always in a position to have his deceit discovered. Many formulaic TV heroes make a kind of joke about having to resort to trickery but are (unrealistically) rewarded for their cutting of ethical and legal corners. By contrast, Colvin continually bumps up against the dissociation of his Dream as he is faced with the complex of contextual circumstances as well as the factions within factions within factions, to use Coates's language.

For example, by isolating the drug traffic in the free zones and cleaning up the surrounding streets for habitation, Colvin creates a festering sewer within the zones. In "Moral Midgetry" (3.8), Colvin speaks with Deacon (Melvin Williams), a local minister, who bluntly tells him that Hamsterdam (nicknamed after Amsterdam, an open city for drugs) is hell and persuades Colvin to provide needle exchanges, free condoms, and offers of counseling in the free zones. Of course, this will not save Hamsterdam. It is caught in a whirlwind of other crime initiatives and increasing political sparring, which attracts the press. The *Sun*, Baltimore's biggest newspaper, learns about the free zones by accident. To save himself once he learns about Hamsterdam, Commissioner Burrell alerts all the media. As a result of the competing but interconnected interests of Burrell, Rawls, and the Baltimore government, Colvin's free zones are leveled like enemy territory in a bombing raid. With a compelling but enigmatic flourish, Simon gives Rawls an ambiguous moment when he raids Hamsterdam, swooping down on the free zones with his car's loudspeaker blasting Richard Wagner's "Ride of the Valkyries."

Simon's articulation of Colvin's and Rawls's actions allows for neither perfect heroes nor perfect villains. There is a splash of fascism across Rawls in his incongruous, almost self-parodying use of the music of Wagner, historically tainted by Adolf Hitler's love of that particular German composer. But Simon himself said that he does not hate Rawls as some viewers may want to. He depicts Rawls as a man in a certain position, here pursuing his idea of what is good for the police with a darkly comic relish. Rawls is not a fascist, even if his Dream may be fascistic. And although Colvin is a good, big-hearted man, Simon does not spare him the consequences of his decisions and behavior. Sometimes characters you like disappoint you, as Simon says, and sometimes characters you do not like surprise you.[7] We as viewers are asked to stop giving easy answers to complex problems and to acknowledge how complex they are even if we cannot find the answers that we and the characters so desperately want.

The morality at play in the series, however, is not relativistic, it is existential. It is certainly unrelated to the reductive morality of the police and the courts in *Law and Order*. Rather, it is evocative of the labors of Sisyphus, the mythic figure who is condemned by the gods to roll a giant stone up a hill only to see it crash back down the hill when he reaches the top and finds himself rolling it back up again. This spirit of ethics as a form of intention, not necessarily achievement, is also expressed eloquently in a quotation from the Jewish holy test *Pirkei Avot* 2:21, to which Simon is sympathetic: "Do not be daunted by the enormity of the world's grief. Do justly now. Love mercy now. Walk humbly now. You are not obliged to complete the work, but neither are you free to abandon it."

A similar narrative process unfolds in season 4, which adds the Baltimore schools as a contextual focus. Prez, hapless as a policeman on the street but adept with the computer, has left the police department and finds his vocation at last as a math teacher in middle school. Colvin, now retired, also drifts toward education. He becomes involved with a pilot project funded by a grant awarded to (white) Professor David Parenti (Dan DeLuca) at the University of Maryland, for at-risk West Baltimore children. The program at first seems promising: Tommy Carcetti (Aidan Gillen) the new (white) mayor announces a new day for Baltimore. But Carcetti is so mired in the city's deep financial problems that it becomes impossible for him to provide whatever support he might have wanted to give Colvin and Parenti. He is too distracted even to know what they are doing.

The school pilot program run by Colvin and Parenti attempts to apply what Coates would call honest thinking that distinguishes itself from the enemy Dream. The program puts a few students identified by their teachers as the ones who are the most disruptive and the most likely to fail into a special team-taught class. Simon calls this using "soft eyes," an expression that he puts into the mouths of the experienced teachers at the school. It refers to not missing the forest for the trees, not getting stuck on a detail and letting all details reflect back on a larger context. Colvin and Parenti's project in many ways does use soft eyes, but Simon makes an interesting distinction between the two men. As a member of the affected community that the program applies to, Colvin is deeply involved in the relationship between the context and the program, while Parenti is a visitor from the detached world of academia. They have different stakes in the pilot program. The nuanced differences in their approaches make it much easier for Parenti to let go when the program fails.

The program's attempt to use soft eyes and see the big picture is hopeful but puts it in conflict with a system that does not favor the long term or the big picture and also with the contextual difficulties of making transitions between classes. Almost all the at-risk children in this season are crushed by the context of their lives, as the pilot program eventually is. Simon balances their blocked lives with the life of Namond Brice (Julito McCullum), a (black) student whose parents are connected to the drug trade. Namond moves toward middle-class success because Colvin personally intervenes and takes him home to raise him. Despite the achievements of the program, however, it remains an ironic success/failure. As an oasis in a highly troubled city, it is a great success. Within the safe area, the kids gain a new understanding of schoolwork and more self-respect; the problem comes from trying to integrate the progress into the world around them.

The problem of the transition between the hopelessness of the ghetto and the possibilities inherent in most middle-class life comes at Colvin full force when he takes children in the program to a very nice restaurant in an attempt to move the kids past the limits of their own neighborhoods and see life within the larger context of the city. The kids get all dressed up, but in ghetto style. They are treated with respect at the restaurant, but the diners there, although an integrated crowd, are not their people, the food is not their food. There is no deceit in this program as there was in Hamsterdam. But there is a similar problem with the way Colvin's effort is imposed on the flow of life instead of growing out of it. It cannot survive its dissociation from what is in progress and flow. It runs counter to both entrenched government and the deeply entrenched experiences of the children who are training for the street as it is. Colvin's Dream has its attractions, but it has the drawback of being disconnected.

The abrupt termination of the program by the city government is inextricably connected with other threads in the season, notably a $54 million shortfall in the budget of the department of education. But no one with power at City Hall will advocate for the change that the program envisions, which is a radical departure from the way education was organized under the George W. Bush administration. Multiple threads in season 4 reflect on, collide with, and intersect with the program to which Colvin and Parenti give so much of themselves and of which they are so brusquely deprived.

Marlo Stanfield (Jamie Hector) rises as the new (black) king of the Baltimore drug trade, filling the vacuum left by the arrest of Barksdale and the death of Bell. Stanfield is a vicious sociopath, while Barksdale and Bell were criminal businessmen. Marlo lacks even the rudiments of empathy and community feeling that we saw in Barksdale. Simon comes close to depicting a perfect villain, but Marlo too is a product of his environment. If he is guilty of heinous crimes, he is not a perfect foil for the perfect hero. Like the characters striving for good, he did not get the way he is by himself; they have all made choices in reaction to circumstances.

The termination of the program reduces everything that the children have done to dust in the wind. Colvin and Parenti have a meeting at City Hall not

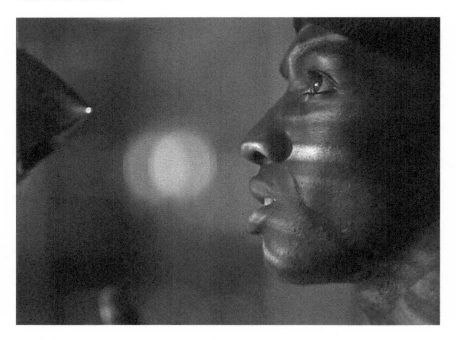

FIGURE 3.3. *Marlo's gimlet eyes reflect the training he has received on the killing streets.*

with Carcetti, who is submerged in the city budget, but with two assistants who dismiss the feasibility of the program within two minutes. They give Colvin and Parenti no chance to create a sense of the reality of the program. The context, the bad Dreams fostered by it, and their pressure on the work and striving of the characters shape the collage narrative of *The Wire*.

In addition to this depiction of systems, *The Wire* also reflects on the addicts and hard-working Baltimore citizens, who live so fiercely in the moment and in such contradiction of the Dream that they often illuminate the destructive function of bad Dreams. One of the most poignant of these is Reginald "Bubbles" Cousins (Andre Royo), a lifelong drug user who has miraculously maintained an active sense of responsibility despite his dependence on drugs. Bubs serves as a touchstone of besieged humanity caught up in the cycles of officialdom. His climactic moment in season 4 is so wrenching in its immediacy that it shakes the detachment of one of the most dedicated soldiers of the Dream.

Throughout the series, Bubs takes young street boys under his wing to try to help them as no one helps him. In each case, despite his best intentions, his protégés fall victim to cultural pressures, as he himself has done to a great extent. Season 4, with its focus on education, places particular emphasis on his protégés, in this case Bubs's protégé Sherrod (Rashad Orange), a young (black) addict. Bubs fails to help Sherrod develop survival skills. Worse, Bubs inadvertently becomes the vehicle of Sherrod's death. The pathetic series of events is a tale of overwhelming context. Bubs has become the victim of a violent street predator, who uses him as his means of survival. He beats Bubs mercilessly and takes away whatever money he has been able to scavenge by stealing metal from construction sites or hawking items like T-shirts and hats. Bubs is a police informer, and the police he works for promise him protection from the predator. But pressures on the police keep them from coming to his aid when he needs them most. In desperation, Bubs decides to poison his archfoe with tainted drugs, but by accident Sherrod smokes the joint and dies. Wracked by guilt and sorrow, Bubs tries to turn himself in as a murderer and in despair over Sherrod's death tries to kill himself while he is in the police station.

Simon portrays Bubs's attempted suicide as a misguided attempt to take personal responsibility for a context that dwarfs him by evoking the overwhelming circumstances surrounding Bubs's concoction of the poisoned joint, which even the most jaded police recognize as paralyzing. The policeman that Bubs surrenders to is Jay Landsman (Delaney Williams), a very cynical (white) enforcer of Major Rawls's departmental narratives of false statistics and clearances. Landsman finds Bubs almost dead after his attempt to hang himself and for that moment makes contact with the reality that the

FIGURE 3.4. *Bubs scours an inhospitable environment to survive.*

police routinely deny. Refusing to prosecute Bubs for anything, despite his confession, Landsman makes sure that Bubs is suitably hospitalized. "What about the clearances?" asks a policeman used to Landsman's sacrifice of any and all things to keep up with the tyranny of the manipulated statistics. "Fuck the clearances," says Landsman in a drastically atypical moment that resonates with hope in the potential for ethical living, despite all the obfuscations of systemic narratives.

On a larger scale, the fourth season also sees an increase in that tenuous hope because of the wire. With the help of the wire Lester Freamon and Bunk Moreland (Wendell Pierce), at times McNulty's (black) partner, locate the place in which Marlo has disposed of the bodies of his many, many victims, which the police suspected existed but could never find. The ensuing publicity about Freamon's major breakthrough forces Commissioner Burrell and Major Rawls to give the Major Crimes unit all the support it needs. Euphoria ensues when it is clearances be damned on a large scale, but, as is always the case in *The Wire*, only briefly. Simon's collage narrative once again encourages the audience to actively balance the dark and light realities of Baltimore when it moves into its fifth and final season. For four seasons, the series has melded its images of the war against drugs with its images of the destruction caused by the grand narratives of the culture. As they overlap, juxtapose, reflect, and collide in collage storytelling, Simon slowly evolves a perspective that reveals the addictive nature of the perfect narrative. This addiction can only be cured by vivid exposure to contextual contradiction of formulaic thinking, often a painful process. The four seasons of that exposure are the preparation for the events of the fifth season, in which Simon adds the institutions of journalism as a new element in his collage, making his vision pointed and explicit and more poignant.

GOING HOME

In season 5, Simon does not permit his series to collapse into a perfect narrative by making the pieces of Baltimore fit in time for final solutions. Instead he brings the audience and the characters into climactic confrontation with how journalists tell and circulate the Official Story. We have already observed two varieties of the perfect story: the grand narrative and the Dream. Season 5 adds the Dickensian effect, a dissociated conception of journalism held by the publisher of the *Baltimore Sun*. It plays a central part that we have not seen before in the shaping forces that aggressively impinge on the characters.[8]

Season 5 begins with an evocation of the failure of the optimism that crests at the end of season 4. Mired in debts and afflicted by old systemic confusion and political enmities between the Democrats and Republicans, Baltimore cannot capitalize on the police victory over Marlo. The city itself begins to seem like a macrocosmic version of the addict immersed in Dreams of freedom from drugs who plunges even further into compulsive need for them. As the hopes raised by the new mayor, Carcetti, are dashed, short-term buy-and-bust policing returns. The Major Crimes unit is shut down along with the wire. All the work of the previous year seems to be going down the drain. At the same time, we are introduced to the city's major newspaper, the *Baltimore Sun*. The (white) executive editor, James C. Whiting III (Sam Freed), announces his preference for narrow-focus journalism, the Dickensian effect, as he calls it, because that is what the public wants to read. Whiting's policies have major consequences for the war on drugs, as the actions of Scott Templeton, a (white) reporter hungry for success at any price, overlap and connect with Jimmy McNulty's similar hunger to make a difference in fighting the structure of drug crime in Baltimore.

Whiting's Dickensian fetish becomes part of Simon's larger portrait of officialdom wielding dissociative power. Whiting adds his special kind of racism combined with his power over the cultural discourse. His name is a

FIGURE 3.5. *James Whiting is the picture of white authority—and a catalogue of its abuses.*

FIGURE 3.6. *Gus Haynes is the picture of the incisive journalist, who struggles to protect the fourth estate.*

racial pun that needs no explanation and suggests some connections between the dominance of white Americans and the increasing tyranny of the perfect narrative over public discourse. We are introduced to the potential disadvantages of Dickensian journalism during an editorial meeting at the *Sun*, early in the season, when the reporters and editors are tossing around the failure of the Baltimore school system. Most of them see a multitude of reasons why the schools are in trouble and include race in the mix, while Whiting immediately dismisses the possibility of feature stories that note the multiplicity of causes, in a display of narrowly focused white privilege. While (black) city editor Gus Haynes (Clark Johnson) insists that a wide-ranging vision of all news is essential to truth, which aligns this character with what the series has shown us, Whiting's journalistic principle is encapsulated in his response to Haynes in "Unconfirmed Reports" (5.2): "If you leave everything in, soon you've got nothing." As it turns out, Whiting means that the public will not read broad-ranging journalism.

In contrast to the reality of the series as Simon has written it, Whiting's Dickensian journalism is contextless and creates a stupid perspective, as encapsulated in Haynes's simile at that same meeting: "It's like you're up on the corner of a roof and you're showing some people how a couple of shingles came loose, and meanwhile a hurricane wrecked the rest of the damn house." Actually, it is worse than that, as we see when the fifth season unfolds. As the episodes continue, Dickensian reporting leads to intentional falsification on the part of Scott Templeton. Templeton's journalism is neither investigated under Whiting's regime nor generally suspected, despite Gus Haynes's insistence that something is wrong with what Templeton is turning in. Whiting smells a Pulitzer prize in Templeton's reporting. The final season of *The Wire* demonstrates the immorality and destructiveness of reducing the complexity of a culture for fast consumption. But Simon refuses to demonize either Whiting or Templeton, because their brand of reporting is what the public wants. The various city bureaucracies want a similar approach to law enforcement. And what are we going to do about that?

In episode 5.2, Templeton makes his first attempt to play to Whiting's preferences by inventing a human interest story instead of finding out what is really out there on the streets. He goes to the local stadium on the first day of the baseball season and comes back with a touching tale that punches all the public's buttons. His story is about a poor black orphan in a wheelchair (called only E. J.) who loves baseball but does not have the price of admission. Haynes does not want to publish the story, being unable to check the details appropriately. But upper management has found its dream reporter. The journalistic abuses get worse and worse in tandem with McNulty's desperate turn toward some Dickensian policing. To get the Major Crimes unit back on its feet, McNulty creates his own grand narrative that at first meshes beautifully with all Dickensian narratives that ignore the bigger reality. Called to look at the corpse of a homeless man who clearly died a natural death, McNulty strangles the man postmortem and arranges his body so that it is face down, in a position that indicates sexual violation. Just as Templeton's false tale opens doors for him with the hierarchy of the *Sun*, McNulty's manipulation of the crime scene opens doors within the police chain of command and the hierarchy of civic government. Between Templeton and McNulty, both reacting to real social pressures, a bad Dream captivates Baltimore. It is both shamefully unethical and the only trigger for getting results—a Pulitzer for Templeton and unlimited money to do real police work for McNulty.

McNulty's invented story is simple and linear, but there is nothing direct or simple about the way he finally puts it into play. McNulty's scam to get money to fight Marlo on the pretext of catching a fictional serial killer, as always in *The Wire*, requires the fortuitous convergences of many different people and motives. McNulty has to convince police associates to join him, no easy feat. To seal his deal, McNulty kidnaps Lawrence Butler (William Joseph Brookes), a severely brain-damaged homeless man, and takes him to a shelter in Richmond, Virginia, under a different name. McNulty uses the *Sun* to terrify the public with a supposed new wrinkle in the case that kicks it into high gear. A crisis arises because Lawrence Butler is nowhere to be found. Now McNulty's fabricated serial killer is no longer leaving mutilated corpses; he is making people disappear.

Once McNulty's fabricated story ripens, it requires a serendipitous intersection with the goals and aspirations of not only Templeton, who has Pulitzers dancing before his eyes, but also Mayor Carcetti, who sees an opportunity to cultivate a signature issue that will propel him into the office of the governor of Maryland in the next election. By this point, we have been trained to look for these intersections that result in inadvertent collaboration among many aspects of the culture and many people who have no idea how they are connected and in many cases believe that they are the ones taking charge of the situation. McNulty's part in the scam turns out to be only one part of the collage. It is a very bad move on the part of a good man, who is never in control, for better or for worse, of how his plan turns out.

At the same time, Templeton's crass ambition is not perfectly villainous, despicable as he may seem to most viewers. It is Simon's desire to present the hustling reporter as part of a context created by the upper newspaper administration, shrinking circulations of print news outlets, competition from electronic news sources, a shrinking pool of jobs for journalists, and the tendency for awards to be garnered by Dickensian reporting. This confluence of forces reflects Simon's real-world experience as a journalist. Whiting's character is based on John Carroll, the executive editor of the actual *Baltimore Sun*. Simon allows that Carroll had an excellent reputation as a journalist but believes that he did not serve journalism well. Collage gives form to Simon's insight that the fragments of human reality never fit well together: only lies generate a story in which they seem to. The confluence of McNulty and Templeton can be nothing but a bogus appearance of progress. And the true story can never be revealed. When the police discover the fraud, they all smile for the cameras and sweep the scandal under the rug. The result is that the unified narrative continues undisturbed and so does crime. Because of the suppression of what McNulty and Templeton did, Templeton gets a Pulitzer and Marlo goes unpunished. There has been no change of any significance in the trafficking in drugs.

Micro-narrative threads add dimension to Simon's depiction of the macro-narratives. One of these is Omar Little's valiant but doomed struggle to beat the odds in the drug trade. Another is Bubs's humble struggle to survive. A third is McNulty's acquisition of some wisdom as a result of his highly flawed attempt at heroism. It all adds up to a series grand finale that tests human action against cultural context and truth. In the tradition of nonformulaic television, it raises more questions than anything it might supply as answers and conclusions. Omar's death in "Clarifications" (5.8), one of the last episodes of season 5, is another distillation of what the individual tends to mean in the larger picture. The charismatic Omar, who has been the gangster equivalent of a code hero, a man who is loyal to his own and only uses violence on those who are a part of the mob world, and then only for cause, has made fools of the leaders of organized drug crime for four seasons. He has played a colorful part in helping the police as part of revenge schemes against mob violence against him and his loved ones. He is a street hero, who walks the depressed and dangerous Western District like a supernatural force and is idolized by the street children, who like to take turns playing the role of Omar in their games.

But Omar is killed as he seeks out Marlo to finish their vendetta while buying cigarettes in a convenience store by Kenard (Thuliso Dingwall), a little (black) boy no more than eight years old. Kenard works as a "hopper" (gofer) for Marlo, has seen Omar in operation, and has internalized the murderous, live fast, die young atmosphere of the streets. With no premeditated plan, Kenard, against whom Omar has no thought of protecting himself, takes a gun lying near him and shoots wildly at Omar, hitting him in the back of the head and creating what looks like a mob hit. Omar dies like dust in the wind. In the end, he is nothing but a police report of "a man" fatally shot in the Western District, a death that is not even reported: Gus Haynes on the spur of the moment picks a story about a fire to insert in the space he has left. Omar is absorbed back into the collage.

Contrasting with these shadows is the light that emerges from Bubs's life and the wisdom that comes from McNulty's failure. In the concluding season, Bubs is part of a drug support group run by Walon (Steve Earle), a dedicated (white) former addict who never preaches and stays true to what he knows from experience. Bubs is also working at the soup kitchen of a church. As he makes his way toward sobriety, Bubs attracts the attention of Mike Fletcher (Brandon Young), a young (black) journalist who is from the school of Gus Haynes. Such journalists are dedicated not to winning prizes but, as Haynes says, getting up in the morning, being surprised by life, and writing about it. Unlike Templeton, Fletcher is looking for what is out there. He has a reporter's instinct for the genuinely astonishing. With respect as well as curiosity, he talks with Bubs, stays with him during his days, and writes a story, which will also see the light of day along with Templeton's prize-winning forgeries.

FIGURE 3.7. *Omar lets down his guard because he sees only a shopkeeper behind protective plastic and a very small boy.*

Bubs puts the period on his own story by asking Fletcher why he should get special attention for doing what he should have been doing all along. It is a lingering question that Simon would not dream of answering. He leaves it to active viewers to suss out for themselves from everything seen and heard. Simon put his own subtle caption on Bubs's story in a moment in the final episode when he and Walon are sitting quietly on a bench, discussing Bubs's recovery. Walon pulls a piece of paper out of his pocket and shows it to Bubs, who reads it aloud. It is a quotation from Franz Kafka, the great Czech modernist, of whom neither Bubs nor Walon has heard. "You can hold back from the suffering of the world and have free permission to do so. It is in accordance with your nature. But perhaps this very holding back is the one suffering you could have avoided." It seems that someone gave Walon this fragment of paper once and he kept it. Neither man knows what it means. Do we?

Kafka's thought on a scrap of paper, compelling to both Walon and Bubs but understood by neither of them, is a kind of answer to what Ta-Nehisi Coates said about the dissociation of the Dream. It is ultimately what McNulty learns, although he has never heard the words. It resonates for us to wonder about. In the end, McNulty's deeply flawed quest to be a perfect hero gives Simon his best opportunity for offering hope, not some formulaic triumph over a perfect villain, but a humane act consonant with reality. As the final act and image of *The Wire*, McNulty goes to Virginia to get Lawrence Butler and bring him home. This time McNulty is not defeating a Stringer Bell or a Marlo Stanfield. There will never be an audience to acknowledge what he has done, but he is making his amends to the human condition that he has so misunderstood and violated. He seems to be at peace for the first time. When he finds Butler, who is so damaged that it is impossible to communicate with him on a verbal level, McNulty is more interested in the simple humanity of the man, which needs no words.

In the last moments of the final episode McNulty pulls over to the side of the highway and stands looking at Baltimore, which he is now approaching, leaving the barely conscious Butler in the car. McNulty's position as he surveys Baltimore at a distance is a 180-degree difference from his fantasy of solving the big problems. It is not a place that he can stay, but it is symbolic of McNulty's development and of where we as the audience have arrived. Ahead lie the ordinary problems of Baltimore as well as a very different path for McNulty and perhaps a new perspective for us.

There is much to wonder at in these final moments and many questions. One of the most prominent is what it can mean to accept everything that we have witnessed in *The Wire* without becoming resigned to the broken nature

FIGURE 3.8. *No longer a perfect hero in his mind, McNulty finally seeks to take in his context.*

of the city and the war on drugs. We are witnessing a decency in McNulty that is achieved by weaning ourselves from our addictions to the retreat from life involved in the simple, grandiose clarity of the Dream. McNulty does—for the moment at least—embody what it may mean to refuse to draw back from the suffering world and that engagement means avoiding your own suffering. *The Wire* leaves us with so many questions in the modernist spirit about conducting life as a moral and ethical person.

YOU CANNOT LIVE IN THE VACUUM OF THE LENS

Beyond Simon's kaleidescopic collage narrative, his aesthetic—developed in concert with his first director of photography, Uta Briesewitz—is the other powerful way that he crafts perspective in *The Wire* to deflect habits inculcated by watching formulaic series TV.[9] *The Wire* is wrongly associated with a flat, vérité visual style, a documentary style in the usual sense of the word. While there is a documentary influence on *The Wire*, it has been augmented aesthetically to create a virtuoso and all-embracing picture of Baltimore. The series has a modernist visual style that keeps the viewer in the moment and by means of its art discourages the dissociation of conventional shot patterns, images, and sound.

Simon was adamant and vocal about what he wanted. He used the word "grandiose" to indicate what he did not want, which translates into his rejection of the visual version of disconnectedness that we find in the Dickensian approach to journalism, policing, or narrative structure. But this does not boil down to the flat photography that many associate with documentary filmmaking. In her own words, in following Simon's dictates Briesewitz was determined to shoot Baltimore as a cinematographic voyage of discovery, guided by what the location showed her, the tone of the scene, and the immediacy of the actions. She dedicated her art to giving viewers a feeling of being present, which is what Simon wished for. Really looking at *The Wire* and engaging the images means recognizing the success of the Simon-Brieswitz collaboration: showing a nonformulaic sense of place that grows out of perception of the locations in which the scenes are shot.

Briesewitz's art, in tune with Simon's vision, combines an eye for the beauty of the environment with a willingness to work extremely hard and a precise understanding of the technology. She not only designed the lighting and the shots but insisted on working the camera herself, an exhausting regimen that paid off brilliantly for the show. She also wore a headphone, which was not necessarily standard procedure for cinematographers at the time, so that she could capture the moment of the action within the lens and could hear the most minute sounds related to the actors when she was located at a distance from the action. "Because what guides me sometimes is to hear somebody breathe. . . . You cannot just look through a lens and live in that vacuum that the lens is giving you. . . . You have to be completely aware of your environment like a documentary filmmaker." This is to say that her conception of creating the look of a television show is about being open to and aware of the environment and making the viewers aware and open too. For example, when producer Robert Colesberry gave Briesewitz tapes of a different show that was shot in Baltimore, she noticed that the night scenes were lit with bright white light. But she had seen that the nighttime streets of Baltimore were bathed in orange sodium vapor light, which gave a warm glow to the city. Colesberry's tapes served to make her aware of exactly what she did not want to do.

The result was a specificity that distinguished Baltimore from anonymous night scenes in story-product television. For that reason, it is rewarding to look at the small moments as well as the big dramatic scenes to appreciate the art involved. In a small sequence of scenes in "Old Cases" (1.4), McNulty is giving Bubs a lift home but has to take a detour on the way to see his son playing soccer in a pretty, affluent, safe white neighborhood. When McNulty then stops in front of an alley in a poor, run-down, dangerous black neighborhood in the Western District, Bubs says to him, "Thin line between heaven and here," an enigmatic reference to the difference between where McNulty's children live with his estranged wife and where Bubs lives. Briezewitz's cinematography beautifully complicates this moment. Of course NcNulty's wife lives in a middle-class suburban heaven, but this block is its own bit of heaven too. The warm sodium vapor light glows in the distance, backlighting some wintery trees that glitter among the shadows. This is an image discovered by Briesewitz, not manufactured according to a convention of glamour shooting. And it raises so many unanswerable questions and unfathomable sensations for the spectators within this context of wealth and poverty and crime and security. The cinematography deepens the collage experience of the episode.

Briesewitz's art complements Simon's. "What the artist does is originate. He keeps surprising you and evolving. When you look at something, it's always changing a little bit and it always keeps you engaged. Whereas I think that those people who just use those stylistic devices [that they import from models exterior to the show that is being lit] very often fail to evolve them further." Briesewitz says that she is inspired by nature. "Many DPs [directors of photography] still try to get a back light on somebody who's in a corner. And I would always ask where's the source of that back light? It looks pretty, but the whole story of the character is that he has his back against the wall

FIGURE 3.9. *Briesewitz found extraordinary beauty on the most ordinary streets.*

and so we should feel that it looks more dim there and not as flattering." We are talking of two different concepts of beauty, one manufactured and the other born from life. The dimly lit scene character has a specific beauty of its own, unlike a standard prettiness that can be and is reproduced from one show to another.

In contrast, some moments in *The Wire*, after Briesewitz left the show in the third season, failed to rise to Simon's expectation and sent him hustling to repair the aesthetic damage, since he could not always be on the soundstage or on location and have a budget for retakes. He gave me an example of what he did not want, referring to a visual in a nighttime scene that was part of the Hamsterdam narrative thread in season 3. Simon's goal in portraying Colvin's plan to clear the residential streets of the drug trade was to show how the area become a pit of all the ills associated with the illegal drug trade as it became a "success." But he did not want to embellish it with formulaic images. The cinematographer who lit Hamsterdam by night, in "Back Burners" (3.7), was Eagle Egilsson. With Simon's ideas about Hamsterdam in mind, Egilsson lit his night scene with trash can-fires and rows of candles that made it look like mythic and poetic depictions of hell, which makes conventional sense. But Simon hated it and thought it grandiose. He did everything he could in postproduction to darken the lurid scenes that emerged in the light cast by the fires and the candles, which he says came as close to ruining his intentions in the series as anything could. Contrasting that episode with the film of Joseph Conrad's *Heart of Darkness*,

Simon told me, "the less you know about what Kurtz is doing at the end of that movie, the better. So don't show me background. I don't want to see it, especially on HD [high-def]." These are the words not of a propagandist or documentarian but rather of a modernist artist who wants the location and the action to speak to the audience through its own immediacy.

Briesewitz and Simon also had specific ideas about how to use a camera. *The Wire* was partial to "oners," scenes filmed in one take. Briesewitz often used only one camera, instead of the conventional two or the three that were sometimes used. Most productions shy away from oners, to give the editors, producers, and directors coverage (fragments of tape for an editor to insert for an intended effect). But Briesewitz does not like to cut a scene up if it is moving along nicely. A oner is a way to tie the action up and stay in the moment. Another aspect that was crucial to Simon is using the camera to find the person who is speaking, not to anticipate the line. Where the formulaic practice is to train the camera on an actor who is supposed to say something of importance to the plot or to emphasize the humor of a character's dialogue, Simon makes sure that the camera "turns toward" the speaking actor, discovering belatedly that something important is being said. As Simon puts it, "The camera can't know everything. If the camera knows everything then the artifice of this incomplete and confusing story that we're going to get a handle on because we're going to stay with these characters is revealed as a lie. It's just a film. It's just a game. Rather than actually capturing life."

Simon gave me an example of a camera with too much omniscience. In "Time after Time" (3.1), we watch the street police, notably Carver and Herc, the characters we know best in this scene, working out a strategy by roughing out a map in the dirt of where each of them is to go.

> In the first episode of season 3, Ed Bianchi had a beautifully composed shot of, it's before they chase the kid they think has the drugs and he leads them on a wild goose chase. And they're drawing a play in the dirt. Carver and the rest of the guys from the Western Division. And they're sort of like in the mud I'll go this way, you go this way. And they're squatting around the play and Herc is standing fully erect and the rest of the guys are on their haunches designing the play and how they're going to do it. Ed was going to shoot the whole scene long lens. He put the camera behind some weeds and trash in the foreground so it was like a blur. And he's like shooting them from the other end of the alley. Beautiful shot. And he said I'm thinking of doing the whole thing long lens without going in for coverage. I said all right let's see how that works. And then he framed it

up in order to get close enough to see what they're doing. Herc is cut off at the waist because he's standing. They start running the scene and then Herc has a funny line. And just before the funny line, the camera, which was at ground level, tilts up to catch Herc in time for the line. And at that moment I realized I can't use that. I can use it up to that moment but then I need to go in for coverage because how did the camera know that Herc was about to speak? All of a sudden you've just revealed you're making a movie, which is the worst thing you can do. Like the camera went, "OK, time for your line. Herc speaks." If the camera goes up because Herc's late and the camera doesn't catch the first couple of words because Herc's late that's okay. But otherwise, let me cut in. Give me a shot of the other guys looking up at Herc while he says the line. And get out of the wide shot and go in. But you must go in. So, I said, no, no, no you're going to have to go in for coverage. The camera can't know everything. If the camera knows everything then the artifice of this incomplete and confusing story that we're going to get a handle on because we're going to stay with these characters is revealed as a lie.

What Simon has in mind is to cleanse the doors of perception to give the audience a more vital connection to the characters that supports the portrayal of life as "incomplete and confusing" in its scale, which is the goal of the series as it portrays crime, punishment, and official and personal life. The kind of spontaneity he has in mind is composed of the appearance of imprecision and never anticipates discovery with the camera. He learned that he wanted an intimate camera that arrives late for a line, as if it is breathlessly catching up with the moment in progress. He wanted to guide the viewers' attention in line with the emotional impact of the moment.

Simon gave me an example of the way the camera was used wrongly in "Refugees" (4.4), in a scene involving two of Marlo's cold-blooded enforcers:

And it bothered me so much I would have gone back and reshot it if we'd had the time and money. It was not so egregious a mistake that I had to correct it, but I thought about correcting it. There's a moment where Snoop and Chris [the enforcers] kill a security guard. And they leave him in a boarded-up vacant house, as they were doing. And as they walk away, Snoop has the badge. And the way that scene should be cut and filmed is I need an insert shot of the badge in her hand or in Chris's. I think he takes it from her and then he throws it into the weeds. And the director, I wasn't out on the set that night, somebody else was covering, the director didn't cover, didn't give me an insert shot of the badge in the hand. It might have been Clark Johnson; I'd have to check. [It was actually Jim McKay.] He gave me the insert shot of the badge lying in the grass. Well, who's looking at it in the fucking grass from up close? Why is the camera there? It's unmotivated. . . . The camera knew too much. So then when you use the piece at the end, the presumption is that that's going to matter. Her fingerprints are on it. People start going *Columbo* on it. Somebody's going to find it. They left it there. It was only meaningful if you knew who they killed. That was a way of saying they could kill that security guard over nothing. It wasn't meaningful that they left it or that they threw it in the weeds. It was the wrong emphasis.

SOFT EYES ON THE PRIZE: WHO ARE ALL THESE PEOPLE?

So, how did the war on drugs become "so fucked"? The answer that Simon proposes demands a lot of work from the viewer and a patient, mature imagination, everything that formulaic TV lacks. The spectator is given the task of living fictionally within the space of seemingly innumerable details that cannot be mastered at one sitting, perhaps cannot be mastered at all. Simon has designed his show as a prompt to active viewing with soft eyes, humbled before the task of the confusions and enormity of life. *The Wire* is the first of Simon's anti-Dickensian collage narratives.

Summing up, *The Wire* artfully breaks a number of television conventions. Simon's series is upsetting rather than reassuring; inquiring rather than definitive; and culturally audacious in refusing to assign the most important roles only to white, middle-class characters. Its nonformulaic storytelling is a bracing narrative of unanswered, perhaps unanswerable questions. As part of the foundation of new modernist auteur television, its collage structure embodies Simon's belief that information, observation, thinking, and uncertainty about how events are structured must be the prelude to ethical action in a world as complex as ours on a subject as labyrinthine as the drug war. *The Wire* is not just a tour de force; it is a storytelling innovation that offers a new way of narrating context, an innovation that has become typical of Simon's television and has proven very effective in avoiding the reductivism of formulaic television.[10]

THE LEGACY

·

New Options, New Questions, Retooled Formulas

CHAPTER 4

DAVID SIMON AND
ERIC OVERMYER, *TREME*

I continue to think that it was really remarkable that HBO let us do a serious program about art and culture. Name another drama show that's ever done that.

—Eric Overmyer

Name another American city like New Orleans or another television series like *Treme*. Nothing comes to mind. The singular *Treme* reflects in its auteur freshness the uniqueness of New Orleans as a child of exceptional circumstances: Hurricane Katrina, post-*Peaks* freedom, and the collaborative skills of an odd couple of writers, David Simon and Eric Overmyer. Simon and Overmyer had worked together on the formulaic series *Homicide* and then on the auteur series *The Wire* and talked for over ten years about creating a show built on their love for New Orleans. The lag time of more than a decade between inception and production benefited *Treme* in two ways. By 2010 Simon's narrative skills had undergone a big, felicitous change as a result of *The Wire*. The distinctly infelicitous Hurricane Katrina, alas, inflicted catastrophic suffering on New Orleans in 2005 but also increased interest in the city. Had Katrina never hit New Orleans, it is not clear (at least to Eric Overmyer) that *Treme* would ever have made it into the HBO lineup, and it might not have been the show that it became.[1]

Or did Katrina have such a profound effect on the way Simon and Overmyer would have pitched the show if the storm had never devastated

New Orleans? In many ways, *Treme* is built on Simon and Overmyer's pre-Katrina idea of juxtaposing a unique arts culture and a severely wanting civic structure, two beating pulses that together animate the Crescent City. Post-Katrina, the situation was the same but more intense. The two aspects of New Orleans, inherently conflicted and inextricably bound by history, were now necessarily in a more dramatic relationship to each other as the challenge of actual survival loomed, so the poststorm story was even more ripe than it had been for the collage narrative that Simon had developed for *The Wire*. Simon and Overmyer were perhaps the only storytellers who could have done it justice.

A New Orleans collage. What else? However, Simon and Overmyer could not employ a collage of concentric circles rippling out from the center, like the collage about drugs in Baltimore in *The Wire*. This had to be a collage juxtaposing diastole and systole, the expansions of the arts and the contractions of civic life. And it could not employ the usual kind of juxtapositions, which conventionally imply sharply defined contrasts and counterpoints. The juxtapositions in a *Treme* series would have to be rivers of fluid interplay among images, people, and systems mercurially in action, as the two vividly contrasting cultures in the city recovered from Katrina.

Simon and Overmyer are in lockstep about the special character of New Orleans, its survival of Katrina, and their preference for nonformulaic narrative. But from what Overmyer told me, it seems that they are an odd couple on many other points. The two men have very different professional backgrounds. As a former police reporter and journalistic commentator on social problems, Simon seems to have been born to see the big political picture. Overmyer, an avant-garde playwright as well as an experienced television writer, is drawn to the micro-details of the emotional level of personal drama. However, Overmyer expressed great satisfaction about his collaboration with Simon, and the way it has developed and changed over the years.

When they were writing *The Wire*, Overmyer told me, Simon had explicitly assigned him the task of writing the emotional—"girly" as Simon called them—scenes. But Overmyer says that on *Treme* Simon demonstrated that he had broadened his own capacity for emotional writing. It is tempting to analogize this syncretistic working relationship with the syncretistic aspects of the series. The New Orleans they portrayed is also about syncretism, a Creole fusion. "Creole," a term endemic to New Orleans culture, is understood differently by different people, but I use it here as Simon and Overmyer use it, as a rich cultural mélange: the fusion of European and African with respect to its music and food arts and also the ethnic composition of its population. The show portrays this fusion as the unique strength and beauty of the city. Similarly, the multiple strengths of Simon and Overmyer made for a strong and vital Creole partnership, a productive richness of differences.

Simon is a writer who is eager to analyze his decisions, while Overmyer tends to explain by saying, "It just feels that way to me." Their collaboration is among the most fascinating in the history of auteur, nonformulaic television. Characteristically, Simon rejects the notion that he is an auteur, even with respect to *The Wire*, saying that he depended on many of his co-workers as much as he depended on himself for creative decisions. An auteur is ordinarily understood as a single creator with a strong hand on the steering wheel. But *Treme* is authentically the result of an auteur partnership, proving that such a thing can exist and demonstrating how two hands on the tiller can work.

Similarly noteworthy is their collage of interpenetrating narratives, which raises the profile of the sensory palette of the storytelling and diminishes the presence of linear storytelling. Much of what there is of narrative linearity in the first two seasons concerns the disappearance of a young (black) man named David Maurice "Daymo" Brooks (Daryl Williams). We never see him alive, only in flashback. As the series begins, he is dead. The discovery of his death and what it entailed is part of the story of his distraught sister, LaDonna Brooks Batiste-Williams (Khandi Alexander), who engages Toni Bernette (Melissa Leo), a (white) civil rights lawyer, to cut through the obfuscations of an unresponsive police force and find him. In the third season, another element of linearity is added to *Treme* when L. P. Everett (Chris Coy), a young (white) reporter comes to New Orleans to consult with Toni on an article he is writing about other disappearances and unexplained deaths associated with Katrina (details to follow below). Other linear stories include conflicts that rattle the New Orleans police hierarchy and the battle between art and finance in some careers. These are the contracting systole of *Treme*. The diastole involves the expansive profusion of characters involved in the arts and culinary life of the city. The life of the arts is circular and cyclic, with the seasonal return to the exhilarating, sustaining energies of Mardi Gras and other communal festivals, as the recovering culture gets a second wind after the trauma of Katrina. The burgeoning reappearance of music and good food through cycles of recovery has a momentum of its own. *Treme* has no dominating linear healing process.

The healing is the upshot of the piquantly counterpointed circular and linear energies. Toni and L. P. Everett seek answers to questions about what happened during the storm; they are on the kinds of quests that American television culture is used to, if not precisely in this complex form. But most of the characters in *Treme* are stumbling from day to day, stunned by the discontinuities in their lives wrought by the storm and by the blows that they receive from the discombobulated, desperate police, flailing out randomly; from the courts; and, of course, from the recalcitrant and duplicitous insurance companies. They seek healing in the cyclic renewal of the music and the food arts of New Orleans (NOLA). The culture comes back to life as the characters prepare for the regenerative pleasures of Mardi Gras and another festival less well known nationally, St. Joseph's Day, which is sacred to the community of "Indians," the name adapted by a particular black community formed in the eighteenth century in resistance to the exclusion of black slaves from creative roles in the white-dominated Mardi Gras. The NOLA Indians have a very precise tradition of costume and music that survives today, even though contemporary Mardi Gras celebrations now include major creative roles for the black citizens of the city. Characters involved with the Indians are central to the *Treme* collage.

An overview of the men and women of the series is in order at this point, because of the richly abundant characters and also because this is the least widely known of the auteur series. The core characters include a disparate and vigorously multiracial group. Davis McAlary (Steve Zahn) is a manic, part-time (white) disk jockey on a local radio station who has intentionally divested himself of his upper-class privileges and immerses himself as much as possible in black culture and authentic New Orleans jazz. Antoine Batiste (Wendell Pierce) and Albert Lambreaux (Clarke Peters) are two (black) musicians with families. LaDonna Williams (already mentioned) is the owner of a bar enigmatically named Gigi's after a progenitor now lost in the mists of time. Janette Desautel (Kim Dickens) is a (white) chef and owner of a local restaurant. The Bernette family consists of Toni (already mentioned), Creighton (John Goodman), a (white) English professor at Tulane University, and their teenaged daughter, Sofia (India Ennenga). There is no perfect hero among them; except for Creighton Bernette, they do not expect or seek heroic control. Complaining and venting as they go, they nevertheless embrace life in all its unpredictability and New Orleans in all its frustrations. Professor Bernette is the exception that proves the rule.

Antoine Batiste is a trombone player, whose post-Katrina days diverge sharply from the usual formulaic story about music makers. Musicians who appear as central characters in formulaic television are all dashing, initially unappreciated but motivated geniuses bound for greatness. Batiste, by contrast, is only competent as a trombone player but filled with the NOLA unstoppable love of life and music. He is important in this narrative even if he is not the next Louis Armstrong: in fact *because* he is not. The opposite of dashing, Batiste is plump and generally uncouth but also generous, warm,

FIGURE 4.1. *Antoine Batiste is the essence of NOLA's hope of recovery as he runs to join the first second line since Katrina.*

and shrewd when he has to be. He is a New Orleans everyman, the loam of the culture to which this series is dedicated. The Creole motto at the core of New Orleans in this show is "always for pleasure," which is Batiste's motto too. He is a near perfect embodiment of this unique part of American culture that lives not for success but for delight in engagement.

But Batiste is not the central character because this collage has no center. Overmyer disagrees: he thinks that the show has a central story line focused on Albert Lambreaux who is just as filled with NOLA culture as Batiste, but in another key. Lambreaux is perhaps one of the last champions of the fierce local tradition of New Orleans Indians and is determined to preserve it against the incursions of Katrina and of modern life. He is the "Big Chief" of one of its tribes, Guardians of the Flame.[2]

Handsome, talented, and fiercely independent, Lambreaux would be the stuff of perfect heroes in a formulaic series, but here he is an equivocal figure, like everyone else. Seductive and courageous, he offers heroic resistance to policies irrationally dedicated to destroying usable housing that make the return of people who left New Orleans before Katrina impossible. As a talented construction worker he has his hands on the nuts and bolts of the recovery. He is involved in both reconstruction and defiance of racist governmental obstruction against preservation of buildings untouched by the storm. But his jealous protection of his traditional role as an Indian gives him a rigidity that threatens the very music and the city he wants to

FIGURE 4.2. *Albert Lambreaux as an Indian chief and the guardian of a very old tradition.*

preserve, putting him at odds with his son, Delmond (Rob Brown), a modern jazz musician who seeks a wider career platform in New York and a national audience for the music of the Indians. Lambreaux's story as a Big Chief places him near the shifting center of the struggle of New Orleans to ensure its survival, but again not at the center.

Audience desire is frequently directed toward the many not the one in *Treme*, emphasizing unforeseen relationships among the multitude of characters. In particular, the juxtapositions of Davis McAlary's story with the stories of Batiste and Lambreaux create highly comic, yet deeply poignant insights into the relationship between the power of white heritage and the very different power and beauty of NOLA music culture. McAlary is a wise fool: hedonistic, often obnoxious, generally awkward, frequently endearing—annoying to Overmyer, but for Simon and for the series, a personification of another fragment of New Orleans as the city of misrule. NOLA inverts normative priorities, through its carnivalesque nature. Davis is a master of misrule, his life an innate satire. With a passion both foolish and sweetly irresistible, he strains for the connection to the arts culture of the city that comes naturally to the musicians, even a charming, extremely talented (white) street violinist named Annie Talarico (Lucia Micarelli), who is not from NOLA but connects to its arts culture in a way Davis cannot.

Standing apart from the unquenchable vivacity and life force in the rainbow of colors, moods, and tones of Batiste, Lambreaux, McAlary, Toni

Bernette—and many more—is Creighton Bernette, white, middle-aged, cynical, and deeply depressed by Katrina and the failure of officialdom to aid his city. He reprises what we have already spoken of in reference to *The Wire*: Simon's fierce code of endurance that also threads through *Treme*. For Simon, taking responsibility is a complex business, and it is not an individual matter. Bernette creates a running YouTube blog in which he curses the failures of the federal and local governments but he also isolates himself from the problems of the world, which is a fatal flaw for Simon. Bernette's counterpoint to the rest of the characters is a significant part of this collage, although not the way Overmyer tells it.

Like McAlary, Bernette is a character about whom the co-creators of the series do not agree. Overmyer deems him unimportant and uninteresting in the long run, but Simon has de facto made him crucial to the storytelling collage. Bernette, as even Overmyer notes, represents the despair that afflicted some in the white creative community after Katrina. For Overmyer, once Bernette was dead, he was gone. This may resonate with some of the audience. However, I would contend that, because of Simon's influence, Bernette's shadow looms enigmatically over the succeeding seasons. His obscene eloquence on the subject of the Katrina tragedy is impotent because it is detached and makes the organic interconnection of multiplicity in the New Orleans context shine more brightly by contrast.

That interconnection is precisely what has been sacrificed to story product when formulaic television series have been located in New Orleans or featured episodes set in the city. New Orleans has tended to figure on TV as the terrain on which standard murder plots unfold, decorated by a generic landscape filled with claptrap about voodoo, the faux erotics of tropical sensuality, and the gothic flavor of a rotting past and a decadent present. Look, for example, at the episode called "Big Easy Murder" in *Murder, She Wrote* (*MSW*) in which series hero Jessica Fletcher (Angela Lansbury) is called upon to solve a murder by avoiding sinister black voodoo men and machete murderers, with the occasional appearance of peripheral black jazz players. *MSW* relies on a Euro-centric picture of the Crescent City as a pit of weird dark magic, stereotypical tragic mulattas, and violent and predatory dusky ethnics victimizing relatively virtuous, or at least not demonically possessed, white people. And, as a perfect hero with a gender twist, white, vaguely rich Jessica Fletcher comes to the city as a disconnected outsider and takes care of it all. Disconnection makes her powerful: the obverse of Simon's vision of life. Whiteness also makes her powerful. Having a woman detective does not in itself make television more inclusive. A white woman detective performing a formulaic role reinforces all the simplistic influence of pre-*Peaks* TV.

Hugh Wilson's *Frank's Place*, a series that aired briefly on ABC eight years before HBO presented us with *Treme*, was centered on a black protagonist: Frank Parrish (Tim Reid), a college professor from Boston who inherits a restaurant in New Orleans. But there is no Creole fusion in the way the show is structured. *Frank's Place* is about the city's black community; the white communities' stories are subordinate in importance. Although that might seem to strike a blow for equality, it does not reflect the Creole nature of NOLA culture. Nor did the show reflect the cultural significance of its musical and food arts, despite the restaurant setting. The title serves as a double entendre that connotes both Frank's ownership of the restaurant and Frank's place in America as a cultivated, intelligent black man. In many ways it depicted what that meant in a way that excludes the primacy of the culture that *Treme* celebrates. *Frank's Place* was a funny, moving, beautifully written and acted show. Formulaic though it was, however, it did not contain enough voodoo or white characters for a standardized audience and was canceled after one year. Had it succeeded, it would still have been only a baby step in the direction of *Treme*. A black perfect hero is still formulaic.

More recent examples of what the perfect narrative does to New Orleans show no changes for the better. "The Man in the Morgue," an episode of *Bones*, is set in New Orleans right after Katrina but features a crime story solved by (white) perfect heroes detached from the culture of the city and knee deep in clichés about voodoo, strange herbs, and snakes. Laughably, "Musician Heal Thyself," an episode of *NCIS: New Orleans*, a spinoff of the heavily formulaic and successful *NCIS*, is not about a musician from New Orleans but about (white) investigators of a murder. It is influenced by *Treme* in a very superficial way, alluding to the Treme section of the city, unheard of before Simon and Overmyer's series. But it could have taken place anywhere; the specifics of the culture are missing. (They kill way down yonder, and, oh yeah, they play a little music too.)[3]

In what follows, *Treme* will be made visible through the eyes of its creators, as a Creole culture peopled by characters of many heritages. As Simon and Overmyer seek to engage us in the struggles of this colorful panoply of Americans, *Treme* implicitly militates against trivialization of the culture and sometimes moves into an explicit critique of any perspective that reduces the humanity of the city to the level of quaint tourist fantasies. For example, in "Right Place, Wrong Time" (1.3), a tourist bus stops to gawk at a group of Indians led by Lambreaux, as they are solemnly preparing for a funeral. He almost wordlessly shames the bus driver for treating them as store-window displays. The driver apologizes and leaves. Acknowledging the driver's humility once Lambreaux makes his point, Simon and Overmyer clearly had no intention of demonizing the tour guide and the tourists. Rather they have created a moment that, in the spirit of nonformulaic TV, encourages viewers to wonder whether they would also have thought of these fellow Americans as curiosities if they had been in the bus.

FUSION: A CREOLE SERIES ABOUT A CREOLE CITY

Count the fusions in *Treme*. The show was made by the fusion of the complementary differences of its co-creators. The show is about a city that fuses European and African cultures and also the newly integrated Latino culture. And it has a narrative structure that fuses the multiplicity of personal heritages and contextual influences with a rapidity that embodies the vitality of the feeling of fusion. Even its visual presentation often reflects this feeling, with its tendency toward quick cuts between images and the abundant use of montage. The opening of the first episode embodies the rhythms of narrative and visuals to follow. We move quickly among a collage of images, often at the expense of the kind of narrative clarity that is obligatory in formulaic entertainment.

The first image in *Treme* is a close-up of a trumpeter putting a reed in his mouth to moisten it so he can play. We do not know who the mouth belongs to and will never know; nor does it matter. This is followed by flashes of extreme close-ups of glasses being filled with beer and liquor, a fluttering feather, a ribbon, white and black flesh, a cigarette, and the sounds of instruments being tuned. There are also flashes of the stoic faces of impassive soldiers looking on, the usual images of order. But at the moment they are purely background. Another image of order is in the foreground: music. Excitement grows at the prospect that a "second line" is about to march through the New Orleans streets, the first since Katrina. That presence invigorates the beginning of the show, that sense of rebirth, of community through music, of people who may or may not know each other but know the importance of the second line.

It is unlikely that most of the audience knows what a second line is. This kind of slippery exposition of terms local to New Orleans is typical of the modus operandi of the series. The viewer is arriving in a strange place and being bombarded by the newness of the context. It is necessary to stick with the narrative until the terrain becomes familiar through exposure and repetition, as in life. It speaks to the traveler in us; it requires work and patience, but it is also immensely rewarding, because it is full of joy. Moreover, it is not an impossible task; there is plenty going on that is familiar. Any American can understand the money troubles and personal allegiances in play. But the ambiguity of *Treme*'s exposition works against the passivity that somatizes

FIGURE 4.3. *What difference does it make whose mouth this is? It is the first second line since Katrina, and he is part of it.*

us in formulaic storytelling when everything is handed to us. It relies on engaging us in the building momentum: when Davis McAlary comes running to join the second line, as does the NOLA community, we do too, out of curiosity if nothing else.

Watching the formation of the second line in progress bombards us with questions. Who are these people? What is a second line? Why do people say "always for pleasure"? Formulaic TV always makes sure that we know the terminology and nomenclature. *Treme* makes us wonder. We are always in the position of trying to figure out the context of this different and tantalizing city. This chapter can help a little. The second line is a street parade of musicians for which they are not paid, a communal event. No one ever explains this during the series. It becomes obvious over time, or viewers can Google it. The phrase "always for pleasure" is the motto of New Orleans Creole culture. All this becomes obvious over time as we watch the show.

The pain of post-Katrina survival is also immediately introduced in the first season. Many of the musicians have had to leave the city. Many who are still there cannot find places to live or jobs. In a cameo role in "Shallow Water, Oh Mama" (1.6) Jacques Morial, a real-world NOLA politician played by himself, gives voice to the sentiments at the heart of the series when he says to Davis, "The culture of New Orleans, that's what's at risk. If they knock out the infrastructure that sustains the culture then it's gone forever." Davis, who is trying to write a song about that risk, replies to him,

"So . . . nothing really rhymes with 'infrastructure.'" Morial is talking about financial recovery; Davis is talking about arts recovery. Together they are a kind of statement and response chorus. These are not the happy little southerners celebrated in "Is It True What They Say about Dixie," laughing and loving "like they say in every song." They bond over music and economics in context with the pain and oppressiveness of the storm and what it did to their lives.

LaDonna's survival story is one of the most poignant, involving much more than the search for her missing brother, "Daymo," and her angst about her mother. Mrs. Brooks (Venida Evans) is almost paralyzed with fear and worry about her absent son. LaDonna, a strong, sensual, and resilient black woman, operates a bar in Treme, which makes her vulnerable to many of the upheavals caused by Katrina, both practical and criminal. She finds herself dealing with a shady contractor who takes her money but does not fix the roof on her bar until he is forced to, insurance money is slow in arriving, and the insurance problems resurface when her brother is discovered dead and the company with whom she has contracted for permanent care of her family's gravesite defines the damage caused by Katrina as not pertaining to their agreement. There is much worse. In the wake of the storm, crime escalates. LaDonna is raped and cannot get justice, despite the strong case built by Toni Bernette. Similarly, others working and living in the parts of the city most affected by Katrina stay this complicated and fraught course. Janette Desautel, a white transplant from Alabama, now intensely connected to New Orleans, is forced to close her very popular restaurant because the insurance money does not come through fast enough. The repairs she must make are major, and she cannot find anyone to borrow money from to tide her over until the insurance money arrives. She gives up briefly and explores New York as a home for her talents, but she returns. A sweet-natured (white) street singer named Harley Watt (Steve Earle) is murdered as violence in broken New Orleans continues to rise.

Our attention jumps among the various threads. Antoine Batiste has nowhere to live inside New Orleans and no way of earning money except by playing whatever band jobs he can get. Lambreaux is also at the mercy of insurance companies to fix his destroyed house, but he cannot leave New Orleans because the Indians rituals mean so much to him. He works on a bar that he does not own, which he fixes up as a place where he and his tribe of Indians can make the elaborate costumes for both Mardi Gras and St. Joseph's Day. He eventually fixes up his own home beautifully. Although no one makes an explicit statement about the fungus and rot permeating the air that he has had to breathe for so long, it is clearly the cause of the lung cancer from which he dies just before the house is completed. Context makes a sinister intervention.

The Creole fusions of narratives of black and white characters reflect on each other to create a large, enveloping contextual perspective. Batiste, Lambreaux, and McAlary all suffer from the disorganized police force of New Orleans. The police are so demoralized because of what has happened to them individually and as a department during Katrina that they strike out even more brutally and capriciously than before. When Batiste accidentally scrapes a police car with the trombone he is carrying, the police beat him, cuff him, jail him, and sell his trombone to a pawn shop. Lambreaux tries to force the city to get the federal government to open federal housing projects barely damaged by the storm and is beaten and jailed for that and for cleaving to the code of the Indians. When the police order him to kneel, he refuses, chanting the code of the Indians: "Won't bow; don't know how." Black residents are more likely to suffer at the hands of the police, but white residents are not immune. McAlary is drinking with a black friend on the street; he resists when the police order them to stop and is roughed up and arrested.

Interconnection is always front and center. Toni's search for LaDonna's brother David is not conclusive so much as it is connective. She exposes the uncooperative police and belligerent district attorney's office. David's bewildered family learns that his corpse was so hard to find because he and another convict exchanged identity bracelets: the corpse was listed as Jerome Cherry, the name of his cousin (Lloyd Watts). Finding David Brooks

FIGURE 4.4. *Toni and LaDonna looking for the truth.*

FIGURE 4.5. *Daymo's festive funeral embodies the survival skills of New Orleans in times of trouble.*

is not as engaging as the route that Toni takes and what LaDonna says when at last she sees his corpse in a FEMA (Federal Emergency Management Agency) trailer. Clearly some kind of foul play led to David's death, but LaDonna refuses to allow Toni to order an autopsy. She does not believe that it will matter to her family to find out how he died; she wants to put the agony of her family's loss behind her and does not see assigning blame as a solution. Right or wrong? The series does not judge. It does not offer the kind of closure so obligatory in formula television. The victory is survival and the unity of the family and the community at David Brooks's funeral.

Juxtaposition with Creighton Bernette's narrative suggests what in him is alien to the flow of New Orleans. His pessimism is celebrated by his You-Tube audience, who like hearing him talk about the "fucking fuckers" who are letting New Orleans down. His suicide is condemned by his wife. But he is neither celebrated nor condemned by the series, which may be difficult for television audiences used to hard and fast judgments and glamorized suffering. Bernette is too shattered to stay connected to the world. His isolationism in the face of the disaster of the storm is carefully articulated as part of the collage, particularly by scenes in which he teaches a class at Tulane soon after Mardi Gras about *The Awakening* by Kate Chopin, a New Orleans writer. In this book a white upper-class New Orleans woman, Edna, commits suicide rather than submit to a repressive society. "That's a tell," as David Simon says. When Bernette answers questions from his class about the heroine's motives for killing herself, he tells them that it is part of her quest for truth: the farther she moves away from social constraints, the closer she gets to freedom. "She's not moving toward the darkness, she's embracing spiritual liberation." This produces a preternatural silence in the class, possibly an acknowledgment on some level that they are watching a man embracing death. Bernette's subsequent suicide can be judged by an active viewer, as it stands in juxtaposition with the story of his wife's search for David Brooks and the stories of Lambreaux, Batiste, and McAlary. Bernette is what they are not: detached. What more powerful statement could there be in support of Simon's belief in the importance of context? To withdraw from it is death.[4]

Simon's interest in context is also depicted through the strangers to New Orleans who work their way into it. For example, Toni falls in love with Terry Colson (David Morse), a (white) police captain, after she makes her peace with the suicide of her husband. The opposite of Creighton, Terry is fascinatingly depicted as a stranger to New Orleans who has started life with conventional expectations about being a man, a husband, and a police professional but changes through an unpredicted intuitive grasp of the New Orleans arts community. As an outsider, he is capable of verbalizing about New Orleans, as Creighton Bernette was, but unlike Creighton, he undertakes the fight in which Toni is also involved, rather than running away. His love affair with Toni is one of the most beautiful in the series, not only because of the sweetness of their connection but because of its larger connectedness as well.

One of the most poignant nuances of Colson's story is Simon's refusal to make engagement in the world a panacea for unhappiness and suffering. Colson eventually has to leave his heart in NOLA because his attempts to do what is right make him a pariah in the police department and he is forced to leave town. Achievement is a mixed blessing because of the complications of context. But it is those complications that make Colson a man rich in understanding. The loss of his job, which he loves despite all the knocks he has suffered, leads Colson to differentiate between himself as an achiever as a police captain and himself as a sentient human being of importance in the grand scheme of things because he is human. His ex-wife and his sons in Indianapolis, where he goes when he leaves NOLA, are imbued with the business view of life and cannot understand what his time in New Orleans has taught him.

Connection is also a part of the depiction of the business community and the civic structure, which are not as detached as Creighton Bernette, although the way they connect is ambiguous in its perspectives and

FIGURE 4.6. *Toni and Terry, a couple uniquely part of the two aspects of NOLA culture.*

impact. The civic stories center primarily on C. J. Liguori (Dan Ziskie), a local patrician (white) investment capitalist, and Nelson Hidalgo (Jon Seda), a dashing and irrepressible young Hispanic Republican Texan. He is looking for riches and fun in New Orleans and makes a beeline for Liguori in hopes of becoming part of the community of movers and shakers in the city. Liguori's attitude toward the possible creation of a jazz center in the neighborhoods where black musicians created New Orleans music is typical of the way he understands the contribution that he can make to the New Orleans recovery. He sees the storm as his chance to clean out the pesky artists that do not seem to him to understand how much better a prestigious jazz center would be than the dirty clubs on Rampart Street. Liguori is charming, but his idea of a legacy is money and buildings. He knows a little something about jazz but not how it grows from the community. We see that he is sincere when he says, as if it were a benediction for his hometown, that Katrina has given the business community a chance to "monetize on the culture in a very, very smart and civic way" ("Knock with Me—Rock with Me," 3.1). Interestingly, while Liguori is the kind of danger to New Orleans that Jacques Morial spoke of to McAlary, he does not commit Simon's three Ds of sin: detachment, disconnection, and despair. When local government bickering defeats the idea of the project, at least for now, Liguori rolls with it, ready to try his hand at some other way to benefit his city as he sees it. He remains undaunted.

The fusion of the pieces of the collage depends on a steady shifting of all of them in relationship to each other. Each shift casts its own complex of illuminations even among characters who never actually meet. Nelson Hidalgo and Terry Colson, for example, cast light on each other without appearing in scenes together. Hidalgo is a stranger, like Colson, a Texan with a Latino background, who also changes as a result of living in New Orleans and makes his own mark on it. A live wire with an enormous zest for living and a real delight in women, he has connected himself to every aspect of the culture that presents itself to him. By the last season, when he has become rich from his dealings in NOLA, it suddenly occurs to him that the way he and Liguori do business makes nothing (but money) and leaves no legacy. While money is very gratifying to him in many ways, New Orleans has taught him other kinds of satisfactions irrelevant to his position as a venture capitalist.

One of the most affecting changes concerns Hidalgo's growing respect and admiration for Janette Desautel's talent as a chef, which leads him to manipulate another venture capitalist who is victimizing her. Janette, who initially is defeated by the insurmountable economic problems caused by Katrina, leaves New Orleans and gains a modicum of success in New York. She is lured back to NOLA by Tim Feeny (Sam Robards), a (white) restaurant empire builder who takes advantage of Janette's strong attachment to the culture of her adopted city. Feeny, the essence of disconnection in the business community, inveigles Janette into partnership with him by offering almost unlimited capital and freedom. While the money does flow, the promise of freedom is a chimera. Feeny has almost no feeling for Janette's talent as anything but a profit-making skill. He so drastically compromises her latitude as a creative artist by hiring conventionally beautiful but inexperienced waitstaff to serve as his sexual harem and by pushing her to virtually mass produce "signature" dishes that will raise the restaurant's profile that she breaks their contract, incurring his wrath as a businessman. Feeny vindictively enforces a clause in the contract that forbids her from using her name on the restaurant that she opens independently. Janette does not understand a man like Feeny, but Hidalgo does and achieves a comic victory over him.

Feeny will continue to rake in money from the restaurant that Janette left, but Hidalgo puts a limit on the collateral damage. When he realizes what Feeny has done, Hidalgo inveigles him into giving Janette back the commercial use of her name by offering him 100 percent of nothing, as he laughingly tells her. Hidalgo has been involved with negotiations to build a jazz center in New Orleans long enough to know that it has no chance of ever being built. But Feeny does not know that and jumps at the chance to get the chimerical restaurant concession in exchange for a concession to Janette. It is a true New Orleans deal from a new son of the city with a unique sense of pleasure in life that equates with strength, community, generosity, resilience, and survival.

ALWAYS FOR PLEASURE: THIS CITY WON'T EVER DROWN

This city won't ever die
Just as long as her heart beats strong
Like a second line steppin' high
Raisin' hell as we roll along

. . .

—This city won't ever drown.

This melancholy, defiant, proud song by Steve Earle inspired by Katrina (which played under the closing credits of the first season finale) expresses the profound importance of pleasure in New Orleans and defines what pleasure is not. It does not conform to the businessman's definition, which dominates formulaic TV: Pleasure is fantasy, extraneous to the serious business of life. It leads to hedonism or at least dangerous excess. Pleasure is merely a commodity. It is what happens in a formulaic series after problems are solved or during breaks in the action. Characters do not stop to sing and dance, to have sex, or to cook a great meal. They wait until the heroic hand has been played, since pleasure is merely indulgence, irresponsibility, losing control. The perfect hero has more important things to do. Not in *Treme*.

Pleasure, in the form of the arts, connects the characters and the culture to the nonverbal wellsprings of human existence that cannot be touched by money and the political jockeying for power. Pleasure in this context is a powerful nexus with reality, not a distraction. It is what sustains our lives when we cannot win, when justice is delayed and denied; it connects us when we are divided. Another singularity of New Orleans is the way it builds survival on pleasure. Nothing in the plot happens because of the force of pleasure in NOLA culture. Rather, pleasure emerges as more forceful than plot as the energy of human interactions. There is nothing like this in formulaic television storytelling—or for that matter in the other auteur series. In *Treme*, everything on the order of human survival happens because of it.

Throughout season 1, the show depicts a complex sense of the pleasure at the heart of any recovery that New Orleans might experience. We watch food being cooked and listen to all kinds of music for no other reason than that it is a major part of the context of New Orleans. No plot points are being made by the experience of the cooking or the music, which could be indicated with just a few shots to give "local color." But these long takes are not just background; they are foreground. They are as much a part of the spectator's experience as the problems and complications of the numerous plots that crisscross as the season progresses. Never in the history of television have the arts played a role like this in storytelling.

Sometimes pleasure seems to be a whimsical presence. When McAlary tries to keep Janette from leaving New Orleans at the end of season 1, she agrees to give him a day in which to immerse her in the pleasures of the town, of which their connection is a part, as he makes very clear to her. He tantalizes her with small experiences of the unique culture of the city, culminating in a scene in which they dance in a jazz club, their bodies in completely delirious harmony that is in many ways more erotic than the overt sex scenes in *Treme*. Janette does leave and McAlary goes on almost immediately to a new romance with Annie Talarico, the street violinist eventually bound for stardom. And it seems that the conventional idea of pleasure as a fleeting, unimportant sensation is in play. But ultimately Davis is right. Janette's commercial success in New York lacks sustaining pleasure. Nor is her connection with McAlary fleeting even if it is composed of moments and goes underground for a while. It is those moments, not the career that Janette briefly thinks of as "a life," that endure. The power of pleasure in these moments asserts itself again when McAlary and Janette reunite in the fourth season.

The serio-whimsy of pleasure in *Treme* is also present in the appearance of Koichi Toyama (Tatsuo Ichikawa), a Japanese aficionado of American jazz who makes his way to New Orleans after Katrina to pay homage to what he loves and to help. One of the most delightful interludes in Batiste's story is Toyama's visit to New Orleans out of pure love for the pleasure that jazz gives him and his respect for its roots in New Orleans. His pleasure in meeting Batiste and seeing New Orleans seems a little foolish at first but not in the end. Toyama is an elegant, generous, wealthy man, with a scholar's knowledge of NOLA jazz history and respect for the artistry that are intellectually well beyond those of Batiste, who knows jazz from being in the trenches. But their rapport in brotherly celebration of a mutual passion for the art creates a dialogue of respect and affection that draws together two vastly different temperaments and cultures through pleasure taken in music. Their friendship is a variation on the NOLA Creole mixture; it is not a fusion of African and European cultures but a fusion anchored in the grounding force of delight.

However, there are also deeply serious manifestations of the power of pleasure as a cultural expression of unity, strength, endurance, and, most surprisingly, responsibility. Pleasure in the same breath as responsibility? Yes, that is the New Orleans way portrayed in *Treme*. The funeral of David

Brooks, the final segment of season 1, begins with a somber religious ceremony then moves into the traditional New Orleans funeral cortege in which all who wish can march behind the coffin to the strains of local jazz. It does not control the situation. David's distraught but conventional mother rejects the musical celebration in the name of respectability, as does her second husband, Larry Williams (Lance E. Nichols), an assimilated, well-to-do (black) dentist. It is available for those open to it. LaDonna and Antoine and their sons take their places behind the funeral band, along with other mourners and strangers who join it spontaneously. The season ends with these grieving bodies moving in time to the jazz strains, flourishing the ritual white handkerchiefs: community is born before our eyes from the union of individuals through the music. It is a unique version of pleasure as the glue that binds people and fills them with renewed strength. We are particularly focused on LaDonna as life returns to her body, exhausted with sorrow. It is momentary; the cortege disperses, but the vitality remains to sustain as the season comes to a close. What has happened is not on the order of justice attained, mysteries solved, punishment meted out as in formula television. It creates a new order of meaning.

The factor of pleasure also is part of the serious career choices of a number of musicians in the show, such as Kermit Ruffins, an actual musician in New Orleans who has gained a modicum of national fame but in real life rejected a national career. Annie Talarico's talent propels her to the attention of hard-driving white manager Marvin Frey (Michael Cerveris). He wants to put her on a career path that would take her out of the NOLA environment and make her rich and famous. Delmond Lambreaux has broken away from New Orleans, his intimidating father, and the family tradition of belonging to the New Orleans Indians but also feels an irresistible bond with everything that he has left behind. The universal wisdom of the American economic system is that we abandon pleasure when we make career decisions as an adult. Money and material success are involved, and it is not prudent to fool around with them. That is what we would be doing if we took pleasure into account when making decisions about our career path. Correct? The answer in *Treme* is a resounding NO!

In the first episode of the series McAlary spots real-world international celebrity Elvis Costello in the audience as Kermit Ruffins performs with his Barbecue Swingers. He tries to persuade Ruffins to network with Costello, who could conceivably connect Ruffins with "big time" national success. Ruffins is utterly unconcerned. He is portrayed as rooted so deeply in the culture that he has an unbreakable organic connection that nurtures his art. It works for him, his family, and his friends. His locality is depth, it is power, it is pleasure. Ruffins makes appearances from time to time on *Treme*, not as a core character but almost as a Greek chorus emphasizing the blood-rush joy of pleasure in locality, its groundedness.

Locality does not have that significance for all the musicians in the series. Annie Talarico, briefly McAlary's love, does decide to try for national stardom when it is offered to her. But her decision is filled with negotiations that she hopes will enable her to stay rooted to her authentic art, leaving many questions hanging about whether that is possible. This is, after all, a series about the necessity of connection to a community, a context, not a celebration of star individualism. Delmond Lambreaux also decides in favor of the "big time," but he is even more determined to stay connected to his father's heritage while he makes the break. In pursuit of that goal, he forges a unique musical alliance between the ancient rhythms of his father's Indian music and the modern jazz that he has connected with in New York. The promise of this dynamic form of syncretism—yes, there is a hint of Creole fusion—invigorates both Delmond and his New York associates. But the power of the past, as creative as it is, is fraught with conflict. It is to the credit of Simon and Overmyer that they are so full of respect for the atavistic pleasure of the local. This rears its head when Albert refuses to stay in New York (with its state-of-the-art recording facilities) and drags the New York musicians to New Orleans, insisting that the music cannot be made out of its place. It would have been easy to laugh at Lambreaux for what would have been his provinciality in a formulaic rendition. But Simon and Overmyer imbue Lambreaux with a gravitas that meshes with the respect for place and locality and the strength of the creative spark ignited by the pleasure of connection that is part and parcel of the series.

In fact, the pleasure of community is not only part of the flowering of art but also part of a deep understanding of morality that liberates the characters from the narrow-mindedness conventionally associated with moralism. Terry Colson's sense of morality develops as a result of his time in New Orleans and his experience of the city's pleasure. In the third season, as he is policing the streets during Mardi Gras, standing in front of a bawdy display by three street performers. he suddenly begins talking to a colleague about the difference between vice and sin. Vice is human, he says, excessive and mistaken but part of what it means to be alive. He is clearly referring to the misrule of Mardi Gras. He likens sin to the actions of a bureaucracy that violates human decency, clearly reflecting on the miscarriages of justice and disrespect for law that he has seen around him since the storm. "New Orleans gets that" and "other cities don't," he adds.

With his expanded vision gained in NOLA, Terry sets a new standard of masculine strength. He throws his manly career away in order to testify about the corruption in the city at the time of the infamous Danziger Bridge massacre and the terrible injustices that took place in the police department in the wake of the hurricane.[5] Colson discovers his personhood in New Orleans as a thing apart from rank and position, which is a mystery to his ex-wife and his sons living a more status-conscious life in Indiana, when he tries to explain to them that his identity does not depend on being a policeman.

Terry's connection of morality to pleasure is unexpected, unusual, and perhaps difficult to fathom for those accustomed to the more diffuse disconnections of money-centered American locales. Similarly, Batiste's connection of maturity to pleasure is unique in television narrative and rich in implications for the puritan culture of America. Batiste begins the series as exactly what America understands as a cautionary figure who exemplifies the problems of living for pleasure. He is undependable, too interested in his own sensory gratifications, and immature. Yet, as the series progresses, we begin to see Batiste as a man who has barely scratched the surface of the Creole outlook: his self-consumed, hedonistic brand of pleasure lacks the communal element of NOLA culture. When Batiste's genuine pleasure takes on communal power, he begins to mature as a man. That process takes place when Batiste becomes associated with the school system in the city as a music teacher. He also discovers the frustrations of the obstacles to the pleasure of community.

A promising young (black) musician, Cherise (Camryn Jackson), whose single-mother family is afflicted by both poverty and crime, is killed in street violence. Robert (Jaron Williams) is a legitimately talented young black boy who is fighting an uphill battle to learn to play the trumpet. Jennifer (Jazz Henry) is a black child shouldering the burden of adulthood with no one to help her. The pleasure of sharing music with these children and others pulls Batiste beyond the limits of the pleasures of individual indulgences. He is no longer the jazz hobo running from club engagement to club engagement and taking all the extras of gambling, women, and liquor on the run. He is connected in a deeper way.

Of course, the Mardi Gras episodes and the scenes of the St. Joseph's celebrations by the NOLA Indians are the pivotal images of pleasure, Creole style. They are the fullest embodiment of the pleasure of the music and food arts in the series writ large. The episodes are filled with a riot of color, carnivalesque disguises, communal music, eating, dancing, reunions, parades, and sensual delights of all kinds. On the margins of Mardi Gras are the selfish people, immersing themselves in pleasure. In the early seasons Annie's initial partner is Sonny (Michiel Huisman), a white musician who indulges liberally in drugs and shallow and degrading compulsive womanizing, while Batiste shucks his parental duties and his loyalty to his (black) partner Desiree (Phyllis Montana LeBlanc) in a greedy search for sex and more sex. But the central celebration is about collectivity and largesse, a generative Bacchanalian release from isolation and the disconnected self, which eventually becomes true of Sonny and Batiste as well.

The Mardi Gras episodes of the first three seasons feature an unchanging rhythm and tone of misrule in the city during carnival. "All on a Mardi Gras Day" (1.8) is the fullest rendition of the pleasure principle of Creole life. The festivities take up almost the entire episode and burst with the diversity of the celebrants swept up in the resilient tide of communal pleasure: the embraces of people long parted; the pathos of those who have returned home just for the day but are forced by the flood to live elsewhere; the hospitality of families and local celebrities who open their homes to crowds that come and go. Koichi Toyama, the Japanese jazz aficionado, "comes home" to celebrate the first Mardi Gras since the flood. The stirrings of loves old and new resonate: McAlary finds himself attracted to Annie; and LaDonna and Batiste, her first husband, find comfort with each other sexually, but just for the moment. The police manifest a momentary openness to the deepest reality of the city with their expert, noninvasive crowd control. The Big Party of New Orleans broadcasts pleasure in survival and survival because of pleasure. Albert Lambreaux's incarceration for getting into a fight with a policeman who was evicting him by force from the project housing seems a true deprivation in the context of this affirmation, and Creighton Bernette's self-willed isolation appears particularly anomalous and ominous.

By the time of the Mardi Gras episodes of the second and third seasons ("Carnival Time," 2.7; and "Promised Land," 3.7), its pleasures have become familiar to the viewer. The power of Albert Lambreaux as the Big Chief of the Guardians of the Flame, withheld from view because of his trouble with the law, is fully visible in episode 2.7, as his tribe moves through the streets in dazzling white costumes at the peak of their virility and Albert's commanding authority. This makes his decline from cancer in 3.7 all the more painful: we see him decked out in the brilliant green that his tribe has chosen for that year but clearly debilitated by his disease. It is testimony to the opposition between death and pleasure in New Orleans, like Creighton Bernette's isolation during carnival in 1.8.

In episode 2.7, the depiction of a Cajun Mardi Gras miles away from New Orleans that Annie has decided to attend becomes a study in contrasts with

New Orleans misrule, offering a fascinating new perspective on the uniqueness of the Creole culture of NOLA. Cajun Mardi Gras is also filled with misrule, but of a complete different character and not always for pleasure. A tone of fear and cruelty dominates the festivities. The celebrants do not wander aimlessly and joyously as in New Orleans but take part in a collective ritual in which mock tyrants demand that they bow before them. The unity of the group is generated around seriocomic rejection of other groups. One of the pretend tyrants spots Annie's Mardi Gras beads and confiscates them in a playful but still ominous fashion, demanding that she atone for bringing New Orleans beads among them. The Cajun Mardi Gras also involves animal sacrifice. The Creole NOLA pleasure principle is absent.

In "Promised Land" (3.7), McAlary has reunited with Janette. Their renewed intimacy is depicted in the way they flow together into the local pleasure of the carnival. The celebration rolls on as we discover that the city is more violent than ever. The police department seems almost as incompetent at dealing with major crime as it was during and right after Katrina. This is not the city that care forgot, as the Chamber of Commerce likes to call it. Creole pleasure is a cultural force but not superglue.

The St. Joseph's celebrations are extraordinary depictions of the least-familiar Creole aspect of New Orleans, the fusion of iron discipline and pleasure. There is barely a trace of the unzipped revelry of Mardi Gras among Lambreaux's Indians, though Overmyer told me that competitive violence can occur among the celebrants as they make their annual festival

FIGURE 4.7. *McAlary suits up as a businessman only for Mardi Gras.*

garments. This is the spartan edge of Creole pleasure, seemingly an oxy-moron and yet representative of a living tradition in New Orleans. The men of the NOLA Indian tribes are almost military in their discipline as they make their flamboyant costumes, which exceed the showiness of any Las Vegas cabaret, and talk about being pretty when they put them on. They are infused with a warrior-like hardness and dedication against all obstacles. Their feather-, sequin-, and bead-studded costumes rival the most extravagant excesses of the legendary Ziegfeld Follies. But they are animated not by the casual, externalized seduction of the imagination, as were those spectacles, but by a fiery energy welling up from the deepest human reserves not only emotionally but historically. Their chants and ritualized gestures are the essence of human connection.

As go the Indians, so go NOLA's links with its most rigorous, primordial, survivalist bonds with pleasure and local history. Terry Colson comes to see Albert about controlling the violence that sometimes erupts between Indians and police during these annual celebrations. The two men try to get past their mutual distrust as members of two historically conflicted com-munities and to tap into their mutual respect for each other. Lambreaux makes it clear that he wants Colson to speak the same cautionary words about violence to the police; Colson wants Lambreaux to honor the wishes of a previous chief to keep civic order. Each man is fighting for his culture, and the obstacles are many. "We're trying to keep something alive here. And y'all trying not to see it," says Lambreaux. When their bargaining pays off on the night of St. Joseph's, the endurance of the Indians, if not a guarantee that NOLA will come back, is a further indication of a revitalizing force at work in the city.

Liguori, the banker, does not understand the sense of responsibility, maturity, and community that goes with pleasure in New Orleans. His motto, although he does not know it, is "always for money." In his ignorance of the wellsprings of his city, he is engaged in plans for the kind of revival that would make New Orleans like any other money-driven city in the country. By contrast, Nelson Hidalgo brings his Latino culture to bear when he takes a more connected attitude toward making money. When he is counseled to join the traditional Zulu parade during Mardi Gras to curry favor with the politicians who are members, he makes a calculated financial connection but does more too. Something in him is awakened to at least some aspect of the spirit of Mardi Gras, and he momentarily joins the community. Nelson grasps that the city is about connection. He makes a speech about it in "Feels Like Rain" (2.6) but is still marked by the business mentality. He does not

FIGURE 4.8. *Treme's scarlet letter, an embellished pothole. NOLA's arts culture adorns the failure of its civic structure.*

really comprehend when McAlary tries to explain why the glitzy jazz center project that Liguori is backing is sterile, a disconnection that would destroy the landmarks of jazz history on Ramparts Street.

McAlary cannot save the city singlehandedly as he would love to for the pleasure he delights in, as might happen in a formulaic comedy. Nevertheless, he is given the last word, so to speak (he is completely silent in his final appearance), on how pleasure works in NOLA and its tendency, though not a certainty by any means, to endure. The last thing we see in the series is McAlary driving up to an immense pothole that has been his nemesis since the storm. It is not fixed yet. After driving into it and wrecking his car, he puts out a ladder and brooms and pails, as a sign of his anger and as a warning to other drivers. As the series finale comes to a close, McAlary drives by and sees that it has undergone a change. Mardi Gras revelers have liberally draped the sign of his wrath with sparkling beads, masks, and colorful headdresses.

Without a single line of dialogue, McAlary's confrontation with the embellished pothole, a nuisance altered by pleasure, embodies a moment of epiphany: nothing fits together in this world, yet that is its charm. The joie de vivre of the town and the essence of the folk bring maturity. Marveling at the sight, McAlary simply gets back into his car and drives on. His front wheel dips into yet another pothole that has appeared since he wreaked havoc on the pothole that is now a work of art. We peek through and around a glittering mask on the pothole sculpture as he goes on his way.[6]

ALWAYS FOR REALITY: AUTHENTIC INDIANS/NO VOODOO IN TREME

Simon's quest for the real in entertainment prompted his co-creation of *Treme*. In a story about New Orleans, Simon discovers a natural subject. In the whirl of the *Treme* collage, Simon and Overmyer find a way to foreground their introduction of the audience to the Creole pleasure principle, unfamiliar to the cultures of other American cities. With the diminished role of linear narrative, screen time became available to give viewers an experience of the vitality of savoring the arts as a humanizing force that strengthens, matures, and sustains as well as delights. But the Simon/Overmyer adoption of collage narrative for a powerful, enlightening, nonformulaic form of entertainment did more. It not only left room for pleasure but also left room for tapping into real elements of New Orleans for the production of the show.

Both Simon and Overmyer incline toward the neorealistic impulse in post–World War II Italian cinema. In applying that aesthetic to New Orleans, they had at their disposal a treasure trove of local arts, a source of Katrina and post-Katrina drama, and gorgeous local festivals. By the time McAlary plays "Do You Know What It Means to Miss New Orleans?" in the final episodes we know it so intimately that we do. "Hey!" he says. "Do you know how sometimes you hear a song you've heard a million times before and maybe you're even tired of hearing it, but this time, maybe because of something you've been through or maybe because of something you now understand, you hear that song again, maybe it's a new version—maybe not—but you realize that there's a fresh world in there to be heard? Yeah, me too." Many in the nondiegetic audience have new eyes and ears and would say that they do.

In *Treme*, we engaged with a strange and bracing, unprecedented blend of fictional characters and situations and the vibrant presence of real Indians, real local and national musicians, real citizens of the town, real locations, and real local history, with only a wisp of reference to the Creole Marie Laveau and her voodoo tradition that haunts clichés of New Orleans on American television. Marie Laveau did exist, and there are voodoo tours for tourists in New Orleans. But these have the relationship to local culture in NOLA that Disney's amusement parks have to California, Florida, and their various international locations. They are given appropriately slight mention in a silly local tour given in his typical style by McAlary. Otherwise Antoine, Albert, Toni, Sofia, Janette, LaDonna, Annie, Sonny, Creighton, Davis, and

Terry talk and work with real-world people and professionals who currently live in New Orleans. Some of the characters are based on real people who lived, suffered, and endured in the city during and after Katrina.

The most spectacular and previously unknown New Orleans reality that Simon and Overmyer brought to their series is the New Orleans Indians. The replication of their costumes and lifestyles defies the pressure to create characters on the basis of patterns tested by previous television shows, representing nothing but a collective fantasy about unfamiliar cultures. Very few had ever heard of a New Orleans Indian culture before. Simon and Overmyer went to the living men themselves in order to give this culture its television debut. The rhythms and tones were provided by the presence of actual New Orleans Indians in Lambreaux's scenes and by the use of a genuine Indian song, "My Indian Red," important to the culture. The lyrics, part of folk history, vary greatly depending on who sings it, but the pounding rhythm informs all versions:

> I've got a Big Chief, Big Chief,
> Big Chief of the Nation, wild, wild creation
> He won't bow down, on that dirty ground
> Because I love to hear him call Indian Red

Some of the dialogue was improvised by the Indians who played Lambreaux's colleagues on the series, just as dialogue was improvised in scenes featuring men from a fleet of fishing boats. A couple of real politicians, Jacques Morial and Oliver Thomas (a New Orleans city councilman), appeared in the series but did not improvise their lines when they spoke on screen about how politics works in New Orleans. Morial, often in trouble with the law in real life, is the son of the city's first African American mayor and the brother of its third. In the first season of *Treme*, he gives a passionate, scripted speech to McAlary about the inherent character of New Orleans that is informed by his family history. His greatest concern is that the destruction caused by Katrina will give the wrong people an opportunity to take away that character in the name of redevelopment and progress, a major concern of the series as well. Oliver Thomas, a popular, capable, crusading politician who served on the city council from 1994 to 2007, would have run for mayor if he had not been convicted of bribery in 2007 and sentenced to thirty-seven months in federal prison. When he played himself on *Treme*, his legal problems were written into the series as a stumbling block for the fictional Nelson Hidalgo, who had been mentored by Thomas for purposes of the story. Hidalgo became business poison for a while on *Treme* because of his association with Thomas. This marks a complex, very unusual interface between fact and fiction in American entertainment.

The jazz musicians, similarly, are members of the New Orleans jazz community: some known nationally, most known only to aficionados. A glittering parade of real-world jazz, blues, and Dixieland musicians sparkles in every season of the show. The credits of every show include at least a half-dozen accomplished musicians, including Kermit Ruffins, Elvis Costello, Allen Toussaint, John Boutté, Tom McDermott, Dr. John, Fats Domino, and Ellis Marsalis. Simon was able to coax chefs from the most famous New York City restaurants to play themselves in some episodes. Major chefs working in the United States today appeared in the series: Eric Ripert of Le Bernardin; Tom Colicchio of Gramercy Tavern; David Chang of the Momofuku Restaurant group; Wylie Dufresne of the wd-50 restaurant; and Emeril Lagasse of the Emeril restaurant empire. Moreover, Anthony Bourdain was a consultant on the scenes in which the chefs appeared and wrote some of them. As Overmyer says, "Simon's very good about bringing people in to do that. That was really crucial."

Several of the central characters are drawn from the lives of real inhabitants of New Orleans. Eric Overmyer told me that McAlary is based on a real man—his name was not specified—and that the set for his house is around the corner from where the real NOLA citizen lives. Toni Bernette is based on Mary Howell, a real-life civil rights lawyer in New Orleans, a friend of Overmyer's. Creighton Bernette is loosely based on Stevenson Palfi, a documentary filmmaker in New Orleans, who made a documentary of which both Simon and Overmyer thought very highly, *Piano Players Rarely Ever Play Together* (1982). Palfi committed suicide in despair after Katrina.

Through its revision of the definition of pleasure and its commitment to the real, *Treme* shifts dependence on winning, the stuff of which formula happy endings are made, to celebration of the recuperative power inherent in the arts as a model for potential American resilience in the United States as a whole in our troubled times. In a Creole town, woven syncretistically out of European, Latino, and African cultures, which inspires all kinds of fusions, nothing is only one thing, not even the city itself. New Orleans is local, but it is also national. It is a culture apart and it is all of us. This series is not about a city cut off from the rest of America, for all its difference and special quality. It is about a city that mirrors one of our deep secrets. When he is trying to get investment capital with the help of Nelson Hidalgo to save the old Rampart Street area, Davis McAlary puts into words this important, all-embracing truth of *Treme*: all of American culture is Creole if we only knew it. From this perspective, while America is focused on its preoccupation with business, a shallow enterprise with no past and no future, only money today, it would do well to acknowledge the significance of our real hope for the future: the fusion of our many cultures, European, Latino, and African. It is a slender hope, but a wild ride.

CHAPTER 5

MATT WEINER, *MAD MEN*

If you can get money, you can reinvent who you are; I think it's an American story that predates *The Great Gatsby*, and we're extremely tolerant of that. . . . In fact, the original script in which Don was developed was based on reading a bunch of biographies of people in the twentieth century: Bill Clinton, Lee Iacocca, Rockefeller. They don't all have fake names, but a lot of them have covered their childhoods.

—Matt Weiner, phone interview, May 26, 2016

I n one important way *Mad Men* is literally, directly, and demonstrably a consequence of David Chase's *The Sopranos*. In many other ways it is very much an auteur's unique response to television's new receptivity to the art of narrative. Created by Matt Weiner, a key member of *The Sopranos* writers' room from 2003 to 2007, *Mad Men* was already in partial draft before Weiner worked with Chase. But, as Weiner has often said, it came to fruition because Chase gave him the confidence to follow his own creative impulses.[1] Having written for formulaic television series, Weiner knew what the "rules" were when he began drafting *Mad Men* and that they worked for mass audiences. But Weiner is an artist who, in his own words, "lives in the not-knowing," his way of alluding to his inclination to work from the subconscious processes that are only slowly—or not at all—verbalized and moved into awareness. This is not the stuff of which formulaic television is made. It has been abundantly productive, however, for this nonformulaic series about Don Draper (Jon Hamm), the creative director of a small but prestigious (fictional) New York advertising agency, Sterling Cooper.

"The not-knowing" is Weiner's vocabulary for speaking about what I am calling the modern indeterminacy of being governed by powerful forces that are both beyond our control and beyond definitive scrutiny. Telling a story about ad men from this point of view has turned out to be fresh, exhilarating, and revealing. The art of Weiner's storytelling flies in the face of cherished cultural stereotypes and sociological truisms about ad men as manipulative, detached Rasputins that have been in vogue since Vance Packard's seminal study of the industry, *The Hidden Persuaders* (1957). In *Mad Men*, ad men do not take charge of the public subconscious from their isolated lairs on Madison Avenue, at the crossroads of shallow American materialism and insidious bigotry, racism, and sexism. Weiner's series does not shrink from portraying their daily indulgences in superficiality and stereotypes, but these ad men are not puppet masters; they too are driven by the subconscious and caught between their own unmanageable depths and their attempts to bemuse and captivate the buying public.

Weiner told me many stories about his own experiences working in the liminality of the not-knowing. One of the most interesting concerns his decision to cast Jon Hamm as Don Draper, an inspired choice on which, arguably, the success of the series hinges; he is comfortable saying that he has never been able to explain it. Similarly, Don Draper's story and the lives of the people around him are filled with such moments. In *Mad Men*, cause and effect are mysterious. Causes begin within dark places in the characters and ricochet forward, backward, and sideways, bouncing unexpectedly off the internal streams of fantasy, emotion, and memory and moving outward as effects. There are no clear straight paths between motivation and act in this series. For this reason, the characters that Weiner has created, who are articulated meticulously by their gender and cultural backgrounds, cannot be fully explained by the usual clichés about gender or those backgrounds. Nothing is a matter of linear cause and effect. These are unfathomable transactions that generate modern questions about identity, indirection, and inconclusiveness.

An important part of the portrait of the not-knowing in *Mad Men* is Weiner's idea about connections between perception and the subconscious and the many ways in which something as seemingly factual as sight is a product of the characters' internal fixations and fetishes projected outward. The possibility for representing such indirection lies, as Weiner sees it, in the nature of the camera. Like David Chase and David Lynch before him, Matt Weiner believes that the logic of the camera (that is to say, of the electronic images it produces) is the logic of the subconscious. From this point of view, one of the most important limitations imposed on a television series by formulaic writing is that it thwarts the connection between the camera and the deepest levels of human nature. The direct linearity of cause and effect in narrative formulas allows little or no time, space, or narrative impetus for the camera to travel the oblique pathways down which Weiner believes we all travel. Formulaic television shoehorns perception into a format in which there are only two options: the "norm" of objective, clear perception of the real and its opposite, the pathology of delusional distortions. By contrast, perceptual norms are illusory in *Mad Men*. It is human to see things as our own subconscious processes project themselves outward. Perception is one of the major wonders central to *Mad Men*, which is much less concerned with the lesser mysteries that preoccupy formula TV: who dunnit or who wunnit?

Don Draper's emotional dissociation from the world around him is front and center, not suspense about whether or not he will sell his agency's advertising plans to the client. Business conflicts are dwarfed by mysteries churned up by our increasing knowledge of his inner struggles. Consider how we learn to know not only Don but also the rest of the series characters and even the agency of Sterling Cooper itself. Roger Sterling (John Slattery) and Bert Cooper (Robert Morse), whose patrician families created the agency, and adman Pete Campbell (Vincent Kartheiser) and Betty Hofstadt Draper Francis (January Jones) are defined as characters born into traditional privileged families. We know them in some ways as such, but we are more engaged by their unique perceptual habits and the odd directions taken by their intentions and actions. Similarly, the characters who, like Don Draper, come from less traditional, less privileged families—for example, office manager Joan Holloway Harris (Christina Hendricks), rising ad woman Peggy Olson (Elizabeth Moss), and star of the art department Stan Rizzo (Jay R. Ferguson)—are known to us less through their identities as outsiders and more by the unpredictable, often liminal portrayals of how they perceive the world and the indirection of their actions. Strikingly, institutions are the sum of this indeterminacy. The very history of Sterling Cooper is shaped by the collective subconscious of its management and employees, as it mutates unsettlingly from season to season—a first in series storytelling.

Change, confusion, blind spots, and ambiguity are the rule in *Mad Men*. There is an external reality, but the characters are at the mercy of subconscious forces in their attempts to see it and to act. To quote Weiner, he does not give the audience a narrative that would "satisfy them any more than their own lives would."

FALLING

The show's main title introduces us to the world of the series as an uneasy space in which perception is mysterious, like a dream of things and bodies plummeting in space. Each *Mad Men* episode opens with the same animated sequence about a featureless black-and-white silhouette of a trim, dapperly dressed male who plunges downward into a maelstrom of images after entering a full-color modern office, which itself quivers in space and then dissipates. As this figure enters the office and puts down his briefcase, the room begins to decompose. Pictures fall from the walls, and the floor disappears as the desk and chairs tumble into a seemingly bottomless void. As the male figure plummets through a world of advertising images and slogans that litter a ghostly external avenue of glass and steel megalith corporate office buildings, we change perspectives often, feeling the fluidity and anxiety of the fall. But, oddly, when all is said and done, we reach a place of peace, when the male figure is suddenly sitting (but on what?), quite relaxed, with an air of curious, quiet contemplation, holding a cigarette at leisure in his outstretched right hand. He looks ahead of him into a blank vista with no spatial depth, a "there" that is not quite there. Nevertheless, somehow this man has landed safely. The world we are entering, though elusive and discombobulating, is not, after all, a ceaseless drop into nothingness.

This main title animation is a visual poem, a prefiguration of Don's story as part of the great tradition of America as a land of new beginnings and upward mobility. But Weiner rings many changes on the familiar American narrative about a poor, disadvantaged boy who rises to success in a land of opportunity. Here, as the main title suggests, rising is also falling: falling into the not-knowing, I would add. The art of Weiner's new beginnings story links American television to some powerful literary traditions, from both popular and high culture, that speak about the American dream.

As a modernist version of that story, however, Weiner's show is never reduced to the level of the many simplistic, formulaic accounts of upward mobility, rooted in the deliriously melioristic low-culture nineteenth-century fictions typified by the wildly popular Horatio Alger stories. These stories appeared between 1866 and 1896 and established powerful but unrealistic images of "making it" in the United States.[2] *Mad Men* has more to do with the modernist high-culture traditions in which America's romantic ideals about endless human possibility and the American image of being chosen to rise to great things have been reenvisioned by modern storytellers as tragic hubris.

Premier among the works in this tradition is F. Scott Fitzgerald's seminal land-of-opportunity novel, *The Great Gatsby* (1925), which is dominated by tragic hubris. Less widely circulated but equally if not more penetrating in its vision of self-made men is William Faulkner's novel *Absalom, Absalom!* (1936). An ill-fated new beginning is at the center of Orson Welles's *Citizen Kane* (1941), one of the films that propelled American movies into the category of cinema art. "Self-made" is the key tragic term, reflecting the creation of dazzling outward success and fatal inner disconnection from the real. The tragic protagonists of these works overlap somewhat with Don Draper: he, like them, claws his way out of a limited, desperate early life that he then hides as he climbs toward the top of the social tree. However, Fitzgerald, Faulkner, and Welles tell tales that substantially differ from that of Don Draper. Through a twist of fate he is able to escape the miserable poverty into which he was born in a whorehouse, with a prostitute mother who died in childbirth.

Don's story has big differences from his high-culture antecedents. He, like them, is catapulted by success into denial of his early life. But, although there is a kind of hubris in *Mad Men*, it is not in the final analysis tragic. While Don exhibits an inordinate and perverse confidence about what he can do to manipulate his reality, his story does not reach a tragic conclusion. Rather, in his happy ending, he more resembles the central figure in a very early American tale of a new beginning, "Rip Van Winkle" (1819) by Washington Irving. This story is one of Weiner's favorites and an important influence on his creation of *Mad Men*. We can push Don's resemblance to the majestically tragic figures created by Fitzgerald, Faulkner, and Welles only so far. Don Draper's saga is ultimately comic. At the same time, there are also limitations to the connections we can make between the tale of Rip Van Winkle and the story of Don Draper.

The tragic and comic tales of new beginnings that preceded *Mad Men* overlap with and interpenetrate each other. Weiner samples a bit of both the comic and tragic traditions. Following in the footsteps of all these stories, *Mad Men* focuses on the links between disconnection and/or dissociation and change. But it departs from the tragic new beginning story, in which the disconnection is a shift in identity during an upward rise that leads to a disastrous fall. Instead *Mad Men* engages the comic trajectory of Irving's story about Van Winkle, a lazy, good-natured slacker. He drinks a magic potion that he believes is only good beer, offered to him by strange, otherworldly men that he meets as he walks in the mountains. After sleeping for twenty years, he wakes up, finding himself out of context but in a much better situation. He is no longer under the tyranny of his abusive wife, the first of the great seminal shrews of American literature.

The specific plot events of Irving's tale are distant from those of Don Draper's story. If Weiner had not been so absolutely clear when he told me about the story's importance to his creative process, I never would have noted the connections between the spirits of the two narratives. They become increasingly visible by the time we reach Don's awakening at the end of his journey, which is unexpectedly a comic one. Until the seventh season, *Mad Men* was almost purely about disconnection and its painful consequences:

"tragic" often seems like a good characterization of the numerous turns of events in Don's story. Born Dick Whitman, son of a prostitute and child of misfortune, Weiner's protagonist joins the army to escape his dead-end life. During a confusing moment at a remote outpost in Korea, he accidentally kills Lt. Don Draper, switches dog tags with him, disavows all connection with his birth family, and leaves Korea with a new name. The new Don Draper arranges things so that the real Draper's widow, Anna (Melinda Page Hamilton), collaborates with his identity switch. He gets her to grant him a divorce so that this boy born in a whorehouse can become the patriarch of an "ideal" American family. Dick Whitman seems dead. But everything about those old days resurges for the new Don Draper with increasing intensity. With apologies to Thomas Wolfe, I note that *Man Men* insists that, paradoxically, you can never leave home, even if you do.

From the first season onward, Don takes time out from his Madison Avenue success and his Connecticut home to carry on sexual affairs with a variety of dark, offbeat, promiscuous women. If they do not remind him of Dick Whitman's mother who died at his birth, they are filaments that shackle him to the mother figures of his boyhood in the brothel. The series is an indeterminate chiaroscuro of Don and Dick, never able to demarcate where one leaves off and the other begins, very much complicating the great American tradition of new beginnings.

THIS DID NOT HAPPEN

Imagine how formulaic television would handle Don's story of borrowed identity. The long story arc would exorcise the ghosts of his earlier life against all odds and tailor the confusions of his subconscious life—maybe through the magic of formulaic therapy—to the needs of a happily conclusive cure and ending. By contrast, the story arc in *Mad Men* bends toward an untailored subconscious life that has both creative and destructive implications: Don and Dick are conflated within the flux of the narrative. The trauma of Don/Dick's history cannot be managed like an inconvenient headache. The importance of the subconscious in Don/Dick's leap from his past is too great. *Mad Men* plunges us into the volatile, unpredictable depths of the subconscious that formula television has chosen to pretend can be groomed.

The indomitable subconscious that disconcertingly weaves fragments of Don and Dick together is the force of Weiner's not-knowing: it is the engine of his new life just as it is the keeper of his old one. The not-knowing is the shining source of Don's impressive creativity, which allows him to make a future for himself very different from his past. But it has another more sinister function, as the source of a process of unknowing: Don attempts to erase Dick, using the incantation "This did not happen." In other words, Don's story is a saga of the incommensurate subconscious levels of his life. As is the case with characterization in modern narratives, there is no fit among all of the pieces of Don Draper/Dick Whitman.

In "Smoke Gets in Your Eyes" (1.1), we are quickly introduced to Don's creativity and his denials, to his impossible plan for his life. We find Don at work. At loose ends, he is trying to plan an advertising campaign for Sterling Cooper's biggest client, Lucky Strike. There's a new government initiative to clamp down on the fake health claims of the cigarette industry, and Don is edgy, flailing. He has no idea what he is doing as he meets with the tobacco kings of Lucky Strike—and it shows. The meeting is about to collapse in futility. Suddenly, as Don blindly prods the stupidly greedy company owners to talk about the product, a moment that perfectly embodies the awkwardness and daring of living in the not-knowing occurs. On the threshold between inspiration and confusion, Don finds the perfect advertising slogan, vague enough to skirt the law but emotionally evocative enough to be attractive: "It's toasted." This is true: the tobacco is toasted, a word that connotes warmth and comfort. No government watchdog can find ways to prosecute something so meaningless. The not-knowing is a state of being connected to the freedom of the subconscious. But Don is also enmeshed in denials of the power that has made him a star, as if he could select only one aspect of his interior forces.[3]

Don's "unknowing" emerges in the pilot. He takes time out from Sterling Cooper to have sex with Midge Daniels (Rosemarie DeWitt), a promiscuous, dark, bohemian artist in Greenwich Village, then returns home to Connecticut to his perfect American wife Betty and his sleeping children. In the Village Don behaves as if Connecticut does not exist, and vice versa. The silence shrouding the disconnect is almost surreal. Figuratively, as he moves among the fragments of his life, one part of Don could almost be asleep in the mountains, as Rip Van Winkle literally was. Psychological denial is in the air. If Don's creativity at the agency is a life lived in the not-knowing that taps into the rich bounty of the subconscious, his unknowing is about blocking it. As the series continues, the fruitfulness of the not-knowing dazzles us with shimmering clouds of glory while the contrasting and contradictory fragile futility of the erasures, the unknowing, raises clouds of disaster around him.

Don rises and falls at the same time. While his magic lifts him past the ties that bind him to his terrible childhood, his denials simultaneously push him toward impending collapse. The first intimations of his inevitable fall come in "5G" (1.5), when Don and the audience are blindsided. We learn that he is living not only a double life but a borrowed life, and he is forced out of denial—to some extent. The man shuttling between Greenwich Village and

Connecticut is not wholly Don Draper, despite the name on his office door and his picture in the newspaper as the recipient of an advertising award.

In "5G," while Don is at an agency meeting, a boy named Adam Whitman (Jay Paulson) appears at the reception desk. Don recognizes the name of Dick Whitman's younger brother. His own brother and not his brother. After all, he has said good-bye to "all that." Or has he? "Who is Don Draper?" Adam Whitman asks of the man he once knew as Dick Whitman. It is the question of the series, never to be answered. Twenty years of being Dick Whitman cannot be erased by twenty years of being Don Draper. But twenty years of being Don Draper cannot be wiped out either. When confronted by Adam, Don's identity war flares up.

Adam becomes collateral damage in this first major skirmish of the series. Erratically, Don offers to meet Adam at a nearby coffee shop, offers to buy him lunch, rescinds the offer, and leaves abruptly, saying, "This never happened." Don (Dick?) bribes Adam with $5,000 to leave town, hugs him with the warmth of a brother, and abandons him. Who is dismissing Adam: Don or Dick? Who is Adam hugging: Don or Dick? Who is offering Adam his own new beginning: Don or Dick? Who weeps brokenly behind closed doors when Adam does not make a new beginning but hangs himself instead? Is Don still there or not? Don and the audience spend seven seasons shuttling between the elation of the not-knowing and the panic inherent in the futility of seeking the erasures of unknowing.

In "Nixon vs. Kennedy" (1.12), the panic crests again. Don's junior colleague, Pete Campbell, is brash, Ivy League, and filled with a sense of upper-class entitlement—unlike Adam, who only wanted family love and connection, Pete discovers Don's secret life and intends to use his newly acquired information as a weapon. Don has decided against giving Pete a promotion. Pete tries to blackmail Don into giving it to him—or else. Pete threatens to "tell all" to Bert Cooper, the patriarch of Sterling Cooper. In a formula TV series, this power struggle would be the crux of the episode. Here the name "Don Draper" once again takes on a Eugène Ionesco surrealism as it ricochets among bodies: in a flashback, for the first time, we see the Lt. Don Draper who was Dick Whitman's commanding officer in Korea. There is a dizzying proliferation of living and dead Don Drapers and Dick Whitmans. Dick in the flashback reaches for the dog tags on the corpse of Don Draper; Dick in present time remembers the real Don Draper. "Who is Don Draper?" The question will always bristle with darkly comic multiple answers.

Pete Campbell's threatened resurrection of Dick Whitman throws the Korean-made Don Draper into a frenzy. The composite Dick/Don cannot switch dog tags with anyone now or send Pete packing with $5,000, so he tries to disappear again. He runs to one of his current lovers, the extremely rich, dark, Jewish Rachel Menken (Maggie Siff), determined to convince her to run away with him. "We'll go somewhere else; we'll start over, like Adam and Eve." Who would he be dislodged from his Connecticut family and his job at Sterling Cooper: Dick, or Don, or Adam? Rachel Menken asks the question somewhat differently when she pulls back from his ease at abandoning his children and breaks off their relationship, asking, "What kind of man are you?" It is a question that goes forever unanswered.

Pete makes good on his threat and tells all to Cooper when Don refuses to give him the promotion. Cooper shocks characters and audience alike by replying, "Who cares?" All but giving a lecture on the American tradition of new beginnings, upward mobility, and the American dream, Cooper says, "This country was built and run by men with worse stories than whatever you've imagined here." He elaborates further: "The Japanese have a saying: a man is whatever room he is in, and right now Don Draper is in this room. I assure you, there is more profit in forgetting this. I'd put your energy into bringing in accounts." (Apparently the Japanese have their own versions of new beginnings.) Don lives in a society that supports his confusion and chaos as its reality. How to live with such knowledge? Desperately and by reliving the moment of unknowing, it would seem.

Don has taught himself to unknow. In addition to teaching Peggy Olson, his office protégé, to work her way up from secretary to copy editor at Sterling Cooper, at a historical time and in a place quite inhospitable to the ambitions of women, he teaches her to unknow too, as we see in "The New Girl" (2.5). It is a part of his ongoing struggle to validate his erasures. Peggy has just given birth to Pete Campbell's baby, conceived the night before his wedding to a woman of his own class. She can neither make claims on Pete nor keep the baby if she wants a career. It is her moment on the battlefield, and Don pays her a visit in the maternity hospital. No one at Sterling Cooper has been given any information about where she is. She has no idea how Don could have found her. Figuratively, he hands her a new set of dog tags. "It never happened," he tells her. "Peggy, listen to me, get out of here and move forward. This never happened. It will shock you how much it never happened." In desperation, she takes his advice. Is there a whiff of Dick Whitman in the air? Is it Dick or Don at her bedside? But unknowing works again, or seems to, and now he has a companion in the twilight zone.

The waves of Don's fantastic disavowals crest again in "The Phantom" (5.13), the fifth season finale. Don's success as part of an expanding Sterling Cooper once again seems to indicate that he has also succeeded in erasing the past. But the past comes roaring back as Don has hallucinations of seeing his dead brother. The ghost he has made of himself through his denials reverberates with intensity. Don stands on the brink of expanding his success as Sterling Cooper expands its success, but his disconnection stares him in the face with increasing ferocity. He visits the set where his second wife, Megan (Jessica Paré), is getting ready to shoot a commercial, a door opened for her by Don's professional success. As the episode and the season come to a close, Megan is being fawned over as she gets ready to be filmed. Don leaves her to her to the newfound success that he has made possible, striding purposefully from a sound stage. The main title from the James Bond feature *You Only Live Twice* (1967) blares nondiegetically on the series soundtrack. The humorous association between Don and Bond, the dashing, professionally invincible, womanizing pop culture hero, would seem to tell us that Don is on his way to some momentous undertaking. But he is not. He is on his way to an upscale bar: on his way, as it turns out, to yet another confrontation with his catastrophic detachment.

The lyric of the Bond song underlines both Don's double and borrowed life in the words "one life for yourself and one for your dreams." The season finale juxtaposes the inherent conflict of those two lives for Don: his appearance of self-assuredness versus his essential solitude. As he sits at the elegant bar, an overdressed party girl approaches and asks him, "Are you alone?" These are the final words of the season. The only response is the expression on Don's face in close-up, a mixture of cynicism and resentment as he turns to her. He is alone and he is not: the moment is Weiner's engagement of

FIGURE 5.1. *"Are you alone?": A glorious moment of Don's undefinable truth.*

the audience in this oxymoron as a prelude to the complexity of the series denouement ahead.

In the final season, Weiner conjures a fitting conclusion to Don's story by bringing him to connection via disconnection, letting him go home via homelessness, and succeed through failure in a way that must make us work, think, question, and accept indeterminacy and wonder. Don's slippage between his old and new identities takes on extreme urgency, as he succeeds and fails at the same time. He has reached the zenith of his advertising career as the new prince of McCann Erickson, the largest of the ad agencies that bought Sterling Cooper. Their clients are the most profitable on the Madison Avenue scene, including Coca-Cola, the acme of the ad man's dream. Don is crowned by its chief executive officer, Jim Hobart (H. Richard Greene), who courts him like a trophy wife. At exactly the same time, Don reaches the nadir of his life: he is swallowed up as never before by an uncontrollable yearning for his roots in the denied past, embodied in another dark lady. Diana Baur (Elizabeth Reaser), an elusive, promiscuous, sadomasochistic, coffee-shop waitress whom he has met by chance, appeals to his Dick Whitman fragment.

Caught between Hobart/Coca-Cola, the apex of his journey upward toward success, and Diana, the personified form of his constantly insurgent inner Dick Whitman, Don/Dick runs away again, but with a difference. He is ostensibly driven to go in search of Diana, who has disappeared suddenly, but is actually taking the last steps of the psychic journey of indefinable reclamation that is *Mad Men*. Without the reductive psychologizing and ultimate diagnosis and cure that would have been mandatory for such a trip in formula television, Don/Dick simultaneously and enigmatically moves closer to both the abandoned life of Dick Whitman and the triumph of Don Draper.

Don does not find Diana when he drives to the place where she once lived in Wisconsin, but he is impelled to keep driving west. In Oklahoma, he revisits the trauma of his actions in Korea. This moment seems like it will exorcise his ghosts, and would have in formulaic TV, but it does not in Weiner's narrative. Don's Cadillac breaks down. While he is having it fixed, he makes an unplanned stop at a rural Oklahoma motel whose owner convinces him to attend an American Legion benefit for one of the local men whose house burned down. Getting drunk with a few of the veterans, he is given partial absolution for Korea. When everyone is completely pie-eyed, an old World War II vet confesses that he and some other starving American soldiers cannibalized some German soldiers they captured, so Don makes his own confession about "killing his C.O." in Korea—without revealing that he switched dog tags with the man he killed. "And I got to go home," he says.

The drunks around the table are very understanding about murder and cannibalism if it helps you come home.

This turns out to be far from an epiphany that brings peace, however. A young Indian boy named Cal (Jack DePew) who works at the motel steals the proceeds from the benefit. In a moment comparable to Don switching the dog tags, Cal makes it look as if Don is the thief, reasoning that this cannot matter to a rich man driving a Cadillac and that he need not respect money given to a man who burned his own house down. In Cal, who wants to get out of Oklahoma as badly as Don wanted to get out of Korea, Don meets his mirror image. He pays the price for Cal, the price that he did not pay in Korea for his own theft of Don Draper's life. When he passively cooperates with Cal's plan, the Oklahoma vets, who are not as understanding about stolen money as they were of cannibalism and a dead commanding officer, break into Don's motel room. They beat him, threatening to hold his car hostage until the money is returned. Don gives Cal his get-out-of-jail-free card: he has to give Don the money so that he can return it to the vigilantes. Cal gets the Cadillac and his liberation from a dead end. But reliving Korea in altered form through Cal and the vets is not the end of Don's pilgrimage.

Don's last stop is California, where he and his inner Dick Whitman reach an indefinable detente. Dick/Don arrives unannounced on the doorstep of the real Don Draper's twenty-something niece, Stephanie Horton (Caity Lotz). She has just had a baby but is suffering from guilt because she does not want to be a mother and has given the baby to the parents of his father, her ex-boyfriend. Don/Dick and Stephanie know each other because of Don/Dick's warm relationship with Stephanie's aunt, the real Mrs. Draper, but they do not know each other well. Stephanie, on her way to a New Age retreat, hoping to achieve some peace about her abdication of maternal responsibility, takes Don with her. Don replays his visit to Peggy in the maternity ward, but this time the outcome is very different. When Stephanie's guilt proves too powerful for the meditations and support groups at the retreat, Don tells her to forget that the baby ever happened. Stephanie stuns Don by tearing into him, angrily reminding him that he is not really her uncle. Stephanie refuses to unknow the existence of her baby boy and leaves Don at the retreat without telling him. Stephanie's rejection breaks the illusion of unknowing, which paves the way for a wave of the creativity of the not-knowing to crest. But only after Don experiences a full collapse. Stephanie literally leaves him a heap on the ground, unable to move.

Are those the crumpled remains of Dick Whitman we see? Or a radically broken Don Draper? What is left? The Don and Dick conundrum is never

FIGURE 5.2. *Dick Whitman/Don Draper recognizes Leonard's suffering.*

settled, but Don does find something to sustain him. Guided in his helplessness to another seminar for want of a better alternative, he hears the
confession of Leonard (Evan Arnold), a man he does not know. Atypically,
in this setting of long-haired hippies in robes, Leonard sports a Madison
Avenue haircut and a Brooks Brothers wardrobe, an alter ego of Don's suave
persona suddenly arising before Don's eyes. As Leonard admits to feeling
empty, invisible, and absent in his own life, he breaks down in sobs. Unexpectedly, Don, who is at this point neither fully in control of himself nor out
of control, neither Don Draper or Dick Whitman, rises and walks over to
embrace Leonard. The two men sob together. Is it Dick who finally finds a
place inside Don that acknowledges his existence compassionately? Is it Don
who compassionately finds his inner invisibility and sense of isolation from
the earlier life he led? Are they integrated with each other so as to be able
to experience a previously unknown humanity and compassion? We do not
know. All we know is that in this comic moment we are in the presence of
the not-knowing fully blessing Don's emotional life at last.

We have traced an interesting line through *Mad Men* that constitutes
the development of Don Draper's internal and external conflicts. However,
we have not exhausted the ways in which Weiner has richly indicated the
presence of inner forces that animate Don's story. It becomes evident after
Don's collapse that he is returning to Madison Avenue at the top of his
game, through the juxtaposition of his life at the retreat with a very famous
television Coca-Cola commercial. This is the climax of a series of unusually

detailed portrayals of Don/Dick's advertising pitches. However, their primary function in *Mad Men* is to serve as maps of Don's inner life.

ADVERTISEMENTS FOR HIMSELF

By his own account, Weiner gives extensive screen time to Don's development of his advertising campaigns as staging areas for revealing his interior life. This is arguably where Weiner's originality, personal approach to narrative, and love of multiplicity shine brightest. Artistically these scenes are dazzling models of Weiner's ideal of achieving multiple narrative purposes simultaneously, especially the campaigns for Kodak, Hershey, Burger Chef, and Coca-Cola, the pièce de resistance. They offer no judgments on the ethics of advertising manipulation that might be involved, which would have been of concern to David Simon if he were writing a series about ad men. The only context that dynamically interests Weiner is Don's inner psychology and the psychological dynamics of perception, which these pitches embody.

We are introduced to the pitches as advertisements for Don's inner life when he woos the men from Lucky Strike in the first episode of *Mad Men*. The evidence is there from the beginning that Weiner is not overstating the case when he says, as he did to me, that he does not care about advertising. Advertising in *Mad Men* is a vehicle of narrative revelation.[4] This could not be clearer than in Don's spectacularly entrancing pitch to Kodak in "The Wheel" (1.13), which registers only slightly as a professional achievement and overwhelmingly as an oblique confession about the painful experience of his Rip Van Winkle–like disappearance from his own life. Similarly, his blighted presentation to emissaries from Hershey's chocolate in "In Care Of" (6.13) is addressed primarily to the nondiegetic audience rather than the Hershey team, as an imaginative foreshadowing of his coming breakdown. The spiel for fast food in "The Strategy" (7.6), when Don is working with Peggy Olson on a pitch for Burger Chef, is a poetic vehicle for undoing their pact of denial and unknowing and transmuting it into a mutual move in the creative direction of not-knowing. In the final episode of the series, "Person to Person" (7.14), the Coca-Cola television ad follows suit, as a payoff for all the pitches that have gone before it.

In pitching to Kodak, Don is establishing an advertising campaign for a new technology, a wheel that can be preloaded with slides that are projected onto a screen with the push of a button as the wheel revolves. This would eliminate the bother of loading each slide separately, projecting it, and removing it to make way for the next one. During the pitch, he is both at the height of Don Draper's charismatic prowess as an ad man and at the depth of Dick Whitman's personal sorrow. As Don uses slides of his own family, clicking by images of his marriage, his children, and family happiness, he renames the wheel for Kodak with a magisterial flare. "It's not called the wheel; it's called the carousel," he says, and the room is filled with magic. But the speech also projects the way he has severed himself from his roots, when he tells the Kodak men that it is nostalgia that makes this carousel turn, "delicate, but potent," the pain from an old wound that enchants. "It's a twinge in your heart far more powerful than memory alone. This device isn't a space ship; it's a time machine. It goes backwards and forwards . . . it takes us to a place where we ache to go again. . . . It lets us travel the way a child travels, round and round and back home again to a place where we know we are loved."[5]

Weiner's intentions for this speech are interesting. He claims it as "an honest acknowledgment of the emotional sacrifice that men make. No one thinks we give a shit. Everyone talks about how hard it is for women to go back to work. But there is a silence about how men feel; it is a social lie that we have no attachment to our families and our kids. Because society assumes that the satisfaction of being the breadwinner is what we are interested in. And that's how you express your love. But it's a huge sacrifice. And when Don is looking at these pictures and remembering how much he loved his wife and that his kids are growing up and that he can't go back there." The pitch is Don's ode to the sorrow of his detachment. It elaborates on the way his personal anguish strikes him more potently as his professional success is enhanced.

Don returns home to an empty house. Betty and the children have gone to her parents' house for Thanksgiving, leaving him alone. He wants to avoid spending time with Betty's family. As Weiner says, "like Rip Van Winkle he comes home to the reality of what he wants [his family], but he has made his own bed and he has to sleep in it . . . emotionally he has missed his life." Some personal angst on Weiner's part is blended in here: he told me that he identified with Don sitting at the bottom of the stairs of his empty home, the final image in the season. So the Kodak pitch is made up to some degree of Don's and Weiner's suffering, but there is also more to it. Weiner told me about that too, but obliquely. Don's sense of being cut off from his family with Betty reopens the wound of being cut off from his own past. At this point, he wrongheadedly sees this as a wound inflicted on him, but he will come to understand it differently.

The inability to go back in time and remake it the way it was supposed to be is key to this amazing speech. In Weiner's words, "And the meta part of it is guess what? This is why you like this show. Not because you're going back in time and I'm telling you how great it was and you were so innocent, but because you can see the fact that you can't go back, which is painful, and also because you're remembering things that are very specific and not necessarily positive." Loss of all kinds, rooted in a horrible childhood and a searingly painful release from that childhood on a Korean battlefield, which is at the bottom of Don's unstable identity, cannot be expressed directly by Don but finds expression through his Kodak ad.

There is not enough space here to mark all of the incremental steps toward Don's final liberating acknowledgment of his pain through the ads that he creates as he approaches the collapse of the house of lies he has built. So we will skip to the Hershey pitch in "The Quality of Mercy" (6.12), which is the next major milestone in revelatory ad campaigns. By this time, the family nostalgia that was so vital and vivid in the Kodak pitch is tired, a pro-forma repetition that Weiner likens to the trap of unrelenting repetitions in *Groundhog Day*.[6] Don begins by wowing the Hershey men with a new version of his customary advertising mythos of the family when he invokes a tableau of a boy and his dad bonding over a Hershey, the father ruffling son's hair affectionately. He gives it the personal touch by passing it off for the Hershey men as a nostalgic scene from his own life and brings his pseudoautobiographical evocation of Hershey's place in the perfect childhood to a crescendo with the campaign slogan: "Hershey's is the currency of affection; it is the childhood symbol for love." This has the desired effect: everyone is ready to shake hands and congratulate Don on another virtuoso performance.

But the creative not-knowing collides in this moment with the denials of unknowing, producing a nuclear explosion. Don recants his pitch and confesses to a very different memory about Hershey's, father, and love—a memory of the whorehouse that his father ran. His advertising colleagues, of course, know nothing about this memory and its connection for him with Hershey's chocolate. As a child, Don learned about Milton Hershey's charitable school for orphans and impoverished children from magazines lying around the whorehouse toilets. He dreamed of going there but got no closer to the Hershey school than the Hershey Bars he got from one of the whores as a reward if he found more than a dollar in the pockets of her Johns while she was having sex with them. Eating it made him feel like a normal child: "It was the only sweet thing in my life."

We can easily imagine a melioristic formulaic television show in which Don is rewarded for his honesty ("My boy, few would have shown the courage you've shown today"). *Mad Men* is not that show. Playing out this pitch is not a matter of standard plot function, although it does result in a crucial plot-related event. Don is sent on leave, tantamount to being fired. One can also imagine a cynical formulaic series in which these events would define how a person is rewarded for lying and punished for telling the truth in our society. But that is the way of formula television with its clarity of causes and effects, whether it comes to a happy or a sad conclusion. By contrast, in *Mad Men*, the Hershey pitch scene is primarily about the many contradictions of the moment. Most of all, it is a brief moment of first contact between Don Draper and Dick Whitman. Shattering as it may be in practical ways, it is also a step forward toward awakening through his creative forces. That leads to an increasing sense of the need to deal with the schism that he created with his new beginning. The trajectory toward the depths is the real direction of the series.

In the final season, an ad campaign is again the occasion for a breakthrough. In "The Strategy" (7.6), Don is in limbo with respect to the externals of his life. The agency has demoted him to being a member of Peggy Olson's campaign team instead of the head of his own. He is now working for the woman who was once his secretary and who joined him in a pact of unknowing denial. As he and Peggy work on a pitch for Burger Chef, their deep connection through the denials—his childhood and her baby—transforms into a new connection, just as deep but positive instead of negative: a connection in the creative not-knowing.

Peggy and Don are doing an all-nighter to perfect the agency's proposal. Peggy already has an idea, but she and Don know that a pitch that would please the client would be full of tired clichés about family, dinner, and mothers and fathers and would not really be the best they can do. The rejection of worn-out successes is very much part of the road back from Don's Hershey disaster after he rejected a tired but effective pitch. In this moment, Weiner comes closer to articulating through Don his core beliefs as an artist than anywhere else in the series. "How do you know?" Peggy asks, exasperated by the blurred boundaries between an easy formulaic idea and a fresh, nonformulaic idea. Don tells her that she cannot know, she must live in the "not-knowing." And Peggy undergoes a transformation. When she lets go and opens up to what might be inside, an idea comes to her, fresh and beyond cliché. The solution, a campaign proposing a new idea about the family, satisfies the needs of the plot. Peggy and Don have hit on the advertising answer. But the more important consequence of this moment is beyond words, beyond answer, and filled with mystery and wonder.

At the moment when Peggy finds her Burger Chef idea, the radio begins to play Frank Sinatra singing his signature song, "My Way." This is an original use of the song, which is generally understood as the anthem of machismo, individualism, and in our vocabulary the perfect hero and external conquest. Here it plays at the moment when "we did it": it is about interiority, empathy, and friendship. It is a moment filled with magic, a pas de deux of friendship, peace, and quiet happiness that is externalized when

FIGURE 5.3. *Peggy and Don face the music and dance—confusedly.*

Don invites Peggy to dance to the music. Their dance is a fascinatingly indeterminate spectacle that in formulaic TV would have been a fabricated prelude to sex and/or a romantic relationship.[7] Here it is the moment of not-knowing again made palpable.

The dance puzzles them both. Peggy is at first hesitant to accept Don's invitation to take a few turns around the office, and Don's expression also reads as confusion. It is not anything that can be easily labeled. Rather it is a strange healing moment that arises from unnamed and unnamable motives within each of them and changes the basis of their emotional intimacy from one based on evasion—this did not happen—to one based on presence—mutual achievement. There is no way to define this intimacy through any of the usual televisual classifications of male-female relationships. Weiner envisions Peggy as a mother figure for Don, despite his unchanging role as her mentor, which might suggest to others that she figures more logically as a daughter figure. Both remain possible in the fluid moment of their celebration. It is a moment bursting with a myriad of questions that need not be answered, just savored and contemplated as we draw closer to Don's equally multivalent comic denouement that lays the groundwork for the last commercial.

We reach that closure in the final minutes of "Person to Person" (7.14), the series finale. It is, indeed, the very last thing we see in *Mad Men*. Rather than any standard scenes depicting Don back in New York with his children or even with colleagues developing the Coca-Cola pitch, this is the vehicle for communicating Don's return. We cut silently from Don's empathetic embrace of the sobbing Leonard (described) above, to Don as part of a group at the retreat, sitting in lotus position and meditating, and then to the Coke ad.

Our last glimpse of Don finds him withdrawn into himself at a New Age retreat in California, meditating alone among other meditators, who are also drawn within. His face is relaxed and peaceful. His lips curve into a gently surprised smile as we cut to an actual print of the famous Coca-Cola commercial picturing a hillside of young people of every race, male and female, singing about Coke being "the real thing." It is a commercial predicated on the yearning for connection, with its sense of universal kinship, and its opening line: "I'd like to buy the world a home and furnish it with love."

The juxtaposition of Don in meditation with the Coca-Cola commercial is highly enigmatic and filled with questions. It has the sweet smell of success, but this is no formulaic happy ending. There is no trace of absolute clarity, as the final moments of *Mad Men* mysteriously merge the power of the subconscious and the materialistic might of commerce. In Matt Weiner's words: "Well, my feeling was that Don's enlightenment would be productive in the origins of that ad when he went back to McCann. And that he was on the team and was influential in it. . . . I hate explaining this, but I don't really care. I don't see why it makes me less of an artist, that he went back and he chose life. The guy who had rejected love in any ad because it was so phony was feeling it in a different way."

Certainly, common stereotypes about advertising do not associate television commercials with love or with choosing life. Certainly, the former McCann Erickson, the name of a real-world ad agency, has loomed as the enemy for Don, as the company he has worked with all his might to avoid. Yet, from the first, the series has depicted unexpected comic connections between means and ends.

The *Mad Men* series finale is the most powerful of Weiner's portrayals of oblique relationships between cause and effect. Triumph is in the air, both interior and exterior, but which one has made the difference? Unspecified intimations of external success? Or intimations of some kind of undefined internal breakthrough? Within the world of the series this is not just a clever solution to the problem of formulaic closure but a summation of the uncertainty of a life like Don's, predicated on discontinuities, and also of the uncertainties and discontinuities of perception in the global world of *Mad Men*. Perception and its mysteries are at the heart of the advertising world represented in the series; they are also central to the way we watch television, although formulaic narratives suppress those enigmas, attempting to persuade us that there is only one way to see things: along the narrative tracks leading toward closure. Weiner, by contrast, encourages us to experience perception in all its complexities as part of the storytelling and as a meta-textual comment on our viewing experiences.

OCULAR CASTLES IN THE AIR

The series has been lavishly and widely praised for its thorough and precise rendition of the look of the 1960s. This may be another way Weiner was influenced and encouraged by his time on *The Sopranos*, studying David Chase's perfectionism with detail. Yet other seminal influences should also be considered, such as Weiner's observation of how perception figures in the dreams that Chase used in *The Sopranos* and influences from Weiner's college days: his fascination with feminist discussions, particularly about the male gaze, and his discovery of the relativity of perception suggested by the discipline of optics. Weiner has been much impressed by studies about sight suggesting that perception of color is subjective: for example, that the color blue is not necessarily a universal experience. He has been particularly interested in the way Edwin Land, the developer of Polaroid technology, explored perceptual relativity. Embedding gendered and scientific subjectivities into *Mad Men*, Weiner has made the visual texture of the series an experience of perceptual ambiguity.

Weiner pointed out to me how he played with Don's attempts to master his own perceptions and those of others through the seasons in order to exercise authority, particularly over women. This meshes narratively with his turmoil about women, which constantly threatens to resurrect the traumas rooted in the discarded life of Dick Whitman. But bringing this to the viewers' attention also meshes with the complexity of the audience's experience of Weiner's art as a storyteller. Weiner depicts Don's visual compulsions as being somewhat sadistic in nature. The way he attempts to subject women to his gaze comes straight out of the feminist discourse he learned in college. At the same time, Don's failure to achieve visual dominance comes straight out of Weiner's speculation about the relativity of sight. Together they create an original texture for Don, whose slippages from control constantly occur when he is most determined to use women as a way of bolstering his denials.

Weiner paid some attention to Don's visual compulsions in the first season, but he began in earnest to form a perspective for the show in the second season, when he felt freer to play with his ideas about perception once he had assurances that *Mad Men* would not be a one-season series. In "For Those Who Think Young" (2.1), for example, Weiner opens the second season with a tantalizing presentation of Don's visual fetishes. He has arranged to meet his wife Betty for a Valentine's Day celebration at her favorite restaurant in a hotel where he has reserved a room for an erotic and sexual tryst, marriage

FIGURE 5.4. *Don's perception of Betty as his creation.*

style. Betty makes an entrance into the restaurant suitable to the occasion, down a long, ornate staircase, looking much like Grace Kelly, in a stunning cocktail gown and expensive fur coat, to the lushly romantic exoticism of the nondiegetic strains of "Song of the Indian Guest," by Nikolai Rimsky-Korsakov. To some extent, she is offering herself as a feast for Don's eyes, but Don sees Betty as his creation. Weiner suggests the way Don sees this moment by superimposing a very large image of his head, as large as Betty's entire body, over her descent, and altering the speed of the camera so that she seems to glide toward Don. But Don's experience of mastery is fleeting.

Once the two of them get up to the hotel room, Betty has a surprise for him that changes the mood. Removing her Princess Grace dress of floating beige chiffon, Betty gives Don an eyeful, standing there for his viewing pleasure in her high heels, a black merry widow corset and stockings, a sudden emergence of the image of a woman in charge of her own sexuality. The operative word is "gives." Although Don dutifully expresses appreciation for Betty's "present" to him, we see that at a much deeper level her display unmans him: he cannot consummate sex with her, a highly atypical moment for a man we have seen make his way through liaisons with many partners with virility and assurance. This is only an introduction to his angst about ocular dominance, as we shall soon note, and only part of the big picture of *Mad Men.* The culture of this fictional universe is one in which men's feeling of well-being is often linked to male delusional normalization of male perceptions as the only reality in a world in which reality is manifold.

FIGURE 5.5. *Betty exuberantly unaware of the dangers for Don in her creation of her own image.*

"Maidenform" (2.6), Weiner's favorite episode in the series, is particularly rich in its portrayal of gender-based perception that builds on Don's visual control issues through exploration of a general inclination in that direction at Sterling Cooper. The episode takes its name from the campaign for Maidenform brassieres that is the priority professional initiative in this episode. However, that campaign is juxtaposed with Peggy Olson's work on a presentation for an auxiliary venture for Mohawk Airlines. The two campaigns in counterpoint combine to call attention to the aggressiveness of male perceptions, the discounting—and fear—of female perceptions, and the show's depiction of a multivalent relativistic fictional universe. Evaluating Peggy's ideas for a Mohawk pitch, Don tells her he does not "feel" her initial ideas; clearly this is a gender divide. He is not compelled by her thinking until she hits on an idea that angles toward Don's fatherly feelings about his daughter. This dramatic preparation pays off handsomely when we watch her experience the same thing on a larger scale: she sits with the men on Don's staff as they brainstorm about a campaign, this time for clothing that only women buy and wear, Maidenform brassieres. With no self-awareness at all, the men in the office presume that their campaign should be based on the premise that we women desire only to see ourselves as men see us.

The men are tickled by their "observation" that all women fall into two categories of contemporary femininity: a Marilyn (Monroe) or a Jackie (Kennedy).[8] Peggy's discomfort with these pigeonholes is obvious, but not to the men, who are so amused with their idea that they make a visual sweep of the secretaries and other women outside of their office, cataloguing each one. The men cannot really collapse women into these two options. But they cling to what they mistake for perception even though they cannot perceive that Peggy, sitting right there with them, is neither a Marilyn or a Jackie. The perceptual disconnect remains. The audience notices, even if the guys in the room do not.

With the air so full of the multiplicity and gendered nature of perception, Don takes time out to take a side trip to the hotel room of Bobbie Barrett (Melinda McGraw), a dangerous affair with yet another dark woman. The scene gives us sudden intimations of not only Don's blindness to evidence that contradicts his beliefs but the fury that ensues if that assumption is shattered or even scratched. As Don and Bobbie engage in foreplay, she babbles distractedly about the widely circulated gossip about his sexual exploits. She intends to excite him with her chatter, but she does not understand him. He will not be the object of what people see and say. Don's ardor turns to cruelty, as he ties Bobbie's hands to the headboard. She initially sees this enthusiastically as a prelude to kinky sex but soon realizes that he is leaving her there, not only sexually unsatisfied but in a state of bondage that confirms that he has the upper hand. She is clueless about his determination that he will be the one who looks at a woman who has no control over what he sees. But the audience has been given a way to actively ponder what Don is about. Such prompts to active thought are all over the series. We find another example in Valentine's Day with Betty, and notably in "A Little Kiss, Part I" (5.1), when Megan, his second wife, throws Don a surprise birthday party and performs a sexy dance for him. He responds with icy fury.

In "Maidenform," Don's colleagues are foils, reflecting his precarious control through optical dominance—and not only during the Maidenform planning session. A subsequent scene features one of Don's colleagues, Duck Phillips (Mark Moses), an alcoholic colleague who is struggling to stay on the wagon, and his dog, who often exist in combination in the series regarding male identity. Pathetically and cruelly Phillips abandons his dog to the streets of Manhattan because he sees the dog looking at him as he reaches for a bottle of liquor. Male ocular issues tantalizingly come to a head in the final moments of "Maidenform." Don's cherished little daughter, Sally (Kiernan Shipka), sweetly comes into the bathroom to watch him shave. Unaccountably, as he is looking into the mirror, he is suddenly unable to stand the pressure of her gaze at him and tells her that she needs to leave him alone.

After Sally leaves the room, Weiner and director Phil Abraham depict Don as he cowers on the toilet seat, caught by the camera in a fit of anguish.

He feels stirrings of a shock of recognition, not yet fully matured, of his false sense of how to hold the world and women under his sway. As he suffers, the camera drifts away from him, as though it will release him from our sight, but it does not. It catches him again in the reflection of a mirror in which he appears, fixed irrevocably beyond his control. His fantasies of dominance are there for us to see as an abysmal hoax of which he not yet aware, which has colored both his marriages. His infantilization of Betty and his abusive games of domination with Megan threaten his bond with his daughter and will appear again in season 6 in the sadistic adulterous games he plays with the wife of the doctor who lives downstairs. This really remarkable episode in which the long arc of Don's external voyage does not advance is rich in its deepening of his internal voyage.[9]

With the passing seasons, Weiner's interest in how Don, the other characters, and the audience see blossoms into a further examination of the role of the subconscious through its evocation of the mind's eye in Don's dreams and visions. At first, dreams and visions are a question of images generated by the subconscious as the tormenting return of the repressed. But ultimately, as Don grows and changes, there is delight for Don and for the audience in what surfaces from the depths. By the time of "Waterloo" (7.7), the approaching sea change in Don's relationship to his inner turmoil is reflected in a new cast to his interior images. In this episode, all America is watching television coverage of astronaut Neil Armstrong's first step onto the moon, using actual period tapes of the event. The news enfolds the American myth of the new beginning so that it reappears, radiating real possibilities, as old limits are broken. In Don's life, this juxtaposition is embodied by Bert Cooper's death right after the moon landing, which generates refreshed productions of the mind's eye. As everyone else attends an office memorial, Don drifts away and in solitude has a vision of Cooper singing and dancing to "The Best Things in Life Are Free," surrounded by chorus girls dressed as secretaries. It is a perfect example of the transformative ways in which the subconscious makes us see. Cooper in life was entirely unrelated to the sentiments of the song: "The moon belongs to everyone; the best things in life are free." Cooper is a bachelor whose days of women and song are long gone. He has never been anything but a materialistic adherent of the ungenerous, inhumane ideas of Ayn Rand, who preached ad nauseam that the best things in life belong to the strongest, most ruthless among us. At Cooper's passing, however, Don's inner life gives Cooper permission to feel joy.

Mad Men, in so many ways, depicts the helplessness of human beings before the subjectivities of perception regardless of class, gender, and status. Creativity simultaneously emanates from the very same subconscious that

FIGURE 5.6. *Don's subjective Cooper.*

brings pain. This hydra-headed relationship to inner processes is at the core of narrative progression in the series, creating a turmoil of highs and lows that the show defines as the stuff of human life. And so we continually wonder if Don's new beginning, and the vicissitudes of all the characters, so soaked in subconscious forces, is a blessing or a curse. *Mad Men* offers no formulaic answers to those questions.

WE REALLY DON'T KNOW LIFE AT ALL

The characters in *Mad Men* are driven by forces over which they have no control, inhabiting a country dominated by a confusing moral relativity. Their very perceptions are often fictions that they unknowingly create. Lack of definitive knowledge characterizes the human condition in this fictional universe. The series suggests that artists of all kinds have been telling us this for a while. Culture also has a subconscious, through its art and music, with which Weiner sprinkles his episodes to form a metatextual commentary that humanizes a frightening world.

The reflexivity of the metatext in *Mad Men* bejewels the episodes from time to time with works of art and music that suggest a wider cultural endorsement of the necessity for internal journeys as we make our way through culture. Culture demands decisions that presuppose clarity and certainty. But the artists tell us that is not true knowledge. This perspective makes an appearance in *Mad Men* through John O'Hara's collection of lyrics, *Meditations in an Emergency*, which accidentally enters Don's life.

Additionally, the audience makes the acquaintance of "The Man with the Miniature Orchestra," a short story written in secret by one of the younger Sterling Cooper account executives, Ken Cosgrove (Aaron Staton), under the pen name Dave Algonquin. We also see an excerpt from *America Hurrah*, a play by Jean-Claude van Itallie. As Don's life begins to turn toward his awakening, for our ears only, Judy Collins's version of a popular song, "Both Sides, Now," written by Joni Mitchell, appears on the soundtrack at a crucial point. In each case, Weiner suggests the cultural discourse about exactly the kind of liminality that we see permeating Sterling Cooper and the lives of those associated with it.

In "For Those Who Think Young" (2.1), a copy of *Meditations in an Emergency* pops up in the hands of a complete stranger in a bar where Don is having a drink. Leaping into the not-knowing, Don buys the book. We are left to wonder about how he is affected by it, particularly by the lyrical "Mayakovsky," an O'Hara poem about identity that invokes "the catastrophe of my personality." Don speaks the poem's final quatrain in voiceover:

> It may be the coldest day of
> The year, what does he think of
> That? I mean, what do I? And if I do,
> Perhaps I am myself again.

Does he send the book to Anna Draper because the poem is a cultural reflection of his identity issues that only she knows about at that point?

In "Signal 30" (5.5), we peek into Ken Cosgrove's short story, "The Man with the Miniature Orchestra." Again, Weiner suggests that art is a steam valve for expressing pent-up angst for people who dare not reveal themselves otherwise. Cosgrove is one of the secondary ad agency characters and frequently behaves like a fraternity boy, often making inappropriately suggestive and sexist comments to the secretaries. His inner world is very different, however; there he is a sensitive commentator on human affairs. The importance of that inner life to this man who seems the essence of superficiality is underlined by the necessity that he write in secret. When he publishes a short story in *Atlantic*, he is chastised by Roger Sterling for spreading himself too thin. Sterling wants Cosgrove's undivided attention for the business of Sterling Cooper and threatens Cosgrove's job if he continues to write and publish fiction. Cosgrove makes a big public show of giving up his sinful engagement in art but covertly clings to expressing behind closed doors the strangeness of human experience that he cannot express in ordinary conversation:

There were phrases of Beethoven's 9th Symphony that still made Coe cry. He always thought it had to do with the circumstances of the composition itself. He imagined Beethoven, deaf and soul-sick, his heart broken, scribbling furiously while death stood in the doorway, clipping his nails. Still, Coe thought, it might be living in the country that was making him cry. It was killing him with its silence and loneliness, making everything ordinary, too beautiful to bear.

But cultural acknowledgment of loneliness and confusion is not always welcome to Don. In a later episode, "Christmas Waltz" (5.10), Don and his second wife, Megan, go to the theater to see a play called *America Hurrah*, by avant-garde playwright Jean-Claude van Itallie. Its exposure of feelings of dislocation enrage Don. The off-Broadway production has no realistic set, just a spare black, white, and gray stage design somewhat recalling the main title of *Mad Men*, and most of the actors wear see-through masks. We only see a small part of the play in which the protagonist, who is not wearing a mask, speaks directly to the audience about his sense of vertigo, which he mysteriously began to experience one evening while watching television and drinking beer. "I smelled the beer in my hand and as I vomited I looked around the living room, I looked for something to grab on to." Don is contemptuous of the play, which is perhaps too close to home.

In "In Care Of" (6.13), the finale episode of the show's penultimate season, teetering on the edge of the Hershey debacle, Don has the urge to run away again. Instead he digs his heels into a moment when Don Draper gazes on the place where Dick Whitman grew up. It is a cold Thanksgiving Day, and Don is unexpectedly in charge of his daughter, Sally, and his two sons. On the way to the family dinner, he shows them the house that he lived in as a child, in what was always the bad side of town. It is now an extremely run-down building in a depressed black ghetto. As the four of them stand before the evidence of the rejected past, Don exchanges a glance with Sally, filled with his embarrassed sense of revelation and her incredulity and disbelief, followed by mutual shock of recognition. It is not a happy gaze and does not contain the promise of resolution of the distance that has opened up between Don and his children, but it is necessary—and strangely a relief. Where there was only illusion and silence, there is now truth and communication. Or can we go that far?

The music with which Weiner scores the scene speaks to illusion and reality, contrasting in a succession of stanzas the ways clouds can be looked at—as fantastic illusions of angel hair and ice cream castles or the pragmatic harbingers of darkness, rain, and snow—and the ways love can be looked at—as the vertiginous illusions of fairy tales and a dancing heart or the

FIGURE 5.7. *Don's daughter controls her gaze as Don moves away from unknowing.*

cynical heartbreak that grows out of ordinary vicissitudes. It is a cultural endorsement of the impossibility of coming to hard and fast conclusions about our lives, which lies at the heart of *Mad Men*:

> I've looked at life from both sides now
> From win and lose and still somehow
> It's life's illusions I recall
> I really don't know life at all.

If the series tells us anything, it is that, of course, we really don't know life at all, not even whether that not-knowing is fortunate or inauspicious. Not-knowing is neither a plus nor a minus in and of itself. Rather, it is when we slip into what might pass for destiny but is in this context letting things happen instead of making things happen. In the great tragedies of American new beginnings, the instant of negation and creation is doomed. In the comic story of Rip Van Winkle, it is instead a mixture of loss and gain. The same is true of its modern incarnation, *Mad Men*, a tale of Dick Whitman/Don Draper and his friends; a tale of America; and a philosophical meditation for the mass media.

CHAPTER 6

LENA DUNHAM, *GIRLS*

The wager is that all the affects of subjectivity, all the significant facets and complexities of subjects, can be as adequately explained using the subject's corporeality as a framework as it would be using consciousness or the unconscious. All the effects of depth and interiority can be explained in terms of the inscriptions and transformations of the subject's corporeal surface. Bodies have all the explanatory power of minds.

—Elizabeth Grosz, *Volatile Bodies: Toward a Corporeal Feminism*

Lena Dunham completes the inner circle of new television auteurs to date. By far the youngest of the group and the only woman, Dunham adds something new and crucial to auteur television, a connection with new feminist ideas about the material, corporeal body. The obvious presence of the body in Dunham's series *Girls* has been abundantly noted by many. But, by and large, the body in *Girls* has been misread as a form of rebellious transgressiveness. This is understandable, because open displays of bodies and bodily functions are transgressive for our culture. Laura Mulvey set the tone in "Visual Pleasure and Narrative Cinema" by defining the mass media as a place within which the female body is inherently transgressive. Formulaic TV feminism subscribes to that perspective. However, there is a problem with viewing Dunham through that lens. That is not how she sees it.

Dunham has repeatedly stated that displaying her body is not transgressive for her. To view *Girls* through that convention is to obstruct our vision of her auteur feminist narrative. The art and originality of Dunham's comic vision in *Girls* depend on her revelations about all bodies as the challenging sites of complexity and indeterminacy that Mulvey ascribed to media presentation of women's bodies alone. We need to look away from Freudian-based feminism to find a different lens for seeing the human comedy, the feminism, the art of Lena Dunham.

Mulveyan feminist theory is appropriate to analysis of formulaic feminist TV narrative, such as *Nurse Jackie* and *Enlightened*. These series observe the traditional bifurcation of body (female) and mind (male), which sets the mind as the natural authority over (female) body. In both of these shows, the female hero's body resists the patriarchal order through the now familiar trope of the "unruly woman," a popular culture type explored by Kathleen Rowe in *The Unruly Woman: Gender and the Genres of Laughter* (1997) and by Linda Mizejewski in *Pretty/Funny: Women Comedians and Body Politics* (2014). Thus, the signature image of *Enlightened*—heroine Amy Jellicoe (Laura Dern) prying open the doors of an elevator with her bare hands in tear-soaked rage, her mascara streaking her contorted face—is also a signature image of the unruly female body in conflict with the male-dominated corporate world. The body of Jackie Peyton (Edie Falco), drug addicted and at war with all the conventions of male-dominated society in *Nurse Jackie*, is also a signature of the unruly woman. But bodies and women remain one rung down.

By contrast, as a storyteller, Dunham resonates with the work of feminist philosophers like Elizabeth Grosz, with her interest in establishing the non-transgressive existence of all corporeality male and female, as we humans stumblingly make our various ways. This view of body challenges the ideas that have depended on our thinking of women's bodies only in terms of the subordination of body to mind within a gendered hierarchy. Such imagined hierarchies do exist within the culture but now so do speculations supported by the scientific work of neuroscientists like Antonio Damasio, whose experiments also make an interesting reference point for thinking about *Girls*. Damasio's work suggests not only that the conventional mind-body hierarchy is erroneous but also that it is impossible to polarize them: in order to function the mind checks constantly with the body for the information it depends on to make decisions. Also pertinent are controversial psychologists pursuing therapies through attention to the body, like Eugene T. Gendlin, who therapeutically ask their patients to examine the often illegible visceral experience of what is happening to them rather than relying exclusively on a mind-centered "talking cure."[1] All bodies make meaning in fraught but fascinating collaboration with minds.

Much feminism casts pregnancy, like female sexuality and procreation, as one more way that patriarchy oppresses women. But new queer perspectives are being developed that reread body, female sexuality, and procreation against the grain of old ideas that link them to patriarchal hegemony. It is true that some important queer theorists simply reread femininity as transgressive from a queer perspective. For example, Lee Edelman based his signature work, *No Future: Queer Theory and the Death Drive*, on the premise that the Child is the cultural abstraction that supplies the force of illusory Western thought systems. In his first chapter, "The Future Is Kid Stuff," Edelman speaks of how Bill Clinton bolstered himself politically against all his attackers on the radical right by insinuating himself into public service announcements for the Coalition for America's Children. Establishing an image of himself as "America's Father," said Edelman, made him unassailable and part of the tyranny of Western ideology. Edelman's conclusion is that procreation is the foundation of illusion in our culture. His idea of the transgressiveness of women and the female body renders us involuntarily compliant in the repressiveness of society as it now exists.[2]

By contrast, Dunham is interested in another kind of discourse in *Girls*. She comes down hard on the side of the physicality of babies and childbirth as a special part of the conversation between verbal constructs and corporeality through which whatever we can know of meaning is made. In this she resonates with nontransgressive perspectives being developed by other queer theorists. I had the pleasure in April 2017 of attending a meeting of the Shakespeare seminar of Columbia's University Seminar Program, where I heard Melissa Sanchez apply queer theory to Shakespeare's sonnets in a way that brings the promiscuity of which the sonnets speak out of the shadow of transgression and into the light of the real. She explored Shakespeare's sonnets with fresh eyes through her assumptions that the secular eroticism within the sonnets registers human desire and subjectivity as "fundamentally promiscuous, a word that I use not only in its sexual sense, but also in its more expansive designation of all that is errant, disorderly, and indiscriminate." Her interpretations of the sonnets as meditations, given the indeterminate nature of desire, and their depiction of the "fantasy that two minds can eternally become one" are expanded upon in her book *Queer Faith: Reading Promiscuity and Race in the Secular Love Tradition*.

Dunham's portrait of sexuality suggests a similar attitude toward the promiscuity of desire. She does not resort to conventional presentation of desire in a positive light by denying that it is inherently indiscriminate and wanton. But, like Sanchez, Dunham finds in promiscuity a way of speaking about how the body makes meaning through unrestricted erotic connection. *Girls* drives toward an understanding of motherhood that is unconstrained by patriarchal hegemony because it is born of a promiscuity that, while it may be confusing and makes relationships discontinuous, is in touch with the flow of life and no longer envisioned as purely perilous. Dunham ends the series with a moment between protagonist Hannah Horvath (Lena Dunham) and her fatherless baby, Grover, whose biological father is just one of the many men she has promiscuously bedded. She thus joins the chorus of body-centric feminists, philosophers, neuroscientists, and queer theorists who have explored the way bodies make nontransgressive meaning.

Dunham may or may not be cognizant of the works of these feminists, queer theorists, philosophers, neuroscientists, and psychologists, but they serve as the appropriate context for *Girls*. They are the complex of ideas to which Dunham's series connects us, as a revision of ideas about body, gender, and transgression. Her auteur series distances the audience from the conventional sitcom narratives of hierarchal mind-body dualisms and the way they have pigeonholed bodies, relationships, family, and procreation.[3]

Bodies are not pigeonholed in *Girls*: all the bodies, male and female, are unruly; the cultural order itself is unruly. This vision may produce anxiety but also the wonder of how bodies, relationships, men, and women make meaning outside of the patterns of middle-class life. Once the gendered hierarchies of men and women, bodies and minds, are leveled in *Girls*, at the very least, stories of women and men become free of those formulaic tracks. At best, the result is a daring and freshly feminist revision of the hierarchal fiction of the American sitcom and its assumption of a comfortable, solid American middle class, with its prescriptive recipes for the maturation process, friendships, male-female relationships, family constellations, and social success. Certainly, friendships, romances, family, and social success are also the central concerns of *Girls*, as they are in formula sitcoms. *Girls* is a sitcom. By contrast, however, *Girls* contains no templates but instead depicts how the indeterminate dynamics of minds and bodies make clarity and definition in all these relationships impossible.

Girls tells the stories of four friends, Hannah Horvath (Lena Dunham), Marnie Michaels (Allison Williams), Jessa Johansson (Jemima Kirke), and Shoshanna Shapiro (Zosia Mamet), living in twenty-first century New York. The series maintains the sitcom emphasis on what is usually depicted as the solid, comfortable middle class but questions whether it is either comfortable or solid. Rather, from a body-centric feminist perspective, all middle-class platitudes are buffeted by the presence of visceral forces in everyday events and their disconnect from logic, ideas, and words. The irreconcilable pressures from both body and mind in each episode leave the characters confused about the nature of relationships and never allow us to be less confused than they are.

The indeterminate, larger reality of New York City is crucial to the modernist narrative context of Dunham's *Girls*. New York culture is a cacophony of social forces; its energetic fluidity is its most distinguishing characteristic. The location of the series is not just a passive setting for the characters. On a micro-level, the lives of Dunham's girls reveal the indeterminate relationship between mind and body that lies at the heart of the ambiguous realities of the metropolis, introducing an entirely new indeterminacy of experience, relationships, and girls into the sitcom genre. If formulaic TV feminism is about the pain and suffering of hierarchical constrictions, *Girls* is about the fear and wonder in the drift and flow of life out of that box.

IDEAS, BODIES, EXPERIENCE, *GIRLS*

Episode 1.1, the pilot, introduces us to the world of *Girls* by sending the standard sitcom structure of the A and B stories (or beats) decisively off the formulaic tracks. In what should be the A story, Hannah Horvath, the main character, two years after graduating from college, is cut off from financial support by her parents. They have come to New York from East Lansing, Michigan, for the purpose of insisting that she now become completely self-supporting. Hannah has been working for free as an intern for a publisher while trying to launch a career as a writer. In what should be the B story, Jenna Johansson returns to New York from many foreign travels, reuniting a group of four friends: Hannah, Jessa, Marnie, and Shoshanna. In formulaic sitcoms the A and B stories mesh like clockwork. In *Girls* they define experience as a chorus of fluid, indeterminate comic conversations between mind and body of whatever gender, as Dunham tries to get her hands around the "wriggling, terrifying monster that is human interaction."[4]

In the A story, Hannah is shocked by the sudden alteration in her life and wants her parents to change their minds. In the B story, Jessa is welcomed home, mostly by an informal party in the apartment shared by Hannah and Marnie. In a formulaic sitcom, the pilot would be organized by a linear narrative about how Hannah devises a plan to continue receiving financial support from her parents in collusion with the now-united quartet of friends. The quartet would be composed of four neatly defined feminine types, as in *Sex and the City*: Carrie Bradshaw (Sarah Jessica Parker), the normal one; Samantha Jones (Kim Cattrall), the sexpot; and Charlotte York (Kristin Davis) and Miranda Hobbes (Cynthia Nixon), two varieties of career girls. If *Girls* were formulaic, one major business of the pilot would be to identify the types and how the series will unfold to reveal predictable plot permutations and combinations.

But the first episode of *Girls* humorously distances itself from the puzzlelike structure of formula TV with its ultimately interlocking pieces. The upshot of Jessa's return and Hannah's dilemma in the pilot is an unredeemable mess.

Illegible meanings implied by the body and mind perform a complex dance. Marnie, for the most part without Hannah's help, gives Jessa a party. Despite Marnie's characteristically organized best efforts, the party is disorganized. Both Jessa, the guest of honor, and the co-host, Hannah, arrive late. A friend of the girls, Ray Ploshansky (Alex Karpovsky), arrives with a stash of opium twigs and causes further turmoil by cooking them up as a tea, which Hannah drinks and becomes extremely high. Under the influence of the tea she goes to her parents' hotel room and incoherently argues in vain for a continued monthly stipend.

Instead of a perfect narrative, we are offered the characters' failed attempts at coherence. In the first scene, the Horvath family is in a restaurant having dinner, as Hannah's parents, Loreen Horvath (Becky Ann Baker) and Tad Horvath (Peter Scolari), attempt to lay out a highly rational plan. Hannah has had two years of a free ride after college at their expense. Living on the extremely moderate salaries of college professors, they cannot afford to continue supporting her. But Loreen and Tad are hard pressed to establish this new policy, as words misfire and visceral responses run wild. Mother and father are not coordinated about how to talk to Hannah. Loreen rather than Tad takes the most direct tone, usually associated with masculinity, while Tad who wants to be more oblique, an attitude often associated with femininity. It is not a fictional world built on reason or linear action or a division of labor assigned according to standard definitions of gender.

Hannah angrily and confusedly rejects her parents. Unable to marshal her own reasons against them and having no idea what to do next, she can neither hold a neat sitcom discussion with them nor formulate a tidy sitcom course of action. Instead, she meanders over to the apartment of Adam Sackler (Adam Driver), with whom she has an undefined emotional relationship but a very clear sexual connection. They have sex orchestrated by Adam. As she tells him about her problem, he is more concentrated on orgasms. Hannah is distracted. But when she leaves, she is no clearer about what kind of relationship she and Adam have or about her relationship with her parents.

The episode moves toward closure of a sort as Marnie and Jessa offer ideas to Hannah about how to handle her parents. These come to nothing because Hannah is physically under the influence of the opium tea. It momentarily fortifies her body with a feeling of connection and purpose and also diminishes her already depleted capacity for thought. Running on purely corporeal energy, she makes her way to her parents' hotel room to make a final plea to continue her regular stipend by showing them a few crumpled pages that she ludicrously presents as evidence that she is a great writer in the making and deserves their continued support. She insists that she may be the voice of her generation—or, on consideration, a voice of a generation. It is an idea, all right, and one calculated to undo her mother's view of the appropriateness of Hannah's fiscal independence. Hannah passes out as her parents confusedly and anxiously look on. Her ideas and plan dissipate as her body takes over. It is a mind-body standoff.

The episode cuts to the next morning: Hannah's parents are gone, having each separately left her an envelope containing money. The gesture speaks, but not clearly: we have no idea—nor does Hannah—why they did it and why they did not use one envelope. There is just Hannah, hungry for breakfast, which she cannot get from room service: she needs to leave because the room account has been closed out.

Welcome to a world of enigmas, shifting perceptions, and uncertain limits, both of the mind and of the body. "What next?" is meant to be the question stimulated by a continuing sitcom pilot. Here the question is "What?" We have seen in other auteur series how the complex impact of the subconscious can derail linear narrative; here we see how the enigmas of the body can do the same, but with one crucial difference. The subconscious packs the punch of crucial absence, while corporeality packs the punch of enigmatic presence. The feminism in the series pilot is not rooted in the expression of neatly framed oppositions. Rather, feminism in *Girls* envelops us in a complex laughter at the parity of men and women in the area of modern confusion.

The pilot humorously and pointedly distinguishes itself from shows about the lives of girls and women that are formulaically clear. In the B story, its distance from *Sex and the City* is made hilariously explicit in the scene in which Jessa, home from her travels, arrives at her cousin Shoshanna's apartment with her luggage, back in New York and set to stay temporarily as a guest. In welcoming Jessa, Shoshanna, who is interested in a career in marketing, makes her first of many vain attempts to give her life the legibility of a consumer item. As the sophisticated Jessa tries to get what a traveler needs when she has just arrived, something to eat and a place to settle in, Shoshanna gets lost in trying to give formulaic shape to the moment by profiling her relationship to Jessa by using *Sex and the City* as her frame of reference. "You're funny because you're definitely a Carrie with like some Samantha aspects and Charlotte hair. That's like a really good combination," she tells Jessa. She wants to tote up her own profile too. "I think I'm definitely a Carrie at heart, but like sometimes, sometimes Samantha kind of comes out. And then I mean, when I'm at school, I definitely try to put on my Miranda hat." Jessa clearly regards Shoshanna as a fool, while she sees herself as a cool, hip cosmopolite more "with it" and attuned to the wisdom of the body. While Shoshanna gets tangled up in her failing analogy, Jessa

FIGURE 6.1. *Jessa unpacks; Shoshanna tries to make her arrival part of Sex and the City.*

keeps grounding the conversation in material basics. Can I come in? Do you have something I can eat? But Jessa is not always in touch either. She is as lost in a world of bodies and minds as Shoshanna is, albeit with more panache, as becomes clear in future episodes and seasons.

The focus on male-female parity in the experiential chaos of bodies, ideas, and experience continues over the course of the series, expanding, deepening, and intensifying, but always leaving questions, not answers. Among the many vivid examples of the expansion over the seasons are "Beach House" (3.7), an episode about a weekend in the country organized by Marnie for the four girls, and "Home Birth" (4.10), in which the A story is about Caroline Sackler (Gaby Hoffmann), Adam's mentally aberrant sister, who goes through the most physical of experiences, giving birth. There are also two other stories about the chaos of experience in which Shoshanna gets a job as a marketer in Japan; and Marnie is forced to go on as a single when her fiancé and partner in the act, Desi Harperin (Ebon Moss-Bachrach), fails to show up at their scheduled gig.

"Beach House" is a particularly evocative depiction of the plight of middle-class men and women plunged into the muddle of words and bodies. Marnie is hell bent on creating order out of what she sees as chaos. She feels that the four friends have grown apart and is particularly unhappy about her ruptured friendship with Hannah, who was very angry when she learned that her one-time boyfriend, Elijah Krantz (Andrew Rannells), who has turned out to be gay, had sex with Marnie. The fluidity of Elijah's and

Marnie's sexuality is humorously presented, as is the transition between avid interest and an encounter that is not satisfying to either of them. Certainly, the episode takes an unusually neutral perspective, for sitcoms, on the liminality of corporeal desire, its indeterminacy.[5] And there is humor in Hannah's unquenchable rage about a very confusing situation. But most humorous of all are the dynamics of mental and material energies.

Marnie's formulaic plan to deal with the distance that has grown among the four girls—who may or may not be friends—is completely satirized. Marnie likes to organize life logically and beautifully if possible, and in this episode (as always in the series) she makes us laugh with her determination to structure the weekend. As Marnie prepares for her friends' arrival, she arranges flowers for each of the guest bedrooms and places handwritten cards to identify room assignments. On the soundtrack we hear the nondiegetic strains of the kind of harpsichord music that is frequently used in movies based on the novels of Jane Austen, often misconstrued as the mother of domestic television comedy. As in standard TV sitcoms, Marnie's preparation reduces the very complex Austen to simplistic ideas of patterned social manners and mores, and for a moment she feels that she has the situation in hand. Gratified by the precision she has created, with chatelaine-like composure and style, she flings open french doors that lead to a balcony and overlooks her domain. Then life takes over.

As soon as the girls arrive, all Marnie's plans begin to fracture, slowly at first and then, as the day wears on, at warp speed. Marnie's stylish expectations

FIGURE 6.2. *Marnie's chatelaine fantasy.*

collide with fractious, irrepressible bodies, male and female. She responds by generating new patterns to impose, which evoke more wild energy. As soon as the girls get into the house, they physically fight to take possession of the rooms, despite the organized plan of the place cards. She is not the only one with abstract expectations: nothing but disorder ensues, as they fight and grumble regardless of where they are: in a pool, on the beach, or shopping for food. When they bicycle into town to get provisions, Hannah refuses to wear shoes or a cover-up over her bathing suit, because, she insists, it is a beach town. But it turns out that she is barred from the food store for inappropriate clothing. By chance, Elijah, his new gay lover, and two gay male friends run into Hannah. She unalterably ruins Marnie's plans by inviting them over to the beach house for dinner. There is not enough food for seven people.

Momentarily it seems that Marnie's weekend plans, destroyed by Hannah's anarchic inclusion of seven people in a four-person dinner, will be partially saved when Elijah's friend Gerald (T. Oliver Reid), who dances when he gets drunk, choreographs a dance number for the girls to the tune of Harry Nilsson's "You're Breakin' My Heart." The song's comical collision of lovelorn lyrics with exhilarating rhythm and upbeat melody contains its own self-parody: "You're breakin' my heart / You're tearing it apart, boo-hoo" and the even more parodic "You're breakin' my heart / You're tearing it apart so fuck you." Gerald's response to the mismatch is to go full throttle with campy choreographic clichés. It works! The bodies of the four girls, now embraced by the looseness of the dance, make hilarious corporeal meaning out of the song's nonsense. The evening seems to have renewed energy. Then Marnie restores rigidity by insisting that they repeat and polish the routine until it is as perfect as it can be. All the energies in the girls' revolt and the evening revert to a rebellious disorder that taps into the girls' resentments that have been simmering for the three previous seasons of the series. The recriminations lead to Shoshanna's climactic tantrum. She has spent the previous episodes desperately trying to curry favor with the three other girls, as she tries to fit their friendship into a meaningful pattern. Now she vents, furiously wondering "if my social anxiety is holding me back from meeting the people who would actually be right for me instead of a bunch of fucking, whining nothings as friends." Marnie has put the finishing touches on the disaster through her misguided yearning for brittle, yes, formulaic order.

Or has she? It is impossible to determine the next morning whether healing took place or not, but some indecipherable meaning has come out of the collisions of ideas and body. It does not betoken reconciliation, but it hints at ongoing connections. In the early light, the recently awakened girls move around in a strangely impersonal spirit of cooperation, cleaning up the

FIGURE 6.3. *Four bodies speak of friendship through spontaneous gestures.*

accumulated garbage of the evening. No one tries to take charge. No one gets in the way. Their bodies are all moving separately but almost as one. A similar process takes place at the bus stop, as they wait to go back to New York City, each staring straight ahead. They begin moving haltingly but in unison through a series of spontaneous motions that they physically sense the others are making rather than seeing and imitating them. And the episode is over. It is a small comic gem that effectively critiques the idea of the transgressive female body that needs to be restrained and controlled—whether by men or by other women.

By the time we get to "Home Birth," we have seen enough of the discrepant multiple levels of mind and body to be ready for a modernist portrayal of the pregnant body as a privileged case of the mind/body dialogue. At the center of the episode, the fourth season finale, is Caroline Sackler's body as she goes into labor. Caroline, who appears and disappears as the seasons unfold, is Adam's manic-depressive sister. Her labor process stands as an image of the murky yet exhilarating interface between body and mind when new situations—and what is newer than birth?—present themselves. Everyone in the episode is affected by the procreative shattering of old realities. In her own thread, Shoshanna is unsure when she receives an unexpected job offer from a company that, even more unexpectedly, will require her to live in Japan but decides to take on the challenge. In a third thread, Desi, without explanation, fails to show up for a performance he and Marnie are scheduled to give: Marnie, terrified, goes on alone, inaugurating her career as a solo performer.

It is a birth of sorts for her. The birth of Caroline's child is no harbinger of the purported bondage that patriarchal culture places on women. Rather, childbirth becomes a renewal, a break in old patterns, a transformative event in which body and mind converge. It is the first of several major allusions in *Girls* to the transformative power of the female body, which take the place of the combative female body—women rebels like Amy Jellicoe and Jackie Peyton and *Xena: Warrior Princess* and *Jessica Jones*—in formulaic attempts at feminist narrative. As she goes into labor, Caroline articulates New Age fantasies about a kind and gentle welcome into the world for her baby at home, in a tub full of warm water, theoretically replicating the environment of the idyllic womb; at the same time, her body speaks of a high-risk breech birth—not so idyllic. The episode comically juggles the abstract romance of the idea of birth, and by extension ideas about the beginning of anything, and the physical reality of birth and all beginnings. In the story thread of Caroline's birth adventure, the camera is trained unwaveringly on her in the tub, as she chants and gives a running commentary on the ecstasies of birth, a perfect narrative that she tells herself, which bears little relationship to the pain she is suffering.

Caroline is not the only one avoiding experience of her body and the uncertainty and wonder of birth. Hannah, Adam, and Hannah's downstairs neighbor, Laird Schlesinger (Jon Glaser), the baby's father, are all trying unsuccessfully to avoid looking at Caroline's corporeal bulk, in labor, as the camera dares an arguably unwilling audience to avert their eyes from the spectacle. It is compelling as well as conventionally transgressive to stare. It is not a sexual spectacle, despite the explicitness of the visibility of the large breasts with large dark aureoles around the nipples, Caroline's abundant pubic hair, and the insistent movement of her torso. Nor is it transgressive in this context. It is a naked body stripped of erotic seduction by its devotion to the hard work of birth and its need for help, because the baby is dangerously in breech position. Caroline's New Age patter morphs into screaming as the body makes its points. Her birth plan dissipates with comic irony. Nothing is left but the insistent reality of Caroline's body, before which all of her narratives are helpless.

Now the dialogue between body and mind turns dynamic: the birth is a cathartic moment of immediacy for Caroline and her friends and breaks open old habits of thinking. There is no abstract Baby, as Lee Edelman theorizes procreation with all its negative implications for him. Instead the physical experience of birth propels the characters to leap creatively into the future, out of their boxes. Jessa makes a sudden decision to study to become a therapist. Hannah, with equal immediacy, leaps into a new romantic relationship with Fran Parker (Jake Lacy), a fellow teacher at the school where she is working. At the same time, Marnie and Shoshanna make their own leaps by giving a solo performance and accepting the job offer in Japan, respectively. The materiality of experience, not the subconscious, is the dancing partner of systems of thought in this series.

But birth does not erase the confusions, paradoxes, and liminalities of modern life. Birth only creates a surge to an ongoing mind/body conversation. Caroline is a manic depressive. What is in store for this baby once the moment of birth, which creates a sudden serenity for Caroline, is past? Similarly, Jessa's postpartum state of bliss and warm camaraderie, which births her revelation that her destiny is to be a therapist, Marnie's solo performance, and Shoshanna's career decision do not bring about neat transformations. Jessa's glow is already fading when Shoshanna tells her, "You're going to be such a good therapist." Jessa responds, "I know. You're going to make a really great geisha." Shoshanna's Japanese idyll will not last; nor will Jessa find that she is meant to be a therapist. Marnie, who breaks an old pattern and gives a solo performance, turns out to be a mediocre talent. She will go nowhere in the music business: it is a physical triumph over fear and just for the moment.

Hannah's afterbirth epiphany with Adam is perhaps the most intriguing of all. What happens when the rupture of old rigidities sends people in opposite directions? In the afterglow Hannah and Adam, whose now ostensibly defunct relationship has left many loose ends, are alone staring into a bassinet at Caroline's baby in the hospital nursery and across it at each other. Adam experiences a deep visceral regret that he terminated his relationship with Hannah and is certain that he made a mistake, as he once experienced a visceral certainty that he wanted a different woman. But Hannah's body is telling her something else. She finds it unusually hard to speak; it is all happening in her viscera. "I can't," she says. Instead, she jumps into a new relationship with Fran. But in the next season Adam is in a hot romance with Jessa and Hannah literally runs screaming from Fran. Out of the vortex of birthing bodies, expectations, idyllic plans, and strong intimations of love, the art of *Girls* pulls a depiction of life as a comic continuum of disconnects—between discursive constructs and feelings and between the organic sensations of the body in time and space.

This sense of life's vicissitudes is part of a larger picture that arises from many such brief interludes. *Girls* emerges with a new perspective on the central preoccupation of sitcoms: the mysteries of relationships, which are more mysterious in Hannah's world than ever. What can they mean in this funny, sad, traumatic, euphoric, inharmonious, rudderless universe?

IF A BODY MEET A BODY

There is no clear answer to this question in *Girls*. Rather, by depicting relationships as bewilderingly shifting and indeterminate, the series works the territory of modern literature and thought, which suggests that human connections may in fact be stories we tell ourselves about a phantom that we have named relationships. The most dramatic portrayal of the dubiousness of the "relationship story" in *Girls* is the breakup of the twenty-five-year marriage of Hannah's parents. Although they are initially the picture of midwestern (read all-American) conventionality, representative of the story of ordinary middle-class marriage, the link between them thins out to a ghostly, unsubstantial apparition when Tad reveals that he is gay. His "story" of a stable marriage with Loreen is in conflict with his physical desires. A similar slippage occurs in Marnie's story threads: she constantly creates stories in her mind about the men she intends to be involved with, which keep breaking down as she experiences disappointment and astonishment at their failure. For example, she is twice oblivious that the men with whom she fabricates romance and intimacy are drug addicted.

Everyone is telling a relationship story to everyone else. When Adam and Hannah are "together" at the beginning of the series, Hannah frequently wonders if they are a couple. She eagerly participates with him in role-playing games that ultimately seem to be her way of trying to answer this question. Similarly, the relationships among the girls often boil down to badly fitting stories. This plays out on *Girls* as a modernist redefinition of relationships on television sitcoms, laying bare the gap between the stories we tell ourselves and reality. When the stories dissipate, nothing is left.

Jenna has her stories too: "I want to have children with many different men of different races," she says. She marries Thomas-John Anderson (Chris O'Dowd), a very eccentric, very wealthy man she hardly knows. She has a lot of sex with him and fantasies of idyllic, unconventional days together. But nothing binds them, engaging that indefinable, mysterious corporeal energy that means relationship in *Girls*. Jenna has the same kind of attraction toward Ace (Zachary Quinto), a hipster who fits her "outsider" self-image, but that attraction too is a chimera.

Relationships among the main characters slip and slide. The series does not encourage bitterness or sadistic laughter, however, but rather the sad, sweet, secret knowledge that we have all been there, despite the persistence of our private mythologies about our personal associations. Nowhere is the elusiveness of what it means to be in a relationship more tellingly depicted than in the digressive episodes, in which one (or two) of the girls takes time off from slipping and sliding around the discontinuities of their usual associations to drift into a brief orbit with a passing stranger. These are the most telling and revealing stories about modern confusions about the differences between phantom connections and solid bonds. Two of the most interesting are "One Man's Trash" (2.5), an atypically bittersweet episode about Hannah's one night stand with an affluent doctor; and "Video Games" (2.7), an atypically painful episode about Jessa's family life.

In "One Man's Trash," Hannah drifts away from her usual circle of associates and into the apartment of a young, handsome, wealthy, kind doctor named Joshua (Patrick Wilson), whose house stands two blocks down the street from Grumpy's, the coffee shop in which she is working temporarily. It is a brief idyll that replicates the isolated relationships of formulaic television but defamiliarizes the anomalous disconnection from the flow of life that conventional sitcoms romanticize as coupledom. Joshua walks into Grumpy's one day to complain to manager Ray Ploshansky that the coffee shop's garbage is winding up in his garbage cans, leaving no room for his own refuse. Ray behaves badly, becoming combative with Joshua, a reasonable man seeking a neighborly discussion. In a grumpy tone that lives up to the name of the establishment, Ray blusters at Joshua, using obscenities and trying to intimidate him, saying that he has his own dumpster for his own garbage and that he has no time for what he is convinced is nonsense. Actually it is not. Hannah has been dumping the garbage at Joshua's house. She does not tell Ray but instead precipitously quits her job and shows up on Joshua's front steps to admit her culpability and apologize. He invites her in.

Her visit turns out to be longer than she expected. She accepts the invitation from this stranger and stays overnight, the next day, and the next night in what turns out to be a strange, fleeting relationship laboratory. Hannah arrives on Joshua's doorstep with almost no idea of why she has come or why she walked two blocks to his trash bins from Grumpy's instead of using the restaurant's dumpster or why she accepts his invitation to come into his home, knowing the danger of strangers. Joshua's male-model looks and expensively furnished domain bring to Hannah's mind the story of the infamous Ted Bundy.[6] But she initiates sex with Joshua anyhow. He does not turn out to be a murderer of women, just a man who, for no apparent reason, is so completely responsive to Hannah's overtures that he decides to skip his work the next day and stay with her in what has now become their bower of bliss. We also have no idea why the connection dissolves silently after a couple of intimate days.

The lack of conventional motivation in this interlude is not a matter of bad writing. It is Hannah's chance, and the show's, to live out the rom-com, formulaic sitcom noncontextual coupledom that is not usually found in *Girls*. Hannah creates that chance out of some combination of the typical story she is creating for herself and the compulsion of corporeal desire. She romps around a beautiful house that she herself describes as resembling the upper-class heaven of a Nancy Meyers movie, drawing Joshua into a number of various roles as lover. What formula TV presents as the zenith of romance can only take place on *Girls* briefly and within brackets: this idyll will not last. Sergio Dias Branco has pointed out that spatial brackets are part of the aesthetics of what I am calling formulaic sitcoms and create the definitions of relationships in those series.[7] For our purposes, Branco's fascinating insight translates into another way we can understand how formulaic conventions limit possibilities and define relationships with clarity. The modernist aesthetics of *Girls* precludes that kind of bracketing. A bracketed relationship in Dunham's series is possible only in minutes and hours as an anomaly, not the basic reality of modernist fiction. However, that said, the bracketed time that Hannah and Josh spend together is a kind of relationship and adds to the complexity of what relationship means in *Girls*, tantalizing us with a phantom appearance of a familiar romance cliché.

As it turns out, before it dissipates, Hannah's attachment to a beautiful man in a beautiful apartment only leads to an experience of her deep loneliness within patterns that culture has idealized and impels her to drift away, after throwing out Joshua's garbage in his garbage bin. The episode raises questions about the formulaic romantic idyll in Joshua's beautiful brownstone, not to answer them. Like Hannah, we have emerged with only questions and a sense of detachment.

The funny paradoxes of connection/disconnection in *Girls* are pushed to reveal the tragedy that underlies all comedy in "Video Games," which takes place entirely in rural upstate New York. Jessa takes Hannah on a trip to meet her father, Salvatore Johansson (Ben Mendelsohn), his new girlfriend, Petula (Rosanna Arquette), and her teenaged son, Frank (Nick Lashaway). As a family visit, it is a painful study in the bizarrely phantom nature of domestic bonding. Most of the episode consists of moments when her father is not there. He is very late to pick the girls up from the train station. He goes to a lecture with Petula that night instead of staying with his daughter, whom he rarely sees. The next day he convinces Jessa to stay for the next night then drives her and Hannah to a grocery store to get food for the meal that he says he will cook for her. He sends the girls in to buy the food then disappears completely from the episode. His corporeal absence is juxtaposed with brief bursts of his verbal declarations of awe at his daughter's beauty, brief moments of repartee between the two, and sudden emotional accusations of abandonment that they level at each other.

The core of this episode is the dialogue of detachment that arises from the collision of verbiage and body, a paradox underscored when Petula tells Hannah that she believes daily life has all the insubstantiality of a video game and behaves in exactly that way. She is right, of course, in describing her life with Jessa's father and Jessa's experience of being his daughter. Yet the video-game sense of family life is repeated between Hannah and her parents at the end of the episode. Jessa abandons Hannah completely, disappearing and leaving Hannah to find her way home by herself. As Hannah waits disconsolately at the station for a train, suffering the sharp pain of an advanced urinary infection, she calls her parents to ground herself and tries to express her gratitude for the way they have loved and protected her. This provokes Loreen's suspicions that Hannah is trying to manipulate her with fulsome praise. Her body is painfully present, her family bonds elusive. Is the phone the problem? Would physical presence involving a context shared with her parents have made a difference?

The interplay that goes into making family disconnection, so intensely depicted in "Video Games," is revealed in varying degrees of pathos throughout the series. Marnie's divorced mother is distracted by her desire to relive her flaming youth while Marnie is most in need of motherly support. Similarly, Shoshanna's divorced parents, glimpsed only briefly when she is picking up her diploma from New York University, are so preoccupied with continuing the battles that broke up their marriage that Shoshanna is barely visible to them, either as a new graduate or a daughter. When Tad Horvath decides to own up to his homosexuality, his conventional parental role with Hannah virtually dissolves. Tad is consumed by experimenting with newfound honesty about his sexuality, while Loreen is filled with self-pity and terror about the future. In "Gummies" (6.5), when Hannah tells her mother in a drunken stupor that she is pregnant, Loreen's fear and melancholy have become so dire that she tells her daughter that every time she looks at her grandchild's face she will see her own death. What does the parental bond mean as families fragment and devolve into individual units? Is family, despite its blood ties, only a story?

Completing its spectrum of relationships, *Girls* also depicts the comedy of overenergetic conversations between mind-body connection in "I Love You Baby" (5.10). Hannah is now suffering as a witness to the story of Adam

FIGURE 6.4. *The horror of relationship.*

and Jessa that is in full swing, as Loreen and Tod are suffering from the dissipation of their marriage story. Hannah turns her jealousy into an actual narrative, which she tells at the Moth, a club that features competitions for writers. Hannah is struggling through her anger, and Loreen and Tod are playing out their confusion about a connection being thinned to noth-ingness. Ironically, behind Adam and Jessa's apartment door, their grand passion is reduced to an uncontrolled clash between ideas about coupledom and corporeal rebellion against them. Their initial low-level bickering about anything and everything from feeding Caroline's baby to the triangle with Hannah escalates to yelling and an orgy of throwing things.[8] The wild and enigmatic nature of the brawl is emphasized by a visual allusion to Stanley Kubrick's *The Shining*. Adam breaks through a locked door behind which Jessa is hiding from him and snarls through the hole, like Jack Nicholson's maniacal, demonically possessed Johnny.

That image is funny here, albeit bordering on frightening, because the allu-sion to Kubrick's great horror film resonates only too well with what has been misunderstood by formulaic sitcoms as the zenith of romance. The bizarre exception to normality in *The Shining* becomes little more in *Girls* than an extreme aspect of ordinary relationships at their most passionate extreme. The mystery of Adam and Jessa's relationship is what endures in the final image of their fight. They end up naked on the floor, surrounded by wreck-age, completely drained of energy. They are not free, only corporeally unable either to continue the fight or to get away from each other. The wreckage is the physical evidence of their connection in a world in which connection, for all the words exchanged, is so difficult to name or analyze. Juxtaposed to these main threads of the episode is a collateral thread about Marnie's absurd stories about her so-called primary romantic relationship with Desi, her partner in a music act that is about to go on tour, and her off-and-on relationship with Ray, her go-to relief from her sexual and professional battles with Desi. When last we see them in this episode, Ray is serving as a battering ram for Marnie. He bangs on the door behind which Desi is being fellated by a groupie he met only a couple of hours before and bellows for Desi to open the door so Marnie can get her open-toed shoes for the performance. As usual, Marnie's relationship narratives are at odds with her life.

The episode is also sprinkled with cameos of two pairs of people happy in their companionship, who have no history and no future. Shoshanna and Hermie (Colin Quinn), Ray's good-natured, middle-aged business partner in a new coffee house called Ray's Place, are closing up the shop after hours. They break into a carefree dance with each other, filled with joy and momentary pleasure because they are not dealing with the expectations of a relationship. Similarly, Loreen and Elijah, uproariously drinking beer together on the street after Hannah's reading at Moth, are filled with laughter and camaraderie as they joke about their nonrelationship. Whatever relationship it may be is complicated and beyond the controls assumed by formulaic sitcoms.

The ironic summation of the episode is a final montage accompanied by the soundtrack music "I Love You Baby." With its bright, bouncy, infectious melodic celebration of the ecstasy of love, it contrasts starkly with what we are shown of relationships. At the same time, it ironically seems more compatible with those pairings that are barely relationships at all. The song reiterates the cultural story about the bliss of coupledom and parenthood, while the episode events suggest that life is a twilight zone. That kind of defined élan is a story that culture tells itself. Such lighthearted joie de vivre only exists in the flesh in moments between people, preferably moments between people who are not involved.

Girls poses questions in each episode about how people connect, asking with a comic insouciance: "What are relationships?" "What do we think they are?" "What bodily experience do we have of them?" These are serious questions, especially in a fictional universe in which relationships and love are almost all that seems to matter yet are almost impossible. This makes Dunham's vision inherently the most scandalous and radical of all the auteurs we have examined, who do not question the very notion of human love and connection despite the troubled relationships that they depict. These questions lead to others about what we glean from the seemingly inexplicable nature of experience. Dunham's equivocal laughter about middle-class life extends to questions about whether, under these circumstances, we can learn and mature as characters do so neatly in pre-*Peaks* domestic comedies.

MATURITY?

Is maturity also a story that we tell ourselves? In the comic world of *Girls*, it would seem to be. In Hannah's world, to be an adult does not equate with the wisdom, responsibility, and the rational management of life that formulaic sitcoms have identified with satisfactory maturity but instead with lengthier experience of the complexity and/or impossibility of relationships. The middle-class characters of whatever age depicted in *Girls* begin as and remain an atomized lot. Age and experience seem to yield little but recurring instances of misbegotten stories told and retold with deepening pain, as in Jessa's experience with her father. Experience does not improve Marnie's relationship stories either. Marnie's first boyfriend, Charlie, who was overly solicitous of approval when they were together, does go on to become a successful businessman after they break up. But if personal growth seemed to be indicated, it all collapses into confusion again. When we last see him, he is living the life of a dissolute drug addict. Marnie's next serious boyfriend, Desi, is a drug addict for the entire time they are together. He successfully hides this problem from her until their final confrontation and cannot extricate himself. Loreen's seemingly stable mature identity as a professional woman, a wife, and a mother cracks when the reality of her ignorance of Tad's homosexuality shatters the image. When the series concludes, we are left with unanswered questions about whether anyone has grown, matured, and/or found some kind of sense to life.

The "Goodbye Tour" (6.9) and "Latching" (6.10) form a two-tiered denouement for the series, with a double layer of comedy about the possibility of growth, development, and maturation. In episode 6.9, Hannah says goodbye to New York City, contemplating her move to a teaching position at a college in upstate New York. We say goodbye to the four girls as they meet at Shoshanna's engagement party. In episode 6.10, Hannah has her first successful connection—to her newborn baby, a success qualified by everything we know of this fictional universe.

When we last see the four girls together (in 6.9), they are at odds with each other as usual. Some things have changed among them, some have not. Only questions remain as to whether we can call the changes maturity. Shoshanna has made her leap away from Hannah, Jessa, and Marnie and is engaged to marry the respectable-looking Byron Long (Ethan Phillips), whom neither the audience nor the other girls know. Shoshanna is poised to enter what she calls, in her distinctive way, the world of pretty girls, "with purses and good personalities." This is the world of public order as Shoshanna understands it, the world as it is presented in formula sitcoms. She is about to leave what she perceives as the shambles of lives that Marnie, Jessa, and Hannah are leading.

In any formulaic sitcom, marriages are happy endings, so Shoshanna, as the one core girl who has attained middle-class marriage, would represent maturity in a story-product sitcom. Here she raises as many questions with her impending spur-of-the-moment marriage as the other girls do as they continue to blunder around in their single lives. In fact, Jessa and Hannah display new capacities for empathy as they make strides past the rupture in their friendship: past Jessa's illusions about herself as the arbiter of how things are and Hannah's judgmental condemnation of Jessa. On the other hand, Marnie remains stuck in her stories that have never served her life, as she swans around at the party as the center of a group of admiring men. She herds Jessa, Hannah, and Shoshanna into the bathroom in one more futile attempt to make them talk out their differences. It does not work.

But, as at the beach house, the episode at Shoshanna's party focuses on the corporeal roots of relationship. In the final moments of the episode, we viewers watch the blur of the girls' bodies as they dance, alone, together, with people we do not know. As the camera moves away, we watch through the windows, as they all become smaller and part of a much bigger picture. With the characters all on the brink of finding new directions and connections, not necessarily what they expected but still open to possibilities, *Girls* makes a penultimate summation of this world at the party, the last time the four girls will be together in the series.

Ultimate closure occurs in "Latching," the series finale, which offers signs that experience may open channels of receptivity to a sense of problems that we all share that passes for a kind of maturation. At the beginning of the episode, Hannah is a single mother. Characteristically, she lashes out at anyone who tries to support her, including Loreen, because no one plays the correct role in the stories that she tells herself about motherhood in general and breastfeeding in particular. However, unlike in previous episodes, Loreen does not go on a counterattack but expresses a fellow feeling for Hannah and for all other human beings. "You know who else is in emotional pain?" she asks. "Fucking everyone!" she answers, unsentimentally but compassionately. Loreen is opening empathetically. By the end of the episode, Hannah too moves in that direction. It is the flowering of maturity as the modernist storyteller of *Girls* imagines it.

Like her mother, Hannah has come a long way from where she began as a spoiled, overprivileged young woman with few responsibilities and less concern for any responsibility she might undertake. She fails at every job she tries in the early seasons once her parents take away their financial support, and she fails at the writer's program at the University of Iowa. She fails again when she decides to try teaching. If "those who can do and those who can't teach," as Hannah reminds her friends, since she cannot do she will teach. She gets a job at a private high school, St. Justine's, for which she needs neither certification nor educational credentials. During her tenure there, she is unprofessional and irresponsible by rational standards. She abandons her classes on impulse and barges into the classroom of another teacher, Fran Parker, her boyfriend of the moment, while he is teaching. She blatantly treats Cleo (Maude Apatow), one of her students, as a personal confidante, as if the two of them were peers, openly discussing personal matters both in class and in the hallways. She chafes at the professional limits and expectations that require preparation of class material and equal treatment of students, blatantly playing favorites and venturing opinions on literature that she has not read in years.

Her immaturity is hilarious but egregious, particularly when she and Cleo go to a tattoo parlor during her break one day, intending to get friendship piercings of their frenums. She engineers it so that Cleo goes first as a guinea pig. When Hannah sees how painful the piercing process is, she backs out without giving a single thought to the way she has used a girl who is supposed to be in her care. During a conversation in the office of Principal Toby (Douglas McGrath), when he is gently critical of her behavior, she flashes him a glimpse of her unpantied crotch to disconcert him. The moment recalls the infamous interrogation scene between Detective Nick Curran (Michael Douglas) and suspected serial killer Catherine Tramell (Sharon Stone) in *Basic Instinct* (1992)—the definitive 1990s backlash film against the progress made by feminists in the 1980s. The allusion is a very funny, if hyperbolic, comparison between one of the most sexist images of a pathological movie seductress and Hannah's effect on St. Justine's.

Yet the resemblance implicates the supposedly formal public realm in its own confusions. Principal Toby is genuinely unhappy when Hannah decides that St. Justine's is not for her and resigns her post, just as Nick Curran is drawn to Catherine despite the mounting evidence that she is a murderess. There is no hard and fast line between personal immaturity and immaturity in the public domain in *Girls*, where the momentary immediacy of the body weighs equally in the scale with the phantomlike quality of rational judgment. Whether this is good or bad is not the point in this series. These are the realities of people in positions of responsibility who are supposed to be mature and in charge.

Questions about maturity revolve to a large extent around Hannah's motherhood in season 6 and sum up everything that has happened in the series. Her pregnancy is the result of promiscuity, which Adam tries unsuccessfully to redeem by building around Hannah and her baby a middle-class narrative of love, marriage, and parenthood. Yet a real connection is the result of Hannah's evasion of the grip of what sitcoms misunderstand as stability. In "All I Ever Wanted" (6.1), Hannah slides into a relationship of sorts with a likeable drifter named Paul-Louis (Riz Ahmed) and becomes pregnant as a result. In "What Will We Do This Time about Adam?" (6.8), she is unable to revisit the possibility of a relationship with Adam, who is suddenly possessed by a need to explore his lingering feelings for her and help her raise her fatherless baby. In "Latching" (6.10), she is swept up in feelings of disconnection from her own child. But, as we shall see, there is more to her maternity than she initially knows.

In episode 6.1, Hannah spends several days with Paul-Louis, who is in charge of teaching surfing at a surf camp. She is on assignment from a trendy online publication named *Slag Mag* to write about his rich, bored female patrons. This interlude is somewhat reminiscent of her time with Joshua in "One Man's Trash," both being inescapably temporary hiatuses. But with time come differences in the two adventures. Hannah emerges more disconnected than ever from Joshua's consumerist paradise. Paul-Louis, by contrast, immerses Hannah in connection not with him but rather with a conscious appreciation of the body of the world, the magnificence of the ocean, and a philosophy of pleasure in experience that finds it easier to love than to hate. That vision of connection is embodied in her pregnancy with his baby. The series does not overlook the symmetries and asymmetries of the two discontinuous interludes in her life. Hannah is surprised to find that Joshua is the doctor assigned to her when she goes to the emergency room because of a painful urinary infection. He reveals to her that she is pregnant.

Adam's decision to help Hannah raise her baby and her surprised openness to his overtures are the last gasp of their role playing, which emerges here as the ultimate disconnect from reality. Adam abruptly terminates his relationship to Jessa and equally abruptly initiates a reprise of his relationship with Hannah. Unlike in the formula sitcom, which thrives on such fantasies, the Hannah-Adam idyll is revealed as an impossibility by Dunham's vision of reality in her fictional universe. Hannah and Adam tenderly have sex and stroll blissfully in Brooklyn and begin to shop for the baby—all sweet and indisputably present moments. The scenes seem to embody what formulaically passes for mature, responsible behavior and the promise of a happy forevermore. But it is all just a formulaic story that, like Hannah's idyll with Josh, cannot withstand the flow of reality.

Reality hits when Hannah's mouth begins to quiver and her eyes water. Not a single word passes between them about the realization rising within her, unbidden, that they have reached the outer limits of a fantasy. Adam knows it too once he sees her body language. This cannot go forward. After six seasons of bodies floundering, staggering, and blundering, we see some young green shoots of wisdom arising in Hannah and Adam from those same bodies. The mind belatedly recognizes this wisdom, much in the mode of models of behavior evolved by neuroscience, which map out human knowledge as a message that passes from body to mind. Here it happens after time and experience. It is some kind of maturity. There is a recognition of the emptiness of the seemingly appropriate words. But that recognition leaves a void. What will Hannah do as a mother?

The question is and is not answered in episode 6.10. Hannah, now confronted with a real child, is still caught between her ever-shifting stories about how things are and her visceral impulses. She is having trouble breastfeeding Grover, her baby boy. The frustration leads to her lashing out in frustration verbally and physically, as she did when we first met her. It would seem that no development has taken place. She is dictatorial with Marnie and contemptuous of her mother. They have both come at some inconvenience to themselves to help her with Grover in her new house in upstate New York, where she has been given an appointment in a small college. Storming out of the house after an argument with her mother, she leaves Grover unceremoniously and irresponsibly with Loreen and Marnie. Hannah's ongoing immaturity is evident—until she comes face to face with a mirror image of herself.

By chance, on the road Hannah meets a nameless, crying teenager (Ruby-rose Hill), who is not wearing pants or shoes. Hannah makes no effort to find out what is happening but immediately enmeshes her in a story of her own invention. She unquestioningly spins a formulaic story around the girl about her putative escape from an abusive home from which she must be rescued. After giving the girl her own jeans and shoes, leaving Hannah in the bad position in which she found the girl, Hannah receives a shock. She discovers that the girl stormed out of her house in a tantrum because her mother insisted that she do her homework before she went to see her boyfriend. She is an ordinary immature teenager, as Hannah was and still is to some extent, stripped of pants and shoes and walking a road in her new home town. An anonymous policeman pulls up next to her in a police car, asking the usual police questions. Inexplicably and comically, he seems to understand this bizarre spectacle when she tells him that she has just had a baby.

The collision between Hannah's mental clichés, her physical plight, and the understanding of the policeman as communal representative yields embodied meaning and transformation. There is no discussion of the change, but Hannah reaches a new point in her conversation with life, maturity, and relationship. Together on the porch of Hannah's new home, she, Marnie, and Loreen all hear Grover cry. Hannah refuses their help but goes to him herself. As Marnie and Loreen contemplate their futures on the porch, Grover latches onto Hannah's breast. We do not see him do it; we see only the look of surprise and pleasure on Hannah's face and then hear his contented gurgling over a black screen as Hannah murmurs and sings to him.[9] The inconclusive but thoughtful conversation between Loreen and Marnie is the acme of their maturity in this series. Hannah's patient nursing of Grover is her zenith. In this fictional world where the flow of life is both physically and mentally chaotic, they have made significant progress.

A NONFORMULAIC FEMINIST FABLE FOR OUR TIMES

Girls gives new meaning to the phrase "the world spins" through its auteur revisioning of the sitcom narrative. Relationships are highlighted as cultural spin about connection and disconnection. Experience highlights the spin about maturity. The series also responds to the spin that passes for feminism in the mass media.[10] Feminism as usually narrated only in terms of systems and rebellion is too removed from the mind-body dialogue that is reality in Dunham's series. Standard feminist concepts abound in *Girls*, but they are thin and comical in contrast to the final images of Hannah, Marnie, and Loreen dealing with themselves, each other, and Grover.

Here it is necessary to make a distinction between Dunham as storyteller and Dunham as feminist activist, which are two different domains for her. This study departs from the bulk of current discussion of Dunham, which is undertaken in a way that makes her life the paratext of her work.[11] However, I would like to suggest a crucial difference: elision of Dunham's life and work is of limited usefulness in illuminating *Girls*. Dunham's well-known and publicly documented controversial and much-criticized activism is sharply defined as to her political goals. Dunham as storyteller, as artist, is in a different position. As the creator of *Girls*, Dunham is a complex observer of women's lives. Her instinct to use the bodies of her characters centrally to depict who they are and how they and everyone else exceed the limits of social discourse and organization of course means that female and male self-assertion alike will be prone to comic confusion. Art is incompatible with the logical linearity of propaganda; political action requires a logically coherent linear agenda. These are unreconcilable differences. Demanding that the pieces fit together is a regressive position that modern frameworks of thought alluded to in this study have rejected. Dunham's art is simply not a piece with her activism, and her activism is not material to this study. Her feminism in *Girls* is.

Dunham's art in *Girls* has resulted in narrative that makes fun of the traps we can fall into if we reduce feminism to slogans and marching orders. This is true and funny when Hannah uses half-baked feminist dogma only for her own selfish purposes in the earlier seasons. It is even truer and more comic in the final season of the series as Hannah moves out into the world and into a more far-reaching domain of reductionist dogma. We can get a handle on how the last season takes comic pleasure in its satire of simplistic feminism by looking at three funny and disturbing scenes relating to Hannah's career in "All I Ever Wanted" (6.1), "American Bitch" (6.3), and "Goodbye Tour" (6.9). In episode 6.1, Hannah is interviewed and immediately hired by Chelsea (Chelsea Peretti), an editor at *Slag Mag*, to write an article about a surf camp. In episode 6.3, Hannah interviews Chuck Palmer (Matthew Rhys), an author she has admired but who has been accused in print of being a sexual predator by a number of women. In episode 6.9, Hannah is interviewed and hired on the spot by the department chair of a small college, a woman with the ominous name of Phaedra (Ann Dowd), the doomed incestuous stepmother of ancient Greek mythology.

The "interview" scenes make us giggle at numerous shifts between an older model of obliviously self-centered, bumptious Hannah not yet fully dead and a new model of savvy, more focused Hannah not yet fully born. They also satirize the rise of an old girls' network as skewed and foolish as the old boys' network of the pre–women's lib days, particularly the episode in which Hannah interviews Chuck Palmer. Hannah is shakily making her way as a feminist, but only two cheers for female liberation. Feminists too are comically embroiled in a confusing mind/body dialogue.

In episode 6.1, Chelsea's enthusiasm about Hannah as a writer for *Slag Mag* thrills Hannah but raises all kinds of alarm bells. Chelsea may be willing to go all out to support her sister writers, but, to put it mildly, she is not a responsible journalist and does not bode well for women in the profession. The interview is funny but also troubling. We watch Hannah jump through hoops for Chelsea, who expresses a voyeuristic, puerile enthusiasm for the story Hannah published based on the Hannah-Jessa-Adam triangle. Chelsea displays no understanding that Hannah regards her article as a deeply felt discussion of emotional complexities. Chelsea also upholds no journalistic standards, blithely ignoring the first rule of responsible reporting: objectivity.

She tells Hannah what to say about the surf camp that neither of them has yet seen. Hannah jumps right on board. She wants the assignment. Chelsea's feminism is everything that *Girls* mocks and everything that sexist authorities have been accused of. It complicates Hannah's success by embroiling her in the kind of dissociated storytelling that has been discredited in every episode of the series.

Something similar happens in episode 6.9, during Hannah's interview with Phaedra. Middle-aged Phaedra wants to energize her department with, as she puts it, "young cock" and the amazing vitality of young mothers and pregnant women. She is interviewing for a faculty member who can bring that energy to teaching students about the Internet. Sold on pregnant Hannah as soon as she walks in the door, Phaedra reverses the long-standing prejudices against women in hiring practices, but is her enthusiasm for Hannah really progress? Indeed her groundless decision to hire Hannah for her pregnant belly and her breasts made fuller by the pregnancy is appallingly funny. Hannah has no credentials. She has no advanced degree, no publishing record, no teaching experience. Too much uncritical sisterhood makes for a very undistinguished moment in feminist history.

But the plight of doctrinaire feminism in an indeterminate world of minds and bodies is most piercingly presented in "American Bitch," when Hannah interviews Chuck Palmer, a highly successful author with charisma to spare. Her arrival in his beautiful apartment has some echoes of her first look at Joshua's apartment in "One Man's Trash." In both cases, she is already seduced by the wealth that passes for satisfaction in materialist America before the action begins. She leaves Joshua with many questions about what relationships are to her. She leaves Chuck's apartment, as we do, with many questions about what feminism is to her and us.

When Hannah arrives, she announces to Chuck that she is appalled by recent claims by many women that he sexually molested them and spouts a fairly standard feminist doctrine about abuse and nonconsensual sexual touching, with which most in the audience will be in agreement. The episode in a darkly comic mode destroys the concept of clarity about what it means to give consent, as Palmer administers a lesson in the complexities of the corporeal experience of sexism. It is not clear whether his "lesson" is premeditated, but Jenni Konner, the executive producer of the series, has expressed a belief that it is unlikely to be. And the episode suggests that she is accurate. The episode raises questions about his behavior and Hannah's behavior rather than certainties.

After Chuck listens politely to Hannah's ideas, she relaxes. He has no trouble leading her to his bedroom as they engage in literary conversation.

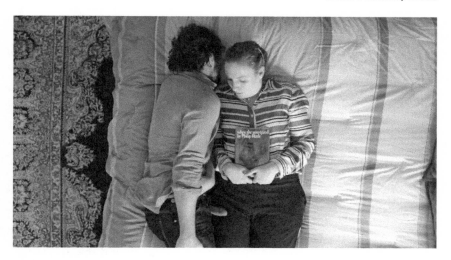

FIGURE 6.5. *What is consent?*

He has a signed first edition of Philip Roth's *Goodbye, Columbus*, originally titled *American Bitch*, that he would like to show her and spontaneously gives it to her as a present. A thrilled Hannah literally clasps the book to her bosom. Then, in an affectless tone, Chuck asks her to lie down on his bed with him and keep her clothes on. He pompously tells her that he just wants to maintain the proper boundaries but also feel close to someone at this moment. When she lies down next to him, he pulls his penis out of his pants so that it rests on her thigh. She looks down to see it, pink against her back stretch pants. She touches it without any invitation from him, surprised to find herself doing so but proceeding anyway, only to pull back in alarm and throw Roth's book away from her.

The question of consent is now fiercely in play, and it is never to be comfortably resolved. Is Hannah manifesting some kind of hard-wiring in women that instantly provides service when men "take care" of us? Or is it some kind of social conditioning to the same effect? Which, if any, of the events in Chuck's bedroom were consensual? Existing on two levels of mind and body that rarely coordinate, the innate behavior of the characters in *Girls* is almost always at odds with ideas, as ideas are at odds with bodies. At that point Chuck's adorable daughter arrives. Hannah's feminist outrage is further complicated by her observation that love for his daughter radiates out of every pore in Chuck's body. Are we in the presence of Lee Edelman's Child syndrome? Doubtful, as it is Chuck who is subdued, rather than empowered. It is Hannah whose doors of perception are opened. As Hannah drifts out of the apartment, while Chuck is obliviously involved with his daughter, Hannah looks behind her and sees a long line of women of all descriptions at Chuck's door, the only moment in the series when a visionary, surrealist image is employed. It is an important moment that I would contend defines the central character of *Girls* as a feminist fable. Instead of concluding with a familiar indictment of Palmer as a sexist, the episode removes us to the plane of imagination and asks us to contemplate as broadly as possible rather than to judge gender relations.

Men, women, abuse, consent. Hannah is lost. Her body has been violated; this much is clear to her. But, as is typical of the series, Hannah has no conceptual, logical, discursive clarity about whether she consented to it or how Chuck feels about female persons. This is an important part of the feminism of *Girls*. Hannah arrives at her own inner analysis of the relationship between what passes for standard feminism and the experience of male authority and power that she has, anchored in her body. This is not activist Lena Dunham speaking, it is contemplative Lena Dunham, the storyteller, who takes the opportunity of the art of her sitcom to plunge into the complexity of the ideas that she more simply cleaves to in the world of action. Should we laugh or cry at the spectacle of Hannah's interview with Chuck? The incongruity of that very pink penis suddenly draped over her black-clad thigh joins the comedy of the failure of families, the dumbing down of social discourse, the collapse of language, the chaotic notions about what relationship means, and the tragicomic possibility that no one actually ever matures. Chuck Palmer is a ruling patriarch, but in the end there is the comic reality of Chuck's divided identity because of his daughter. This is Dunham's comic take on what Lee Edelman envisioned tragically as the procreativity that cements the tyranny of patriarchy.

In Laura Mulvey's "Afterthoughts on 'Visual Pleasure and Narrative Cinema,'" the mother of feminist film criticism identifies as the quintessential female tragedy the death of Pearl Chavez (Jennifer Jones) because she is unable to establish a stable identity in a hierarchal patriarchal world. In Lena Dunham's comic televisual vision, Pearl would just be one of the befuddled guests dancing at Shoshanna's engagement party or one of the crowd of "American bitches" that Hannah imagines converging on Chuck Palmer's apartment. In the groundbreaking modernist television of *Girls'* feminist auteur, you know who cannot establish a stable identity? In Loreen Horvath's comically mournful words, "Fucking everyone!"

·

CHAPTER 7

BACKLASH! FORMULA 2.0

If you look carefully at *Breaking Bad* and any given episode of *The X-Files*, you will realize the structure is exactly the same.

—Vince Gilligan, IMDb (International Movie Database)

The post-*Peaks* evolution of the formulaic American television series is also part of the legacy of the David effect. TV 1.0 began to undergo a transformation almost as soon as *Twin Peaks* went on the air in 1990. Indeed, by the turn of the twenty-first century, we no longer had TV 1.0. We had its successor, henceforward to be known as 2.0, a many-faceted reaction to and against auteur television that mingles the appearance of expanding aesthetic possibilities with a resolute preservation of the perfect hero and perfect narrative—and its disconnection from the cultural ideas that now shape modernity.

With good reason, 2.0 has intrigued many serious television critics through its delight in playing with special effects, inventive framing, and trendy editing. It has brought a stylishness to American television that was previously lacking. But it is necessary to stand back and note that in virtually all cases this is a matter of form divorced from function. The glittery but superficial aesthetic effects are virtually never in the service of storytelling that moves beyond the constraints of story product. We see this most blatantly in the new fantasy/horror/sci-fi super hero series and in the updated pseudo–socially conscious series. In the new super hero series, all problems are ultimately managed by superperfect heroes, male and female, who exceed the purely human talents of the 1.0 perfect hero.[1] The characters represent a spectrum of races, ethnicities, and genders in the allegedly more socially responsible 2.0 series. But any problems, discontinuities, or fragmentations that might occur as a result of diverse histories are ultimately shaved down to become smooth interlocking pieces of the narrative puzzle, as in the amiable caper series *Leverage*, created by Chris Downey and John Rogers. This 2.0 upgrade is about charming former criminals of diverse ethnicities, races, and genders who band together to save ordinary people from the abuses committed by the rich and privileged. All this is posed in transgressive terms, as 2.0 social issues generally are, to fit the needs of story product. Transgressive battles lend themselves to the perfect narrative, which is continuous, well defined, and definitively resolved, unlike the liminal visions of culture in auteur storytelling.[2] However, a small group of 2.0 series manifests stylish innovations and suggests larger ideas through apparent rebellions against old mass-media taboos, but almost always without engaging the audience in the destabilizing confusions that connect viewers with fearful and wonderful modern speculations about reality.

While this group of 2.0 shows continues the formulaic tradition of the perfect hero, it offers two variations on the old recipe for story products. One variation incorporates into perfect narratives a perfect enough but eccentric hero, of which Fox Mulder (David Duchovny) in Chris Carter's *X-Files* is the template, an outsider in conflict with a problematic social structure, David against Goliath. The eccentric hero breaks the mold of the 1.0 perfect hero as a flawless representative of an innately good society while continuing the formulaic perpetuation of narrative complications cut to suit the powers of the hero. The other type offers what appears to be a much more dramatic change in televisual entertainment: narratives about the almost total corruption of an antihero swaggering around in an almost totally corrupt society, such as Walter "Walt" White (Bryan Cranston) in Vince Gilligan's *Breaking Bad*, Al Swearengen (Ian McShane) in David Milch's *Deadwood*, and Annalise Keating (Viola Davis) in Peter Nowalk's *How to Get Away with Murder*. But here, too, the fictional universe tailors the corrupt society to the dimensions of its antiheroes' control. The term "antihero," which was inapplicable to our discussions about nonformulaic television, is well suited to the corrupt swaggerers of 2.0, as will become apparent. The term "antihero" nicely involves a villainy that provokes no discontinuities, fragmentation, or paradoxes and assures definitive closure.

The new league of perfect-enough Fox Mulder–like eccentrics and the perfectly imperfect antiheroes keep alive the spirit of 1.0 protagonists that tower over their circumstances. They protect audiences from wonder or deep fears whether they are scapegoated by dangerous authorities or conduct cultural business by vicious and depraved means.

THE JOURNEY OF THE ECCENTRIC HERO—AND HIS GIRLFRIEND

Fox Mulder in *The X-Files*, the *ur*-eccentric hero and model for all eccentric heroes, is a story-product version of David Lynch's Dale Cooper in the 1990–1991 *Twin Peaks*, but not because Carter took inspiration from Lynch. Carter's official story is that he was inspired by *Kolchak: The Night Stalker*, a formulaic, darkly comic 1.0 attempt at science fiction created by Jeffrey Grant Rice featuring Carl Kolchak (Darren McGavin), a rumpled, offbeat reporter who notices deviations from normal life that others do not and copes with them.[3] And Carter is right. Mulder is much more a descendant of Kolchak than of Cooper. The connection between Carter and Lynch is that *Twin Peaks* cleared the way for formulaic television to play offensively with a reductionist version of Lynch's genuine mysteries. Moreover, like *Kolchak*, *The X-Files* understands mystery as a deviation from the "norm," not as the core of human existence.

Twin Peaks is a visionary work of art that dissolves 1.0 ideas of "the norm." Carter's series only proposes mutant and alien disturbances of the norm. Cooper hazards the overwhelming mysteries of the cosmos beyond marketplace norms; Fox Mulder, like Kolchak, is a champion dedicated to saving "normal" life from mutants and conspirators and functions as a Sherlockian clue hound. But Mulder has something that neither Cooper nor Kolchak can boast of: a female sidekick, Dana Scully (Gillian Anderson). There, as we shall soon see, lies Carter's real originality.

Mulder and Scully have more frustrations than the 1.0 perfect hero, but not because of the mutants and aliens: they make all the pertinent discoveries about them and find the necessary answers. Rather, they are thwarted by a government that considers them oddballs—Mulder has a reputation as a fool at the FBI—and conspires for nefarious reasons to prevent them from achieving acknowledgment for their success. This is the business of storytelling with a twist. Carter's only slightly skewed story products are available in two templates: the episodes that form a conventional long arc story in which Mulder and Scully repeatedly find evidence for a criminal conspiracy between the government and aliens and a plethora of stand-alone episodes about human oddities here on earth.[4]

The government conspiracy story arc identifies perfect villains, not the inherent, unsolvable mysteries that nonformulaic television depicts as complicating our understanding of life. The stand-alone episodes initially suggest some odd pieces of the puzzle of existence but turn out to be 2.0 *X-File* "freaks" that can be culled from the herd to protect the normal world. The long arc is a tale of perfect heroes and perfect villains, of which more below. All the stand-alones are similar tales about some form of freakish deviant that violates the basic normality of the real world.

"Small Potatoes" (4.20) is a particularly good example of the formulaic nature of the stand-alones, notwithstanding their attention to seemingly out-of-the-box situations. It is a lovely mélange of the actors' personal charm and onscreen couple chemistry, the show's humor, its imaginative invocation of a world beyond the usual expectations, and a reassuring conclusion that confirms unbroken formulaic normality. Eddie Van Blundht (Darin Morgan), a janitor at a fertility clinic, uses his strange ability to shape-shift into the likeness of anyone he chooses in order to impregnate four clinic patients and his high school girlfriend who long ago rejected him. Scully and Mulder turn up at the fertility clinic suspecting the doctor, like all the people involved in this unhappy turn of events. But Mulder, in perfect hero fashion, is onto Van Blundht as the culprit in minutes.

Wandering through the hallways, while Scully attends to the uproar between unhappy couples and the clinic doctor, Mulder conveniently spots Van Blundht involved in janitorial duties, at the precise moment when he bends over to reveal, just above the division between his posterior cheeks, the scar where his vestigial tail was removed. It is not long before Mulder is able to connect this deformity to Van Blundht's shape-shifting powers. Mulder may be an outsider in the FBI, but he is an insider on the terrain of clues, possessing the perfect hero's uncanny ability to narrow down the fictional universe to precisely the details necessary to perfect closure. This episode avails itself of the new freedom to use previously taboo images by visualizing the first clue with bawdy humor: the plump, gaping buttocks of Van Blundht that will put Mulder and the show on the narrative track. (In the spirit of the 2.0 version of the liberated woman, it is sometimes Scully who "finds the buttocks," so to speak.)

Nevertheless, the more seemingly deviant the situation appears, the more potent Mulder and Scully seem. In this episode, Mulder looms large indeed when he has to deal with being imprisoned by Van Blundht in a locker in the deepest recesses of the clinic basement. Van Blundht transforms into a clone of Mulder, leaving Scully vulnerable to the Mulder look-alike. In the spirit of 1.0, we never learn how Mulder extricates himself from the subterranean locker to get to Scully "just in time" and capture Van Blundht. But what would the details matter? His propitious arrival is destined in story-product land. While Mulder is a 2.0 eccentric hero, he reproduces the omnipotence of the perfect hero over context, with a vengeance. Once apprehended, Van Blundht is put on tranquilizers so that he cannot continue to morph. Case closed.

Here and in the long story arc episodes about alien invaders, *The X-Files* tacks a veneer of superficially bizarre incidents over a highly formulaic plot structure and takes the urgency out of all questions it may raise about matter or aliens and governments. Indeed, the aliens on *The X-Files* may be the least mysterious creatures from outer space in the history of the American mass media. If that is a slight overstatement, it is nevertheless true that *X-Files* aliens are well defined. As the series unfolds, the audience is fed a well-articulated story about two tribes of aliens. One is composed of small gray hominoids with large insectlike black eyes (and a capacity for shape shifting) that control the government on their home planet. The other is composed of rebellious full-sized humanoid aliens with sealed facial orifices (to make it harder for the grays to identify and catch them), who attempt to thwart the grays' plans to colonize earth. We learn much about the long-standing historical connection between aliens and earth cultures and the current goal of this cabal to fabricate a human/alien hybrid, ideal for colonization.

Behind the corruption of government in *The X-Files* stands the standard issue "bad guy" common to 1.0. Mulder's archnemesis is C. G. B. Spender (William B. Davis), an inordinately perfect villain. He is the source of both the hidden evil in American government and the hidden evil in Mulder's personal life and as such handily facilitates the linear plots of the episodes and their definitive closures. As a shadow force behind the powers that be, Spender is responsible not only for every terrible aspect of the pact between the villainous human conspirators and the aliens, but, as we learn in "Musings of a Cigarette Smoking Man" (4.7), also for every terrible event of post–World War II American history. We discover that he orchestrated the assassinations of President John F. Kennedy, Martin Luther King Jr., and Robert Kennedy and lurked as the dark force behind the injustices that surfaced in the Anita Hill case and in the Rodney King case. With a dash of playful "coolness," the series adds that he is also the reason why the Buffalo Bills will never win the Super Bowl.

Spender, not the beloved Bill Mulder (Peter Donat), also turns out to be Mulder's biological father. This explains away the odd circumstance that Mulder is never killed or fired despite his constant challenges to some very merciless evildoers at the FBI. The manipulative Spender protects his son and torments him at the same time, by destroying all the evidence that Mulder finds about his despicable machinations with the aliens. Very evil— and also the stuff of paranoia. The institutions in which we place our trust are not what they seem. And yet, considering that all the problems narrow down to one villain, not the structure of reality, are we really in a different position than we were in *Columbo*?

Some of the shows that were inspired by *The X-Files* further exacerbated the paranoia, while falling short of the charisma of *The X-Files*, such as *Eureka*, *Warehouse 13*, and *Falling Skies*, and Carter's own successors to his series: *Harsh Realm*, *Millennium*, and *The Lone Gunmen*. These were even more simplistic than *The X-Files* in their plotting. But *The X-Files* also inspired a wide assortment of other kinds of 2.0 eccentric heroes who face down a variety of Goliaths, including Will Schuester (Matthew Morrison) in *Glee* and Daniel Holden (Aden Young) in *Rectify*. Schuester's alternative sensitive masculinity as a music teacher had to stand strong against a school administration more conventionally dedicated to the machismo of sports and ultimately quite consolingly reconfigured his initially abusive educational environment as a place with a new respect for difference. Holden, an innocent victim of cruel (southern) patriarchal authority, begins the series suffering from the trauma of a prison experience that he did not deserve but ends by having quite reassuringly conquered his demons and exonerated himself.

It was predictable that the success of *The X-Files* would open the door to new opportunities for formulaic science fiction on television and to anti-authoritarian male eccentrics. What was not predictable was the immense impact that Scully and her relationship with Mulder would have on TV 2.0. The self-assertive Scully did not alienate viewers and in fact became an object of fan adoration, so producers began to feel safe including strong-minded women and even female versions of the perfect hero in their shows. Most likely it never occurred to the creators of shows about deviant and/or strong women in 2.0 shows like *United States of Tara* and *Weeds* that they were indebted to *The X-Files* for the welcoming climate it created for women in Formula 2.0 television who were either absent from or demonized in 1.0. But they too were cut to fit the dimensions of the story product.

The Scully repercussions extend all the way to the goofy female heroes of *Parks and Recreation* and *30 Rock*, which can be labeled stories of the eccentric hero—and her boyfriend. They extend also to Rayna Jaymes (Connie Britton), the perfect hero of *Nashville*, whose eccentricity consists simply of being a heroine rarely visualized on television outside of daytime soap opera in its heyday: the benign, sexual, yet highly competent woman who keeps order in a world only nominally run by patriarchs. Two other shows that visualize similarly capable and simultaneously desirable women are *Scandal* and *The Good Wife*. And, of course, *Orange Is the New Black* is set in a women's prison, an unprecedentedly secluded feminine world. Almost all of the important intimate and collaborative relationships are among women of highly diverse races, ethnicities, and socioeconomic classes. Its narrative structure is formulaic but hybridized by its initial presentation of nuanced, ordinary problems and how women work together to solve them, like the real-world context in the autobiography on which it was based. Unhappily, it became increasingly formulaic over time, wading into grandiose high melodrama that violated the intent of the book and disconnected its characters from reflecting on human situations, even in its earlier, limited way.[5]

Just as consequential for 2.0 is Scully's relationship with Mulder, which generated a new kind of story-product romantic story. Questions about what Scully and Mulder are to each other as colleagues, friends, and potential lovers, which in one way or another resonate throughout the series, are the reduced 2.0 version of Dunham's much more searching, expressive, and imaginative exploration of the nature of relationships in *Girls*. The nature of the Scully-Mulder personal-professional alliance has a limited indeterminacy but ultimately turned toward manipulation of the audience. Carter repeatedly broke the rules of the fictional universe he had created to lure viewers back for the next installment of the continuing story.

The curious tale of Scully's pregnancy is the most blatant example of how Carter turned intriguing questions about where collegiality ends and intimacy begins into bad storytelling and confusion. The descent into narrative nonsense begins in "En Ami" (7.15), when Scully is taken away for a weekend by C. G. B. Spender, lured by the promise of a cure for her cancer that resulted from her abduction. After a dinner for two, the next morning Scully cannot remember the night before and believes that she was drugged by Spender, who did not give her the promised cure. Later, in light of Scully's inexplicable pregnancy, viewer speculation began that Spender had raped her or given her some kind of treatment based on alien technology that impregnated her. A different sexual possibility was also thrown into the mix at about the same time. In the opening scene of "All Things" (7.17), two episodes after Scully's weekend with Spender, we see Scully getting dressed, while a naked sleeping Mulder, tastefully draped by sheets, is visible behind her. All the signs of consummation are there, but the elliptical tease denies us the formulaic certainty typical of 2.0, while generating hopes and questions about Mulder's part in her pregnancy.

This is not an example of the art of indeterminacy but a version of the highly formulaic manipulative "who's the daddy?" ploy employed by 1.0 melodrama. In this case, the ploy was shamelessly embellished with a very suspect use of religious metaphor. The mystery of a woman giving birth despite the impossibility of impregnation in the usual way connects the series not to cutting-edge thinking of any kind but either to the possibility of a benign mutation in a fictional universe of one-off mutations or to a crass use of the seminal Christian story of divine birth. Indeed, in "Existence" (8.21), Scully's baby is born in a structure that looks very much like a manger, with allusions to the birth of Jesus. Scully has hidden herself from potential dangers to her baby from aliens. She and Mulder agree that even he should not know where she is, but he arrives in time to see the newborn, quipping that he followed a star that led him to her.

The chemistry of the actors renders the episode charming and enthralling, but as a narrative this episode is hardly up to Dunham's art when she played with the enigmas of parenthood and love. It throws all the clichés it can at the audience, hoping that "love is the answer" (divine or human), a pseudo-clarity if ever there was one, will placate the viewers. The 2017 reprise of the series moves from cliché to craven deviousness in its attempt to get more mileage out of the original mechanical, formulaic complications of the birth mystery. Spender claims that he is the father, abetted by alien technology. It then tops its chicanery by ending the series with yet another impossible Scully pregnancy. This time Mulder is proclaimed the father for certain.

Generally speaking, the initial nine seasons of *The X-Files* are a mélange of bogus science, convenient religion, and groundbreaking romance: now giving us conventional detection in a science fiction context, now regaling us with conventional dystopian images, now whispering in our ears a version of *amor vincit omnia*. The cynical 2017 series does not make the original sentimentality more complex; it only piles on more layers of mismatched clichés to exploit audience affection for its innovative couple. This reduction of questions of intimacy to the dimensions of the perfect narrative engendered a series of similar seemingly ambiguous professional/erotic relationships in *Bones, Burn Notice, Masters of Sex*, and *Castle*. *Masters of Sex*, like *Orange Is the New Black*, is based on a biographical account, in this case of the male/female partnership of the pioneers of sex therapy, intuitive and promiscuous Virginia Johnson (Lizzy Caplan) and icily cerebral Bill Masters (Michael Sheen). As with *Orange*, the series gives a particularly clear look at how 2.0 disconnects the complexities of life from television through perfect narrative.

Yet the very power of art television has also meant that the most inventive of the 2.0 series occasionally veers into something very close to auteur TV. Three reflexive *X-File* episodes do just that. "The Post-Modern Prometheus" (5.5), the story of a scientist who fancies himself a twentieth-century Dr. Frankenstein, is the most fantastic of the three. "Jose Chung's 'From Outer Space'" (3.20), a story about a writer whose research on alien abduction uncovers numerous unreconcilable perspectives on a Mulder/Scully case, is the wittiest. "Milagro" (6.18), the story of a writer who unleashes his unsatisfied urges as an evil inflicted on the world through his fiction, is the closest *The X-Files* ever came to being auteur television.

"Milagro" authentically troubles the line between the imagination and the external world in both its plotting and its sensory palette. The spectator is haunted long after the episode has concluded by a variety of modern philosophical and psychological speculations about how we human beings create our own reality. This episode does not proceed from the point of view of Mulder and Scully but from the perspective of Phillip Padgett (John Hawkes), a writer who has moved next door to Mulder in order to meet Scully. "Milagro" destabilizes the very clichés about love on which the series is built, not as a matter of an atypical mutation but as a way of depicting human reality. While Scully and Mulder are on the trail of a serial killer who mysteriously removes the hearts of his victims in lovers' lanes, Padgett is in the process of writing a novel. It combines a horror story about a serial killer named Ken Naciamento (Nestor Serrano) who, not coincidentally, extracts the hearts of his victims through psychic surgery and a love story that fictionalizes his own passion for Scully.

Mulder's next-door neighbor is the criminal they are searching for. Or is it Naciamento who crosses the line between fiction and reality and performs the psychic surgery that Padgett recounts in his manuscript? Indeterminate. Regardless, Scully and Mulder (uniquely resembling the nonformulaic protagonist here) are consistently unable to find or follow reliable clues. When Padgett's various obsessions lead him to merge with his creation Naciamento, who directs him to kill Scully, Mulder is not only unable to save Scully himself but accidentally almost facilitates her death. Mulder, convulsed with jealousy because of Padgett's interest in Scully and certain that the manuscript is evidence, chases Padgett down to the apartment house furnace room to prevent him from burning the manuscript. But only burning the manuscript can stop him, as Padgett knows, so Mulder is prolonging Naciamento's ability to kill Scully by preventing it. This unresolved, liminal situation is only brought to a head when Mulder finally realizes that Scully is in mortal peril and forgets his vendetta with Padgett. Mulder returns to his apartment to find Scully apparently moribund, her white blouse soaked in her red blood. But many floors below in the furnace room, Padgett breathes life back into her by burning the manuscript and pulling his own heart out of his chest, still pulsating and dripping. With Scully's sudden intake of breath, she and Mulder reach for each other, their bodies entwining. But if love has conquered in this episode, it is a deeply enigmatic victory.

FIGURE 7.1. *Scully lives because Mulder loses perfect control.*

"Milagro," a fascinating anomaly in *The X-Files* fictional world, blurs the boundaries between formula television and art television, as Padgett's imagination stymies the ability of Scully and Mulder to reduce their fictional world to the size of their deductions. The indeterminacy begins almost immediately, while Scully is on the phone with Mulder as he calls from the scene of a second strange death in which a victim has been discovered without a heart. Scully has found an unmarked envelope on the floor of Mulder's office containing a *milagro*, a religious medal picturing a burning heart, and the two of them wonder if it has a bearing on their case. After Scully hangs up and looks at the *milagro* in puzzlement, Padgett's voiceover begins to describe her every action, which we can see, and her purported internal thoughts about the relationship between the medal and the crime, which we cannot. At this point the narrative bolts the narrative tracks that had seemed to be under construction. The scene cuts between Scully and Padgett as his words fill the soundtrack. Although the montage clearly began in external reality, it has become impossible to tell whether at some point it seamlessly morphed to his imagination of her while they are spatially far apart. Are we witnessing a swerve of time and space described by quantum science as part of the modern understanding of how the universe functions? (See the discussion of entanglement in chapter 1.) A trace of cutting-edge storytelling is in the air.

This kind of violation of traditional expectations of time and space erupts at other times during the episode. It is compounded by the other crucial violation of ordinary physics and the logic of materiality: the entrance into the world of matter of the psychic surgeon Naciamento, whom Padgett has written into his pages, based on a real psychic surgeon who is now dead. The liminality of the relationship between a fictional character and the real world Naciamento's embodiment is never explained away by the episode. The line between imagination and reality is severely troubled when Naciamento kills and when Mulder and Scully observe Padgett through a camera that they have rigged up to monitor his actions and see nothing but Padgett sitting at his desk. The writer's process is invisible to the eccentric heroes.

The episode is filled with a wonder that is not far from what Lynch proposes in both the original series of *Twin Peaks* and *Twin Peaks* (2017), discussed in the coda. In "Milagro," questions are raised about imagination and reality that are never answered. But because the episode is part of a 2.0 fictional world, unlike in Lynch's works, we are saved from the truly extreme possibilities of the human condition proposed here by a reassurance about the unconditional, ineradicable love between Mulder and Scully, the truth of which they do not yet fully know. The episode closes on an affirmative note. Padgett's sacrifice is the perplexing liminality of human creativity that supports this love. It is a deeply emotional closure for *X-Files* fans that satisfies all our longings for perfect and eternal love after a brief hiatus into a more challenging mode of storytelling.

Mulder and Scully and their descendants do ring a few changes on the perfect hero of 1.0 but do little more than embroider the 1.0 perfect narrative. However, the transformation of the perfect villain into a 2.0 antihero is another story. The new depiction of cynicism, brutality, and criminality in a 2.0 antihero television series is such a stunning departure from the conventional story product that it bellows for our attention. Most insistently, it requires that we think about what happens when you shoehorn an evil character into the role of hero in an American TV story product. But before we go further, we need to clarify an important point. There is no such thing as *the* 2.0 antihero.

THE JOURNEY OF THE VILLAIN: NEGATIVE EXAMPLES

Formula 2.0 offers more than one kind of antiheroic narrative. It always offers the audience identification with a criminal protagonist, a genuine, significant, and startling change in storytelling from 1.0. However, crime does not pay for some of these antiheroes, while it does for others. Crime does not pay for the antihero who functions as a negative example. This more familiar version of the antiheroic narrative tells its tales from the point of view that we have often seen before in old gangster movies if not in television. This update of the flamboyant men played by James Cagney and Edward G. Robinson for Warner Bros. offers a chance for audiences to identify unapologetically with bad guys at the top of their game while preserving conventional story product norms when they fall spectacularly.

By contrast, crime pays abundantly for the antiheroes of *Deadwood* and *How to Get Away with Murder*, who tower over extremely corrupt fictional worlds as the lesser of the many evils of a brutish reality in a troubling way that we have never seen before in popular culture. In *The Wire*, David Simon created an antihero in vigilante drug dealer Omar Little, a corrupt man taking charge of a corrupt situation. But in this nonformulaic series the social system is too vast for the symmetry of fighting fire perfectly with fire. By contrast, 2.0 stories about the ascendance of the perfect villain to a position usually held by the perfect hero narrow their corrupt fictional universes to the dimensions of their antiheroes.

The more familiar 2.0 antihero who gives us an oblique lesson that crime does not pay takes the shape of Vic Mackey (Michael Chiklis) in Shawn Ryan's *The Shield*; Dexter Morgan (Michael C. Hall) in James Manos Jr.'s *Dexter*; and, most of all, Walt White in Vince Gilligan's *Breaking Bad*, which is the most important and brilliant of the 2.0 negative example series, as we shall see. Giving this kind of 2.0 antihero story its due, it does display a modicum of trust in the audience. As we follow the rise and fall of the 2.0 antihero, we are given the freedom to make a leap toward an active understanding of morality when the party ends in death or incarceration instead of being spoon-fed morality through a 1.0 straightforward model of goodness in the person of a police officer, detective, or reporter.

It is Gilligan who brings his formulaic crime tale most tantalizingly close to reality when he motivates Walt to become an almost omnipotent meth lord by tapping into the financial conditions faced by so many hardworking American people. Walt begins the series as a kind, educated, loving husband and father, a high school chemistry teacher who was a prodigy early in his career but was cheated out of the fame and fortune he deserved by a couple that he had considered his best friends. The measure of Walt's original integrity is that those injustices did not catapult him into a life of crime. Similarly, he and his wife, Skyler White (Anna Gunn), are financially strapped by the expenses of having a teenaged son, Walter White Jr. (R. J. Mitte), who was born with cerebral palsy. That also did not cause Walt to cease his struggle to live by humane, ethical values in a world that does not respect knowledge or teachers and is built on injustice and brute force. Walt reaches his limit when he is diagnosed with stage four cancer. How will his family live once he is gone? Now he uses his education to become the country's most eminent, successful, and feared meth lord. At the same time, Gilligan's hybridized formulaic narrative gives some play not only to fiscal realities but also to a connection in the American imagination between crime and masculinity.

Initially, masculinity figures ambiguously as we are prodded to think, at least in a limited way, about whether Walt becomes more of a man when he makes a 180-degree turn toward the life of a feared and admired meth lord and away from his life as a teacher, mocked by his students and sexually dominated by his beautiful wife. As a meth lord, Walt begins an immediate transformation, ascending toward the dominant role of the hierarchal male. He partners up with Jesse Pinkman (Aaron Paul), the worst student he ever taught, now a petty criminal, to assist him in meth production. Walt has never dominated anyone before. He was barely able to keep order in his classroom. He also emerges as a newly dominant husband. At the end of the pilot episode, the previously deferential Walt makes an aggressive sexual overture to Skyler, flipping her over to penetrate her anally. "Walt," she gasps. "Is that you?"

Ultimately, however, Gilligan's series does validate the illusion that crime is indeed manly. Walt is not only more macho than he was as a teacher but ultimately more virile than even his butch Drug Enforcement Agency brother-in-law, Hank Schrader (Dean Norris). And the series never backs down on its postulation of the superior masculinity of the antihero. When Walt turns meth lord, he immediately begins to loom larger and larger as a powerful figure. Then his masculinity quotient skyrockets further. In "Cornered" (4.6), when Skyler tells Walt that his life of crime has made her afraid of the danger he has brought into their lives and afraid of who will knock on the door, he is able to say, "I am the danger; I am the one who knocks." Walt's menace builds until he is able to destroy Gus Fring (Giancarlo Esposito), a cold-blooded, fastidious, deadly, and powerful drug empire head masquerading as a pillar of the community. And he finally obliterates a degenerate gang of American Nazi psychopaths through scientific genius.

Buying into the way Walt is made unquestionably more virile and powerful by crime points the series toward its destiny as perfect narrative. Walt's climactic battle with the white nationalists, his final assertion of his power, engages his perfect scientific expertise in the time-tested manner of story product. The self-starting, repeat-firing mechanism that he rigs to kill the entire coven of Nazis depends on the narrowing of the fictional universe to precisely the conditions that Walt postulates in setting it up, erasing the endless details that might have gone wrong in a universe that genuinely observes scientific understanding of matter and mechanisms. His last triumph kills him along with the white nationalists, but he does take a lot of them with him. It is the old, traditional consolation from gangster movies, where the protagonist goes down in a blaze of glory or at least after achieving a lot of glory.

Nevertheless, just as in *The X-Files*, an authentic moment or two of modernism does seep into *Breaking Bad*, this 2.0 crime story in the wake of the David effect. The most interesting of these concerns the moments when ordinary life genuinely spirals out of Walt's grasp. Most spectacularly, a spiral begins in "Phoenix" (2.12), when Walt argues with Jesse and Jane Margolis (Krysten Ritter), the love of Jesse's life, about money. Walt and Jane are in competition over Jesse's loyalty and his right to have more control over the money he has helped Walt make. When he gets to Jesse's house, Walt finds the two of them in a heroin stupor on her bed. He inadvertently knocks Jane onto her back as he tries to wake Jesse, and she begins to vomit right back into her windpipe and choke. With some difficulty, Walt wills himself to watch Jane choke to death instead of turning her over and forcing the regurgitated food out of her. Problem solved? No. If an obstacle has been removed from his life as a meth lord, collateral damage to others and interminable anguish for himself are set in motion.

Letting Jane die causes the death of hundreds of innocent people because her father Donald Margolis (John De Lancie) is an air traffic controller. Distraction resulting from his grief leads him to make a mistake in the control tower that results in a terrible plane crash. The elegance of Gilligan's storytelling interweaves Walt's act of omission and Donald Margolis's tragic mistake.[6] Ironically, Walt supervises Jane's death after talking to a stranger in a bar, who is Donald Margolis, although Walt does not know it. The irony is compounded, as they talk about children and family just before Walt allows Jane to die. The ripple effect of her death and the depiction of Walt as a negative example continues in "Fly" (3.10), the most ingenious episode in the series and arguably the closest that Formula 2.0 has yet come to the vision and complexity of art.

In episode 3.10, all linear progress of the story of Walt's career of crime is put on hold as he drives Jesse and himself crazy in their meth lab trying to kill an elusive fly that Walt compulsively insists is an unacceptable contaminant. The irony of a man whose life is polluted by crime obsessing over a contaminant as small as a fly will not be missed by anyone. Astonishingly, this episode devoted to two men killing a fly never becomes boring but rather bores into the love-hate relationship between an intellectual baby boomer and an uneducated, goofy millennial who are partners in crime. Most important, it tantalizes us with complex insights into how compromised Walt's intellect has become by his life choice.

Midway in their battle with the fly Walt and Jesse take a time-out. Jesse, unconvinced that the fly will matter, wants to get on with making the new batch of meth and drugs Walt's coffee, hoping that Walt will fall asleep so that Jesse can get on with business. But the drug stupor makes Walt reflective in a way that captivates Jesse's curiosity and ours. The episode halts the linear thrust of the series to play with the tension between Jesse's economically motivated determination to get the meth into production and Walt's drug enhanced need to deal with interior psychological forces of guilt and helplessness. Anguish over the corruption of his life takes a circuitous, fascinatingly indirect route: his obsession with the corruption that a tiny speck of a fly might cause in the batch of meth that he is supposed to cook. His thoughts become even more intriguingly byzantine when he wishes for death, groggy from the drug, or at least regrets that he has missed the perfect moment to die, now that he has amassed enough money for his family come what may. Not that he knows when that moment might have been. After some woozy speculation he decides that the perfect moment to die would have been the night Jane died.

Walt keeps Jesse enthralled by giving him new information about the most terrible night of his partner's life. He tells the story of meeting Donald Margolis in the bar, without revealing his own part in Jane's death. Tantalizingly, Walt is caught between what science has taught him and the way the world now looks at him in his new identity as a criminal. "The universe is random. It's not inevitable, it's simple chaos. It's subatomic particles in endless, aimless collision. That's what science teaches us. But what does this say? What is it telling us that on the very night that this man's daughter dies it's me who's having a drink with him? How can that be random?" Indeed, how can there be any perfection in a random universe?

Gilligan gives us a truly reflexive moment here that seems to connect us briefly with the conflict between the concepts of perfection in Formula 2.0 and the cultural conception of a universe that would seem to deny the possibility of perfection. But it is only a brief hiatus. The fly dies. And meth production and the linear narrative resume. Nevertheless, Gilligan has teased us with something more, just as he did in the pilot, when Walt challenges his incurious students to think about the nature of chemistry, which he tells them is about change. "Electrons change their energy levels. Molecules change their bonds. Elements combine and change into compounds. But that's all of life. Right? It's the constant. It's the cycle. It's solution, dissolution over and over and over. It is growth and decay, then transformation." *Breaking Bad* gives us whiffs of something much greater than the linear story of an antihero. They linger, if only as fragments, as at the end of "The Fly" when Walt is lying in bed after finishing the meth production and hears the buzz of another fly contaminating the peace that should be sleep.

The increased importance of questions in *Breaking Bad*, while it never reaches the level of artistry in nonformulaic TV, is buttressed by a magnificent

FIGURE 7.2. *Walt hears the buzz of the inevitable loose end.*

sensory palette that is only partly designed to serve the perfect narrative as a setting for crime. Without disrupting the linearity of the narrative, it also exists in itself as an element of the show that makes us wonder along the way. By and large, what we see smooths Walt's journey along the narrative tracks of Formula 2.0, but sometimes it suggests that things look different from different angles, a moderately disruptive approach to the sensory palette that adorns Gilligan's series with a splash of artistry.

Many episodes of *Breaking Bad* begin with images that tease us visually with surprising revelations of the limits of only one point of view. Some of the most evocative of these occur in season 2. They both prepare us for events to come and complicate the show's sensory palate. Numerous episodes in this season open with flash-forwards to the plane crash that is the result of Walt letting Jane Margolis die when he could have saved her. On first viewing, these opening shots are impenetrable. We have no way of knowing what they are about. We see black-and-white images of Walt's pool, in which objects are floating, notably a damaged child's stuffed toy, bearlike in shape, magenta in color, the only object that is not black-and-white. The mysterious images do not suggest that we will never know what they mean; they are not a visual sign of a limitless modern universe. But they do suggest that it can be impossible to know what a detail means until you know the whole story, that perspective matters. These fragmentary glimpses ultimately do become a coherent whole when Margolis causes a plane crash right over Walt's house and we understand that we are seeing the wreckage of that crash.[7]

Similarly "No Más" (3.1) begins with one of the most visually uncanny sequences in Formula 2.0 television. It is a sequence only obliquely connected to the narrative of Walt, which makes it all the more revolutionary in a 2.0 series. We begin panning down from a cloudy yellow sky to the rocky terrain endemic to the New Mexico of the series. Here it is a terrain inhabited by poor Hispanic families. Now down on the dusty ground, the camera sees only a gloved hand clawing its way along the dehydrated soil. The camera pulls back slightly to reveal a grizzled, weatherbeaten man crawling on his stomach, his face contracted with the pain of his efforts. All around him, we see people walking by casually, paying him no attention, cars driving by, chickens scratching for corn in the dust. Suddenly about a dozen such people are crawling, surrounded still by unconcerned bystanders. A car pulls up. It is much more expensive and sleek than anyone in this vicinity can afford, and now the people standing and sitting around pay attention, as they do not to their fellow townsfolk struggling on the ground.

Will the car run these people over and kill them without a second thought? No. Two gangsters get out of the car wearing expensive suits. They, alone among the onlookers, look at the spectacle in the dust. Then they drop to the ground and start to crawl forward ahead of the pack, on their stomachs, pulling themselves forward with their elbows. This three-minute sequence culminates at a shrine, a shabby wood shack, roughly tacked together, filled with the bric-a-brac associated with voodoo. The gangsters light new candles and make an offering of money while staring at a piece of rumpled lined paper torn from a notebook with a pencil drawing of Walt White. Narratively, this sequence turns out to be about a simple attempt by the gangsters to placate their gods to grant them success in their vendetta against Walt. Nevertheless, it brings into the mix an invocation of the problem of perception, perspective, truth, which leavens the certainties and resolutions of the series. Unparalleled to date in 2.0 programming, this segment and several others like it in *Breaking Bad* create a kind of richness for the post-*Peaks* upgrade of the formulaic American series television. Gilligan's series, an intriguing part of the legacy of the "David effect," lifts the bar very high, for new ways of telling a fairly pedestrian, formulaic story about the conventional wages of sin.

AN ALTERNATE VILLAIN'S JOURNEY: ANTIHEROICS

The more sinister variety of 2.0 antihero is embodied most perfectly in *Deadwood* and *How to Get Away with Murder*, each of which is misleading in its claims to be a harshly real approach to race, gender, and social negotiations. Rather it stands in the service of a darkly tweaked product of the business of storytelling. The American TV series has never been more formulaic than it is in the antiheroics of *Deadwood* and *How to Get Away with Murder*. It has also never been as amoral.

The picture of the old West in *Deadwood* exemplifies the use that the 2.0 antihero series makes of context to fabricate a world as saturated by toxicity as the world of 1.0 was filled by wholesomeness—and just as cut off from any real link to historical/social context. David Milch aims to burst the bubble of the 1.0 frontier tale, sanitized for TV, by being "honest" about its "real" history. However, his series reduces the town of Deadwood, set on the American frontier of the 1870s, to the dimensions of its antihero, Al Swearengen. By real, Milch means that the frontier was so completely chaotic and so conducive to the reduction of human beings to almost total greed and violence that only a man who nakedly outstrips everyone in selfishness and cruelty can create any form of order. On the one hand, it is true that Milch used historical documents as the basis of his portrait of the infamous city of Deadwood in the Dakota territories. On the other hand, there is as much manipulation of the historical facts of the Dakota territories as there was of the context of Los Angeles in *Columbo*.[8] The difference is that Columbo is impossibly effective as a crime fighter by means of highly moral and principled values, while Al Swearengen is impossibly in control of the chaotic western outpost of Deadwood by means of vicious racism, sexism, and violence.

Swearengen's base of operations is his saloon. The Gem, a center for gambling, whoring, and drugs, is the social hub, such as it is, of the lawless Deadwood mining camp. In concocting his episodes and narrative arcs, Milch used diaries and documents contemporary with frontier Deadwood containing interesting historical figures, including the much-storied Wild Bill Hickok, Wyatt Earp, and Calamity Jane Canary; and real people of the era who are known only to historians, including Seth Bullock, Sol Star, Al Swearengen, Charlie Utter, Joanie Stubbs, and George Hearst. The actual documents, however, do not support the extreme characterizations of these people as either good or as evil as Milch draws them. The result of Milch's reductive tinkering with history is his complete repudiation of Hollywood happy-ending frontier stories about wholesome, family-oriented, Christian pioneers and substitution of a dystopic vision of American history as a sink of degenerate liars and brutal cheats in the process of establishing the reign of vice and violence from the Mississippi River to the Pacific Ocean. Milch's series is an inversion of the equally extreme and unrealistic portraits of the honorable American West of TV shows like *Gunsmoke*, created by Charles Marquis Warren. But, as David Chase said to me, pure good and pure evil are the same thing, narratively speaking.

Deadwood is built on the oppositions between pure good and pure evil characters. The good characters are losers, frustrated by this filthy swamp of ignorant predatory men and victimized martyred women motivated by the craven lust for money. The series draws its line in the sand immediately, by opening with one of the core characters, Canadian Seth Bullock (Timothy Olyphant), a marshal in the Montana territory in 1876, a good man who will stand in clear contrast to bad men. When we meet him, he is in the midst of performing his last act as a lawman, keeping a lynch mob from punishing a horse thief. He is leaving to become a storekeeper in the Dakota territory. We can see why he is tired of trying to impose the law, which he believes in, over a lawless people. Things being what they are, he has no recourse but to prevent the lynching by hanging the man himself, under "cover of law" as he says. He and his friend Sol Star (John Hawkes), a Bavarian Jew raised in Chillicothe, Ohio, with whom he plans to open a hardware business in Deadwood, get out of town as fast as they can.

When Bullock and Star arrive in Deadwood, the point of view of the series is that there is really no difference between the thugs of Montana and the thugs of Deadwood. Now they are forced to deal not with a lynch mob but with Al Swearengen, a British immigrant who rules Deadwood. They are forced to negotiate with this anti-Semitic, racist bully who never negotiates in good faith for the land on which they plan to build their hardware store. It is all downhill from there.

Swearengen's motives are two: greed and order. He will steal, kill women and children, foment racial and ethnic violence, and betray any personal commitment if it will forward those ends. But in this upside-down formula western, if Swearengen's means are despicable, his situation pleads for them, or so the series would have it. The unruly mass of gold miners in town justifies Swearengen's exercise of power by any means possible. The beatings and murders of men and women alike that Swearengen sometimes performs and often orders proliferate through the three seasons of the series, notably the extreme abuse of a whore named Trixie (Paula Malcomson) because she defended herself against a homicidal john. The methods are repulsive, but at the same time the series asserts that, whether or not we approve of Swearengen's methods, there would be complete chaos without him because people are innately selfish and prone to degeneracy. It is Swearengen or nothing. And then things get worse.

Swearengen becomes visible as the alter ego of the rulers of the more "civilized" society of the better-clothed and better-fed East. Eventually we see that they do the same on a larger scale with more organization and wealth and to the same nasty effect. When Swearengen tricks naïve, pompous Brom

FIGURE 7.3. *Swearengen is exposed as a bully but excused.*

Garret (Timothy Omundson), the son of a very wealthy eastern family based in Manhattan, into buying one of the gold claims at an outrageously bloated price in the early episodes, we see the stupid greed of the better educated. After Swearengen orders one of his henchmen to kill Garret to defend his fiefdom, we learn that the bigger manipulators higher on the food chain do exactly the same. By the end of the series we have seen worse violence than Swearengen's inflicted by George Hearst (Gerald Lee McRaney), a cold-hearted, tyrannical California businessman with a national mining empire who works his miners to death and imports whores from China who are starved and used up like waste paper and burned when they can no longer perform sex for ten cents a time. In the series finale, *Deadwood*, now annexed to South Dakota, is under the rule of martial law imposed by the federal government and in worse circumstances than ever. Swearengen is now by far the lesser of two evils, which is the best that is possible in this series. At closure, he is no better than he ever was, but he is now allied with Bullock and Star against Hearst, the federal government, and the Pinkertons. What's a town to do?

Milch's revisionist history of the American frontier in *Deadwood* opens up narrative space for characters often omitted from TV 1.0, but their inclusion does not add up to a renewal of the art of storytelling on American television, just a more sinister perfect narrative. While Milch does include once-forbidden images and characters, they remain formulaically reductive. Yes, the depiction of Calamity Jane in his series as a physically filthy, miserably unhappy alcoholic is a far cry from the sanitized version of this character as played by Doris Day in *Calamity Jane* (1953) and theoretically closer to history. And Jane is embodied in a brilliant performance by Robin Weigert. But the rumpling of Jane's character is as simplistic and ahistorical a portrait as Day's clean-scrubbed portrayal. While the 2.0 Jane may seem to offer a more inclusive representation of femininity, both Jane's attempts at being an independent woman and her lesbian sexuality are narrated as pathetic and pathological. A butch loner, hopelessly infatuated with the dashing Wild Bill Hickok (Keith Carradine), Jane ultimately forms an unhappy lesbian relationship with Joanie Stubbs (Kim Dickens), an ultra femme prostitute who arrives in Deadwood to help the dashing Cy Tolliver (Powers Boothe), set up a whorehouse in competition with Swearengen's Gem. The lesbianism of both Joanie and Jane is presented as the result of abuse by the world. Jane cannot hope to attract the real object of her passion, Bill Hickok, and Joanie has been so physically abused by her father that she cannot form what this series characterizes as a normal romantic allegiance to men. *Deadwood* similarly reprises a panoply of clichés in its punishment of Alma Garret (Molly Parker), the stunningly beautiful and brilliant widow of the spoiled, doomed Brom Garret, when she comes into her own as a businesswoman after Brom's death. Successful women must pay the price of sacrificing personal gratification. And the black characters are just as constricted by the limits of formula. Hostetler (Richard Gant) is unorthodoxly in charge of the livery stable but nevertheless a product of the worn-out cliché of the "magic Negro" who is pure of heart despite his challenging social situation. Aunt Lou Marchbanks (Cleo King), a conventional "mammy" who is Hearst's cook; her son, Odell Marchbanks (Omar Gooding); and Samuel Fields (Franklyn Ajaye) a con man who is sometimes known as the "Nigger Captain," are also familiar clichés.

The manipulations of the *Deadwood* narratives are complemented by its sensory palette, which is a triumph of the old Hollywood zero degree aesthetic. The visual textures of *Deadwood* are the opposite of those of Baltimore in *The Wire*, lit by Uta Briesewitz (see chapter 3), who found the beauty of the world using only real light sources. In *Deadwood*, great effects are created through light emitted from places where there are no actual light sources. Light shines up from the floors or in corners where there are no windows, lanterns, or candles, or shines too brightly for what we see of the light sources. Torches that burn in the nighttime streets of Deadwood provide unrealistically effective lighting for the faces of the characters and the muddy thoroughfares. In its insistence on its monolithic "reality," *Deadwood* is a fictional world that is reliably rotten and corrupt, providing the old formulaic reassurances that reality can be known perfectly as a perfectly awful place. It is a perversely manipulated form of certainty that found its audience in TV 2.0.

Another series that demands our attention because of its antiheroically juggled formulaic "consolations" is *How to Get Away with Murder*, a series with a black heroine created under the imprimatur of Shonda Rhimes. The startling, groundbreaking African American antihero, Annalise Keating, cries out for inclusion here as one of the more important antiheroes of 2.0 formula TV, both for her originality and for the limits placed on that originality by 2.0.

Annalise Keating is a wealthy lawyer, glamorous in the style dictated by white culture, who doubles as a law professor at fictional Middleton University in Philadelphia. Annalise has a well-earned reputation for both ruthlessness and winning her cases. The two are connected. Periodically she regales whoever will listen with an array of rationales for her tactics of bullying, lying, intimidation, framing innocent bystanders, and covering up murder to acquit her clients. But the series refuses to judge her for that because it portrays a society where the chips are stacked against her as a woman and a black person—and against everyone else but the power elite: surely all is fair within a framework like that. Annalise's most explicit defense of her nefarious methods appears in "It's All My Fault" (1.15), the first season finale, when she explains to her students that truth and justice do not exist. There are only individual stories, and whoever tells the most convincing story wins.

Annalise represents two important cultural institutions, the law and the university, but neither she nor they uphold their purported standards and ideals. So if winning is all that matters for her, the series is at a loss to dispute her position. Each episode contains a weekly case, and in each season they are juxtaposed with long arc stories about the personal dilemmas of Annalise, her students, her associates, and her family. In the cases of the week, the killers are all identified eventually by Annalise, her staff, and the "Keating 5," an elite group of law students that Annalise has selected to work with her in her law practice while they take courses and learn the art of survival that is Annalise's trademark, by abandoning the values of truth and honor.

The students are a formulaic, carefully typed diverse rainbow of workplace colleagues/friends/lovers and a basket of ethnic and racial clichés: Laurel Castillo (Karla Souza), an intense Hispanic beauty; Michaela Pratt (Aja Naomi King), a gorgeous, overly ambitious young black woman; Wes Gibbins (Alfred Enoch), a handsome, sincere, and talented young black man toward whom Annalise frequently shows much partiality; Asher Millstone (Matt McGorry), a conniving, materialistic Jewish student; and Connor

Walsh (Jack Falahee), an opportunistic, chic, oversexed gay man. Annalise's personal life involves ongoing angst about her double dealing, which only propels her toward more and more chicanery. It is the way of this world.

The through line of the first three seasons, which we are fed in flashbacks and flash-forwards as well as in the present time of the weekly story, is lashed to the mast of formulaic narrative of the murder of Lila Stangard (Megan West), a pretty, wealthy white co-ed at the university where Annalise and her husband, Sam Keating (Tom Verica), teach. Sam Keating, who is suspected of an affair with Lila and of her murder, is subsequently murdered. Annalise has her hands full lying and betraying in any way she must to maintain her ascendance in this murky mess. "The Night Lila Died" (1.14) interestingly exemplifies Annalise's modus operandi, juxtaposing how she betrayed one of her lovers and the case of a Catholic priest accused of murder. As part of the long arc story of the deaths of Lila and her husband, Annalise has allowed the police to jail her former lover, Nate (Billy Brown), on grounds she knows to be false. They had an affair while his wife was suffering with advanced cancer. The case of the week involves Father Andrew (Tom Everett Scott), who is accused of killing another priest, Father Bernard (Lou Richards). He is very reluctant to accept Annalise's strategy for winning an acquittal because it involves lying.

Father Andrew makes a useful foil for Annalise. He *did* kill Father Bernard. But from his point of view he did so as a pure deed. It is a convoluted situation and completely in sync with the "by any means necessary" amorality of the series. Father Andrew is as pure as Annalise is corrupt. He refuses to let Annalise use information obtained during a confession that would exonerate him because it would violate his oath as a priest. We discover that Father Andrew killed Father Bernard after hearing his confession that he had sexually abused one of the boys at the parish school. The boy subsequently killed himself as a result of the trauma. Andrew believes that the murder was justified because of the corruption of the church hierarchy. He knows that if he reports the abuse Bernard will only be transferred to another church, where he will continue his predatory career. What is a priest to do?

While the episode seems not to condemn the murder, it does seem to be critical of Andrew's fidelity to the confessional. "Life is messy, Father," Annalise says. "We all have to make compromises in order to be happy." Kill, if nothing else will work. Betray the confessional for the same reason. Just look at the context! Father Andrew endorses this philosophy in regard to the murder but not in regard to the confessional. The show backs him up on both counts but also endorses Annalise's stance. There is something praiseworthy but otherworldly in Andrew. Those of us who live in this world would be lucky to do as Annalise does, but few can perform such antiheroics. This problematic amoral yet formulaic depiction is miles away from the art of David Simon's storytelling in *The Wire*, in which he explicitly refuses to justify amoral acts in the name of a corrupt society and depicts the harsh necessity to accept frustration as we oppose the evils of the world in the name of morality.

On the other hand, there is no denying that *How to Get Away with Murder* alters the racial TV landscape with the power of Annalise Keating. It makes a big change from the easy milk and water optimism of Formula 1.0: easy integration of minority and female heroes into the perfect narrative. But in Annalise's story, the rigidities of formula generally succeed in enforcing old patterns in some ways as they are breaking them up in others. What some might call honest depiction of the modern world of corruption others will call the intentional fabrication of a corrupt world to justify the amoral machinations of its antihero, another form of formulaic manipulation.

However, the series offers some original and real moments in its depictions of the liminal, indeterminate situation of a black woman in a white society. One of the most startling takes place at the end of "Let's Get to Scooping" (1.4). Bombshell Annalise, seated at her dressing table in her bedroom in all her full glory, begins to get ready for bed. We are suddenly made aware that little about her appearance is as it has seemed. In a shocking moment, she removes her wig, revealing that under the "mask" of a straight, long, high-style coiffure is her unadorned hair, short, curly, and unstyled. She peels off her false eyelashes and creams off her glamour makeup. Underneath her alluring but false surface, the reality of a natural black woman exists, still sexy but challenging all our *Vogue*-inspired ideas about female beauty. In the second season we discover that her real name is "Anna Mae," not quite her distinctly Hollywoodish pseudonym, "Annalise."

Does the way Annalise has been forced to deny her reality as a black woman really justify her constant use of the strategy that the one who tells the best story wins whether it is true or not? This simplification fits the neat structure of story product; it is no revolution in televisual storytelling. The moments that confront racial realities come and go without forming an organic nonformulaic narrative. They are just interesting breaks in a show that uses shock and moving back and forth in time only to reinforce linearity and the resolution of a story product. *How to Get Away with Murder* teases us with the kinds of questions that the auteur nonformulaic series ask in earnest—and the auteurs find it more interesting and more real *not* to provide simplistic answers.

How many viewers are inspired by *Deadwood*, *How to Get Away with Murder*, and other 2.0 shows generated on this antiheroic model to ask

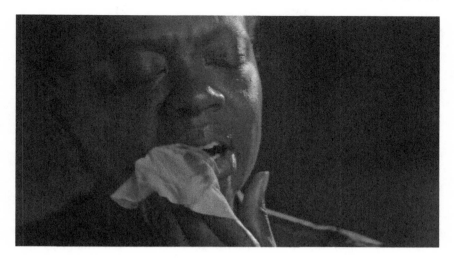

FIGURE 7.4. *Anna Mae comes out.*

questions about their moral relativism? How many are prompted to connect these shows with the increasing rejection of evidence in the United States when coming to conclusions, the rampant, intentional generation of lies by some news sources that began to be demonstrated in earnest in 2016 in the United States? To date, there are no studies of the sinister aspects represented by this turn of formulaic entertainment, although by 2017 the counterpoint between art television and the business of storytelling was sufficient to provide a basis for drawing some conclusions.[9]

There was also sufficient evidence for drawing some conclusions about the evolution of all formulaic televisual entertainment in the direction of obscenity and violence. What have we gained, what have we lost, as the American story machine cranks out hyperviolent and often obscene story product like *Game of Thrones*, with its grandiose overstuffed pseudomythology; the antiheroic sewer of *House of Cards*; and the sad disappointments of Chris Carter's return to television with seasons 10 and 11 of *The X-Files*, after a hiatus of fifteen years. Carter's new but unfortunately misshapen, shrill, and hyperbolically simplistic perfect narratives were made watchable only by the enduring chemistry of David Duchovny and Gillian Anderson.

At the same time, we are also confronted with a more promising prospect. Television was also offering some fascinating new experimentation with fresh ways of animating the perfect narrative, as in *Mr. Robot*, with its innovative approach to our increasingly technological culture; and *Westworld*, with its careful probing of the boundaries between living organisms and humanmade artificial intelligence. Some series feature eccentric heroes like Amazon's *The Marvelous Mrs. Maisel*, with its interesting use of a perfect hero that makes comedy out of female liberation and ethnicity, and *Mozart in the Jungle*, a formulaic series that is charmingly balanced by its use of music and art in a way approaching the innovations of *Treme*.

In comparison with the first surge of creative energy after the appearance of *Twin Peaks*, however, even the television auteurs were treading water. David Simon's *Show Me a Hero*, about the uproar over integrated housing in Yonkers, New York, and *The Deuce*, about the pornography industry of the 1970s in New York, display brave uses of his collage narrative and encyclopedic examinations of the many sides of cultural events. But Simon was not challenging himself in regard to narrative invention. A surprise auteur online miniseries independently written, produced, and directed by Louis C. K., *Horace and Pete*, brilliantly chronicled the history of the ownership of a bar in Manhattan streamed online, reminiscent of the great American theater we used to see, provoking questions of where Louis could go from there. A new series, *The Romanoffs*, from Matt Weiner is promised. But none of this activity has yet risen to the heights of the imaginative life of the television we saw in *Twin Peaks*, *The Sopranos*, *The Wire*, *Mad Men*, *Treme*, and *Girls*.

And then David Lynch came back.

CODA

The Return of David Lynch

I believe there are rules to follow which apply to painting and cinema.
These rules are very friendly and abstract. The rules make us feel there are
infinite possibilities. They make us feel that even there are no rules! Yet
the rules are there. They are not in a book but exist inside us in the mind
and heart. They reveal themselves through intuition just before and just
after each action or decision. These rules apply to all mediums. Following
them brings happiness.

—David Lynch, *David Lynch: Chaos Theory of Violence and Silence*

D avid Lynch's declaration lays bare in its essence the distinction
between the expansive horizons of the new auteur series and the
contracted limits of formulaic American television. The rules to
which Lynch refers open up infinite possibilities. The similarly
unwritten rules of formula TV impose generally stultifying restrictions. The
declaration also reveals the optimism that Lynch fervently holds to in a
universe in which no one is driving the chariot. Order is inherent; it is just
not the rigid order imposed by network practices. *Twin Peaks* was the first
revelation of what that could mean to popular entertainment. *Twin Peaks*
(2017) constitutes the beginning of a second wave and a fuller realization of
Lynch's aesthetic for television.[1]

The 2017 series does not just repeat Lynch's original challenge to formulaic storytelling. It performs modernist magic in its expansion of the
possible connotation of the word "sequel," which has historically had deeply
formulaic, linear implications. Simple linearity has no bearing on Lynch's
return to *Twin Peaks*. Much more applicable is the line spoken by the Little
Man in the Red Room at the end of the 1990 series: "When you see me
again, it won't be me." When Lynch brings us back to *Twin Peaks*, the return

is both familiar and strange, particularly in the changes that it rings on his use of Special Agent Dale Cooper. Lynch's more complete unpacking of the rules of nonformulaic narrative connects the audience with a narrative desire intensely attached to the failure with which the original series ended. Instead of using his "sequel" for conventional purposes as might well have been expected, to detail Cooper's conquest of the forces that previously divided and detained him, Lynch uses his return to *Twin Peaks* to invite us to simultaneously stand back from and engage with a Cooper who blindly and increasingly perpetuates evil. And he does it in the form of an epic.

A modernist epic story for television! In *Twin Peaks* (2017), Lynch pushes television with dramatic intensity even further away from the consolations of the perfect hero, almost unimaginably by means of a genre that classically elevated its protagonist to extreme heroism in the face of evil, sometimes to near divinity, turning television into the kind of site of discovery previously reserved for classical literature. As Lynch moves the mass audience toward a modernist reconsideration of the problem of evil on a prodigious scale, he provides an audience with perspectives on the action informed by the materiality, energy, and temporality at the heart of the cutting-edge zeitgeist.

In 2017 Cooper's already fragmented nature shatters further, making it impossible for him to achieve closure and to set things right, the two desires that are an uncontested given for perfect heroes in formula television but are precluded by a modernist view of human capacity. As the eighteen parts of the new season unfold, Cooper is increasingly a conglomerate of mysteriously opposing and conflicting fragments that sidetrack, impede, and imperil his continuing mission to make sense of the cosmic dimensions of Laura's death. Joined in fraught dissonance are Cooper's determined FBI-motivated fragment and his high-octane equally intelligent doppelgänger, Mr. C, a continuation of the division that we saw in 1990–1991. Reflecting the quantum nature of Lynch's universe, they are each more than one and less than two. This intricate jumble is further complicated by a third enmeshed "particle" of the Cooper identity, Dougie Jones, a lower-energy, lower-intelligence manufactured version of Cooper, not another doppelgänger but a tulpa. If Cooper's doppelgänger was the result of possession by demon BOB, tulpa Dougie is enigmatically manufactured in some way that is never explicitly revealed but may well be part of Mr. C.'s plans. Mr. C looms darkly as an obstruction to Cooper's sense of mission; he is as narratively determined to tyrannize the marketplace as Cooper is to guard and protect it. But Dougie is even more obstructive, albeit passively. As the Dougie tulpa is destroyed, Cooper takes his place as a feckless bumbler in no condition to pursue Cooper's goals. As we shall see, Cooper's time becalmed as Dougie may be in part a result of

Mr. C's machinations, but it is also the consequence of Cooper's continuing propensity for making the wrong choice.

Doppelgängers are a form of doubling familiar to Western literature and thought, and we saw them in the 1990 *Twin Peaks*. Lynch's addition of the tulpa to the third season embroiders it with a new kind of twinning replicant. Tulpa is a term adapted from the Tibetan *sprul-pa*, used by early twentieth century mystics for a thing given animation by spiritual powers, which Lynch has borrowed for his series.[2] Mr. C. is not the only doppelgänger on the series event horizon; nor is Dougie the only tulpa. They are part of a general quantum fragmentation of identity in the narrative. Doppelgängers are inevitably negative and enduring doubles, while tulpas run the gamut of the negative and positive permutations of being, existing only until they fulfill the purpose for which they were created. Cooper's doppelgänger and tulpa create difficult times for him. They get worse once we reach an apparent happy ending at the opening of the season finale, part 18, and Lynch goes on to complete his story by posing enormous and troubling questions. But we are not ready to deal with that yet. The journey of *Twin Peaks* (2017) exists to detail that progression, and this exploration of Lynch's magisterial work exists to explore how the precipitous fall of Dale Cooper changes the televisual experience.

Epics are about establishing order across earthly and superhuman levels of reality, the kind of order based on premodern ideas about time and identity. Homer's noble Odysseus, a seminal example of the classical epic hero, made his journey home as a unified identity battling gods and demons. He reconstitutes his home after it has been shattered by the violence of war, despite being detained by one obstructive external situation; his homecoming is an inevitable arrival along the linear path of time. In *Ulysses*, James Joyce's modernized version of *The Odyssey*, he depicts a plebeian epic hero whose obstructions are all ordinary and human. But even his deflated Odysseus, Leopold Bloom, who traverses a fragmented terrain during his journey, comes home along a linear trajectory. Cooper, Lynch's much more daring creation, can make only an epic attempt at going home and redeeming Laura's suffering. He is overwhelmed, as Homer's and Joyce's heroes are not, by both the obstructive fragments of himself and the even more debilitating modern mysteries of nonlinear time.

The epic travels of both Odysseus and Leopold Bloom take place within the linear context of the arrow of time, the name given by Arthur Eddington to the concept of a conventionally forward-moving temporality that both Homer and Joyce understood as a crucial part of the shape of reality and as the guarantor of the hero's arrival at his intended goal. Cooper's journey, shaken by time shifts between past and future, must inevitably and spectacularly derail. Here Lynch channels a contemporary (unproven) speculation of modern physics. Not content with proving that seemingly solid matter is actually a vortex of swirling particles, physics has begun to entertain the possibility that the arrow is also an illusion. Lynch, who has been playing with questions of that kind since *Eraserhead* (1977), narratively embraces alternate temporal possibilities full throttle in *Twin Peaks* (2017).

As I have often noted, Lynch does not know either the mathematics of physics or the complicated processes of its laboratory experiments, with respect to either matter or time. And, certainly, Lynch has no acquaintance with Eddington's speculations about the possibility that the arrow might go the way of previous ideas about materiality. But as an artist within the modern zeitgeist of such ideas, he has intuited the possibility and has imagined the consequences according to his own vision. If Eddington was filled with mere anxiety when he contemplated images of the random motion of particles that renders solid matter nothing more than a cultural myth, he regarded with full-blown dread the possibility of reversible time. As he wrote in *The Nature of the Physical World*, "The reversal of the arrow would render the external world nonsensical."[3] By contrast, Lynch has imaginatively grasped this destabilizing possibility without abandoning his faith in meaning or the unwritten rules of art.

Reversible time structures the narrative of 2017 and discombobulates the comfortable sense of a stable landscape that is unquestioned by formulaic TV. The series ends with a Kafkaesque vision of Cooper marooned in a temporal cul de sac. But Lynch questions even Cooper's experience of destabilization. As an artist, he is not daunted by the possibility that the arrow is just a dream of our waking lives. David Chase has likened Lynch to an astronaut because of his bounding liftoffs into public space.[4] And Lynch returns to *Twin Peaks* with an enormous leap. Lynch has been hopeful about leaping into the end of illusion in all his film and television and here too. Certainly, in 2017, as in all his work, the end of illusion is painful. But Lynch believes that there is a sense to the universe generated from within a unified field at its center and meaning beyond the hallucinatory logic of our rules once the sleeper awakens from the false symmetries of marketplace dreams. How is it possible to deny that Cooper's failure to awaken can be read as an assertion of that faith? Any response to that question lies ahead of us.

We must first look into the way *Twin Peaks* (2017) shuttles Cooper along the disorienting twists and swerves of a temporal Möbius strip, engaging him in the tumult of the time loop of future-past. The question is often asked as the epic unfolds, "Is it future or is it past?" And who can say with clarity which it is, as the Möbius twists affect both the marketplace and the many spaces beyond it—the Red Room, a strange palace inhabited by the Fireman, and the space bunker that Cooper falls into on his way to the marketplace. He fully expects to redeem Laura's life and return her to her home, at least at first. Those hopes are dashed when our wandering through all the Möbius reversals of all the spaces in Lynch's epic brings a harvest of inversions. Cooper ultimately finds himself with Carrie Paige (Sheryl Lee), a woman who looks like Laura but has no reason to think she is, in front of what looks like Laura's home but is not, unable to be certain of what year it is. In the deep structure of this narrative, past and future have lost their comfortable relationship. And we have lost our comfortable assumptions about human control over circumstances.

The intriguing Möbius loop challenged the arrow of time before the discipline of quantum mechanics even existed. It was arrived at separately by two German mathematicians, Ferdinand Möbius and Johann Benedict Listing, in 1858.[5] A temporal curvature, the Möbius strip is a continuous loop with one twist that makes it resemble the shape of both the number 8 and the sign of infinity, two figures that recur in *Twin Peaks* (2017) and in some of Lynch's other works.[6] Merely an oddity back in its day, the Möbius strip has become increasingly relevant in the age of modern physics as quantum scientists struggle with the fact that they really have no theoretical basis for belief in the irreversibility of linear time. While it appeared only in the Red Room at the end of the original *Twin Peaks*, which for the most part had proceeded in a conventionally linear fashion, Möbius time is the prevailing temporal shape in the epic landscape of *Twin Peaks* (2017).

In the language of mathematics, the Möbius shape is "unorientable." A line drawn down the seam of the continuous Möbius strip will end up where it started, but on the inverse side of the loop. This is the foundation of Cooper's ultimate dilemma: when he gets where he is going, he is not there yet he is there too. With Cooper's new adventures, Lynch casts his glance along time with an intuition similar to the one that guided Möbius and Listing toward their temporally reversible 8-shaped image of eternity.[7]

Projecting our vision along the loop, Lynch asks us to think anew not only about time but also about energy. Of necessity, the Möbius loop renders energy equally reversible. As a result, since Lynch understands human behavior in terms of energy surges, the characters in 2017 become functions of invisible underlying motives, causes, and dynamics implied through images of multidirectional electricity that crackles all around the temporal twists of 2017. Theoretically, electrical energy can only move from negative to positive. But the opposite is conceivable in a world of unlimited possibility. Electricity, a presence in all of Lynch's *Twin Peaks* stories, serves as the embodiment of the way energy and matter oscillate wildly between positivity and negativity as time swerves. (The 2017 series features numerous electrical transformers, generators, and sockets that serve poetically to convey the presence of the changing shape of narrative energy.) All the characters in 2017 exist from the first moments not only in an immense universe of bewildering time/space mutabilities but in a universe of unorientable electrical forces. The impetus toward forward narrative motion is continually deflected by electrical surges of all types and in all directions, which has major implications for the multitude of characters in this epic, especially for Cooper.

COOPER'S CHOICE

The unorientable direction of Cooper's epic voyage is immediately present in the series. Its articulation begins immediately in part 1, when Cooper fails to take charge of his return to the marketplace. Instead, it happens to him and batters him with troubling intimations and violent discontinuities. Before any action starts, Cooper is given an enigmatic audience with an authoritative figure called the Fireman (Carel Struycken), a new version of the Giant from the original *Twin Peaks*, then apparently only a messenger and now a figure of cosmic importance. Cooper, who is in two places at once, both the Red Room and the Fireman's palace, is exposed by the Fireman to an unidentified scratching sound that summons up thoughts of static electricity and perhaps insect activity. Insects have been an ongoing Lynchian image, suggesting buried, unseen dark energies. Here that allusion takes on the form of a sound, something negative scratching at the periphery of perception. It moves toward center stage for Cooper as the series unfolds.

If Cooper is bemused by the troubling sound, he is shaken by the clear presence of a strikingly bewildering negative, unstable cosmic force that first violently ejects Laura from the Red Room as she is telling him that he can leave and then catapults him back toward the marketplace. The force that envelops Laura is never identified. The force that propels Cooper is associated with the negative doppelgänger of the "arm," which suddenly appears spitting negative electricity and intoning the word "Nonexistent!" Cooper's return to the marketplace is thus heralded by a cry that negates being. The less than auspicious nature of Cooper's return becomes more pronounced in part 3: instead of seamlessly arriving in Twin Peaks, he falls into a strange bunker in space where he makes a grave mistake.

The bunker epitomizes the Lynchian nature of reality; it is simultaneously both enclosed and open to limitlessness. The inside of the bunker has the appearance of an ordinary grounded home, complete with cozy living room and fire burning in the fireplace. Within this seeming comfort and security, however, bodies move in a disjointed, spasmodic way as though they were experiencing Möbius reversals simply as part of moving in this space. By contrast, the outside of the bunker is a vertiginous balcony overlooking the infinite reaches of the star-sprinkled cosmos. In the face of limitlessness, bodies move naturally and fluidly. Both spaces are "electrified." A bell-shaped electric generator stands on the dizzying balcony, and an electric socket emanates a powerful magnetic electrical charge in the firelit parlor. The electricity on the balcony on the edge of forever offers the daunting possibility of leaping into the unknown, while the electrical socket inside the cozy bunker suggests seemingly less fearful containment of energy. During Cooper's experiences with both aspects of the bunker, he arrives at the Lynchian moment of choice, the threshold where the Lynchian protagonist takes on limitlessness and all its expansive tremulous potential or chooses the limited marketplace, with all its deceptive reassurances. With slippery time and the threat of nonexistence buffeting him with a vengeance, Cooper opts for limits, a bad choice from which he will never recover.

Cooper gets his chance at expansiveness but rejects it. In the bunker Cooper finds a strange, eyeless woman who is unable to speak except in high-pitched cries and rhythmic expulsions of breath. She leads him out of the seemingly secure room and away from a large electrical socket to which he is drawn. Instead, she guides him out onto the frighteningly exposed balcony to help him escape from the sinister approach of some never-identified, unseen, very loud menace. The woman throws the switch on the generator and is catapulted into the boundless, starry night. Cooper is daunted and terrified. Did she fall into nothingness? A ghostly image of the head of that intrepid explorer of what lies beyond the marketplace, Maj. Garland Briggs (Don S. Davis), appears in the limitless space, intoning the words "Blue Rose." The words seem to be a message for Cooper, perhaps about what he should do next. Blue Rose is the name of an FBI task force that investigates the limits of ordinary life, so this might be a warning or it might be an invitation. It is not clear how Cooper construes it, but it is clear that he chooses to retreat when he goes back into the bunker.

At this point, he and we do not know the implications of his withdrawal to the enclosed space within which he once again hears the approach of a sinister energy. Nor can we yet discern the implications of his succumbing to the energy rushing out of the electric socket on the wall of the bunker room, which breaks him down into particles that move into the electrical outlet. But there are signs that he has chosen badly. Cooper's energy is immediately reduced to the confines of the wall socket, a inversion of the liberation of

FIGURE C.1. *Cooper chooses an energy reduction.*

Henry Spencer in *Eraserhead*, when electricity burst the confines of wires and outlets. Ultimately, it is clear that Cooper's rejection of the path of infinite possibilities has ensured the futility of his quest.

During this expository phase, the action not only serves as a jumping-off point for the consequences of Cooper's choice but also recalibrates the definition of a clue for our detective in regard to our own journey into mystery. Clues, those reliable compasses for formulaic detectives, lose all sense of stability as guideposts in the 2017 series. Clues in the original *Twin Peaks* are little bricks of meaning, not as effectual as Cooper's access to his subconscious but well defined. In the 2017 series, they contain their own mystery and their own multivalence. In this initial stage of the narrative, Cooper has received clues from the wraithlike presence of Major Briggs and both the Fireman in his palace and the one-armed man, Philip Gerard (Al Strobel), who serves as the guide in the Red Room. But the clues may potentially mean anything. When the Fireman tells Cooper in part 1 to remember 430, Linda and Richard, and killing two birds with one stone, the clues are as bewildering as the shaking, destabilizing floor of the Red Room through which Cooper falls when he is catapulted into the space bunker. Similarly, Gerard's insistent questioning of whether "it" is future or past is a new frontier. It requires the audience to divest itself of the reassuring prediction of solution and conclusion of the conventional Sherlockian clue.

The first consequences of Cooper's choice in this multivalent, multidirectional universe of mysterious clues are both comic and dire. As a much reduced version of himself, Cooper emerges from a marketplace wall socket in Las Vegas, just in time to take the place of tulpa Dougie, who is called back to the Red Room to be broken down into his particles and destroyed. The energy compression caused by his route to the marketplace has left Cooper almost completely inert, a comical cipher who seemingly can do no more than play out Dougie's futile, limited life in a barren Las Vegas subdivision. Dougie has a history of cheating on his wife and deserting the family for gambling casinos, hardly the hero role that we expect of Cooper. Worse, Cooper's choice has also saved the violent, homicidal Mr. C. from being called back into the Red Room. Cooper is trapped once again, this time within Las Vegas, the home of marketplace illusions and the node of American materialism, as he was twenty-five years earlier when he let fear overwhelm him into making a bad choice. As he continues his adventures, he continues to make bad choices on both an ordinary and a cosmic level. In his diminished form he is further than ever from his initial mission, and the specificity of his mission becomes murkier and murkier. In the original series, he was on assignment from the FBI to solve the mystery of Laura Palmer's murder. His responsibilities concerning Laura's disappearance from the Red Room as he watches entail no such specificity. There is vagueness as well as compulsion as Cooper stumbles through his epic journey. This fictional universe, in contrast with formulaic TV, does not offer heroic clarity, even about the protagonist's mission.

EPIC LYNCH

Epics are context heavy, spend a lot of time mapping out the entirety of the cosmos on all its levels, and create a humbling portrait of the place of the individual in the whole of creation. When classical epics ask the big questions about good and evil, a solid answer is provided by classical epic heroes, who succeed through the help of forces much larger than themselves. The epic importance of larger forces dovetails with the inclusive and ego-curbing contexts that are the hallmark of the new nonformulaic American television. But the modernity of Lynch's epic envisions those forces in Kafkaesque terms as enigmatic and not particularly conducive to the success of the epic protagonist or even the definition of his goal.

The classical epic reveals how all the pieces of the universe and culture, seemingly in conflict, are actually part of a harmonious whole in which the epic hero is able to fulfill epic tasks. The opposite is true in Lynch's modern American epic. Misrule through discontinuity and fragments that are incapable of fitting together is the rule on all levels of reality. The cosmic levels of the 2017 series are unfathomable, and the marketplace is chaos. The familiar shapes of diners, hospitals, police stations, family homes, gambling casinos, and the like, whether in the marketplaces of Twin Peaks or Las Vegas, at first glance seem solid and coherent, just as the Möbius strip looks perfectly unambiguous if a mathematician looks at only a small section of it. A little section of the strip appears to be a square in which everything seems, but only seems, "orientable." However, that appearance of linear regularity disappears once the bracketed segment is reinserted into the entire strip. This is also the situation of the marketplace in *Twin Peaks* (2017); it has the appearance of what has conventionally been visualized as normal life but experiences quite a lot of the unorientable, puzzling, disturbing action of the time and energy of the entire cosmos.

The twists of time and energy are most fully revealed in the cosmic levels of the 2017 series, unencumbered by the illusions of the marketplace. And what a cosmos Lynch gives us! The infinite regions beyond the marketplace in 2017 are not just the single space of the Red Room as in 1990 but many spaces. As the series unfolds, we often visit the Red Room, with its rabbit warren of scarlet-curtained corridors in which time and space contradict themselves and its floor patterned like a symbolic representation of the jagged flow of electricity. But the ambiguity of the Red Room, present in the original series, is much magnified in 2017 in Philip Gerard's insistent question: "Is it future or is it past?" and in the multivalence of the "arm." It is an ineffable icon of power that once served the demon BOB but became a potentially positive, force when Gerard tore it off his body as a rejection

FIGURE C.2. *Is it future or is it past in the Fireman's palace?*

of BOB's negative energy. The twists and turns of the bunker lead to the wrong road home, an enigmatic space that we never saw in 1990. The palace inhabited by the mysterious Fireman is filled with unstable clues and illegible appearances. It is a strange potpourri of futuristic machines and antique contraptions—an encapsulation of the fusion of past and future.

Moreover, we are introduced to yet another mysterious space beyond the marketplace in part 8, this one suffused by a pervasively sinister, hellish aura: the grimy, dark, and decrepit "convenience store." It is a portal to both infinity and curved time that is charged with a sense of evil. It opens up for us first in 2017 in the testing of the atomic bomb in 1945, at White Sands, New Mexico, but we have seen it in the vicinity of Twin Peaks in *Twin Peaks: Fire Walk with Me* (1992) and will see it again in a number of moments when space and time are not clearly orientable. The convenience store is occupied in 2017 by missing special agent Phillip Jeffries (David Bowie) of the FBI. Jeffries in 2017 is not a person but a voiced mechanism enlivened by a special kind of electricity that controls a portal into the slippery coils of time, marked with an icon that is interchangeably the number 8, the sign of infinity, and a pictograph of the Möbius strip. In their ambiguity and illegibility, the slippages of time in the convenience store complement the other major slippages in 2017.

These shifts contextualize Cooper's travels through cosmic portals that receive a great deal of traffic. The town of Twin Peaks is especially rich in portals, but they also exist all over America and the world, though the

FIGURE C.3. *The convenience store is the home of negative energy.*

FIGURE C.4. *Phillip Jeffries is the gatekeeper of negative Möbius time. The black dot is the clue.*

international portals are hinted at rather than shown. The energy, space, and time inversions in 2017 are bewildering and disorienting. At the same time, however, being trapped within marketplace limits, the essential condition of the audience of a formulaic series, is also a form of being lost.

LOST IN THE MARKETPLACE

Cooper, trained and bred by the marketplace, is lost when he enters the cosmic levels of his epic world, as are all the characters who engage however briefly with the perplexing thresholds that emerge unexpectedly at the far end of ordinary limits. However, ordinary life is actually not very much less perplexing; it is actually a place of immense discontinuities. Filled with snippets of stories, it is a virtually endless parade of characters, of whom we get merely fragmentary glances. They are in some sort of turmoil about ordinary desires that turn out to be not quite ordinary and leave them in a constant state of confusion. We shall never know the conclusions of these partial narrative snippets, which convey the feeling of random human particle life inside the ordinary marketplace limits. We saw hints of this in the 1990 series, but here it is multiplied many times: more vivid, sizzling with careening negative and positive energies that often metamorphose into each other. This is also true of the reverses involving already familiar characters and some new characters to whom we are exposed at some length.

Shelly Briggs (Mädchen Amick) is still the waitress we knew at the Double R diner in 1990, no longer abused by Leo Johnson (Eric Da Re) but still leading an emotionally fraught life. We watch her shift back and forth between an intense, warm, loving energy toward her daughter, Becky (Amanda Seyfried), and positive energy for Becky's father, Bobby Briggs (Dana Ashbrook), and a negative attraction to Red (Balthazar Getty), a gangster and drug dealer. With similar precipitousness, the once unhappy triangle of Norma Jennings and Ed and Nadine Hurley shifts from Nadine's negative desire to entrap Ed in a loveless marriage to a sudden positive desire to free him to enjoy love with Norma. Nadine slips from negative to positive under the influence of Dr. Amp, the new identity of Dr. Jacoby (Russ Tamblyn), once an eccentric psychiatrist and now a hysterical radio talk show huckster, "electrified," in his own words. He dispenses violently abusive tirades against the government and golden shovels, at a price, which he claims will enable his listeners to dig their way "out of the shit" in which he claims the powers that be are burying them. We feel the mysteries of shifting energy and time as they appear within the characters we already know well but now see from an expanded perspective.

The same applies to some new marketplace characters whom we get to know well. The most foregrounded are the people Dougie/Cooper gets involved with in Las Vegas: Janey-E Jones (Naomi Watts) and Sonny Jim Jones (Pierce Gagnon), the wife and young son of tulpa Dougie, and a pair of gangsters, the Mitchum brothers (Jim Belushi and Robert Knepper), all tainted and tinged by the mercurial flow of a town that distills the marketplace desires for sex, money, and power. Cooper's helpless sojourn there as Dougie, a result of his characteristic inability to encounter the boundlessness of reality no matter how often he is instructed about what lies beyond the marketplace threshold, puts into perspective the limited possibilities offered to human beings by the marketplace, which lead Cooper to misunderstanding and tragedy once he gets his full energy back.

Lynch's epic presents us with a spectrum of comic and tragic American marketplace limitations. While these boundaries always end in diminished possibilities, they vary in style, depending on location. Twin Peaks and Las Vegas are the two most crucial human habitations on this spectrum in 2017. Their incompatible profiles as habitations make it impossible to arrive at a definition of America, except as a place in which the pieces of the country do not fit together to make a homogeneous context. American history and geography are visible as limited fragments suffused by the constantly reversing energy of infinity. Las Vegas stands at the extreme negative end of the marketplace, a consumerist bulwark against the magic of the infinite. Twin Peaks stands at the opposing positive extreme of the marketplace spectrum, less limited, more in harmony with nature, and more nurtured by the magical if confusing world beyond ordinary boundaries.

The depressed possibilities of the Las Vegas characters are inherent not only in their behavior but also in their evocative names.[8] Janey-E Jones's odd, parodic name defines her as a woman almost totally swallowed up by clichés. "Jane" is a slang name for a random ordinary woman. The diminutive "Janey" thins the character even further, as does her surname, Jones, a hallmark of anonymity that she acquired through marriage to a manufactured man. The name of her son, Sonny Jim, is generic in its own right. "Sonny Jim" is a demeaning term for a boy child, and sometimes for a man, which Lynch has used before. The night porter (Michael Elphick) in *The Elephant Man* (1980), with ironic pseudo-geniality, calls himself "your own Sonny Jim" as he prepares a crowd to pay him to smuggle them into John Merrick's hospital room to gawk at and terrorize him.

Janey sees the world and people as a collection of generic objects. When Cooper/Dougie first takes the place of tulpa Dougie, she is unable to take in that he is not her husband no matter how obviously he differs from the man that she has been living with for fifteen years. (Almost everyone in Las Vegas has a similar tendency to accept Cooper as Dougie, all evidence to the contrary.) At the same time, Janey-E sees Cooper/Dougie primarily in terms of what he means for her in terms of the values of money, sex, and power that define the marketplace and are rendered illusory in her marriage and family. Janey-E is filled with anger at Dougie when she feels that he seems to be lacking in the power to provide her with desirable consumer goods. She is filled with love after he bumbles into a position at the Lucky 7 Insurance Company that makes him rich and influential by default—and after she notices Cooper's muscular body, not in the privacy of her home but when a doctor is examining him.

The sudden wealth for the Joneses is to some degree the result of similar knee-jerk materialist reflexes in the gangsters. They are hell bent on murdering Cooper/Dougie when they think he has caused them to lose money but become his enthusiastic benefactors when he brings them a check for over thirty million dollars from the Lucky 7 Insurance Company.[9] These and other examples of the ironies of materialism within an unorientable marketplace have a satiric edge. But Lynch complicates his parodic picture of consumerism, refusing to let us stand back from these people and feel detached from or superior to them. There is real emotion attached to their spasmodic zigs and zags, with particular attention to the pathos of Sonny Jim.

The Twin Peaks characters, cradled by nature not by casinos, have greater depth in their attachments than their human counterparts in other places in the United States. They offer the very few moments of profound human friendship and love in the series. Bumbling Deputy Andy Brennan (Harry Goaz), a decent simpleton, and his wife, Sheriff's Station receptionist Lucy Brennan (Kimmy Robertson), a maddeningly literal dimwit, display kindness, decency, and a strangely instinctive tendency to be at the right place at the right time, doing the right thing. The most conventionally sympathetic characters in the series live in the town of Twin Peaks, particularly Sheriff Frank Truman (Robert Forster), a cornerstone of American humane decency, like his brother, Harry Truman. Frank has taken over the position of sheriff while Harry is sick. His deputy chief, Tommy "Hawk" Hill (Michael Horse), is an intuitive, rock solid, and comforting presence, who offers a channel to the stabilizing force of ancient wisdom from his American Indian heritage. They are not the heroes of this epic but rather touchstones for the viewers of the grace under pressure that we would all like to have as they become aware of being caught up in the unfathomable nature of life. Norma Jennings, the owner of a reassuring, literally nourishing town gathering place, is completely unseduced by the profit motive as she runs her diner and in her relationship with Big Ed Hurley, one of the very few abidingly loving couples. Contrast this with Janey-E in Las Vegas, who ultimately is thrilled to be the wife of a tulpa clone of himself that Cooper orders to be fabricated to replace him in her life when he leaves on his mission. (Is this a suggestion that a part of Cooper will always be married in some way to the vacuous comforts of the marketplace?)

The appealing closeness of *Twin Peaks* to the larger forces in the cosmos is also indicated by the pilgrimage of Freddie Sykes (Jake Wardle), a London cockney, to the town when he receives a summons from the Fireman to find his destiny there. The Fireman tells him how to find and make his own magic green rubber gardening glove that will serve his purposes in his new home. When peripheral Freddie destroys BOB with the power of the glove in part 17, this adds a further complication to the relationship between the Fireman and marketplace characters. Why is protagonist Cooper not given that power and that destiny? The equivocal nature of the Fireman and indeed everyone beyond the marketplace points increasingly beyond our belief systems and toward the unorientable.

We see ambiguity in the marbling of both positive humanity and negative energy in Las Vegas and Twin Peaks alike. Negativity roils the town in the fights that break out at the Bang Bang roadhouse, where people congregate to hear music but also to tangle with each other; in Audrey Horne's

FIGURE C.5. *Sarah Palmer has become a threshold between the marketplace and the beyond.*

relationship with her husband, Charlie (Clark Middleton), which has the toxic claustrophobia of Jean-Paul Sartre's *No Exit*; in the marriage of Shelly Briggs's daughter to a self-destructive man; and in the murderous destructive self-involvement of Audrey Horne's son, Richard (Eamon Farren). The most sinister negativity emerges in Sarah Palmer, Laura's mother. She was an oppressed wife with psychic sensibilities in the 1990 series. Her husband abused their daughter and died, both as a result of his possession by demon BOB. In 2017 Sarah herself has become a person to whom something has happened, as she states hysterically. "Something" has forced her into an inversion of her former identity and left her in darkness and isolation, trapped within reversible Möbius time that repeats itself like a horrible version of *Groundhog Day* (1993), enclosed in the cage of her home. We observe her sitting on her couch in an airless, lightless living room, avidly watching a televised boxing match that we suddenly understand is stuck in a time warp, an infinitely repeating loop of the moment when one boxer is knocked down by his opponent. Living on the threshold between the marketplace and infinity, she occasionally displays knowledge of her plight. To defend herself from a sexual predator, she removes the front of her face as if it were a mask to expose herself as a portal to dark and violent cosmic energies.

The characters who form the Blue Rose task force at the FBI suggest another fragment of the modern American crazy quilt and another nuance to the epic drama of the series. Without personal lives that we know of, they jointly fabricate a version of family that is ironically a branch of government, the FBI. From this platform they investigate the unorientable marketplace, the strangeness that they alone, among marketplace characters, consciously recognize and hunt for as the source of evil in human life. In addition to Cooper, the special Blue Rose agents include Albert Rosenfield, Tammy Preston (Chrysta Bell), Gordon Cole (David Lynch), deputy bureau chief, and missing agent Phillip Jeffries. Conscious of the illegibility and dangers of events that contradict what is supposed to be the nature of the marketplace, they strive to understand them and find a way to exert control over them. But they are too caught up in the chaos of adjusting to the existence of tulpas and doppelgängers to succeed.

They are, for the most part, comic foils for Cooper's epic debacle as an agent. They are amusing bunglers on a smaller scale as they fly around the country trying to figure out why dead bodies are turning up in strange places and following up on their hunches that it is all somehow connected with the mysteries of Cooper's disappearance and his possible return after twenty-five years. Yet, with all the technology and power of the FBI at their disposal, explanations are (humorously) always just beyond their grasp. Also beyond them are the swirling passions of the other marketplace characters that contain a modicum of something beyond the illusions of the quest. Their less extreme disconnections are the comic relief for Cooper's profound isolation, especially Cole's antic episodic adventures in brief, fragmented consenting-adult romance.

FIGURE C.6. *Gordon Cole's Frenchwoman raises her leg for him.*

The fragmented Cooper, at the center of Lynch's epic, stands not only as the most extreme case of the fragmented identities of marketplace characters subject to temporal and energetic inversions but also as the most extreme case of the isolation that the marketplace misprisions breed and the toll exacted by commitment to dealing with evil. As Cooper's detachment and division intensify toward the end of the 2017 series, the terrible evolution of Sarah Palmer becomes clearer as a parallel of where Cooper ends up at the closure of this tale. It is no coincidence that she is the other character as intimately connected to Laura. Yet she provides only an evocative image rather than answers to the questions that grow exponentially out of the darkening of Cooper as he pursues his dubious mission and of Laura as she becomes more embroiled in his plans. But it is Cooper's relationship to Diane Evans (Laura Dern), his assistant at the FBI, that prefigures his ultimate envelopment by negativity and disorientation. Cooper returns to her at last in part 17, like Odysseus to Penelope in Homer's epic poem of homecoming, only to lose her in a vortex of fragmentations and inversions on all levels of cosmic reality.

In Lynch's modern epic, Cooper finds his female other to be a match for his own fractured identity. In 1990 Diane was Cooper's silent partner back at the FBI offices, a running gag: Cooper's frequent communication with her left her completely invisible. At the same time, as the silent companion to whom he dictated his personal thoughts as well as the data for his expense account by voicemail, she was also a comic evocation of a major absence in Cooper's life. In 2017 Diane is embodied—indeed has too many bodies. And this raises many distinctly unfunny questions.

The four Diane fragments, like Cooper's scraps, can neither fit together to form a whole, harmonious identity nor fit into any relationship or situation. The main Diane particles are Naido (Nae Yuki), a blonde tulpa Diane, and an ostensibly real Diane. The Naido fragment of Diane is introduced early in the series, in part 3, but neither we nor Cooper recognize her. She is the woman in the space bunker, a bizarre mutant tulpa whose eyes are covered over with skin and who lacks the capacity for human speech. She offers herself to Cooper through the brave, if equivocal, model of a leap into boundlessness. Naido is a mass of mysterious, disorganized intuitions, unable to make either visual or aural contact with the marketplace but apparently in touch with knowledge that comes from beyond its limitations. She does not see, hear, or speak, but she senses presence, evil, and danger. When she turns out to be a vessel for "real" Diane to protect her from the evil intentions of Mr. C., she adds fascinatingly to the repertoire of possible purposes of tulpas. She also stands interestingly as a kind of mirror image of the inchoate Dougie, who is a vessel for Cooper while Mr. C. stalks him.

Blonde tulpa Diane is surly and foul mouthed as well as alcoholic and tobacco addicted. She is somewhat mannequin-like in appearance due to her geometric haircut and heavy makeup. She alone among the series tulpas is self-aware as a fabrication and as a betrayer of the people who are supposed to be her friends. She works for Mr. C. as a spy and was most likely created by him for the purpose—we are not sure. But she does not belong with him: she

FIGURE C.7. *A positive tulpa Diane cannot make herself understood to a frightened Cooper.*

FIGURE C.8. *Mr. C. has created a negative tulpa Diane.*

has conflicting feelings about serving him and about the Blue Rose agents she has been designed to kill.

Real Diane emerges after both Naido and blonde tulpa Diane disappear. The blonde tulpa is killed when she attempts to shoot Gordon Cole. After Mr. C. is killed when he tries to kill Sheriff Truman, a supposedly nontulpa Diane emerges from the shell of the eyeless mutant tulpa. The real Diane? Reality is a much larger concept in 2017 than it has ever been on American TV. "Real" Diane possesses the means of communication—eyes and a human voice—but she is even more artificial looking than the treacherous blonde tulpa. The "real" Diane's geometrically styled hair is an impossibly synthetic looking Day-Glo orange, and her extreme makeup makes her face look like a full-fledged mask. Is there a real Diane? Near the end of Cooper's quest, in part 18, they ask each other: "Is it really you?" Both answer "yes," but the show's answer is much less certain. Shortly before she disappears from the epic, this version of Diane glimpses her own doppelgänger, the fourth fragment, about which we learn nothing further. What had seemed to be the prelude to Cooper getting the girl and solving the mystery à la formulaic television is quite the reverse. As we shall soon see, it ultimately seems that Diane and Cooper are not *really* anything. Moreover, on both occasions when Cooper might have accepted Diane's invitation to relationship, he does not, opting for a course of action without her that leads to nonbeing.

But before we trace the final narrative thinning of Cooper's heroism into nothingness, we must first take a detour to ponder one more crucial

FIGURE C.9. *Real Diane's reality is visually questioned.*

presence. It surges along the Möbius twist that foments human perplexity and alienation and unfathomable negative and positive reversals, degrading matter and contaminating energy. It alienates people and lures heroes to their destruction—and may be indestructible: Judy.

WE *ARE* GOING TO TALK ABOUT JUDY

In *Twin Peaks: Fire Walk with Me*, Lynch's film companion to his two television series about Cooper and the death of Laura Palmer, Phillip Jeffries, the missing FBI agent, introduces Lynch's audience to "Judy." Appearing suddenly to Gordon Cole's Blue Rose team in the FBI offices in Philadelphia, Jeffries blurts out, "We're not going to talk about Judy," then disappears. In the same film a monkey that we first saw behind a plaster mask suddenly appears without plaster camouflage, fully revealed, and says, "Judy." Bafflement ensues.[10]

Part 17 reveals to us that Gordon Cole was not as baffled as he seemed. He already knew about Judy when Jeffries made his bizarre appearance; Judy—the raw denial of being, the degradation of being into nothingness and positive into negative—was the reason he originally organized the Blue Rose team. As Cole explains, he long since decided that such a team was necessary when he was made aware of Judy by Major Briggs. Judy, he adds, is the modern name of this energy; the ancient name is Jou-dei. It is of interest, with respect to Lynch's vision, that Cole's embellishment of his Blue Rose history with its ancient name was not in the shooting script, as I was told by Michael Barile, Lynch's personal assistant. Lynch improvised that name on the set and added it to Cole's "big reveal." For that reason, the spelling of the name does not appear anywhere (but here) on paper. However, we have Lynch's word on the way it would have been spelled: "Jou-dei." The improvised addition of Jou-dei tells us that Lynch wanted to create a vivid story about the evil being hunted by his Blue Rose team, to make it clear that it was not some purely modern force born in 1945 with the explosion of a bomb in New Mexico. Lynch's vision defines the nuclear explosion of matter in the service of warfare as a contemporary extension of a negative energy buried in the mists of time. It is also interesting to consider how belated the FBI is in adding to its mission a mandate to investigate Jou-dei/Judy.

The audience too is belated in hearing the name "Judy"; however, its spirit inheres continuously in the series as a presence of nonexistence. It is almost immediately sensed when Laura is pulled violently out of the Red Room in part 2, dissolving into terrified shrieks and fragmented particles. It is almost the first thing we see of the marketplace in part 1, when we observe a young man named Sam Colby (Ben Rosenfield). He has been hired by an anonymous employer in New York City for the enigmatic task of keeping watch for anything that might appear in an empty, large glass box isolated in a windowless building. When he and his girlfriend Tracey (Madeline Zima) begin to have sex while he is on duty, a force previously unsuspected by Sam explodes from the box, mutilating and killing them. It is Judy. Judy's extreme negativity as the inversion of being is, as a matter of course, the enemy of human connection. Someone is looking for that power, apart from the Blue Rose task force. When we see a photograph of Mr. C. in front of the glass box, we know who the anonymous employer is. As the parts of the 2017 series unfold, we become privy to his desire for Judy but never to his specific intentions. Nor is Mr. C. any more successful in his search than Gordon Cole.

An untrammeled Judy looms over the epic. When Cooper is shunted out of the Red Room as the doppelgänger of the arm cries "Nonexistent!" he is in the clutches of Judy. This becomes clearer when we see him pass through the sinister glass box on his way back into the marketplace. In an even more overwhelming form, Judy is behind the nonexistence initiated by the testing of the atom bomb in White Sands, New Mexico, that dominates the sublime part 8. Judy is the unnamed negative presence that we feel when the dying Log Lady speaks to Hawk in elegiac tones in part 10 about electricity, the dream of time and space, and the sad fading of the universal light.[11]

Cole's preoccupation with what he calls Judy is reflected in the images on the wall of his office: the 1945 bomb test; a blighted, black ear of corn; and a photograph of Franz Kafka, the Czech surreal poet of modernist absurdity

FIGURE C.10. *Once again Cooper is overwhelmed by a doppelgänger.*

that we see in parts 3 and 7. The unarticulated malevolence of the owl icon on the green ring that has moved through all of the parts of the *Twin Peaks* saga is an emblem of Judy.[12] It is behind all of the cosmic manifestations of negative energy that we see and experience throughout 2017 as it travels along the routes of electric poles, emanates from transformers along the road, sizzles in wall sockets, bursts forth in part 17 during the fight between demon BOB and the characters at the Twin Peaks Sheriff's Station, and finally flares up and pulls everything into darkness at the end of the series finale, part 18. It is all evoked as a special kind of electricity, not the charge that makes your toaster work, but pernicious energy.

We are taught about that other electricity in part 11, when Deputy Sheriff Hawk gives Sheriff Truman and the audience a map-reading lesson as they are about to go on a mission in uncharted territory. Truman prepares by looking at a conventional map showing latitude, longitude, and miles. It ultimately suggests that there is no path through the forest that they have to cross to arrive at their destination. Hawk has another way of talking about paths. He unrolls his sacred ancient map of the Twin Peaks area, drawn on animal skin, which doubles as a map of the cosmos, and the baffling explosions of electricity and the smoke and/or magnesium glare of light that often accompany it throughout the series. It is always current because it maps the energy in the universe, which is unchanging, unlike the conventional map that changes with changes in culture. As Sheriff Truman watches Hawk plot the nature of the energy that they are about to encounter, he sees an image of what he thinks is a campfire. Hawk explains it as a fire symbol for energy that is "more like modern-day electricity," neither good nor bad in itself. Negativity and positivity depend on the intention behind the energy. The map, says Hawk, indicates a connection between their destination and blackened corn, something that should be positive and nourishing but is unnatural and deadly. Putting together the fire symbol and the blackened corn, Hawk arrives at a third pictorial icon: black fire. When Truman asks about a picture on the map of the owl-like pictogram that was also on Briggs's message, Hawk closes up. It is not a subject for discussion, forbidden knowledge. Are we to understand a wisdom in Hawk's refusal to engage in any way with the terrors of deep negativity and a foolishness in Cooper's rush to confront it? This is a question that hangs over Lynch's epic. What are we to do in the face of evil: close down or stand to? There will be no simple answers. However, one thing is sure. If Hawk turns his face from even naming the force, *Twin Peaks* (2017) names and observes it. That may be as far as Lynch dares to go this time around. Nevertheless, the epic is fearless in its attentiveness.

FIGURE C.11. *Deputy Hawk's cosmology lesson.*

By the time we seek Hawk's map, we have already had a taste of the inversions embedded in negative energy, particularly when we cut in part 8 to the countdown at White Sands to the testing of the atom bomb in 1945. The countdown backward from 10 has a special meaning within the context of Möbius time in this series. It is standard in military operations, but in this context it evokes the twist in Möbius time toward the negative. When the explosion reduces matter to waves, particles, and black fire in a long montage, it resonates with the cry "Nonexistent!" as Cooper left the Red Room. The nonexistence created by the nuclear blast is also visualized by the scorched oil in a gas station/convenience store in the White Sands desert. Scorched oil is a contaminant, the negative degeneration of fuel, analogous to the blackened corn as the degeneration of food into putrefaction. Putrefied beings emerge as part of this de-creation process, concentrated negative energies covered in scorched oil, who congregate around the convenience store. The most prominently featured of these scorched oil men is called the Woodsman (Robert Broski). He and the iconic BOB are among the images generated by the de-creation of the nuclear blast. In response, the Fireman emits a golden flux of particles from his head, creating a positive energy that he conveys to earth to balance the degenerative force of the bomb.

These imbalances between negative and positive energies are not at all comforting. We cut from 1945 to 1956 in the New Mexico desert. Though we see a sweet scene of teenagers exchanging their first kiss in this segment of part 8, we also observe a mutant bird/frog/insect creature emerge from an egg, a dark, unsettling liminality. While no explicit connection is made between the creature and the atomic explosion, there is a strong implicit connection. The suggestion of its negativity is unmistakable after the grim Woodsman appears on the desert sands. He invades a local radio station playing the song "My Prayer," a marketplace ode to the sublime connections made possible by love, and horribly kills the people in the station. The Woodsman replaces the affirmative song with his own inscrutable, repetitive hymn to negativity: "This is the water and this is the well. Drink full and descend. The horse is the white of the eyes and dark within." "The horse" uncertainly resonates with images of a white horse that appear from time to time in the *Twin Peaks* saga: when Leland Palmer is drugging Sarah so he can molest Laura undisturbed; in part 2 of *Twin Peaks* (2017) right after Laura is abducted by an invisible power; and later in the series in a small plastic model of a white horse that appears in part 18 on the fireplace mantel of the house that Cooper enters when he encounters the Laura look-alike Carrie Paige on the last leg of his epic journey. The statuette is part of a collection of visual clues, ambiguous as all clues are in this epic, that Carrie is a negative presence (of which more below).

Random, impenetrable traces of malignancy abound. This chant; the bodiless, phantom sound of a horse neighing as the Woodsman disappears from the desert terrain; the images of the bomb's degeneration of matter to particles and waves; the birth of a monstrous creature; and the intrusion into the marketplace of the Woodsman are generally illegible modernist evocations of the problem of evil. Krzysztof Penderecki's *Threnody to the Victims of Hiroshima*, which accompanies the images of matter decomposing into particles, is itself the decomposition of music into silences and sound particles. If there is positive brilliance in art that can convey the energy of nuclear weapons, it is nevertheless a portrait of negative sound. The putrefied Woodman's silencing of the regular rhythms and soaring melodic line of "My Prayer," which invoke the characteristically defined and bounded structures of the marketplace, yields dark consequences. As ordinary people listening to the broadcast are cut off from a sustaining energy when the song is interrupted, they lose consciousness. The young girl who has just had her first kiss goes to sleep listening to the sound of the Woodsman's voice. In an unconscious state, she opens her mouth to the mutant creature, which enters it. Nothing seems to be a sufficient counterforce: not even the golden energy of the Fireman—whose name takes on ambiguous implication in the light of Hawk's map.

Hope surges in part 17 that the Blue Rose agents with some help from the beyond can get a handle on Judy. A no-holds-barred battle at the Twin Peaks

Sheriff's Station against Mr. C. and BOB ends in the seriocomic death of Mr. C. at the hands of resident silly person Lucy Brennan, who uncharacteristically shoots him as he is about to kill Sheriff Truman, and in the equally mixed absurdity and drama of the pulverizing of BOB by the gardening glove–empowered fist of ordinary bloke Freddie. In the aftermath Cole and his team show up for a cheerful reunion with Cooper. The eyeless tulpa dissolves to release Diane into Cooper's arms. Bafflingly, disconnection literally raises its head just when Cooper connects with Diane and a satisfying conclusion to all problems seems to be in the offing. An image of Cooper's head, large and disconnected from his body, is superimposed over the figures of Cooper and Diane and intones in a slurred, basso profundo voice, "We live inside a dream." This resonates with part 14, in which Gordon Cole talks to Albert and Tammy, his Blue Rose team, about his recent Monica Bellucci dream, in which she says to him, "We are like the dreamer who dreams and then lives inside the dream." She asks, "But who is the dreamer?" Cooper here is distinctly separate from the large speaking Cooper head. At the moment of his reunion with Diane, he is in the process of fragmenting so as to live inside his dream, but it is not clear who is the dreamer. It is and is not Cooper, just as Cooper and Diane are and are not connected. Judy's denials and degradations are in the room, and we shall soon discover that Judy only lost foot soldiers when BOB and Mr. C were destroyed. Because this moment of Cooper's further entrapment in the marketplace dream shapes the rest of his mission, Judy prevails.[13]

FIGURE C.12. *A fragmented Cooper dreams and then lives inside his dream.*

What happens to the familiar, formulaic desire for conclusive happy endings that this moment has raised and immediately begins to prohibit? We are encouraged to move toward a very different kind of desire, unfamiliar and in opposition to every yearning to which we have been trained by formula TV.

PARADISE LOST

"Did I do it?" asks a bloodied Freddie after his powerful gloved fist shatters the demon BOB into pieces. "You did it, Freddie," says Cooper. But Freddie has been successful only in part. The nonexistence of which BOB and Mr. C. are made—the essence of Judy—remains. Cooper is about to be engulfed by it when he takes the last leg of his journey.

A warning sign of what lies ahead pops up when Cooper abruptly leaves the scene of his triumph and any commendation from Gordon Cole and the FBI, as well as any joy that he and Diane might have experienced there. Truncating those potential moments, Cooper seeks to do some time traveling toward Laura and her redemption. But he enters into the past to change the future through a demonic space, which he reaches by going through a door in the sub-basement of the Great Northern Hotel: its heating system suggests the black fire in Hawk's map.[14] We want to be optimistic when the guide who now leads Cooper as he pursues his quest is Philip Gerard, whom we have regarded as a positive mentor. But a Möbius reversal is in progress. Gerard leads Cooper through the sinister portal that is the convenience store, intoning the ode to bad energy that echoes through all the *Twin Peaks* stories: "Through the darkness of future-past the magician longs to see, one chance out between two worlds. Fire! Walk with me," Referring back to Hawk's map, this is not the fire of good intent. As Phillip Jeffries opens the flow of time for Cooper to insert himself into it to erase Laura's death from the year 1989, he marks the Möbius sign of infinity on the air into which Cooper enters with the same black dot that Mr. C. used to mark his death threats in the marketplace. Cooper is walking into the wrong side of infinity and cannot get to where he thinks he is going.

If this is not clear when Cooper walks through a questionable portal in the basement of the Great Northern Hotel in order to reach Jeffries, it later becomes probable. Although Cooper's machinations mean that he finds Laura and that she neither goes to the cabin where she met her death nor becomes a corpse wrapped in plastic, she slips from his grasp as he leads her toward home. We then hear the sinister insect sound to which the Fireman called Cooper's attention in part 1. Do we recognize it now as the quietly terrible sound of nonexistence? Possibly, as it is followed by Laura's shriek of fear and pain, reverberating horribly, which we have heard before at every instance in which she suffers. It becomes certain that Cooper has taken a wrong turn when he tries again to find and redeem Laura after he loses her in part 17. This time his epic quest patently leads to nothingness.

Disconnection and radical negativity rule part 18, the final episode, in which Cooper destroys his connection with Diane as the prelude to his final misbegotten attempt to complete his linear quest in a Möbius universe. Part 18 begins summoning up images of a happy ending. Mr. C. is in the Red Room burning to ash in black fire. The tulpa Dougie that Cooper ordered for Janey-E and Sonny Jim shows up at the red door of their home, joyously uniting the family. Cooper and Diane meet again to work together. They are all false hopes. All are diminished versions of formula closure. The Jones family has been completed by a manufactured man. And Cooper and Diane fall prey to the Fireman's clues, which turn out to represent a deepening of disorientation, not signposts along a road to victory. As they combine forces, Cooper and Diane drive on an enigmatically unidentified road, a new version of a lost highway: the number 430 mentioned by the Fireman marks a place where they pass through a storm of sizzling negative energy emitted by a forest of electrical transformers as the light darkens. Transformation does ensue, but it is all negative. When they stop at a motel, Cooper seems to have merged with the energy of the supposedly defeated Mr. C. In their room, before sex, Cooper orders Diane to come to him, as we have previously seen Mr. C. command women. During sex, like Mr. C. and unlike "Coop," he is unreceptive, and worst of all, disconnected. In her distress, Diane looks

FIGURE C.13. *Real (?) Diane has bad sex with a much-changed Cooper.*

more like a mannequin than ever. The nondiegetic sounds of "My Prayer," recalling part 8 and the negative energy of the atomic test, reverberate over the scene. It is very negative sex.

By the next morning their union has been destabilized completely. Diane has disappeared. In her place is a note from someone named Linda to someone called Richard, breaking off the relationship. Arguably, the Fireman's clues about Richard and Linda and killing two birds with one stone turn out here to be an equivocal reference to the dissolution of both the identities of Cooper and Diane and their connection. Not even their own names remain. Nor does Laura's. Cooper leaves the motel, which is clearly not the motel that he and Diane entered the night before. Having no obvious direction, he drives until he sees Judy's Coffee Shop, where he gets the address of a woman who looks like Laura. Cooper is sure that she is Laura, but she claims to be named Carrie Paige. "Carrie" agrees to go with Cooper back to Laura's mother and home because, well, she needs to get out of town. Cooper asks for no explanation even when he sees a male corpse stiffening with rigor mortis in a chair in her living room, with a bullet hole in his forehead, blood on the wall in back of him, and an automatic rifle on the floor near him. Cooper now travels with "Carrie" further down the lost highway that he has committed to, which terminates exactly nowhere. When he and "Carrie" pull up at a building that looks like the Palmer house, they are told by the woman who opens the door, Alice Tremond (Mary Reber), that no one named Palmer lives there or has ever lived there. (Mary Reber is the actual owner of the house that Lynch used as the Palmer house. So what she tells Cooper and "Carrie" is true in both real and fictional time. The scene is simultaneously comic and tragic.)

Lost in time, Cooper stands in the middle of the street uncertain of even the year as "Carrie" hears a faint voice, familiar to viewers, calling "Laura." It is Sarah Palmer's voice emerging from 1990 when she called for her daughter, not knowing that Laura was already dead. Is it future or is it past? Time turns in on itself as Laura's horrible scream once again reverberates, now emitted from "Carrie's" lips, this time on the flip side of the Möbius twist. The brightly lit windows in the "Palmer house" suddenly go black. A brief magnesium flash explodes in the darkness, reminiscent of the magnesium flashes in the desert convenience store after the first atomic test. Then everything disappears. Cooper's choice of marketplace limitations over possibility (in the bunker) and decision to live in his dream instead of living (in the Twin Peaks Sheriff's Station) have landed him on the other side of Möbius time and in a state of nonbeing. Has he found Judy as a victim instead of as a savior? Is all lost? Yes.

FIGURE C.14. *Stranded on the wrong side of Möbius time*

And no. Cooper's fall does not define the absolute limits of his narrative reality. At the same time that he and Carrie implode, the side of Möbius time where Laura and Cooper began and Cooper's mission originated as a positive goal still exists somewhere, as evidenced by the faint echo of Sarah calling Laura's name. So if we as audience external to the fiction have lost the dream of the conventional quest and the illusions of conventional fiction, we have not necessarily found nothingness. And here is where narrative desire becomes complicated. Yes, *Twin Peaks* (2017) can be read as a nihilistic Kafkaesque epic about a world that is at base a vacuum of absurdity and horror. If this is what the pictures of Kafka, the atom bomb blast, and the putrefied black corn in Cole's office indicate, then the dream of the marketplace *is* fatal. The attempt of Gordon Cole's Blue Rose task force to protect the marketplace is an exercise in futility and worse, as Cole himself fears from time to time. But Lynch's series can also be read, as I prefer to read it, as a prompt to a desire for a new and more profound liberation from formulaic story products: a reply to the illusions of the bunker (mentality) that formulaic television still represents, to which Cooper capitulated at the outset of his voyage.

From this perspective, Lynch aggressively models freedom, like nothing television has ever seen, even in the original *Twin Peaks*. *Twin Peaks* (2017) can be seen as an even more complex incitement to think outside the box (the pun is irresistible) or bunker toward a fuller inhabitation of our boundless reality with all its charm, fear, and strangeness, without any model to imitate. Would imitation, after all, not defeat the freedom that Lynch espouses? Indeed, the 2017 series can be read as a call to reclaim the human in the universe he has depicted by distancing ourselves from recipes for action summed up by the formulaic hero that can only lead to nonexistence. The epic hero as a liberating negative example! Lynch in conversation often uses parables that harness negative images to make a positive point. He spoke to me of the parable of the coiled rope and the snake. If we choose to see a snake, he said, then that is the negative universe we create. In other words, the universe of the coiled rope remains. In his epic *Twin Peaks* (2017) parable, Lynch connects Cooper's bad choices to the power of Judy and non-existence. Judy is only a failure of the art of living.

Lynch believes that we are all artists in our own ways if we can unblock ourselves and listen to the "rules" within, not only as painters and auteurs. The modern epic journey of Dale Cooper, a hero who did not listen but rather chose to live inside a marketplace dream, offers the pain of loss, the loss of old habits of mind and beliefs. But it also offers the pleasure of recognizing the wrong road toward nothingness so as to open up the option of a better path toward being. It infuses the medium anew with a courageous imaginative energy that deepens its connections with the power, mystery, and beauty of art.

CONCLUSION

The creation of television art is not the goal of most of those who control the mass media. Nor is art the preoccupation of a vast percentage of the mass audience. Both tend to remain on the shallow side of the three ways of understanding how a television series can be of value and significance. First, it can be financially significant by the numbers and valuable monetarily. This is the most obvious form of success in America, and the one to which the business end of television has been addicted from the beginning. Second, it can also be culturally significant in a limited way when it introduces, albeit in simplistic form, social ideas or images and characters that delight or intrigue the audience in substantial numbers, giving it a temporary power to popularize clothing, music, colloquial expressions, platitudes, attitudes, and actors. Third, it can be significant as art, rarely a question of numbers and rarely recognized with awards, which almost always celebrate significance by the numbers.

The shallow reduction of value to little beyond short-term financial and faddish cultural importance will probably always be popularly and industrially misrecognized by the numbers, as the crucial benchmarks of American television. And the fortunes built by formulaic successes are facts of economic life. But importance by the numbers fades and leaves in its wake sterility, no matter how inventive the initial creative energy behind the business of storytelling is—and some of it has been prodigious. Formulaic limits inevitably produce entropy. By contrast, whether or not an auteur television series is significant financially or culturally in this short-term sense, whether or not it garners awards, and even if it does all that (as *The Sopranos* did), its crucial importance is that art is a matter of the enduring long term.

Twin Peaks (2017) may mean unlimited things to some or all and to Lynch himself—who, after all, insists that he does not know what he is doing when he creates. So do the works of Joyce, Kafka, and Faulkner. So do all works that come from the rules of the mind and heart, make contact with that part of us that is not conditioned by the externally imposed rules of the story product, and give America a link to the nurturing stamina of the internal rules, the unabated imaginative restructuring of what it means to be human without which all cultures perish. I once claimed the mantle of Alfred Hitchcock for Lynch.[15] *Twin Peaks* (2017) suggests that I underestimated him. Perhaps it is the mantle of James Joyce, William Faulkner, and, even more to the point, Franz Kafka that now belongs to Lynch for his transformation of American television into a medium that can provide both the humanizing influence of modern art and its mind-expanding visions. Lynch and the other new auteurs have risen to the challenge with stunning results. But can they continue to do so within an industry that neither understands nor values the modern experience of doubting the delusions of the marketplace?

The auteur challenge to old, established desires is formidable, more so since *Twin Peaks* (2017), but so is the power of habit. What if the challenge proves to be too great for both the limited concepts of those who control the mass media and the habitual responses of too many in the mass audience?

ACKNOWLEDGMENTS

To David Lynch and David Chase, who beautifully changed my life with every encounter: what a privilege to enjoy deepening conversations over many years; to David Simon for allotting time in his very busy life; to Matt Weiner for the pleasure of butting heads with a passionate artist; to Eric Overmyer, a gentleman and a poet; to Uta Briesewitz, inspirational lightning in a bottle. To the industry voices of hope and striving: Allen Coulter, Tim Van Patten, Mark Johnson, Brad Anderson, Terry Winter, Steven Van Zandt, Michael Imperioli, Eigil Bryld, Sidney Wolensky, Howard Korder, Steve Kornacki, John Magaro, and Bella Heathcote. To the helpers who make the connections: Sabrina Sutherland, who moved heaven and earth in record time for this book; Mindy Ramaker and Michael Barile, keeping order at the gate at the "Lost Highway House"; to Nicole Lambert, Jason Minter, Gabrielle Altheim, and Reena Rexrode. To the administrators: Richard Plepler, the late Brad Grey, and Nina Kostroff Noble. To Columbia University Seminars: Bob Pollack and Alice Newton, my colleagues in the seminar on Cinema and Interdisciplinary Interpretation, especially Cindy Lucia and Bill Luhr, as well as Melissa E. Sanchez, for her provocative presentation at the Shakespeare seminar.

I would like to express my appreciation to the Schoff Fund at the University Seminars at Columbia University for their help with this publication. The ideas presented here have benefitted from discussions in two university seminars: Cinema and Interdisciplinary Interpretation and Shakespeare.

I am indebted to the expanding field of television studies, but a practical word limit imposed by my contract prevents me from a full dialogue with those pioneers who have come before me in their explorations of television aesthetics, including Christine Geraghty, Jason Mittell, Martin Shuster, Jason Jacobs, Steven Peacock, Jane Feuer, Kim Akass, Janet McCabe, George Toles, Sarah Cardwell, and so many more. However, they are ever present as part of the context from which this study grows. To Cantor Cathy Lawrence, M. M., for the *Pirkoi Avot* translation in chapter 3.

To my editor at the University of Texas Press, Jim Burr: We have worked together since 1995, and the unfolding years continue to reveal new and special aspects of our collaboration. To Robert Kimzey, managing editor at the press; Kathy Lewis, freelance copy editor; and the talented and patient Amanda Weiss, freelance designer. To my dear, generous, talented, supportive friends Debarati Biswas and Arthur Vincie for their many contributions to the research and the illustrations; Kim Akass for her support and collegiality; Sarah Stemp for her contributions to my research; Ken Provencher for his support and assistance in nervous times; and to my class at the David Lynch Graduate School of Cinematic Arts, whose questions and lively cinematic imaginations continually pushed me to reexamine old assumptions.

To my cherished family: my son David Nochimson, because I love him and for his valuable help with my research and for his technical support; my treasured daughter Holly and immensely loved granddaughter Amara, for bringing the light; and to my dear, husband Richard, my BFFEAE.

NOTES

INTRODUCTION: THE DAVID EFFECT

1. A useful reference for surveying the field of television studies concerned with televisual aesthetics is the anthology *Television Aesthetics and Style*, edited by Steven Peacock and Jason Jacobs. Also useful are Martin Schuster, *New Television: The Aesthetics and Politics of a Genre*; and, of course, Jason Mittell's seminal publications, *Genre and Television: From Cop Shows to Cartoons in American Culture* and *Television and American Culture*. My claims for the aesthetics of soap opera are explored in *No End to Her: Soap Opera and the Female Subject*.

2. There is a lively dialogue in process about when and how the newer developments in American television began. In *New Television*, Martin Schuster argues, as do I, that it started with David Lynch and *Twin Peaks*. A host of television writers, directors, and producers concur, including David Chase, who identifies Lynch as his inspiration for breaking free of formulaic television, and director Allen Coulter. By contrast, David Simon identifies the series *Oz* as his inspiration, not necessarily as the beginning of auteur television but as the show that gave him confidence that a gritty story about real world problems is possible on television. For the opinions of two representative entertainment journalists on the history of the changes in American TV, see David Bianculli, *The Platinum Age of Television: From* I Love Lucy *to* The Walking Dead, *How TV Became Terrific*; and Alan Sepinwall, *The Revolution Was Televised: The Cops, Crooks, Slingers and Slayers Who Changed Television Forever*. For an interesting discussion of the question of aesthetics and television in general, see Sarah Cardwell, "Television Aesthetics: Stylistic Analysis and Beyond," pp. 23–44.

3. Shonda Rhimes, *Year of Yes: How to Dance It Out, Stand in the Sun and Be Your Own Person*, p. xviii. Rhimes's enthusiasm for formula writing is filled with the ecstasy of achievement according to external rules: "There's a hum that happens inside my head when I hit a certain writing rhythm, a certain speed. When laying

track goes from feeling like climbing a mountain on my hands and knees to feeling like flying effortlessly through the air."

4.   David Simon, in-person interview with author, January 21, 2016. Unless otherwise specified, all Simon quotations are from this interview.

5.   Consideration of film as a modern tributary of the literary tradition has become commonplace. There is no other sustained consideration of American television as a new branch of our national literature, as far as I know, though something of the sort is alluded to by Alan Sepinwall in *The Revolution Was Televised*, when he speaks in passing of *The Wire* as being structured like a novel (p. 76). However, Sepinwall seems not to have a concept of the structural modernity of the series; he judges the pilot to be badly written because it does not conform to the rules of formulaic writing (p. 70).

6.   Matt Weiner, phone interview, May 26, 2016.

7.   The dreamlike elements of life and of storytelling were part of every in-person conversation I had with David Chase, and of some of our e-mails, as is evident from the e-mail of October 28, 2013, quoted above.

CHAPTER 1: DAVID LYNCH, *TWIN PEAKS*

1.   Mark Frost, in-person interview with author, November 22, 1991. In this interview Frost expressed surprise that I did not see Cooper as coming from the detective tradition of Sherlock Holmes, since that was the image of Cooper that he had. When I spoke to him of Cooper's most un-Sherlockian methods, like throwing stones at bottles and consulting with the Giant, he shrugged his shoulders.

2.   Elsewhere I have explained in great detail the influence on Lynch's worldview of quantum mechanics and the cosmology of the ancient Hindu Vedas: "The Perplexing Threshold Experience," in *David Lynch Swerves: Uncertainty from Lost Highway to Inland Empire*, pp. 1–11, 14–18. The influence of the Vedas resulted from Lynch's exposure to meditation, which he began in the mid-1970s, through his guru, Maharishi Mahesh Yogi. The influence of quantum mechanics was a result of Lynch's exposure to physics through his friendship with physicist John Hagelin, who summarizes his basic approach to physics in *Is Consciousness the Unified Field? A Field Theorist's Perspective*, pp. 29–87. Neither of these influences should be construed to be intentionally and didactically embedded in *Twin Peaks* or in any of Lynch's other works. Rather, the ideas that he has gleaned have found their way into his work only after they have been trans-formed at a very deep level of his creative process, when he gets out of the way of subconscious creation. I discussed that process with Lynch and wrote about it in *The Passion of David Lynch*, pp. 1–15.

3.   In *Inland Empire*, Lynch uses the word "marketplace" for the first time in dialogue to represent the level of reality on which daily cultural transactions take place. He does not use that precise term in *Twin Peaks*, but it is the way he thinks of the bracketed cultural context in which business, law, and science are carried on. For Lynch, the marketplace offers stultifying constraints that cut his characters off from the larger realities of the universe. If there is no recourse to the unified field beyond the marketplace, life is stunted and blighted.

4. It has been clear from all of my discussions with Lynch that he is suspicious of theoretical psychology and finds support for his interest in dreams and visions in other artists. Interviews: phone, January 31, 1992; in person, March 29–31, April 1, 1993, January 15–18, 1996 (set visit while Lynch was filming *Lost Highway*), January 13, 2006, March 18, 2010. This was particularly central to our conversations from March 29 to April 1, 1993, when we looked at paintings and films together. However, a number of distinguished critics have opted to read Lynch through Freudian and Lacanian theory. See Todd McGowan, *The Impossible David Lynch*; Michel Chion, *David Lynch*; and Slavoi Zizek, *The Art of the Ridiculous Sublime: On David Lynch's Lost Highway*. It is possible to say that McGowan, Chion, and Zizek are proposing another way of talking about how Lynch's art links us to the great ideas in our culture, but some might wish that these critics had explored the validity of interpreting Lynch through theoretical frameworks that he disclaims interest in or a relationship to.

5. Lynch has spoken to me about the Unified Field for decades; recently he has begun speaking about it in public. His retrospective at the Pennsylvania Academy of the Fine Arts in 2014 was called "David Lynch: The Unified Field" and featured much discussion of the role of this concept in his thinking.

6. Uta Briesewitz, in-person interview with author, June 28, 2015.

7. Lynch is not versed in the theory of superposition, but his creation of the relationship between BOB and Leland Palmer reflects precisely that state of a particle that is both itself and its double, a phenomenon for which we have no language except to say that it is midway between one and two. This is a bewildering concept of modern physics that I discussed with David Z. Albert, director of the M.A. Program in the Philosophical Foundations of Physics at Columbia University. Lynch might have had exposure to it through Hagelin or might simply have intersected with this cutting-edge physics through his own intuition, as artists often connect independently with the thinking of the Zeitgeist. David Z. Albert, in-person interviews with author, January 4, 2010, February 12, 2010, and May 7, 2010.

8. Kate McQuiston, *We'll Meet Again: Musical Design in the Films of Stanley Kubrick*, p. 45.

9. Ibid., p. 53.

10. The Internet is full of material about Rakshasas, as Lynch referred to them when he spoke to me of the turmoil that they create. It is also possible to find allusions to Rakshasas in the Rigveda, one of the books of the Vedas, where they are referred to as Rakshas:

    Rigveda 7.104.18
    O Powerful Ones! You should stand up to protect the masses and capture the Rakshas who intend to kill and destroy peace in night.
    Rigveda 7.104.22
    Destroy the Rakshas who attack like an owl, hound, wolf, eagle or vulture.

11. In my interview with Mark Frost on November 22, 1991, he went out of his way to praise ABC for unfailingly supporting Lynch and himself and to commend the

way they honored their promise never to impose any network pressure on them to make story decisions. This was a lie. And it made me question everything that he asserted about his relationship with Lynch and with ABC.

12. Mark Frost, in-person interview with author, November 22, 1991. When I asked for a copy of each of the two final episodes of *Twin Peaks*, he told me I would have to "ask David." Providing scripts for an article is almost always a matter of course, so I knew that some interesting situation lay behind Frost's reticence. In contrast, Lynch without hesitation authorized his assistant to send me the scripts. I was stunned to discover that they had not been used for the on-screen episodes. During an in-person interview with Catherine Coulson, March 30, 1993, she told me at great length how Lynch had improvised the final two shows.

13. Mark Frost, Harley Peyton, and Robert Engels, *Twin Peaks* #29 (Episode 2.022) First Draft: February 14, 1991; Rewrite/Dept. Heads; Distribution: February 25, 1991; Revised February 29, 1991. For excerpts that make clear the descent into formula in this script, see Nochimson, *The Passion of David Lynch*, pp. 94–95. Lynch's total discarding of the script when he taped the last episode implicitly attests to how much it violated his vision of the series. Lynch made his anger with the script explicit in our phone conversation on January 18, 2018: "I hate it. They [the authors of the script] don't understand the Red Room at all."

CHAPTER 2: DAVID CHASE, *THE SOPRANOS*

1. Between 1984 and 1990, I took brief leaves from my academic career, to write and edit for five network soap operas: *Ryan's Hope, Guiding Light, As the World Turns, Loving*, and *Santa Barbara*.

2. Richard Plepler (CEO of HBO), phone interviews with author, January 29, 2014, and February 10, 2014. Those interested in the history of HBO's production of the series will find valuable information in Gary R. Edgerton's *The Sopranos*.

3. David Chase, in-person interview with author, January 27, 2014.

4. In *Dying to Belong: Gangster Movies in Hollywood and Hong Kong* I compared American and Hong Kong gangster films in terms of their moral and ethical perspectives. While gangster movies in Hong Kong affirm ancient values, American gangster films are culturally subversive. I defined gangster films as being only those in which the stories are told from the point of view of a gangster protagonist. Films that contain gangsters but are structured from the point of view of a detective, police officer, or reporter attempting to bring the gangster to justice reinforce conventional social values, while gangster films interrogate them.

5. For good discussions of the relationship between the gangster film and America as a country built by immigrants, see Jonathan Munby, *Public Enemies, Public Heroes: Screening the Gangster from Little Caesar to Touch of Evil*; Thomas Leitch, *Crime Films*; Lee Grieveson, Esther Sonnet, and Peter Stanfield, eds., *Mob Culture: Hidden Histories of the American Gangster Film*; Nochimson, *Dying to Belong*.

6. David Chase, in-person interview with author, January 27, 2014. Chase had consulted a psychiatrist about professional responsibility to report to the

authorities on crimes revealed during psychiatric sessions covered by doctor-patient confidentiality. He was amused by the psychiatrist's description of the responsibility as a technical one. Melfi's line was intended as a humorous and ironic comment on her professional ethics.

7. David Chase, in-person interview with author, October 29, 2008. An early revealing moment in my conversations with Chase occurred when he spoke to me of how flawed Melfi was as a therapist. I had initially idealized her, an example of how easy it is to fall into the trap of reading auteur television through old formulaic habits. Our conversation helped me to look with fresh eyes at the series.

8. Tim Van Patten, in-person interview with author, January 16, 2014. A writing decision was made to intensify the experience of Ralph's death by giving him a sympathetic moment concerning his son right before Tony kills him.

9. Chase frequently pointed to the anonymity of "Mama" Corleone in speaking to me over the years of the roles for women in gangster films; he spoke of it again on September 7, 2017, during an appearance "in conversation" with me at the Columbia University Seminar on Cinema and Interdisciplinary Interpretations.

10. David Chase, in-person interview with author, October 29, 2008.

11. The study Melfi reads is a real study, famously conducted by psychologists Stanton Samenow and Samuel Yochelson over sixteen years, which led to their three-volume work *The Criminal Personality: A Profile for Change.*

12. David Chase, in-person interview with author, January 27, 2014.

13. Allen Coulter, in-person interview with author, December 16, 2013.

14. David Chase, e-mail with author, October 29, 2013.

15. David Chase, in-person interview with author, May 30, 2014.

CHAPTER 3: DAVID SIMON, *THE WIRE*

1. David Simon, in-person interview with author, January 21, 2016. Unless specifically indicated otherwise, all statements by David Simon come from this interview.

2. Other statements by Simon also make clear that he is not a producer of propaganda. His dedication to complexity and a 360-degree view of an issue come out loud and clear in this statement he made to me: "Context is everything. . . . Everything is messy. Everything's a tangle. I can't help but be a reporter."

3. Ta-Nehisi Coates, *Between the World and Me*, p. 47.

4. Ibid., p. 53. Simon told me that these ideas were consistent with the point of view of *The Wire*; he also made a point of letting me know that he does not agree with all the ideas in the book. "What I agree with is the intellectual rigor that he applies to himself and to his arguments as he reaches them. I find him to be one of the least susceptible essayists, modern essayists when it comes to cant and ideology. And I say that knowing how vulnerable civil rights issues are to seeing villains and heroes. He is much more sophisticated about his sociological and historical perspective . . . I don't think he reaches his conclusions without a great deal of rigor. . . . Coates is clearly an advocate for the African American community. . . . And yet at points he will stand back from the advocacy and argue in

political and practical humanistic terms." Rigor, one of Simon's goals for himself, similarly requires standing back from advocacy: "I'm always getting in trouble with ideologues because nothing is clean."

5. David Simon, *Homicide: A Year on the Killing Streets*. Simon's account of his firsthand experiences riding with the police in Baltimore is dense, thorough, and fascinating and provides further evidence for his collage-like approach to context.

6. There are not many book-length studies of *The Wire*. Two of note that take a different approach from mine are Linda Williams, *On the Wire*; and Rafael Alvarez, *The Wire: Truth Be Told*. Alvarez's book is for the official HBO series and constitutes a detailed recapping of each episode. Williams's book is a thoughtful attempt to establish *The Wire* as a tragedy. She pays her respects to the series as an artistic achievement but not to Simon's ideas about his work. Williams calls him a better artist than a critic. I think her interpretation undervalues Simon's perspective and also its discontinuity and collage structure in her effort to relate the series to a classic literary structure. More recently, Jonathan Abrams, *All the Pieces Matter: The Inside Story of* The Wire, is an extensive collection of interviews with members of the creative community that made the series.

7. As a result of a spirited interchange about Rawls during our interview, Simon ultimately won me over from my initial simplistic anger at the character. The following excerpt makes it clear that Simon has a very complex idea about this abrasive, almost always obscene character: "I'm trying to make arguments about why the world is what it is and why it isn't something else. I've seen my world-view described in misanthropic terms, and I don't feel that. I have great affection for even—I like Rawls. I understand Rawls. Rawls isn't corrupt. He's personally ambitious, but he's committed himself to this institution." The standout moment when Rawls reveals his commitment is in "The Hunt" (1.11), in which Rawls consoles McNulty, whom he emphatically detests, out of pure professionalism. When McNulty becomes morose after his colleague Kima Greggs suffers near-fatal injuries during a police action, Rawls unexpectedly comes to his aid as a comrade in arms:

> Listen to me, you fuck. You did a lot of shit here. You played a lot of fucking cards and you made a lot of fucking people do a lot of fucking things they didn't want to do. . . . You, McNulty, are a gaping asshole. . . . But fuck if I'm going to stand here and say you did a single fucking thing to get a police shot. You did not do this. You fucking hear me?. . . . And the motherfucker saying this? He hates your guts, McNulty. So, you know if it was on you, I'd be the son of a bitch to say so. Shit went bad. She took two for the company. That's the only lesson here.

This was not the formulaic beginning of a beautiful friendship, merely a moment when complex levels of Rawls's humanity are revealed.

8. During the interview, Simon explained to me the difference between the kind of journalism that he believes makes a difference in society and Dickensian journalism. Dickensian journalism is not "the whole picture. I've had editors

say that's amorphous, we can't—Just give us the hunger, give us the kid dying of hunger. Don't explain to us how agricultural policy and capitalism have produced such extraordinary excess in one part of the human race and—I've seen this happen time and again. The hard work of explaining the how and the why of journalism which are the two questions." Yet Dickensian journalism is currently winning the Pulitzers. Simon referred me to an award-winning story about a canine unit in Philadelphia that had bitten more people than any other canine unit. "It was certainly reported in great and elongated detail. And it was so perfectly contained. We used to joke it was the ultimate dog bites man story. But he pounded on that one nail until the board split. But the idea that the whole Philadelphia police department was in adversarial stance against its inner city and what that meant and how we got to this point, that never entered into the realm of the *Philadelphia Enquirer*." Simon gives this journalism its due. "Look, you can feel the dog's teeth sink into the flesh in the Pulitzer story. *The Wire*, by contrast is grown-up shit. . . . It was a story about this is why we are the way we are. It was trying to stand back and say, 'Can we fix this?'"

9. Uta Briezewitz, in-person interview with author, June 28, 2015. The following Briezewitz quotations are also from this source.

10. David Simon told me that he "was always amazed when people watched *The Wire* and were like, 'Well, there's nothing to be done.' That it was urging that everything is fucked. No, this is an argument for society, for the city. This is an argument for us. This is what needs to be attended to. To me, I have the same tonalities [in *The Wire*] that I had when I was a journalist. Let's go look at what's actually happening on the ground and write about it and make people give a shit."

CHAPTER 4: DAVID SIMON AND ERIC OVERMYER, *TREME*

1. All quotations from David Simon and Eric Overmyer are from in-person interviews with them: David Simon, January 21, 2016, and Eric Overmyer, February 18, 2016. Some production history about pitching *Treme* to HBO:

MARTHA NOCHIMSON: Did you bring this idea to David or did he bring it to you?

ERIC OVERMYER: I think it was kind of mutual. We started talking about it during *Homicide*. That's where we really met and worked together. I've had a house there [New Orleans] since 1989. And David and I got friendly on *Homicide* and we started to talk about wouldn't it be great to do a show set in New Orleans. And how all the shows that have ever been there have been terrible, the fictional shows. And they always shoot the same five things, the streetcar, the French Quarter, blah blah blah. And then when I did a season on *The Wire*, which was the summer of the storm, before that happened, we started to talk a little more seriously about it. And David said that it should be about musicians. And I thought, "Well, yes, that's right." Then that became the larger idea after the storm. Everybody who makes culture down there in the bigger sense. And I have to say it was David who saw the potential. I was so distressed about the storm. I said that we had missed our chance. And David said, "No, this is our chance." And he was right. It would have been a very different show if the storm hadn't happened and we were doing a show about the city before the storm happened.

MARTHA NOCHIMSON: What would it have been like?

ERIC OVERMYER: It would have been about the chronic problems of the city.

2. Michael Smith, *Mardi Gras Indians.* The extensive depiction of the importance to New Orleans of a subculture known as the Indians is one of the most original aspects of the series. The Indians date from the eighteenth century, when slaves developed their own music and dance ritual celebrations parallel with those of Mardi Gras, which, as Overmyer says, has been a long-standing cause of conflict with authority and the city government, especially the second line of the Indians. (During Mardi Gras season, numerous second lines are formed when groups of people coalesce independently of the large parades and take to the streets with singing, dancing, and sometimes costumes.)

3. The discussion of racism as a spatial issue in George Lipsitz, *How Racism Takes Place*, has interesting ramifications for the achievement of Simon and Overmyer in *Treme*. Lipsitz has coined the very useful terms "black spatial imaginary" (pp. 51–70) and "white spatial imaginary" (pp. 25–50). His discussions of the issue of race-defined space primarily address socioeconomic problems in the United States. However, these terms also give us a way to discuss what happens to New Orleans in the formulaic American series. In *Murder, She Wrote, Bones,* and *NCIS: New Orleans*, this Creole city is reduced to a white spatial imaginary. In *Frank's Place*, it is reduced to a black spatial imaginary. The collage design of *Treme* prohibits such simplistic depiction and endows television with one of its very few complex, multiracial, multiethnic spatial imaginaries.

4. The importance of refusing despair by opting out of the context is a continuing theme in Simon's television. It is especially prominent in the series he wrote after *Treme, Show Me a Hero*, about a racially charged uproar about housing in Yonkers, New York. At the end of that series, we are asked to ponder the implications of the suicide of Nick Wasicsko (Oscar Isaac) because of the political pressures brought to bear on him.

5. The massacre on the Danziger Bridge in New Orleans took place in the chaotic aftermath of Katrina, when New Orleans police fired on a group of unarmed black citizens of New Orleans, killing two of them. None of the citizens had any criminal records. The victims of the police attack claimed that they were trying to get help for their families. The police falsely claimed that they had been summoned to the scene because of a report that a policeman had been shot and were fired at when they arrived at the bridge. The policemen in the case were eventually forced to plead guilty to various charges related to the shooting, including obstruction.

6. Some production history about the pothole:

MARTHA NOCHIMSON: The last image is of Davis. I love that last image.

ERIC OVERMYER: It was inspired by a pothole in front of David Simon's house. But they were also all over town. Potholes are routinely decorated with beads from Mardi Gras. So that was no aberration on the New Orleans phenomenon. Which is a lot of what the show was. Elaborating on strange and wonderful things that happened in New Orleans. There's a sort of sense of humor in the midst of all this catastrophe. And an inside factoid about it that tickles us is that it's a pothole in front of John Boutté's house. [Boutté is a New Orleans musician who is prominently featured in *Treme* and wrote the main title song.] And John Boutté directed us to that pothole. And then we enlarged it, which the neighbors thought was really hot.

MARTHA NOCHIMSON: Did you fill it back up?

ERIC OVERMYER: Yeah, we did. John and his mother had been complaining to the city about that pothole for ages. The decorated potholes are among the things we liked about the culture, how participatory it is. You don't just watch a parade, you jump in.

MARTHA NOCHIMSON: You don't just stumble over a pothole, you decorate it.

CHAPTER 5: MATT WEINER, *MAD MEN*

1. Matt Weiner, phone interview, May 26, 2016. The foundation of David Chase's influence on Weiner involved many practical and theoretical issues. First of all, the way Chase ran his writers' room was a model for Weiner. He saw in Chase a writer following his creative impulses and at the same time maintaining a level of focus and commitment, which meant discipline in writers' meetings and writing one series at a time. Obviously, writing a formulaic series leaves a writer free to put together other formulaic series at the same time, but auteur television means undisturbed concentration. At the same time, Weiner understood from Chase that although "no one wants to write to the cliché, your first mistake is to write to the opposite of a cliché. And David was really good at pointing out to me that that was also a cliché. You didn't have to go to Mars to find the next beat. You had to think about the characters in the situation. You had to find something that was true or interesting. As opposed to what's normal or what's the opposite of normal." All subsequent quotations of Weiner are from this interview.

2. George Toles, "Don Draper and the Promises of Life." In his insightful and eloquent essay, which is primarily a close reading of the pilot of *Mad Men*, Toles is also interested, as I am, in the connection between *Mad Men* and American literature (pp. 168–169). But Toles emphasizes very different texts than those toward which Weiner directed me in our interview.

    MARTHA NOCHIMSON: Don seems to grow out of a central literary tradition. The phantom new beginning that Don is struggling in vain to create grows out of the Great Gatsby tradition. Did you think about this when you were creating *Mad Men*?

    MATT WEINER: If you can get money, you can reinvent who you are; I think it's an American story that predates *The Great Gatsby*, and we're extremely tolerant of that. I am very much aware of that. In fact, the original script in which Don was developed was based on reading a bunch of biographies of people in the twentieth century, Bill Clinton, Lee Iacocca, Rockefeller. They don't all have fake names, but a lot of them have covered their childhoods.

They are from rural poverty or scandal and they spent a lot of their life trying to hide it.

MARTHA NOCHIMSON: That's the American immigrant story.

MATT WEINER: It's kind of the tradition of Casanova, which influenced our choice of music. We started using music from the late nineteenth century, *Song of India, Peer Gynt*; these are all stories about men who abandoned their families and then came back. Part of it was personal experience. I worked in a place in which a man said he went to Harvard. And we found out he didn't go to Harvard and nobody cared. We're totally tolerant of this. . . . We are extremely tolerant of that. In fact, we admire it.

MARTHA NOCHIMSON: And what about Huck Finn? Huck is always trying to escape, and in the end he lights out for the territories.

MATT WEINER: I have to say that that was not part of my education. The world had turned away from Huck Finn. I was embarrassed not to have read it, but there was no influence from Huck Finn.

The literary influences on Weiner are surprising, especially the story of Rip Van Winkle and Charles Dickens's *A Tale of Two Cities*:

> I read *Tale of Two Cities* before we wrote season 6, and season 6 is sixty years from the 1960s just as Dickens's novel was seventy years from the French Revolution. I loved the parallel. In season 6 and in *Tale of Two Cities* you have a device of two men who look the same but are very different. And as a writer you say when you have twinning you're talking about two parts of the same person. Sydney Carton and Charles Darnay. One is a virtuous aristocrat and one is a grimy, dishonest lawyer. But they look the same, and there's a great scene in which Carton looks in the mirror and says who is this man, I hate this man. That doppelgänger effect goes back to everything, to Gatsby, to all of it. There's a devil inside me. That is at the heart of Don Draper.

Curious readers may also want to check out Horatio Alger's stories about how poor boys struck it rich in America, which, ironically, are simultaneously part of the mythology of the American dream and a refutation of it: luck rather than hard work is generally the reason for his hero's success, as in his novel *Ragged Dick: Or, Street Life with the Boot Blacks* (1868).

3.   Toles, "Don Draper and the Promises of Life, pp. 147–155. Toles, in an admirably insightful close reading of Don's process of arriving at a successful pitch, emphasizes Don's helplessness, a deficit reading of his character that contrasts with my reading of Don as a model of the creative person, as Weiner would have it, living in the not-knowing. A still more contrasting approach to Don as an ad man can be found in Kevin Guilfoy, "Capitalism and Freedom in Affluent Society," in *Mad Men and Philosophy: Nothing Is as It Seems* (Wiley, 2010), pp. 34–52. Guilfoy takes a purely sociological look at advertising.

4.   Weiner has some complex feelings about advertising:

> **MATTHEW WEINER:** I accept it as what it is. I think there's too much of it and I dislike it as too much or a distraction, and I hate that the bargain has been

broken which is that you used to watch advertising in exchange for free entertainment and that's been broken now that you have to pay for the shows and the advertising. And you can't choose to ignore it and get it out of your life. And that it's everywhere and that we cannot get rid of it. That bothers me. It bothers me as urban blight. There used to be rules about how it could be and where it could be and what you could sell to children. All gone. And it's a free for all, and there's plenty to criticize, but to say that the amount of art work that is in people's homes in the United States that is some form of artistic expression paid for by a consumer product; I'd say it's up around 80 percent. . . . I'm not saying it's good or bad. It's just the way it is. So when I hear superiority about the valuelessness of the message because [of] who is paying for it and how we're getting it, I would say: you may feel that way, but Don doesn't. And in the end you certainly aren't behaving that way. You would have never watched *Mad Men* if it weren't for advertising.

MARTHA NOCHIMSON: Why not?

MATTHEW WEINER: You'd have never known about it.

5. When Weiner learned long after Don's Kodak speech went on air that Don had the wrong definition of nostalgia, he thought it served the scene even better as a mistake on Don's part.

6. Weiner's discussion of the Hershey pitch:

And I feel like in the Hershey thing, he's just going through the motions. . . . He's just giving this phony story because he's so ashamed that he can't tell his personal relationship to this thing. And then he realizes he has to. And it was hard to have to put him in such a horrible place, but we had to. But I felt like it was a matter of what Sally [his daughter] had seen. And if you recall after Grandma Ida breaks into the house, Sally says to Don, "I don't know anything about you." And then she knows everything about him. She sees him cheating on her stepmother, who she is friends with. And then he insists that she be with him in the lie. "You saw nothing." And I think that comes out in the most supreme crisis of self-hatred when he does the usual advertising thing in creating a beautiful Don Draper story. He realizes he is a liar.

7. WEINER: We wanted Don working for Peggy, which we went out of our way to do. And I thought that half of that scene was Don working his way up in his business and making amends to Peggy. He really makes amends with Peggy as part of the end of their story. Because Peggy is a significant woman in his life. She's really his friend. She's definitely grown up and she's definitely a cheerleader but she's also a critic, all the things you would want in your friend. There's a big age difference, but I never saw her as a romantic possibility. Everyone was always going, "When is Don going to sleep with Peggy?" And I said, you know what? I hate to disappoint anyone, but never.

8.   Weiner was interested in unmasking as delusional the fantasies men cling to
      about their control over women:

      MATTHEW WEINER: I wanted the male sense of power over women to be at odds with
          reality. That by the time you get to "Jet Set" [2.11] you can see that Don has
          no control of anything.
      MARTHA NOCHIMSON: Like Tony Soprano, who despite all his seeming machismo
          had no control of anything.
      MATTHEW WEINER: Well, honestly, the fantasy of control is the foundation of the
          formula of men on TV. And you see it even more with the woman charac-
          ters, who [formulaically] want to have it all and they do [formulaically]
          have it all. So once your hero isn't in control, you're breaking a big rule.
      WEINER: The bra story. The Jackie/Marilyn thing. It's very important in the second
          episode of the show. In the television world, all anyone wants is males from
          eighteen to forty-nine. And I've done shows that are opposite Monday
          night football and are totally for women. And then later on they say, well,
          those men don't watch TV except for Monday night football. When you say
          your show is female or skewed female, it's considered a failure. There is a
          misconception that advertising should appeal to women and that a woman
          wants to be seen the way a man sees her. Whether it's true or not that's
          definitely the way they think it works. The absurdity of appealing to men
          about a product when it will only be women who are buying the product,
          that was part of the Maidenform thing.
9.   WEINER: I had had that experience. I was extremely sleep deprived. And I went
          into the bathroom at work late at night. And it's a fluorescent lit bathroom.
          The building is from 1957 and hasn't been remodeled since. When you see
          a bathroom on the show it's usually one of those bathrooms. But I had this
          experience of looking at myself and seeing myself for a second. This is what
          I look like to other people. And I heard this noise. And I could not take that
          feeling for very long. Bobbie doesn't want to be seen as a mother, and Betty
          doesn't want to be seen as a mother. And Don doesn't want to be seen as
          what he is, a liar. . . . I credit that shot to Phil Abraham, our director. That
          was not in the script. The music is related to the music that was on the train
          leaving his brother behind.

CHAPTER 6: LENA DUNHAM, *GIRLS*

1.   For more exposure to new theories of mind and body, see Antonio R. Damasio,
      Descartes' Error: Emotion, Reason, and the Human Brain; Antonio R. Damasio,
      *The Feeling of What Happens: Body and Emotion in the Making of Conscious-
      ness*; Jane Gallop, *Thinking through the Body*; Eugene T. Gendlin, *Focusing-
      Oriented Psychotherapy: A Manual of the Experiential Method*; and Elizabeth
      Grosz, *Volatile Bodies: Toward a Corporeal Feminism*.
2.   Lee Edelman propounds his transgressive reading of procreation in *No Future:
      Queer Theory and the Death Drive*. Edelman calls the "rhetoric of The Child"
      a political Möbius strip, only permitted one side. His use of that imagery is

unfortunate, since he means to say that the image of a child allows only one, compulsively positive and sympathetic reaction. By contrast, the Möbius strip suggests an enigmatic co-presence of *two* sides of a closed loop with a twist. Ironically, Edelman's invocation of the wrong image accurately reflects the dubiousness of his theory. When Donald Trump as president put policies in place in 2018 that resulted in babies being warehoused in detention centers without their parents and toddlers being forced to appear in court without any advocate to protect them, a significant number of Americans remained indifferent to the suffering of those immigrant children. Indeed, American history shows that some Americans have never had a compulsively positive reaction to children of color and/or children of ethnicities perceived as alien. The Child would not seem to be a universal lever, as Edelman would have it (pp. 1–3).

3. Lena Dunham, *Not That Kind of Girl: A Young Woman Tells You What She's "Learned."* Dunham's very early memoir makes no allusions to the collection of theorists I have invoked. Rather, it points toward her sensitivity to liminality and her lack of inclination to speak in transgressive terms. The title itself tells us that she is questioning what we mean by maturation, and she questions the nature of relationship throughout, beginning with her prefatory remarks (pp. xii–xiii). She ends the book by placing the words "true friends" in quotation marks, still unsure of what that might mean or what she has learned (p. 246).

4. Lena Dunham, "Introduction," in *This Is 40: A Screenplay by Judd Apatow*, p. vii.

5. Sexual liminality pops up from time to time in *Girls*, always with a comic twist that nevertheless suggests wild energy making itself manifest in a way that complicates formulaic ideas of identity that define people as either gay or straight. Some interesting moments of sexual fluidity are depicted in episodes 1.8, 3.1, 5.5, and 5.9, which run a gamut of feelings about breaking boundaries. In "Weirdos Need Girlfriends Too" (1.8), Marnie and Jessa put on a lesbian display for Thomas-John, a man they meet in a bar. In "Females Only" (3.1), Jessa, in rehab for a drug problem, "therapeutically" performs cunnilingus on a fellow inmate to help her with her identity problems as a lesbian. When Hannah and her mother go to a health spa in "Queen for Two Days" (5.5), one of the women employees seduces Hannah into a sexual moment that leaves Hannah scared and confused. In "Love Stories" (5.9), Hannah smokes marijuana with Tally Schifrin (Jenny Slate) an old high school friend, with whom she has always felt competitive. Feeling a new sense of kinship with Tally, Hannah wonders out loud if they should have sex, but they both laugh off the idea.

6. Ted Bundy is the pseudonym adopted by Theodore Robert Cowell (1946–1989), one of America's most notorious serial killers. Outwardly a model of clean-cut normality, he was actually a psychopath who is known to have murdered thirty people and believed to have murdered many more about whom we will never know. In 1989 he was executed in the electric chair in Florida.

7. Sergio Dias Branco, "Situating Comedy: Inhabitation and Duration in Classical American Sitcoms." This excellent essay convincingly explodes the idea that television sitcoms are produced with a zero degree aesthetic, when in fact they

have a very well-defined style of their own. "This is a piece of television criticism that aims at illuminating the nuanced uses of these techniques calling attention to the way the 'stagey' feel of these series is connected with the closeness of the characters and with their delimited, intimate world" (p. 95).

8. Adam and Jessa are the most violent example of a relationship that bodies distinctly speak of, in their own visceral vocabulary, as confining and oppressive, but it is not the only one. For the first two years of the series, Marnie is involved with Charlie Dattolo (Christopher Abbott) in an inexplicable round of approach-avoidance couples cycles; Hannah is involved with Fran Parker in a similar way in season 5. In both cases, the bodies involved push back against the defined shape of continuous coupledom, as the concept of relationship boggles and slips. In Hannah's case, she is unable to explain why she suddenly finds herself leaning out the window of the passenger seat to get air as she and Fran are leaving New York for a vacation together or why she literally runs away from him at a highway rest stop and continues to flee from him until he gives up and drives away. Hannah's revulsion against defined couple claustrophobia pours out of her body; no words that they utter speak louder than her corporeality.

9. Opting for a sound image leaves the mother-child link on the threshold between the gratified union of these very early days of Grover's life and the future, in which Grover will find himself as do all people in Dunham's universe, in the grip of undefinable, unsatisfying situations.

10. Maria Sulimma, "Lena Dunham: Cringe Comedy and Body Politics." Sulimma's essay is rooted in what I see as a mistaken reading of Dunham's work through paratext.

11. Dunham's public political statements are a mélange of categorical pronouncements and finely nuanced statements. She has never presented herself publicly in as many shades of gray as she does as a storyteller and has often had to apologize. See Tom Sykes, "Lena Dunham Accused of 'Hipster Racism' by Black Ex-Coworker in Explosive Resignation Letter"; and Lena Dunham, "Harvey Weinstein and the Silence of the Men." See also Lena Dunham, "Why I Chose To Speak Out"; and an article in Huffpost, in which she is quoted as angrily dismissing those who "go through his [Woody Allen's] work and comb through it for references to child molestation, that's not the fucking point." Rather, she points to "the actual evidence that exists in the world, which I think strongly suggests that Woody Allen is in the wrong." Cavan Sieczkowski, "Lena Dunham Is 'Nauseated' by Woody Allen, But Won't Indict His Work."

CHAPTER 7: BACKLASH! FORMULA 2.0

1. Even the best of the 2.0 superhero shows (such as *Jessica Jones*, which has pretensions to feminist and antiracist storytelling) feature win-lose situations that exclude any consideration of the nuanced aspects of new ideas about the world, the challenges faced everyday by women and minorities, or the resources of people facing social challenges.

2. *Leverage* is an updated version of the 1.0 caper series *Mission Impossible*.
    Leverage features a very appealing group of characters involved in crime fighting,
    which updates *Mission Impossible* with narrative threads in which the team
    members move toward satisfying romantic and collegial bonds with each other.
    The team is spearheaded by the main potential love interest, team leader Nathan
    Ford (Timothy Hutton), an attractive master of manipulation and organization,
    and Sophie Devereaux (Gina Bellman), a failed but sexy actress, brilliantly
    capable of assuming a multitude of identities to support team efforts. The other
    members of the team are Eliot Spencer (Christian Kane), a typical hunk and
    former special forces muscle man who loves to cook; Parker (Beth Riesgraf) a
    platinum blonde acrobat of prodigious flexibility and physical stamina; and Alec
    Hardison (Aldis Hodge), a wisecracking black computer genius. It is a major 2.0
    upgrade from the humorless, wooden characters of *Mission Impossible*. Still,
    Leverage is essentially about invincible, "perfect teams" solving problems in a
    perfect narrative that leaves no room for the complexities of human contexts.
3. Kolchak's editor, like Mulder's superiors at the FBI, never believes that he
    has actually encountered the *X-Files* variety of mutants and monsters that he
    reports on.
4. The original *X-Files* has generated a cottage industry of very popular collateral
    merchandise, like coloring books, posters, puzzle and activity books, and pro-
    fessionally written versions of "fan fiction" that employ Scully and Mulder in all
    varieties of independently conceived adventures. Critical literature about Chris
    Carter's series, however, is in short supply but includes the following works. Dr.
    Anne Simon contributed *The Real Science behind the X-Files: Microbes, Meteor-
    ites, and Mutants* (Simon and Schuster, 2001). Jason Davis, who worked at Ten
    Thirteen Productions as an intern but spent most of his time working on *Harsh
    Realm*, provided some interesting production history in *Writing the X-Files:
    Interviews with Chris Carter, Frank Spotnitz, Vince Gilligan, John Shiban,
    and Howard Gordon* (Create Space Independent Publishing Platform, 2016).
    Darren Mooney wrote *Opening the X-Files: A Critical History of the Original
    Series* (McFarland, 2017). Dr. Dean A. Kowalski examined *The Philosophy of the
    X-Files* (University Press of Kentucky, updated edition, 2009).
5. Piper Kerman's book *Orange Is the New Black: My Year in a Women's Prison*
    is an autobiographical study of her yearlong, life-changing lesson in the conse-
    quences of actions. It is an honest examination of the limits of Kerman's ability
    to manipulate her circumstances once she gets involved with the international
    drug trade. The television series *Orange Is the New Black*, created by Jenji
    Kohan, is not about the events of a year; not about Piper Kerman but about
    Piper Chapman (Taylor Schilling); and not about the situations that Kerman
    reported in her portrait of prison life. To keep its narrative on the formulaic
    tracks, the series disregards not only the story of personal growth in the book
    but also the context of the subculture of prison life that Kerman richly depicted.
    That said, as a 2.0 upgrade of the American formulaic television series, it is
    much more inclusive than the usual formulaic series in its casting of women of

all physical types and ethnicities and abundantly passes the Bechdel test. (The Bechdel test, named in honor of lesbian cartoonist Alison Bechdel, evaluates the feminism of a mass-media entertainment by counting not only how many women are in the cast but how many times they talk to each other and whether they talk about anything besides men and romance.)

6. Bryan Cranston, *A Life in Parts*. Cranston's memoir begins with a moving recounting of his experience of playing the scene in which he allows Jane to die. He gives us insight into the ability of *Breaking Bad* to capture emotional reality within its formulaic limits.

7. Elliott Logan, "Flash Forwards in *Breaking Bad*: Openness, Closure, and Possibility." Logan has written an extraordinary analysis of the uses of Gilligan's breaking of the time line in *Breaking Bad*, paying particular attention to the flash-forward in "Crazy Handful of Nothin'" (1.6). His analysis is a telling evocation of how the freedom modeled by the new television auteurs opened up pockets of new flexibility for authors of formulaic TV to achieve depth and originality innovatively in their storytelling within the parameters of the perfect narrative.

8. Mary Franz, "The Real Men of Deadwood." The historical Al Swearengen was at the center of prostitution, gambling, drugs, and liquor in Deadwood, but there is no evidence that he controlled the town or that Seth Bullock was the noble loser presented in Milch's series. He did not become friends with Wild Bill Hickok and the two did not try in vain, as they do in the series, to maintain law in the town. Hickok was killed less than a day after Bullock arrived in Deadwood. On the contrary, the evidence suggests that Bullock was an effective sheriff and more than held his own with Swearengen. Bullock was also not the progressive, sympathetic character presented in the series but a union buster. Bullock married not his brother's widow but his childhood sweetheart, with whom he lived a satisfying life. He was not part of a doomed affair with the glamourous, passionate Alma, his true love, as presented in the series. In other words, Milch's antihero is as much a formulaic concoction as the perfectly virtuous force for good in *Gunsmoke*, Matt Dillon (James Arness). Milch's perfect narrative of perfect corruption in *Deadwood* represents a dissociation from the history that he purports to represent.

9. Willa Paskin, "How to Get Away with Hyperdrama"; Willa Paskin, "What I Got Wrong about *How to Get Away with Murder* and Fall's Other New TV Shows." In "How to Get Away with Hyperdrama," Paskin notes the grindingly manipulative nature of Annalise's story. "Given all the room TV has made for a seemingly endless number of white male antiheroes, there is certainly room for more than one addictive, morally skewed, fast-paced soap opera with a diverse case led by a great black actress. But the pilot of *How to Get Away with Murder*, entertaining as it sometimes is, seems constructed almost entirely out of the building blocks from the Shonda Rhimes Build-a.show Kit." However, she retracts her objections in her November 3 column, saying that the show has turned out to be about Annalise's identity, featuring such catchy lines as her question to her husband, "Why is your penis on a dead girl's phone?" Paskin got it right the first time,

though she later became diverted by one-liners and a pseudo-search for the "real" Annalise. Annalise wears a wig and false eyelashes, but there is no need to search for who she really is. The series is powered by her definition as an amoral opportunist.

CODA: THE RETURN OF DAVID LYNCH

1. There seems to be some confusion about the title of *Twin Peaks* (2017). It is always *Twin Peaks* in the main title onscreen, but the series is referred to in numerous places as *Twin Peaks: The Return*, including Amazon Prime Video and *TV Guide*. Sabrina Sutherland, executive producer of the series, asked me to use the correct title, *Twin Peaks* or *Twin Peaks* (2017).

2. Resource materials for reading about tulpas are available at en.wikipedia.org /wiki/Tulpa and tulpa.info/what-is-a-tulpa. Resource materials for reading about doppelgängers are available at en.wikipedia.org/wiki/Doppelgänger and in Vardoulakis, *The Doppelgänger*.

3. Arthur S. Eddington, *The Nature of the Physical World*, pp. 325–329 (quotation on 325).

4. David Chase, in-person interview with author, May 30, 2014.

5. Basic information about the Möbius strip is readily available at en.wikipedia .org/wiki/Möbius_strip and mathworld.wolfram.com/MoebiusStrip.html (with mathematical equations). A more comprehensive article can be found at math .hmc.edu/~gu/curves_and_surfaces/surfaces/moebius.html.

6. Set visit with David Lynch, January 15–18, 1996 (while he was filming *Lost Highway*). Lynch spoke about his interest in the Möbius strip and his intention that this would be the shape of *Lost Highway*. Only in retrospect, with the full flowering of Möbius time in *Twin Peaks* (2017), do I see its traces in his earlier work.

7. David Lynch, in-person interview with author, March 18, 2010. When Lynch spoke to me about historical cycles in Vedic mythology, he was not alluding to linear time but to the circular cycles of change on a very large scale, discussed by students of the Vedas. The time he was invoking was circular not Möbius time, but to date I do not see Vedic cycles in his film and television. However, the large nonlinear loop of time in *Twin Peaks* (2017), characteristic of the Möbius strip, seems to me to be consistent with the reversals that characterize the Vedic cycles and inconsistent with the narrative conventions of linear time. For a readable exploration of time by a contemporary physicist, see David Z. Albert, *Time and Chance*. In a more recent book (*After Physics*), Albert has considered the future-past and the relationship between physics and narrative, with the caveat that it involves advanced mathematical equations.

8. We arrive at the happy conclusion of the love triangle involving Norma Jennings, Ed Hurley, and Nadine Hurley because all of them reject the delusional, consumerist marketplace version of values that take the form of money, materialist power, and commodity sex. By contrast, the other "happy ending" in 2017 comes about when Cooper, in part 17, asks Philip Gerard to make a new tulpa for Janey-E and Sonny Jim Jones to take the place of the old, now destroyed tulpa Dougie. The

completion of the Jones family, far more dubious, is based on an embrace of all the materialist values of the marketplace.

9. David Lynch, in-person interview with author, March 18, 2010. In trying to explain the desires stimulated by the marketplace, Lynch gave me an anecdote of the desire for a new car, which is all-consuming at first but degrades with the passage of time, to be replaced by other similarly temporary sensations of yearning. It is of interest that Janey-E, in her desire for a wonderful car, perfectly embodies his parable.

10. One of the few questions that Lynch ever asked me was "What did the monkey say?" (in reference to the talking monkey in *Fire Walk with Me*). When I unhesitatingly answered "Judy," he seemed very pleased. He never explained why he asked, but I do not think it was because he knew then how important Judy would become. He explained to me once in a different context the way that his creative process worked. An image or idea would appear to him and he would not know why it seemed important, but over time other images or thoughts would join it. Then he would know that they were supposed to work with each other as part of some creation. I suspect that when "Judy" appeared in *Fire Walk with Me*, it was a beginning, of which he was not conscious at the time, of an evolution that yielded Judy a crucial place in 2017.

11. The dying Log Lady speaks mysteriously and prophetically to Hawk:

> Hawk, electricity is humming. You hear it in the mountains and rivers. You see it dance among the seas and stars and glowing around the moon. But in these days, the glow is dying. What will be in the darkness that remains? The Truman brothers are both "true men." They are your brothers, and the others, the good ones who have been with you. Now the circle is almost complete. Watch and listen to the dream of time and space. It all comes out now, flowing like a river. That which is and is not. Hawk, Laura is the one.

The Log Lady is speaking of the flow of energy in the cosmos, of illusions about space and time, but not in a way that is legible. What does it mean for a circle to close? Circles appear as sinister, entrapping configurations from the unproduced *Ronnie Rocket* script to *Twin Peaks* (2017). How does the closed circle bear on energy, possibility, freedom, and the power of Judy? Then there is the mystery of why she calls Laura "the one," since she is not just one. In the prologue to the pilot of the original *Twin Peaks*, the Log Lady speaks of Laura as the one who leads to the many, and perhaps that is what she means here too. What is most pertinent to the narrative flow of 2017 is her elegiac tone, a melancholy that prefigures Cooper's impending failure. If there is another *Twin Peaks* series we may learn more about the other mysteries as well.

12. The gold ring with a flat, oval, green stone inscribed with an abstract symbol of an owl (the Judy icon?) haunts Lynch's film and television about Twin Peaks, still unexplained and complex in its associations with positive and negative energy, another potentially fruitful area of discovery in a possible future series.

13. Mark Frost's two companion books to *Twin Peaks* (2017), *The Secret History of Twin Peaks: A Novel* and *The Final Dossier*, raise serious questions about

the collaboration between Frost and Lynch, as the books inhabit an utterly different level of storytelling than the series. There is no dream, no dreamer, in Frost's companion books. They arise out of a completely different sensibility than we see in the series. While *Twin Peaks* (2017) constitutes a new frontier in television art, *The Secret History* conveys "abnormal" events (UFOs and people who encounter warps in time and space) from the standard perspective of the mass-entertainment norm, like *The X-Files*. The radical contrast between the formulaic mass-media universe of Frost's *The Secret History* and the liminal, ambiguous, nonformulaic enigmas of Lynch's auteur universe of 2017 creates a nonproductive, confusing, and potentially destructive tension with what audiences saw on television.

14.   The basement of the Great Northern Hotel as a portal beyond the marketplace has been prepared for in two ways. We have already heard a mysterious tone that puzzles Ben Horne and his new secretary, Beverly Paige (Ashley Judd). It vibrates in Ben's office, but neither of them can find the source. And we have already seen the door juxtaposed with the mysterious sound, when James Hurley (James Marshall), Laura Palmer's secret boyfriend in the 1990 series, now on the staff of the Great Northern, checks on the furnace in the hotel basement.

15.   Martha Nochimson, *The Passion of David Lynch: Wild at Heart in Hollywood*, pp. 19–20.

BIBLIOGRAPHY

BOOKS AND SCRIPTS

Abbot, H. Porter. *The Cambridge Introduction to Narrative*. Cambridge: Cambridge University Press, 2008.

Abrams, Jonathan. *All the Pieces Matter: The Inside Story of* The Wire. New York: Crown/Archetype, 2018.

Albert, David Z. *After Physics*. Harvard University Press, 2016.

———. *Time and Chance*. Cambridge, MA: Harvard University Press, 2001.

Alger, Horatio. *Ragged Dick; Or, Street Life with the Boot Blacks*. New York: Signet, 2014.

Alvarez, Rafael. The Wire: *Truth Be Told*. New York: Grove Press, 2009.

Archive of American Television, "David Chase." Part 1 of 6 Interviews. emmytvlegends .org.

Baudrillard, Jean. *Simulacra and Simulation*. Translated by Sheila Faria Glaser. Ann Arbor: University of Michigan Press, 1994.

———. *The System of Objects*. Translated by James Benedict. 9th ed. London: Verso, 2006.

Berger, John. *Ways of Seeing: Based on the BBC Television Series* (1972). Reprint, London: Penguin Books, 1990.

Bianculli, David. *The Platinum Age of Television: From* I Love Lucy *to* The Walking Dead, *How TV Became Terrific*. New York: Doubleday, 2016.

Bloom, Harold. *The Daemon Knows*. New York: Spiegel and Grau, 2015.

Bolton, Andrew. Rei Kawakubo: *Comme des Garçons: Art of the In-Between*. New York: Metropolitan Museum of Art, 2017.

Bordo, Susan. *Unbearable Weight: Feminism, Western Culture, and the Body*. Berkeley: University of California Press, 2003.

Bradbury, Malcolm, and James McFarlane, eds. *Modernism: A Guide to European Literature, 1890–1930* (1976). With a new preface. London: Penguin Books, 1991.

Brumberg, Joan Jacobs. *The Body Project: An Intimate History of American Girls*. New York: Vintage, 1998.

Butler, Jeremy G. *Television Style*. New York: Routledge, 2009.

Carveth, Rod, and James B. South, eds. *Mad Men and Philosophy: Nothing Is as It Seems*. Hoboken, NJ: Wiley, 2010.

Castleman, Harry. *Watching TV: Six Decades of American Television*. 2nd ed. Syracuse, NY: Syracuse University Press, 2010.

Chion, Michel. *David Lynch*. London: British Film Institute, 1995.

Coates, Ta-Nehisi. *Between the World and Me*. New York: Spiegel and Grau, 2015.

Cozzolino, Robert. *David Lynch: The Unified Field*. Berkeley: University of California Press, 2014.

Cranston, Bryan. *A Life in Parts* (2016). Reprint, New York: Scribner, 2017.

Creeber, Glen. *Serial Television: Big Drama on the Small Screen*. London: British Film Institute, 2005.

———. *The Television Genre Book*. 2nd ed. London: British Film Institute, 2009.

Csikszentmihalyi, Mihaly. *Flow: An Illuminated Training Manual: How to Thrive in Love, Work and Play*. N.p.: Steve Budden, 2013.

D'Acci, Julie. *Defining Women: Television and the Case of Cagney and Lacey*. Chapel Hill: University of North Carolina Press, 1994.

Damasio, Antonio R. *Descartes' Error: Emotion, Reason, and the Human Brain*. New York: G. P. Putnam's Sons, 1994.

———. *The Feeling of What Happens: Body and Emotion in the Making of Consciousness*. New York: Harcourt Brace, 1999.

Dow, Bonnie J. *Prime Time Feminism: Television, Feminism, and the Women's Movement since 1970*. Philadelphia: University of Pennsylvania Press, 1996.

Dukes, Brad. *Reflections: An Oral History of Twin Peaks*. Nashville, TN: Short/Tall Press, 2014.

Dunham, Lena. *Not That Kind of Girl: A Young Woman Tells You What She's "Learned."* New York: Random House, 2014.

Eddington, Arthur S. *The Nature of the Physical World*. New York: Macmillan Company, 1929.

Edelman, Lee. *No Future: Queer Theory and the Death Drive*. Durham, NC: Duke University Press, 2004.

Edgerton, Gary R. *Mad Men*. London: I. B. Tauris, 2011.

———. *The Sopranos*. Detroit, MI: Wayne State University Press, 2013.

Feminist Television Criticism. Edited by Charlotte Brunsdon and Lynn Spigel. San Francisco: Open University Press, 2007.

Feynmann, Richard P. *The Strange Theory of Light and Matter*. Princeton, NJ: Princeton University Press, 1985.

Frost, Mark. *The Final Dossier*. New York: Flatiron Books, 2017.

———. *The Secret History of Twin Peaks: A Novel*. New York: Flatiron Books, 2016.

Frost, Mark, Harley Peyton, and Robert Engels. *Twin Peaks* #29 (Episode 2.022) NP: First Draft: February 14, 1991; Rewrite/Dept. Heads; Distribution: February 25, 1991; Revised February 29, 1991.

Gallop, Jane. *Thinking through the Body*. New York: Columbia University Press, 1988.

Gendlin, Eugene T. *Focusing-Oriented Psychotherapy: A Manual of the Experiential Method*. New York: Guilford Press, 1996.

Gilder, Louisa. *The Age of Entanglement: When Quantum Physics Was Born*. New York: Vintage Books, 2008.

Goren, Lilly J., and Linda Beall, eds. *Mad Men and Politics: Nostalgia and the Remaking of Modern America*. London: Bloomsbury Academic, 2015.

Grieveson, Lee, Esther Sonnet, and Peter Stanfield, eds. *Mob Culture: Hidden Histories of the American Gangster Film*. New Brunswick, NJ: Rutgers University Press, 2005.

Grosz, Elizabeth. *Volatile Bodies: Toward a Corporeal Feminism*. Bloomington: Indiana University Press, 1994.

Hagelin, John. *Is Consciousness the Unified Field?: A Field Theorist's Perspective*. Modern Science and Vedic Science, vol. 1, no. 1. Fairfield, IA: Maharishi International University, 1987.

Halskov, Andreas. *TV Peaks: Twin Peaks and Modern Television Drama*. Odense: University Press of Southern Denmark, 2015.

Hersey, John. *The Child Buyer*. New York: Alfred A. Knopf, 1960.

Jenkins, Henry, Sam Ford, and Joshua Green. *Spreadable Media: Creating Value and Meaning in a Network Culture*. New York: New York University Press, 2013.

Rowe, Kathleen. *The Unruly Woman: Gender and the Genres of Laughter*. Austin: University of Texas Press, 1997.

Kerman, Piper. *Orange Is the New Black: My Year in a Women's Prison*. New York: Spiegel and Grau, 2011.

Kristeva, Julia. *Powers of Horror: An Essay on Abjection*. New York: Columbia University Press, 1982.

Kulzer, Dina-Marie. *Television Series Regulars of the Fifties and Sixties in Interview*. Jefferson, NC: McFarland, 2012.

Kumar, Manjit. *Quantum: Einstein, Bohr and the Great Debate about the Nature of Reality*. New York: W. W. Norton, 2010.

Kumar, Shashiprabha, ed. *Veda as Word*. N.p.: Special Centre for Sanskrit Studies, Jawaharlal Nehru University in association with D. K. Printworld, 2006.

Lavery, David, and Christy Desmet, eds. *Full of Secrets: Critical Approaches to Twin Peaks*. Detroit, MI: Wayne State University Press, 1994.

Leitch, Thomas. *Crime Films*. Cambridge: Cambridge University Press, 2002.

Lipsitz, George. *How Racism Takes Place*. Philadelphia: Temple University Press, 2011.

Lucretius Carus, Titus. *On the Nature of the Universe*. Translated by Sir Ronald Melville. New York: Oxford University Press, 1999.

Lynch, David. *The Air Is on Fire*. London: Thames and Hudson, 2007.

———. *Catching the Big Fish: Meditation, Consciousness, and Creativity*. New York: Tarcher, 2007.

———. *David Lynch: Chaos Theory of Violence and Silence* (catalogue for his exhibition). Tokyo, Japan: Laforet Museum Harajuku, 2012.

———. *Images*. New York: Hyperion, 1994.

Mander, Jerry. *Four Arguments for the Elimination of Television*. New York: William Morrow Paperbacks, 1978.

Martin, Brett. *Difficult Men*. New York: Penguin Press, 2013.

McCabe, Janet, and Kim Akass, eds. *Quality TV: Contemporary American Television and Beyond*. London: I. B. Tauris 2007.

McGowan, Todd. *The Impossible David Lynch*. New York: Columbia University Press, 2007.

McQuiston, Kate. *We'll Meet Again: Musical Design in the Films of Stanley Kubrick*. New York: Oxford University Press, 2013.

Miller, Toby. *Television Studies: The Basics*. New York: Routledge, 2010.

Mittell, Jason. *Genre and Television: From Cop Shows to Cartoons in American Culture*. New York: Routledge, 2004.

——. *Television and American Culture*. New York: Oxford University Press, 2009.

Mizejewski, Linda. *Pretty/Funny: Women Comedians and Body Politics*. Austin: University of Texas Press, 2014.

Mulvey, Laura, ed. *Visual and Other Pleasures* (1989). 2nd ed. London: Palgrave, 2009.

Munby, Jonathan. *Public Enemies, Public Heroes: Screening the Gangster from Little Caesar to Touch of Evil*. Chicago: University of Chicago Press, 2002.

Newman, Stephanie. *Mad Men on the Couch: Analyzing the Minds of the Men and Women of the Hit TV Show*. New York: St. Martin's Griffin, 2012.

Nochimson, Martha. *David Lynch Swerves: Uncertainty from Lost Highway to Inland Empire*. Austin: University of Texas Press, 2013.

——. *Dying to Belong: Gangster Movies in Hollywood and Hong Kong*. Malden, MA: Wiley-Blackwell, 2007.

——. *No End to Her: Soap Opera and the Female Subject*. Berkeley: University of California Press, 1992.

——. *The Passion of David Lynch: Wild at Heart in Hollywood*. Austin: University of Texas Press, 1997.

O'Reilly, Julie D. *Bewitched Again: Supernaturally Powerful Women on Television, 1996–2011*. Jefferson, NC: McFarland, 2013.

Packard, Vance. *The Hidden Persuaders* (1957). Reprint, Brooklyn, NY: IG Publishing, 2007.

Payne, Robert. *The Promiscuity of Network Culture: Queer Theory and Digital Media*. New York: Routledge: 2015.

Peacock, Stephen, and Jason Jacobs, eds. *Television Aesthetics and Style*. London: Bloomsbury Academic, 2013.

Potter, Tiffany, and C. W. Marshall, eds. The Wire*: Urban Decay and American Television*. New York: Continuum, 2009.

Pullman, Barry. *Twin Peaks* #28 (Episode 2.021); First Draft: February 5, 1991; Second Draft/Dis. To Dept. Heads: February 8, 1991; Revised/General Distribution: February 14, 1991; Revised: February 14, 1991; Revised: February 20, 1991; Revised: February 21, 1991; Revised: February 22, 1991.

Rhimes, Shonda. *Year of Yes: How to Dance It Out, Stand in the Sun and Be Your Own Person*. New York: Simon and Schuster Paperbacks, 2015.

Rodley, Chris. *Lynch on Lynch*. London: Faber and Faber, 2005.

Rose, Frank. *The Art of Immersion: How the Digital Generation is Remaking Hollywood, Madison Avenue, and the Way We Tell Stories*. New York: W. W. Norton, 2012.

Said, Edward. *On Late Style: Music and Literature against the Grain*. New York: Vintage, 2007.

Sanchez, Melissa E. *Queer Faith: Reading Promiscuity and Race in the Secular Love Tradition*. New York: New York University Press, 2019.

Schuster, Martin. *New Television: The Aesthetics and Politics of a Genre*. Chicago: University of Chicago Press, 2017.

Sepinwall, Alan. *The Revolution Was Televised: The Cops, Crooks, Slingers and Slayers Who Changed Television Forever*. New York: Touchstone, 2012.

Simon, David. *Homicide: A Year on the Killing Streets*. New York: Henry Holt, 1991.

Smart Chicks on Screen: Representing Women's Intellect in Film and Television. Edited by Laura Mattoon D'Amore. Lanham, MD: Rowman and Littlefield Publishers, 2014.

Tindall, Blair. *Mozart in the Jungle: Sex, Drugs, and Classical Music*. New York: Grove Press, 2005.

Tolman, Deborah L. *Dilemmas of Desire: Teenage Girls Talk about Sexuality*. Cambridge, MA: Harvard University Press, 2005.

Turnbull, Sue. *The Crime Drama*. Edinburgh: Edinburgh University Press, 2014.

Vardoulakis, Dimitris. *The Doppelgänger: Literature's Philosophy*. New York: Fordham University Press, 2010.

Weinstock, Jeffrey, and Catherine Spooner, ed. *Return to Twin Peaks: New Approaches to Materiality, Theory, and Genre on Television*. New York: Palgrave Macmillan, 2016.

Williams, Linda. *On the Wire*. Durham, NC: Duke University Press, 2014.

Wittern-Keller, Laura, and Faymong J. Haberski Jr. *The Miracle Case: Film Censorship and the Supreme Court*. Lawrence: University Press of Kansas, 2008.

Wolf, Naomi. *Promiscuities: A Secret History of Female Desire*. London: Chatto and Windus, 1997.

Yochelson, Samuel, and Stanton Samenow. *The Criminal Personality: A Profile for Change*. Lanham, MD: Jason Aronson, 2000.

Zizek, Slavoi. *The Art of the Ridiculous Sublime: On David Lynch's Lost Highway*. Seattle, WA: Walter Chapin Simpson Center for the Humanities, 2000.

INTERVIEWS

Albert, David Z. (director of the M. A. Program in the Philosophical Foundations of Physics at Columbia University). In person: January 4, 2010; February 12, 2010; May 7, 2010.

Anderson, Brad. In person: December 8, 2014.

Barile, Michael. E-mails: September 3, 2018; September 4, 2018.

Briesewitz, Uta. In person: June 28, 2015.

Bryll, Eigil. Phone: June 15, 2014.

Chase, David. In person: October 29, 2008; January 27, 2014; May 30, 2014; September 7, 2017 (chairing a presentation for the Columbia University Seminar

on Cinema and Interdisciplinary Interpretations). E-mail correspondence:
October 30, 2008; December 19, 2008; January 28, 2010; January 29, 2010;
March 4, 2010; March 22, 2010; April 8, 2010; April 11, 2010; April 12, 2010; May
6, 2010; July 13, 2010; July 14, 2010; July 28, 2010; July 30, 2010; September
24, 2010; September 25, 2010; October 28, 2013; November 30, 2013; December
1, 2013; December 4, 2013; December 11, 2013; January 28, 2014; March 2,
2014; September 8, 2014; September 18, 2014; September 28, 2014; October 5,
2014; October 14, 2014; December 31, 2014; January 18, 2015; January 19, 2015;
January 20, 2015; January 24, 2015; January 25, 2015; April 16, 2015.

Coulson, Catherine. In person: March 30, 1993.

Coulter, Allen. In person: December 16, 2013.

Cox, Deb (head writer, *Miss Fisher's Murder Mysteries*). E-mail: April 25, 2015.

Eagger, Fiona (producer, *Miss Fisher's Murder Mysteries*). E-mail: May 17, 2015.

Frost, Mark. In person: November 22, 1991.

Grey, Brad. Phone: January 15, 2014.

Heathcote, Bella. Phone: March 2016.

Imperioli, Michael. Phone: December 4, 2013.

Johnson, Mark. Phone: March 23, 2016.

Korder, Howard. In person: December 11, 2011.

Kornacki, Steve. In person: November 16, 2011.

Lynch, David, Phone: January 31, 1992; January 18, 2018. In person: March 29–31,
1993; April 1, 1993; set visit: January 15–18, 1996 (while Lynch was filming *Lost
Highway*); January 13, 2006; March 18, 2010.

Magaro, John. In person: March 15, 2016.

Overmyer, Eric. In person: February 18, 2016.

Plepler, Richard (CEO of HBO). Phone: January 29, 2014; February 10, 2014.

Simon, David. In person: January 21, 2016.

Van Patten, Tim. In person: January 17, 2014.

Van Zandt, Steven. Phone: January 10, 2014.

Weiner, Matt. Phone: December 11, 2013; May 26, 2016.

Winter, Terry. In person: December 14, 2011.

ARTICLES

Booth, Wayne C. "Point of View and the Control of Distance in *Emma*." *Nineteenth-
Century Fiction* 16, no. 2 (September 1961): 95–116.

Branco, Sergio Dias. "Situating Comedy: Inhabitation and Duration in Classical
American Sitcoms." In *Television Aesthetics and Style*, edited by Steven Peacock
and Jason Jacobs, pp. 93–102. New York: Bloomsbury Academic, 2013.

Branham, Matt. "10 Thoughts and Prediction Going into the 'Mad Men' Series
Finale." *Crave*, May 15, 2015.

Cardwell, Sarah. "Television Aesthetics: Stylistic Analysis and Beyond." In *Television
Aesthetics and Style*, edited by Steven Peacock and Jason Jacobs, pp. 23–44. New
York: Bloomsbury Academic, 2013.

Dunham, Lena. "Harvey Weinstein and the Silence of the Men." *New York Times*,
October 9, 2017.

———. "Introduction." In *This Is 40: A Screenplay by Judd Apatow*. A Newmarket Shooting Script Series Book, 2012.

———. "Why I Chose to Speak Out." *Buzzfeed*, December 9, 2014.

Fallon, Kevin. "All the Signs That Don Draper Will Die." *Daily Beast*, April 14, 2014.

Franz, Mary. "The Real Men of Deadwood." *Wild West* (August 2006), historynet.com.

Kozloff, Sarah, "Social Problem Film." In *An Introduction to Film Genres*, edited by Lester Friedman, David Desser, Sarah Kozloff, Martha P. Nochimson, and Stephen Prince, pp. 446–483. New York: W. W. Norton, 2014.

Logan, Elliott. "Flash Forwards in *Breaking Bad*: Openness, Closure, and Possibility." In *Television Aesthetics and Style*, edited by Steven Peacock and Jason Jacobs, pp. 219–226. New York: Bloomsbury Academic, 2013.

Mittell, Jason. "All in the Game: *The Wire*, Serial Storytelling, and Procedural Logic." In *Third Person: Authoring and Exploring Vast Narratives*, edited by Pat Harrigan and Noah-Wardrip Fruin, pp. 429–438. Cambridge, MA: MIT Press, 2009.

Mizejewski, Linda, and Victoria Sturtevant. "Introduction." In *Hysterical: Women in American Comedy*, edited by Linda Mizejewski and Victoria Sturtevant, pp. 1–34. Austin: University of Texas Press, 2017.

Mulvey, Laura. "Afterthoughts on 'Visual Pleasure and Narrative Cinema' Inspired by King Vidor's *Duel in the Sun*." In *Visual and Other Narrative Pleasures*, pp. 31–40. 2nd ed. London: Palgrave, 2009.

———. "Visual Pleasure and Narrative Cinema." In *Visual and Other Pleasures*, pp. 14–30. 2nd ed. London: Palgrave, 2009.

Nochimson, Martha P. "*Boardwalk Empire*: America through a Bi-focal Lens." *Film Quarterly* (Fall 2012): 25–39.

———. "Brightness Falls from the Air: Ally McBeal." *Film Quarterly* (Spring 2000): 38–39.

———. "Desire under the Douglas Firs: Entering the Body of Reality in *Twin Peaks*." *Film Quarterly* (Winter 1992–1993): 31–40.

———. "Did Tony Die at the End of *The Sopranos*?" Vox.com, August 27, 2014.

———. "Genre Out of the Box in Miss Fisher's Murder Mysteries: The Evolution of a Critic, Parts 1 and 2." *Critical Studies in Television Online*, May 29, 2015, and June 5, 2015.

———. "Substance Abuse: Special Agent Dale Cooper, What's the Matter?" In *Return to Twin Peaks: New Approaches to Materiality, Theory, and Genre on Television*, edited by Jeffrey Weinstock and Catherine Spooner, pp. 47–70. London: Palgrave, 2016.

———. "Tony's Options: *The Sopranos* and the Televisuality of the Gangster Genre." *Senses of Cinema Online* (2003).

———. "Waddaya Looking At?: Re-Reading the Gangster Genre through 'The Sopranos.'" *Film Quarterly* (Winter 2002): 2–13.

O'Hehir, Andrew. "Fake News, a Fake President and a Fake Country: Welcome to America, Land of No Context." Salon.com, December 3, 2016.

Paskin, Willa. "How to Get Away with Hyperdrama." Slate.com, September 25, 2014.

———. "What I Got Wrong about *How to Get Away with Murder* and Fall's Other New TV Shows." Slate.com, November 3, 2014.

Sieczkowski, Cavan, "Lena Dunham Is 'Nauseated' by Woody Allen, But Won't Indict His Work." Huffpost.com, March 18, 2014.

Smith, Michael. *Mardi Gras Indians*. Gretna, LA: Pelican Publishing, 1994.

Sulimma, Maria. "Lena Dunham: Cringe Comedy and Body Politics." In *Hysterical: Women in American Comedy*, edited by Linda Mizejewski and Victoria Sturtevant, pp. 379–402. Austin: University of Texas Press, 2017.

Sykes, Tom, "Lena Dunham Accused of 'Hipster Racism' by Black Ex-Coworker in Explosive Resignation Letter." dailybeast.com, November 20, 2017.

Toles, George. "Don Draper and the Promises of Life." In *Television Aesthetics and Style*, edited by Steven Peacock and Jason Jacobs, pp. 147–174. New York: Bloomsbury Academic, 2013.

Trow, George W. S. "Within the Context of No-Context." *New Yorker* (November 17, 1980).

Wallace, Kelsey. "'How to Get Away with Murder' Gives Us a Female Anti-Hero We Can Root For." *Bitchmedia*, September 26, 2014.

Wallace, Phil. "King of His Castle." *Columbia College Today* (Summer 2015): 22–24.

TELEVISION SERIES

30 Rock (2006–2013)
77 Sunset Strip (1958–1964)
All in the Family (1971–1979)
Ally McBeal (1997–2002)
Battlestar Galactica (2004–2009)
The Beverly Hillbillies (1962–1971)
Blake's 7 (1978–1981)
Boardwalk Empire (2010–2014)
Bones (2005–2017)
Borgen (2010–2013)
Breaking Bad (2008–2013)
Buffy the Vampire Slayer (1997–2003)
Burn Notice (2007–2013)
Cagney and Lacey (1981–1988)
Car 54, Where Are You? (1961–1963)
Castle (2009–2016)
Cold Lazarus (1996)
Columbo (1971–2003)
The Corner (2000)
The Cosby Show (1984–1992)
Dallas (1978–1991)
Deadwood (2004–2006)
The Deuce (2017–)
Dexter (2006–2013)
Doc Martin (2004–)
Doctor Who (1963–1989); (2005–)
East Side/West Side (1963–1964)

Empire (2015–)
Engrenages (2005–)
Enlightened (2011–2013)
Eureka (2006–2012)
Falling Skies (2011–2015)
Foyle's War (2002–2015)
Frank's Place (1987–1988)
Friday Night Lights (2006–2011)
Game of Thrones (2011–)
The George Burns and Gracie Allen Show (1950–1958)
Girls (2012–2017)
Glee (2009–2015)
The Good Wife (2009–2016)
Gunsmoke (1955–1975)
Happy Days (1974–1984)
Happyish (2015)
Harsh Realm (1999–2000)
Hill Street Blues (1981–1987)
Homicide: Life on the Street (1993–1999)
The Honeymooners (1955–1956)
Horace and Pete (2016)
The Hour (2011–2012)
House, MD (2004–2012)
House of Cards (2013–)
House of Lies (2012–2016)
How to Get Away with Murder (2014–)
I Love Dick (2016)
I Love Lucy (1951–1957)
Inside Amy Schumer (2013–2016)
Inspector George Gently (2007–2017)
Inspector Lewis (2006–2015)
Inspector Morse (1987–2000)
In Treatment (2008–2010)
I Spy (1965–1968)
The Jeffersons (1975–1985)
Kolchak: The Night Stalker (1974–1975)
Law and Order (1990–2010)
Leave It to Beaver (1957–1963)
Leverage (2008–2012)
The Lone Gunmen (2001)
Louie (2010–2015)
Mad Men (2007–2015)
The Marvelous Mrs. Maisel (2017–)
The Mary Tyler Moore Show (1970–1977)
M*A*S*H (1972–1983)

Master of None (2015–)
Masters of Sex (2013–2016)
Matlock (1986–1995)
Maude (1972–1978)
Max Headroom (1987–1988)
McCloud (1970–1977)
McMillan and Wife (1971–1977)
Midsomer Murders (1997–)
Millennium (1996–1999)
Miss Fisher's Murder Mysteries (2012–2015)
Modern Family (2009–)
Moonlighting (1985–1989)
Mozart in the Jungle (2014–2018)
Mr. Robot (2015–)
Murder, She Wrote (1984–1996)
Murphy Brown (1988–1998)
Nashville (2012–)
NCIS (2003–)
NCIS: New Orleans (2014–)
Northern Exposure (1990–1995)
Nurse Jackie (2009–2015)
Orange Is the New Black (2013–)
Parks and Recreation (2009–2015)
Peaky Blinders (2013–)
Pennies from Heaven (1978)
Perry Mason (1957–1966)
The Prisoner (1967–1968)
Rectify (2013–2016)
The Rockford Files (1974–1980)
Scandal (2012–2018)
Seinfeld (1989–1998)
The Shield (2002–2008)
Show Me a Hero (2015)
The Singing Detective (1986)
Six Feet Under (2001–2005)
Slings and Arrows (2003–2006)
Sons of Anarchy (2008–2014)
The Sopranos (1999–2007)
Space 1999 (1975–1977)
Top of the Lake (2013)
Top of the Lake, China Girl (2017)
Transparent (2014–)
Treme (2010–2013)
Turn: Washington's Spies (2014–2017)
The Twilight Zone (1959–1964)

Twin Peaks (1990–1991); *Twin Peaks* (2017)
The Unbreakable Kimmy Schmidt (2015–2019)
United States of Tara (2009–2011)
The Untouchables (1959–1963)
Warehouse 13 (2009–2014)
Weeds (2005–2012)
Westworld (2016–)
The Wire (2002–2008)
Wiseguy (1987–1990)
WKRP in Cincinnati (1978–1982)
Xena: Warrior Princess (1995–2001)
The X-Files (1993–2002); (2016–2018)

INDEX

Note: page numbers in *italics* refer to illustrations.